JOSEPHUS

LCL 487

JOSEPHUS

THE JEWISH WAR
BOOKS III–IV

WITH AN ENGLISH TRANSLATION BY

H. ST. J. THACKERAY

HARVARD UNIVERSITY PRESS
CAMBRIDGE, MASSACHUSETTS
LONDON, ENGLAND

First published 1927, 1928
Reprinted 1957, 1961, 1968, 1979, 1990, 1997
Jewish War bound in three volumes beginning 1997

LOEB CLASSICAL LIBRARY® is a registered trademark
of the President and Fellows of Harvard College

ISBN 0-674-99536-8

Printed in Great Britain by St Edmundsbury Press Ltd,
Bury St Edmunds, Suffolk, on acid-free paper.
Bound by Hunter & Foulis Ltd, Edinburgh, Scotland.

CONTENTS

THE JEWISH WAR

ΒΙΒΛΙΟΝ Γ

1 (i. 1) Νέρωνι δ' ὡς ἠγγέλη τὰ κατὰ τὴν Ἰουδαίαν πταίσματα, λεληθυῖα μὲν ὡς εἰκὸς ἔκπλη-
ξις ἐμπίπτει καὶ δέος, φανερῶς δ' ὑπερηφάνει καὶ
2 πρ σωργίζετο, στρατηγῶν[1] μὲν ῥᾳστώνῃ μᾶλλον
ἢ ταῖς τῶν πολεμίων ἀρεταῖς γεγονέναι τὰ συμ-
βάντα λέγων, πρέπειν δ' ἡγούμενος ἑαυτῷ διὰ τὸν
ὄγκον τῆς ἡγεμονίας κατασοβαρεύεσθαι τῶν σκυθρωπῶν καὶ δοκεῖν δεινοῦ παντὸς ἐπάνω τὴν
3 ψυχὴν ἔχειν. διηλέγχετό γε μὴν ὁ τῆς ψυχῆς
θόρυβος ὑπὸ τῶν φροντίδων (2) σκεπτομένου[2] τίνι
πιστεύσει κινουμένην τὴν ἀνατολήν, ὃς τιμωρή-
σεται μὲν τὴν τῶν Ἰουδαίων ἐπανάστασιν, προ-
καταλήψεται δ' αὐτοῖς ἤδη καὶ τὰ πέριξ ἔθνη
4 συννοσοῦντα. μόνον [οὖν][3] εὑρίσκει Οὐεσπασιανὸν
ταῖς χρείαις ἀναλογοῦντα καὶ τηλικούτου πολέμου
μέγεθος ἀναδέξασθαι δυνάμενον, ἄνδρα ταῖς ἀπὸ
νεότητος στρατείαις ἐγγεγηρακότα καὶ προειρη-
νεύσαντα μὲν πάλαι Ῥωμαίοις τὴν ἑσπέραν ὑπὸ
Γερμανῶν ταρασσομένην, προσκτησάμενον δὲ τοῖς
5 ὅπλοις Βρεττανίαν τέως λανθάνουσαν, ὅθεν αὐτοῦ

---

[1] PA: στρατηγοῦ the rest (perhaps rightly).
[2] σκεπτόμενος δὲ C.
[3] MA (corrector) Lat.: om. the rest.

BOOK III

(i. 1) The news of the reverses sustained in Judaea
filled Nero, as was natural, with secret consternation
and alarm, but in public he affected an air of disdain
and indignation. " These unfortunate incidents,"
he said, " were due to remiss generalship rather than
to the valour of the enemy ; " and the majesty
of empire made him think it became him to treat
black tidings with lofty contempt and to appear to
possess a soul superior to all accidents. His inward
perturbation, however, was betrayed by his anxious
reflection.

(2) He was deliberating into whose hands he should
entrust the East in its present commotion, with the
double task of punishing the Jewish rebels, and of
forestalling a revolt of the neighbouring nations,
which were already catching the contagion. He
could find none but Vespasian a match for the
emergency and capable of undertaking a campaign
on so vast a scale. Vespasian was one who had been
a soldier from his youth and grown grey in the
service ; he had already earlier in his career pacified
and restored to Roman rule the West when con-
vulsed by the Germans ; he had by his military
genius added to the Empire Britain, till then almost
unknown, and thus afforded Claudius, Nero's father,[a]

---

[a] Step-father ; he adopted Nero (cf. B. ii. 249).

3

καὶ τῷ πατρὶ Κλαυδίῳ παρέσχε χωρὶς ἱδρῶτος
ἰδίου θρίαμβον καταγαγεῖν.

6 (3) Ταῦτά τε δὴ προκληδονιζόμενος καὶ σταθε-
ρὰν μετ᾽ ἐμπειρίας τὴν ἡλικίαν ὁρῶν, μέγα[1] δὲ
πίστεως αὐτοῦ τοὺς υἱοὺς ὅμηρον καὶ τὰς τούτων ἀκμὰς χεῖρα τῆς πατρῴας συνέσεως, τάχα
τι καὶ περὶ τῶν ὅλων ἤδη τοῦ θεοῦ προοικονο-
7 μουμένου, πέμπει τὸν ἄνδρα ληψόμενον τὴν ἡγεμονίαν τῶν ἐπὶ Συρίας στρατευμάτων, πολλὰ
πρὸς τὸ ἐπεῖγον οἷα κελεύουσιν αἱ ἀνάγκαι μειλι-
8 ξάμενός τε καὶ προθεραπεύσας. ὁ δ᾽ ἀπὸ τῆς
Ἀχαΐας, ἔνθα συνῆν τῷ Νέρωνι, τὸν μὲν υἱὸν
Τίτον ἀπέστειλεν ἐπ᾽ Ἀλεξανδρείας τὸ πέμπτον
καὶ δέκατον[2] ἐκεῖθεν ἀναστήσοντα τάγμα, πε-
ράσας δ᾽ αὐτὸς τὸν Ἑλλήσποντον πεζὸς εἰς
Συρίαν ἀφικνεῖται, κἀκεῖ τάς τε Ῥωμαϊκὰς δυνάμεις συνήγαγε καὶ συχνοὺς παρὰ τῶν γειτνιώντων
βασιλέων συμμάχους.

9 (ii. 1) Ἰουδαῖοι δὲ μετὰ τὴν Κεστίου πληγὴν
ἐπηρμένοι ταῖς ἀδοκήτοις εὐπραγίαις ἀκρατεῖς
ἦσαν ὁρμῆς καὶ ὥσπερ ἐκριπιζόμενοι τῇ τύχῃ
προσωτέρω τὸν πόλεμον ἐξῆγον· πᾶν γοῦν εὐθέως
ὅσον ἦν μαχιμώτατον αὐτοῖς ἀθροισθέντες ὥρ-
10 μησαν ἐπ᾽ Ἀσκάλωνα. πόλις ἐστὶν ἀρχαία τῶν
Ἱεροσολύμων εἴκοσι πρὸς τοῖς πεντακοσίοις ἀπ-

---

[1] Destinon : μετὰ MSS.
[2] καὶ δέκατον Niese, etc., cf. B. iii. 65 (and Tacit. Hist. v. 1):
καὶ τὸ δέκατον MSS.

---

[a] He was sent by Claudius to Germany and subsequently,

the honours of a triumph which cost him no personal exertion.[a]

(3) Regarding, therefore, this record as of happy augury, seeing in Vespasian a man with the steadiness resulting from years [b] and experience, with sons who would be a sure hostage for his fidelity, and whose ripe manhood would act as the arm of their father's brain, moved, may be, also by God, who was already shaping the destinies of empire, Nero sent this general to take command of the armies in Syria, lavishing upon him, at this urgent crisis, such soothing and flattering compliments as are called for by emergencies of this kind. From Achaia, where he was in attendance on Nero, Vespasian dispatched his son Titus to Alexandria to call up the fifteenth legion from that city ; he himself, after crossing the Hellespont, proceeded by land to Syria, where he concentrated the Roman forces and numerous auxiliary contingents furnished by the kings of the neighbouring districts.

(ii. 1) The Jews, after the defeat of Cestius, elated by their unexpected success, could not restrain their ardour, and, as though stirred into activity by this gust of fortune, thought only of carrying the war further afield. Without a moment's delay their most effective combatants mustered and marched upon Ascalon. This is an ancient city, five hundred and twenty furlongs from Jerusalem,[c] but the hatred

Unsuccessful Jewish attack on Ascalon.

---

in A.D. 43 (aet. 34), to Britain, where his career of victory, which included the reduction of the Isle of Wight, was " the beginning of his fortune " (Tac. *Agric.* 13 ; Suet. *Vesp.* 4).

[b] Vespasian, born in A.D. 9, was now 57.

[c] About fifty-nine miles (the *stade* being rather longer than our " furlong ") ; the distance as the crow flies is just over forty miles.

ἔχουσα σταδίους, ἀεὶ διὰ μίσους Ἰουδαίοις γεγε-
νημένη, διὸ καὶ τότε ταῖς πρώταις ὁρμαῖς ἐγγίων
11 ἔδοξεν. ἐξηγοῦντο δὲ τῆς καταδρομῆς τρεῖς ἄνδρες ἀλκήν τε κορυφαῖοι καὶ συνέσει,[1] Νίγερ τε ὁ
Περαΐτης καὶ ὁ Βαβυλώνιος Σίλας, πρὸς οἷς
12 Ἰωάννης ὁ Ἐσσαῖος. ἡ δὲ Ἀσκάλων ἐτετείχιστο
μὲν καρτερῶς, βοηθείας δὲ ἦν σχεδὸν ἔρημος·
ἐφρουρεῖτο γὰρ ὑπό τε σπείρας πεζῶν καὶ ὑπὸ
μιᾶς ἴλης ἱππέων, ἧς ἐπῆρχεν Ἀντώνιος.[2]
13 (2) Οἱ μὲν οὖν πολὺ ταῖς ὁρμαῖς[3] συντονώτερον
ὁδεύσαντες ὡς ἐγγύθεν ὡρμημένοι καὶ δὴ παρῆσαν.
14 ὁ δὲ Ἀντώνιος, οὐ γὰρ ἠγνόει μέλλουσαν ἔτι τὴν
ἔφοδον αὐτῶν, προεξήγαγε τοὺς ἱππεῖς, καὶ οὐδὲν
οὔτε πρὸς τὸ πλῆθος οὔτε τὴν τόλμαν ὑποδείσας
τῶν πολεμίων καρτερῶς τὰς πρώτας ὁρμὰς ἀν-
εδέξατο καὶ τοὺς ἐπὶ τὸ τεῖχος ὡρμημένους ἀν-
15 έστειλεν. τοῖς δὲ πρὸς ἐμπείρους πολέμων ἀπείροις
καὶ πεζοῖς πρὸς ἱππεῖς, ἀσυντάκτοις τε πρὸς
ἡνωμένους καὶ πρὸς ὁπλίτας ἐξηρτυμένους εἰ-
καιότερον ὡπλισμένοις, θυμῷ τε πλέον ἢ βουλῇ
στρατηγουμένοις πρὸς εὐπειθεῖς καὶ νεύματι πάντα
16 πράττοντας ἀντιτασσομένοις πόνος ἦν ῥάδιος·[4] ὡς
γὰρ αὐτῶν ἅπαξ ἤδη συνεταράχθησαν αἱ πρῶται
φάλαγγες, ὑπὸ τῆς ἵππου τρέπονται, καὶ τοῖς
κατόπιν αὐτῶν ἐπὶ τὸ τεῖχος βιαζομένοις περι-

[1] PA: σύνεσιν the rest.
[2] + ἡγεμὼν (ὁ ἡγ. P) PAM.
[3] PAL (corr.): ὀργαῖς the rest with Lat. (perhaps rightly).
[4] I retain with hesitation the text of PAM (Lat.): for
πόνος ἦν ῥάδιος the rest have πονοῦσιν ῥᾳδίως, beginning the
sentence with οἱ δὲ and replacing the subsequent datives by
nominatives.

6

with which the Jews had always regarded it [a] made
the distance of this, the first objective selected for
attack, seem less. The expedition was led by three
men of first-rate prowess and ability, Niger of Peraea,
Silas the Babylonian,[b] and John the Essene.[c] Ascalon
had solid walls, but was almost destitute of defenders,
its garrison consisting of but one cohort of infantry
and one squadron [d] of cavalry under the command of
Antonius.

(2) The ardour of the Jews so accelerated their
pace that they reached the spot as though they had
just issued from a neighbouring base. But Antonius
was ready for them ; informed of their intended
attack he led out his cavalry and, undaunted either
by the numbers or the audacity of the enemy, firmly
sustained their first charge and repulsed those who
were rushing forward to the ramparts. It was a case
of novices against veterans, infantry against cavalry,
ragged order against serried ranks, men casually
armed against fully equipped regulars, on the one
side men whose actions were directed by passion
rather than policy, on the other disciplined troops
acting upon the least signal from their commander.
Thus outmatched, the Jews were soon in difficulties.
For, once their front ranks were broken by the cavalry,
a rout ensued, and, the fugitives falling foul of those
in their rear who were pressing forward to the wall,

[a] Philo, *Legat. ad Gaium*, 205 (Cohn), mentions this irre-
concilable feud ; the Jews had recently devastated the town
(*B.* ii. 460). It had since 104 b.c. been independent.

[b] Both these distinguished themselves in the first engagement with Cestius, ii. 520 ; Niger was the governor, or ex-
governor, of Idumaea, ii. 566.

[c] Recently appointed general for N.W. Judaea, ii. 567.

[d] *ala*, a body of auxiliary cavalry.

πίπτοντες ἀλλήλων ἦσαν πολέμιοι, μέχρι πάντες
ταῖς τῶν ἱππέων ἐμβολαῖς εἴξαντες ἐσκεδάσθησαν
ἀνὰ πᾶν τὸ πεδίον· τὸ δὲ ἦν πολὺ καὶ πᾶν ἵπ-
17 πάσιμον. ὃ δὴ καὶ τοῖς Ῥωμαίοις· συνεργῆσαν
πλεῖστον εἰργάσατο τῶν Ἰουδαίων φόνον· τούς τε
γὰρ φεύγοντας αὐτῶν φθάνοντες ἐπέστρεφον καὶ
τῶν ὑπὸ τοῦ δρόμου συνειλουμένων διεκπαίοντες
ἀπείρους ἀνῄρουν, ἄλλοι δὲ ἄλλους ὅπῃ τρέποιντο
κυκλούμενοι καὶ περιελαύνοντες κατηκόντιζον ῥᾳ-
18 δίως. καὶ τοῖς μὲν Ἰουδαίοις τὸ ἴδιον πλῆθος
ἐρημία παρὰ τὰς ἀμηχανίας κατεφαίνετο, Ῥωμαῖοι δ᾽ ἐν ταῖς εὐπραγίαις, καίπερ ὄντες ὀλίγοι,
τῶν πολεμίων[1] καὶ περισσεύειν σφᾶς αὐτοὺς ὑπ-
19 ελάμβανον. καὶ τῶν μὲν προσφιλονεικούντων τοῖς
πταίσμασιν αἰδοῖ τε φυγῆς ταχείας καὶ μετα-
βολῆς ἐλπίδι, τῶν δὲ μὴ κοπιώντων ἐν οἷς εὐ-
τύχουν, παρέτεινεν ἡ μάχη μέχρι δείλης, ἕως ἀν-
ῃρέθησαν μὲν μύριοι τῶν Ἰουδαίων τὸν ἀριθμὸν
ἄνδρες καὶ δύο τῶν ἡγεμόνων, Ἰωάννης τε καὶ
20 Σίλας· οἱ λοιποὶ δὲ τραυματίαι τὸ πλέον σὺν τῷ
περιλειπομένῳ τῶν ἡγεμόνων Νίγερι τῆς Ἰδουμαίας εἰς πολίχνην τινά, Χάαλλις[2] καλεῖται, συν-
21 έφυγον. ὀλίγοι δέ τινες καὶ τῶν Ῥωμαίων ἐπὶ
τῆσδε τῆς παρατάξεως ἐτρώθησαν.
22 (3) Οὐ μὴν οἱ Ἰουδαῖοι τηλικαύτῃ συμφορᾷ
κατεστάλησαν τὰ φρονήματα, μᾶλλον δ᾽ αὐτῶν
τὸ πάθος ἤγειρε τὰς τόλμας, ὑπερορῶντές τε τοὺς
ἐν ποσὶ νεκροὺς ἐδελεάζοντο τοῖς προτέροις[3]
23 κατορθώμασιν ἐπὶ πληγὴν δευτέραν. διαλιπόντες

---

[1] Conj. Niese: τῷ πολέμῳ mss.
[2] PAM* Lat. (Challis): Σάλλις the rest.
[3] προγενεστέροις PAM.

they became their own enemies, until at length the whole body, succumbing to the cavalry charges, were dispersed throughout the plain. This was extensive and wholly adapted to cavalry manœuvres, a circumstance which materially assisted the Romans and caused great carnage among the Jews. For the cavalry headed off and turned the fugitives, broke through the crowds huddled together in flight, slaughtering them in masses, and, in whatever direction parties of them fled, the Romans closed them in and, galloping round them, found them an easy mark for their javelins. The Jews, notwithstanding their multitude, felt themselves isolated in their distress ; while the Romans, few as they were, imagined, in their unbroken success, that they even outnumbered their enemies. However, the former continued to struggle on under their reverses, ashamed of being so quickly routed, and in hopes of a return of fortune, while the latter were indefatigable in pushing their success ; so that the combat was prolonged till evening, when ten thousand of the Jewish rank and file, with two of the generals, John and Silas, lay dead upon the field. The remainder, most of them wounded, took refuge with Niger, the one surviving general, in a country town of Idumaea, called Chaallis.[a] The Romans, on their side, had but a few wounded in this engagement.

(3) Far, however, from the spirit of the Jews being crushed by such a calamity, their discomfiture only redoubled their audacity ; and, disregarding the dead bodies at their feet, they were lured by the memory of former triumphs to a second disaster. ^{Second Jewish attack on Ascalon repulsed.}

---

[a] Unidentified.

γοῦν οὐδ' ὅσον ἰάσασθαι τὰ τραύματα καὶ τὴν
δύναμιν πᾶσαν ἐπισυλλέξαντες ὀργιλώτερον καὶ
πολλῷ πλείους ἐπαλινδρόμουν ἐπὶ τὴν Ἀσκάλωνα.
24 παρείπετο δ' αὐτοῖς μετά τε τῆς ἀπειρίας καὶ
τῶν ἄλλων πρὸς πόλεμον ἐλασσωμάτων ἡ προτέρα
25 τύχη· τοῦ γὰρ Ἀντωνίου τὰς παρόδους προ-
λοχίσαντος ἀδόκητοι ταῖς ἐνέδραις ἐμπεσόντες καὶ
ὑπὸ τῶν ἱππέων πρὶν εἰς μάχην συντάξασθαι
κυκλωθέντες, πάλιν πίπτουσι μὲν ὑπέρ ὀκτακισχιλίους, οἱ λοιποὶ δὲ πάντες ἔφυγον, σὺν οἷς
καὶ Νίγερ, πολλὰ κατὰ τὴν φυγὴν εὐτολμίας ἐπι-
δειξάμενος ἔργα, συνελαύνονταί ⟨τε ⟩[1] προσκειμένων
τῶν πολεμίων εἴς τινα πύργον ὀχυρὸν κώμης Βελ-
26 ζεδὲκ καλουμένης. οἱ δὲ περὶ τὸν Ἀντώνιον,
ὡς μήτε τρίβοιντο περὶ τὸν πύργον ὄντα δυσάλωτον μήτε ζῶντα τὸν ἡγεμόνα καὶ γενναιότατον
τῶν πολεμίων περιίδοιεν, ὑποπιμπρᾶσι τὸ τεῖχος.
27 φλεγομένου δὲ τοῦ πύργου Ῥωμαῖοι μὲν ἀνα-
χωροῦσι γεγηθότες ὡς διεφθαρμένου καὶ Νίγερος,
ὁ δὲ εἰς τὸ μυχαίτατον τοῦ φρουρίου σπήλαιον
καταπηδήσας ἐκ τοῦ πύργου[2] διασώζεται, καὶ
μεθ' ἡμέρας τρεῖς τοῖς μετ' ὀλοφυρμὸν πρὸς
28 κηδείαν αὐτὸν ἐρευνῶσιν ὑποφθέγγεται. προελθὼν
δὲ χαρᾶς ἀνελπίστου πάντας ἐπλήρωσεν Ἰουδαίους
ὡς προνοίᾳ θεοῦ σωθεὶς αὐτοῖς στρατηγὸς εἰς τὰ
μέλλοντα.
29   (4) Οὐεσπασιανὸς δὲ τὰς δυνάμεις ἀναλαβὼν
ἐκ τῆς Ἀντιοχείας, ἣ μητρόπολίς ἐστι τῆς Συρίας,
μεγέθους τε ἕνεκα καὶ τῆς ἄλλης εὐδαιμονίας

---

[1] ins. Destinon (after Lat.) : om. mss.
[2] πυρὸς conj. Destinon and Niese.

Without even leaving time for wounds to heal, they reassembled all their forces and, more furious and in far greater strength, returned to the assault on Ascalon. But, with the same inexperience and the same military disqualifications, the same fortune attended them as before. Antonius had placed ambuscades in the passes ; into these traps they inconsiderately fell, and before they could form up in battle order they were surrounded by the cavalry and again lost upwards of eight thousand men. All the remainder fled—including Niger, who distinguished himself in the retreat by numerous feats of valour—and, hard pressed by the enemy, were driven into a strong tower in a village called Belzedek.[a] The troops of Antonius, unwilling either to expend their strength upon a tower that was almost impregnable, or to allow the enemy's general and bravest hero to escape alive, set fire to the walls. On seeing the tower in flames, the Romans retired exultant, in the belief that Niger had perished with it ; but he had leapt from the tower and found refuge in a cave in the recesses of the fortress, and three days later his lamenting friends, while searching for his corpse for burial, overheard his voice beneath them. His reappearance filled all Jewish hearts with unlooked-for joy ; they thought that God's providence had preserved him to be their general in conflicts to come.[b]

(4) Vespasian had now set in motion his forces assembled at Antioch, the capital of Syria, and a city which, for extent and opulence, unquestionably ranks

Vespasian advances from Antioch to Ptolemais.

---

[a] Unidentified.
[b] He was murdered by the Zealots during the siege of Jerusalem (B. iv. 359).

τρίτον ἀδηρίτως ἐπὶ τῆς ὑπὸ Ῥωμαίοις οἰκουμένης ἔχουσα τόπον, ἔνθα μετὰ πάσης τῆς ἰδίας
ἰσχύος ἐκδεχόμενον αὐτοῦ τὴν ἄφιξιν καὶ Ἀγρίππαν τὸν βασιλέα κατειλήφει, ἐπὶ Πτολεμαΐδος
30 ἠπείγετο. καὶ κατὰ ταύτην ὑπαντῶσιν αὐτῷ τὴν
πόλιν οἱ τῆς Γαλιλαίας Σέπφωριν νεμόμενοι,
31 μόνοι τῶν τῇδε εἰρηνικὰ φρονοῦντες· οἳ καὶ τῆς
ἑαυτῶν σωτηρίας καὶ τῆς Ῥωμαίων ἰσχύος οὐκ
ἀπρονόητοι πρὶν ἀφικέσθαι Οὐεσπασιανὸν Και-
σεννίῳ Γάλλῳ πίστεις τε ἔδοσαν καὶ δεξιὰς ἔλαβον
32 καὶ παρεδέξαντο φρουράν. τότε γε μὴν φιλο-
φρόνως ἐκδεξάμενοι τὸν ἡγεμόνα προθύμως σφᾶς
αὐτοὺς ὑπέσχοντο κατὰ τῶν ὁμοφύλων συμ-
33 μάχους· οἷς ὁ στρατηγὸς ἀξιώσασι τέως πρὸς
ἀσφάλειαν ἱππεῖς τε καὶ πεζοὺς παραδίδωσιν
ὅσους ἀνθέξειν ταῖς καταδρομαῖς, εἴ τι Ἰουδαῖοι
34 παρακινοῖεν, ὑπελάμβανεν· καὶ γὰρ οὐ μικρὸν
ἐδόκει τὸ κινδύνευμα πρὸς τὸν μέλλοντα πόλεμον
ἀφαιρεθῆναι τὴν Σέπφωριν, μεγίστην μὲν οὖσαν
τῆς Γαλιλαίας πόλιν, ἐρυμνοτάτῳ δ᾽ ἐπιτετειχισμένην χωρίῳ καὶ φρουρὰν ὅλου τοῦ ἔθνους ἐσο-
μένην.

35 (iii. 1) Δύο δ᾽ οὔσας τὰς Γαλιλαίας, τήν τε
ἄνω καὶ τὴν κάτω προσαγορευομένην, περιίσχει
μὲν ἡ Φοινίκη τε καὶ Συρία, διορίζει δ᾽ ἀπὸ μὲν
δύσεως ἡλίου Πτολεμαῒς τοῖς τῆς χώρας τέρμασι
καὶ Κάρμηλος, τὸ πάλαι μὲν Γαλιλαίων, νῦν δὲ
36 Τυρίων ὄρος· ᾧ προσίσχει Γάβα,[1] πόλις ἱππέων,
οὕτω προσαγορευομένη διὰ τὸ τοὺς ὑφ᾽ Ἡρώδου

[1] So Lat. (cf. A. xv. 294, Vita 115): Γαβαὰ, Γάβαλα etc.
MSS.
12

third [a] among the cities of the Roman world. Here he had found, among others, king Agrippa awaiting his arrival with all his own troops. From Antioch Vespasian pushed on to Ptolemais. At this city he was met by the inhabitants of Sepphoris in Galilee, the only people of that province who displayed pacific sentiments. For, with an eye to their own security and a sense of the power of Rome, they had already, before the coming of Vespasian, given pledges to Caesennius Gallus, received his assurance of protection, and admitted a Roman garrison ; [b] now they offered a cordial welcome to the commander-in-chief, and promised him their active support against their countrymen. At their request, the general provisionally assigned them for their protection as large a force of cavalry and infantry as he considered sufficient to repel invasions in the event of the Jews causing trouble ; indeed, it appeared to him that the loss of Sepphoris would be a hazard gravely affecting the impending campaign, as it was the largest city of Galilee, a fortress in an exceptionally strong position in the enemy's territory, and adapted to keep guard over the entire province.

(iii. 1) Galilee, with its two divisions known as Upper and Lower Galilee, is enveloped by Phoenicia and Syria. Its western frontiers are the outlying territory of Ptolemais and Carmel, a mountain once belonging to Galilee, and now to Tyre ; adjacent to Carmel is Gaba, the " city of cavalry," so called from the cavalry who, on their discharge by King Herod

[a] After Rome and Alexandria.
[b] Cf. ii. 510 (Caesennius was commander of the 12th legion) with Vita 394 (Sepphoris asks for and obtains a garrison from Cestius Gallus).

βασιλέως ἀπολυομένους ἱππεῖς ἐν αὐτῇ κατοικεῖν·
37 ἀπὸ δὲ μεσημβρίας Σαμαρεῖτίς τε καὶ Σκυθό-
πολις μέχρι τῶν Ἰορδάνου ναμάτων. πρὸς ἔω
δ' Ἱππηνῇ τε καὶ Γαδάροις ἀποτέμνεται καὶ τῇ
Γαυλανίτιδι·¹ ταύτῃ καὶ τῆς Ἀγρίππα βασιλείας
38 ὅροι. τὰ προσάρκτια δ' αὐτῆς Τύρῳ τε καὶ τῇ
Τυρίων χώρᾳ περατοῦται. καὶ τῆς μὲν κάτω
καλουμένης Γαλιλαίας ἀπὸ Τιβεριάδος μέχρι
Χαβουλών, ἧς ἐν τοῖς παραλίοις Πτολεμαῒς
39 γείτων, τὸ μῆκος ἐκτείνεται. πλατύνεται δ' ἀπὸ
τῆς ἐν τῷ μεγάλῳ πεδίῳ κειμένης κώμης, Ξαλὼθ²
καλεῖται, μέχρι Βηρσάβης, ᾗ καὶ τῆς ἄνω Γαλιλαίας εἰς εὖρος ἀρχὴ μέχρι Βακὰ κώμης· αὕτη
40 δὲ τὴν Τυρίων γῆν ὁρίζει. μηκύνεται δὲ μέχρι
Μηρὼθ ἀπὸ Θελλᾶ κώμης Ἰορδάνου γείτονος.
41 (2) Τηλικαῦται δ' οὖσαι τὸ μέγεθος καὶ τοσούτοις ἔθνεσιν ἀλλοφύλοις κεκυκλωμέναι πρὸς πᾶσαν
42 ἀεὶ πολέμου πεῖραν ἀντέσχον· μάχιμοί τε γὰρ ἐκ
νηπίων καὶ πολλοὶ Γαλιλαῖοι πάντοτε, καὶ οὔτε
δειλία ποτὲ τοὺς ἄνδρας οὔτε λιπανδρία τὴν χώραν
κατέσχεν, ἐπειδὴ πίων τε πᾶσα καὶ εὔβοτος καὶ
δένδρεσι παντοίοις κατάφυτος, ὡς ὑπὸ τῆς εὐ-
πετείας προκαλέσασθαι καὶ τὸν ἥκιστα γῆς φιλό-
43 πονον. προσησκήθη γοῦν ὑπὸ τῶν οἰκητόρων
πᾶσα, καὶ μέρος αὐτῆς ἀργὸν οὐδέν, ἀλλὰ καὶ
πόλεις πυκναὶ καὶ τὸ τῶν κωμῶν πλῆθος πανταχοῦ
πολυάνθρωπον διὰ τὴν εὐθηνίαν, ὡς τὴν ἐλαχίστην

¹ Γαυλωνίτιδι PA.
² Ἐξαλὼθ PAL : Ξαλὼθ the rest, cf. Vita 227.

---

[a] Cf. A. xv. 294 ; called Geba by Pliny, Nat. Hist. v. 19.
75.

settled in this town.[a]   On the south the country is
bounded by Samaria and the territory of Scythopolis
up to the waters of Jordan ; on the east by the
territory of Hippos, Gadara, and Gaulanitis, the
frontier-line of Agrippa's kingdom ; on the north
Tyre and its dependent district mark its limits.
Lower Galilee extends in length from Tiberias to
Chabulon, which is not far from Ptolemais on the
coast ; in breadth, from a village in the Great Plain
called Xaloth [b] to Bersabe.   At this point begins
Upper Galilee, which extends in breadth to the
village of Baca, the frontier of Tyrian territory ; in
length, it reaches from the village of Thella, near the
Jordan, to Meroth.

(2) With this limited area, and although surrounded by such powerful foreign nations, the two
Galilees have always resisted any hostile invasion,
for the inhabitants are from infancy inured to war,
and have at all times been numerous ; never did the
men lack courage nor the country men.   For the
land is everywhere so rich in soil and pasturage and
produces such variety of trees, that even the most
indolent are tempted by these facilities to devote
themselves to agriculture.   In fact, every inch of the
soil has been cultivated by the inhabitants ; there is
not a parcel of waste land.   The towns, too, are
thickly distributed, and even the villages, thanks to
the fertility of the soil, are all so densely populated

---

[b] Mentioned as on the southern frontier in *Vita* 227, " I
ought to have gone to Xaloth or beyond " (to meet a deputation coming from Jerusalem to Galilee) ; lying on the
" flanks " of Mt. Tabor, it is the O.T. Chisloth-tabor, Jos.
xix. 12, modern *Iksal*.   Josephus by " length " here means
the measurement from east to west, by " breadth " that
from south to north.

ὑπὲρ πεντακισχιλίους πρὸς τοῖς μυρίοις ἔχειν
οἰκήτορας.

44 (3) Καθόλου δ', εἰ καὶ τῷ μεγέθει τις ἐλαττώ-
σειε τῆς Περαίας τὴν Γαλιλαίαν, προέλοιτο δ' ἂν
τῇ δυνάμει· ἡ μὲν γὰρ ἐνεργὸς ὅλη καὶ συνεχές[1]
ἐστιν καρποφόρος, ἡ Περαία δὲ πολὺ μὲν μείζων,
ἔρημος δὲ καὶ τραχεῖα τὸ πλέον, πρός τε καρπῶν
45 ἡμέρων αὔξησιν ἀγριωτέρα (τό γε μὴν μαλθακὸν
αὐτῆς καὶ πάμφορον, καὶ τὰ πεδία δένδρεσι ποικίλοις κατάφυτα τὸ πλεῖστόν τε ἐλαίαν [τε][2] καὶ
ἄμπελον καὶ φοινικῶνας ἤσκηται) διαρδομένη
χειμάρροις τε τοῖς ἀπὸ τῶν ὀρῶν καὶ πηγαῖς
ἀεννάοις ἅλις, εἴ ποτ' ἐκεῖνοι σειρίῳ φθίνοιεν.
46 μῆκος μὲν [οὖν][3] αὐτῆς ἀπὸ Μαχαιροῦντος εἰς
Πέλλαν, εὖρος δ' ἀπὸ Φιλαδελφείας μέχρι Ἰορδά-
47 νου. καὶ Πέλλῃ μέν, ἣν προειρήκαμεν, τὰ πρὸς
ἄρκτον ὁρίζεται, πρὸς ἑσπέραν δὲ Ἰορδάνῃ· μεσημβρινὸν δ' αὐτῆς πέρας ἡ Μωαβῖτις, καὶ πρὸς
ἀνατολὴν Ἀραβίᾳ τε καὶ Ἐσεβωνίτιδι,[4] πρὸς δὲ
Φιλαδελφηνῇ καὶ Γεράσοις[5] ἀποτέμνεται.

48 (4) Ἡ δὲ Σαμαρεῖτις χώρα μέση μὲν τῆς Γαλιλαίας ἐστὶ καὶ τῆς Ἰουδαίας· ἀρχομένη γὰρ ἀπὸ
τῆς ἐν τῷ [μεγάλῳ][6] πεδίῳ κειμένης Γιναίας[7]

---

[1] Destinon, cf. Lat. assidue: συνεχής MSS.
[2] ἐλαίαν (om. τε) PAM: εἰς ἐλαίαν τε the rest.
[3] om. PAL.
[4] Reinach after Schürer (Σεβωνίτιδι): Σιλωνίτιδι or Σιλ-
βωνίτιδι MSS.
[5] VR: Γεράροις the rest.   [6] om. PAL.
[7] C: Γηνεὼς or Γηνέας the rest: the place is called Γήμα(ν)
B. ii. 232, Γιναῆ(ς) A. xx. 118.

---

[a] We may suspect exaggeration.   There were 204 towns

that the smallest of them contains above fifteen thousand inhabitants.[a]

(3) In short, if Galilee, in superficial area, must be reckoned inferior to Peraea, it must be given the preference for its abundant resources ; for it is entirely under cultivation and produces crops from one end to the other, whereas Peraea, though far more extensive, is for the most part desert and rugged and too wild to bring tender fruits to maturity. However, there, too, there are tracts of finer soil which are productive of every species of crop ; and the plains are covered with a variety of trees, olive, vine, and palm being those principally cultivated. The country is watered by torrents descending from the mountains and by springs which never dry up and provide sufficient moisture when the torrents dwindle in the dog-days. Peraea extends in length from Machaerus to Pella,[b] in breadth from Philadelphia [c] to the Jordan. The northern frontier is Pella, which we have just mentioned, the western frontier is the Jordan ; on the south it is bounded by the land of Moab, on the east by Arabia, Heshbonitis, Philadelphia, and Gerasa. Peraea

(4) The province of Samaria lies between Galilee and Judaea ; beginning at the village of Ginaea [d] situate in the Great Plain, it terminates at the Samaria and Judaea.

and villages in Galilee (*Vita* 235); the largest village was Japha (*ib.* 230), the largest town Sepphoris (*ib.* 232).

  [b] Including Machaerus, but excluding Pella (mod. *Fahil*) which was in Decapolis ; Peraea is the Jewish province, not comprising the northern trans-Jordanic region (Decapolis).

  [c] The O.T. Rabbah of Ammon, called Philadelphia after Ptolemy II Philadelphus, modern *Amman* ; it was in Decapolis, but a neighbouring village was the scene of a bloody boundary dispute between its citizens and the Peraean Jews (*A.* xx. 2).   [d] *Cf. B.* ii. 232 (Gema).

JOSEPHUS

ὄνομα κώμης ἐπιλήγει τῆς Ἀκραβετηνῶν τοπ-
αρχίας· φύσιν δὲ τῆς Ἰουδαίας κατ' οὐδὲν διά-
49 φορος. ἀμφότεραι γὰρ ὀρειναὶ καὶ πεδιάδες, εἴς
τε γεωργίαν μαλθακαὶ καὶ πολύφοροι, κατάδενδροί
τε καὶ ὀπώρας ὀρεινῆς καὶ ἡμέρου μεσταί, παρ'
ὅσον οὐδαμοῦ φύσει διψάδες, ὕονται δὲ τὸ πλέον·
50 γλυκὺ δὲ νᾶμα πᾶν διαφόρως ἐν αὐταῖς, καὶ διὰ
πλῆθος πόας ἀγαθῆς τὰ κτήνη πλέον ἢ παρ'
ἄλλοις γαλακτοφόρα. μέγιστόν γε μὴν τεκμήριον
ἀρετῆς καὶ εὐθηνίας τὸ πληθύειν ἀνδρῶν ἑκατέραν.
51 (5) Μεθόριος δ' αὐτῶν ἡ Ἀνουάθου Βόρκαιος
προσαγορευομένη κώμη· πέρας αὕτη τῆς Ἰουδαίας
τὰ πρὸς βορέαν, τὰ νότια δ' αὐτῆς ἐπὶ μῆκος
μετρουμένης ὁρίζει προσκυροῦσα τοῖς Ἀράβων
ὅροις κώμη, καλοῦσι δ' αὐτὴν Ἰαρδὰν[1] οἱ τῇδε
Ἰουδαῖοι. εὖρός γε μὴν ἀπὸ Ἰορδάνου ποταμοῦ
52 μέχρις Ἰόππης ἀναπέπταται. μεσαιτάτη δ' αὐτῆς
πόλις τὰ Ἱεροσόλυμα κεῖται, παρ' ὃ καί τινες οὐκ
ἀσκόπως ὀμφαλὸν τὸ ἄστυ τῆς χώρας ἐκάλεσαν.
53 ἀφῄρηται δ' οὐδὲ τῶν ἐκ θαλάσσης τερπνῶν ἡ
Ἰουδαία τοῖς παραλίοις κατατείνουσα μέχρι Πτολε-
54 μαΐδος. μερίζεται δ' εἰς ἕνδεκα κληρουχίας, ὧν

---

[1] C : Ἰορδὰν the rest.

[a] South-east of Shechem.
[b] The Lat. has "Anunath which is also called Borceas";
Borcaeus is the modern *Berkit*, nine miles due south of
Shechem.   [c] Or, perhaps, "at its greatest length."
[d] Or Iarda ; perhaps the modern *Tell Arad*, sixteen miles
nearly due south of Hebron.
[e] Strictly, rather to the north-east of the centre of Judaea.
The usual Rabbinic tradition, however, was that (like Delphi
to the Greek) Jerusalem was the navel (*ṭabur*) of the whole
world, a position assigned to it in some mediaeval maps.
See the *Book of Jubilees*, viii. 19, " Mount Zion, the centre of

18

toparchy of Acrabatene.[a] Its character differs in no
wise from that of Judaea. Both regions consist
of hills and plains, yield a light and fertile soil for
agriculture, are well wooded, and abound in fruits,
both wild and cultivated; both owe their productive-
ness to the entire absence of dry deserts and to a
rainfall for the most part abundant. All the running
water has a singularly sweet taste; and owing to the
abundance of excellent grass the cattle yield more
milk than in other districts. But the surest testi-
mony to the virtues and thriving condition of the
two countries is that both have a dense population.

(5) On the frontier separating them lies the village Judaea.
called Anuath Borcaeus,[b] the northern limit of Judaea;
its southern boundary, if one measures the country
lengthwise,[c] is marked by a village on the Arabian
frontier, which the local Jews call Iardan.[d] In
breadth it stretches from the river Jordan to Joppa.
The city of Jerusalem lies at its very centre,[e] for
which reason the town has sometimes, not inaptly,
been called the "navel" of the country. Judaea is,
moreover, not cut off from the amenities of the sea,
because it slopes down towards the coast on a ridge
extending as far as Ptolemais.[f] It is divided into

the navel of the earth," Talm. Bab. *Sanhedrin*, 37 a, with
other passages cited by Charles (on *Jub.* viii. 12); the idea
was based, *inter alia*, on Ezek. xxxviii. 12.
  [f] A difficult clause. Not "having a coast extending as
far as Ptolemais," for the maritime plain was not in Jewish
possession; and Ptolemais, in Phoenician territory, was far
north, not only of Judaea, but of Samaria. The reference,
it seems, is to the central mountain chain, which, sloping
westwards to the Mediterranean and extending northwards
through the Judaean plateau and Mt. Ephraim, terminates
in Mt. Carmel, a little south of Ptolemais; perhaps also to
the *view* obtainable therefrom.

ἄρχει μὲν βασίλειον τὰ Ἱεροσόλυμα προανίσχουσα
τῆς περιοίκου πάσης ὥσπερ ἡ κεφαλὴ σώματος·
αἱ λοιπαὶ δὲ μετ' αὐτὴν διήρηνται¹ τὰς τοπαρχίας,
55 Γόφνα δευτέρα καὶ μετὰ ταύτην Ἀκράβετα,
Θάμνα πρὸς ταύταις καὶ Λύδδα, Ἀμμαοῦς καὶ
Πέλλη καὶ Ἰδουμαία καὶ Ἐνγαδδαὶ καὶ Ἡρώδειον
56 καὶ Ἱεριχοῦς· μεθ' ἃς Ἰάμνεια καὶ Ἰόππη τῶν
περιοίκων ἀφηγοῦνται, κἀπὶ ταύταις ἥ τε Γαμα-
λιτικὴ καὶ Γαυλανῖτις Βαταναία τε καὶ Τραχω-
νῖτις, αἳ καὶ τῆς Ἀγρίππα βασιλείας εἰσὶ μοῖραι.
57 ἀρχομένη δὲ ἀπὸ Λιβάνου ὄρους καὶ τῶν Ἰορδάνου
πηγῶν ἡ χώρα μέχρι τῆς πρὸς Τιβεριάδι² λίμνης
εὐρύνεται, ἀπὸ δὲ κώμης καλουμένης Ἀρφᾶς
μέχρις Ἰουλιάδος ἐκτείνεται τὸ μῆκος. οἰκοῦσι
58 δ' αὐτὴν μιγάδες Ἰουδαῖοί τε καὶ Σύροι. τὰ μὲν
δὴ περὶ τῆς Ἰουδαίων τε καὶ πέριξ χώρας ὡς
ἐνῆν μάλιστα συντόμως ἀπηγγέλκαμεν.

59 (iv. 1) Ἡ δ' ὑπὸ Οὐεσπασιανοῦ πεμφθεῖσα
Σεπφωρίταις βοήθεια, χίλιοι μὲν ἱππεῖς ἑξακισχίλιοι δὲ πεζοί, Πλακίδου χιλιαρχοῦντος αὐτῶν,
ἐν τῷ μεγάλῳ πεδίῳ στρατοπεδευσάμενοι δι-
αιροῦνται, καὶ τὸ μὲν πεζὸν ἐν τῇ πόλει πρὸς
φυλακὴν αὐτῆς, τὸ δ' ἱππικὸν ἐπὶ τῆς παρεμβολῆς

¹ κατὰ has possibly dropped out.
² πρὸς Τιβεριάδι Niese : πρὸς Τιβεριάδα or Τιβεριάδος the rest.

ᵃ Or " allotments." Viewed from the Jewish standpoint
they are κληρουχίαι (cf. B. v. 160 ἡ Ἑβραίων κληρουχία and
often in A. of the allotments of the tribes in Canaan), from
the Roman standpoint, for administrative and revenue-
collecting purposes, τοπαρχίαι. Pliny, Hist. Nat. v. 14. 70,
mentions the division of Judaea into ten toparchies ; he omits
Idumaea and Engaddi, inserts Joppa (incorrectly), and sub-

eleven districts,[a] among which Jerusalem as the
capital is supreme, dominating all the neighbourhood as the head towers above the body ; in the case
of the other minor districts the divisions coincide
with the toparchies. Gophna is the second, then
come Acrabeta, Thamna, Lydda, Emmaus, Pella,[b]
Idumaea, Engaddi, Herodion, and Jericho. To these
must be added [c] Jamnia and Joppa, which have
jurisdiction over the surrounding localities, and lastly
the territories of Gamala, Gaulanitis, Batanaea, and
Trachonitis, which form, moreover, part of Agrippa's   Kingdom of
kingdom. That kingdom, beginning at Mount   Agrippa II.
Libanus and the sources of the Jordan, extends in
breadth [d] to the lake of Tiberias, and in length [e] from
a village called Arpha [f] to Julias [g] ; it contains a
mixed population of Jews and Syrians. Such, in
briefest possible outline, is my description of the
country of the Jews and of their neighbours.

(iv. 1) The supports sent by Vespasian to the people   The Roman
of Sepphoris [h] consisted of a thousand cavalry and   garrison at
                                                       Sepphoris
six thousand infantry under the command of the   ravages
tribune Placidus ; the troops at first camped in the   Galilee.
Great Plain and then divided, the infantry taking up
quarters in the town for its protection, the cavalry

stitutes (correctly) for Pella Betholethephene (= Bethleptepha,
B. iv. 445).
  [b] See previous note.
  [c] Josephus here appends to the four main provinces of
Jewish territory (1) the only two maritime towns whose
population was predominantly Jewish, (2) Agrippa's kingdom in the north, also containing a large Jewish element.
  [d] From north to south.   [e] From east to west.
  [f] Unidentified (east of Trachonitis).
  [g] Bethsaida Julias at the head of the Sea of Galilee.
  [h] Resuming the narrative of §§ 33 f.

60 αὐλίζεται. προϊόντες δὲ ἑκατέρωθεν συνεχῶς καὶ
τὰ πέριξ τῆς χώρας κατατρέχοντες μεγάλα τοὺς
περὶ τὸν Ἰώσηπον ἐκάκουν, ἀτρεμοῦντάς τε κατὰ
πόλεις[1] ἔξωθεν ληζόμενοι καὶ προθέοντας ὁπότε
61 θαρρήσειαν ἀνακόπτοντες. ὥρμησέ γε μὴν Ἰώσηπος ἐπὶ τὴν πόλιν αἱρήσειν ἐλπίσας, ἣν αὐτὸς
πρὶν ἀποστῆναι Γαλιλαίων ἐτείχισεν, ὡς καὶ
Ῥωμαίοις δυσάλωτον εἶναι· διὸ καὶ τῆς ἐλπίδος
ἀφήμαρτεν, τοῦ τε βιάζεσθαι καὶ τοῦ μεταπείθειν
62 Σεπφωρίτας ἀσθενέστερος εὑρεθείς. παρώξυνεν
δὲ μᾶλλον τὸν πόλεμον ἐπὶ τὴν χώραν, καὶ οὔτε
νύκτωρ οὔτε μεθ᾽ ἡμέραν ὀργῇ τῆς ἐπιβολῆς[2] οἱ
Ῥωμαῖοι διέλιπον δηοῦντες αὐτῶν τὰ πεδία καὶ
διαρπάζοντες τὰ ἐπὶ τῆς χώρας κτήματα, καὶ
κτείνοντες μὲν ἀεὶ τὸ μάχιμον, ἀνδραποδιζόμενοι
63 δὲ τοὺς ἀσθενεῖς. πυρὶ δὲ ἡ Γαλιλαία καὶ αἵματι
πεπλήρωτο πᾶσα, πάθους τε οὐδενὸς ἢ συμφορᾶς
ἀπείρατος ἦν· μία γὰρ καταφυγὴ διωκομένοις αἱ
ὑπὸ τοῦ Ἰωσήπου τειχισθεῖσαι πόλεις ἦσαν.

64 (2) Ὁ δὲ Τίτος περαιωθεὶς ἀπὸ τῆς Ἀχαΐας
εἰς τὴν Ἀλεξάνδρειαν ὠκύτερον ἢ κατὰ χειμῶνος
ὥραν, παραλαμβάνει μὲν ἐφ᾽ ἣν ἔσταλτο δύναμιν,
συντόνῳ δὲ χρώμενος πορείᾳ διὰ τάχους εἰς
65 Πτολεμαΐδα ἀφικνεῖται. κἀκεῖ καταλαβὼν τὸν
πατέρα δυσὶ τοῖς ἅμα αὐτῷ τάγμασιν, ἦν δὲ τὰ
ἐπισημότατα τὸ πέμπτον καὶ τὸ δέκατον, ζεύγνυσι
66 τὸ ἀχθὲν ὑπ᾽ αὐτοῦ πεντεκαιδέκατον. τούτοις

---

[1] text Niese : ἀτρεμοῦντα τάς τε πόλεις most mss.
[2] Destinon : ἐπιβουλῆς mss.

remaining in camp. Both divisions made constant
sallies and overran the surrounding country, causing
serious trouble to Josephus and his men : if the latter
remained stationary in their cities, the Romans
ravaged the surrounding district ; whenever they
ventured out, the Romans beat them back. Josephus
did, in fact, attempt an assault on the city in hopes
of capturing it, although he had himself, before it
abandoned the Galilaean cause, so strongly fortified
it as to render it practically impregnable even to the
Romans ; consequently his hopes were foiled and he
found it beyond his power either to compel or to
persuade Sepphoris to surrender.[a] Indeed he drew
down fiercer hostilities upon the country ; for the
Romans, enraged at his enterprise, never ceased,
night or day, to devastate the plains and to pillage
the property of the country-folk, invariably killing
all capable of bearing arms and reducing the in-
efficient to servitude. Galilee from end to end
became a scene of fire and blood ; from no misery,
no calamity was it exempt ; the one refuge for
the hunted inhabitants was in the cities fortified
by Josephus.

Josephus unsuccessfully attacks Sepphoris.

(2) Meanwhile Titus,[b] after a swifter passage from
Achaia to Alexandria than is usual in the winter
season, had taken command of the forces which he
had been sent to fetch, and by a forced march soon
reached Ptolemais. There he found his father with
his two legions, the most distinguished of all, the
fifth and the tenth, and now united to them the
fifteenth which he had brought himself. These

Titus joins Vespasian at Ptolemais.

Total strength of the Roman forces.

---

[a] A similar, though apparently distinct, attack of Josephus
on Sepphoris (*before* the arrival of Vespasian) is recorded in
Vita 395 ff. [b] § 8.

εἵποντο ὀκτωκαίδεκα σπεῖραι· προσεγένοντο δὲ
καὶ ἀπὸ Καισαρείας πέντε καὶ ἱππέων ἴλη μία,
67 πέντε δ' ἕτεραι τῶν ἀπὸ Συρίας ἱππέων. τῶν δὲ
σπειρῶν αἱ δέκα μὲν εἶχον ἀνὰ χιλίους πεζούς,
αἱ δὲ λοιπαὶ δεκατρεῖς ἀνὰ ἑξακοσίους μὲν πεζούς,
68 ἱππεῖς δὲ ἑκατὸν εἴκοσιν. συχνὸν δὲ καὶ παρὰ
τῶν βασιλέων συνήχθη συμμαχικόν, Ἀντιόχου μὲν
καὶ Ἀγρίππα καὶ Σοαίμου παρασχομένων ἀνὰ
δισχιλίους πεζοὺς τοξότας καὶ χιλίους ἱππεῖς, τοῦ
δὲ Ἄραβος Μάλχου χιλίους πέμψαντος ἱππεῖς ἐπὶ
πεζοῖς πεντακισχιλίοις, ὧν τὸ πλέον ἦσαν τοξόται,
69 ὡς τὴν πᾶσαν δύναμιν συνεξαριθμουμένων τῶν
βασιλικῶν ἱππέας τε καὶ πεζοὺς εἰς ἓξ ἀθροίζεσθαι
μυριάδας δίχα θεραπόντων, οἳ παμπληθεῖς μὲν
εἵποντο, διὰ δὲ συνάσκησιν πολεμικὴν οὐκ ἂν
ἀποτάσσοιντο τοῦ μαχίμου, κατὰ μὲν εἰρήνην ἐν
ταῖς μελέταις τῶν δεσποτῶν ἀεὶ στρεφόμενοι,
συγκινδυνεύοντες δ' ἐν πολέμοις, ὡς μήτ' ἐμπειρίᾳ
μήτ' ἀλκῇ τινος πλὴν τῶν δεσποτῶν ἐλαττοῦσθαι.

70 (v. 1) Κἂν τούτῳ μὲν οὖν θαυμάσαι τις ἂν
Ῥωμαίων τὸ προμηθές, κατασκευαζομένων ἑαυτοῖς
τὸ οἰκετικὸν οὐ μόνον εἰς τὰς τοῦ βίου διακονίας
71 ἀλλὰ καὶ πρὸς τοὺς πολέμους χρήσιμον. εἰ δέ τις
αὐτῶν καὶ εἰς τὴν ἄλλην σύνταξιν τῆς στρατιᾶς

---

^a The cohort was the tenth part of a legion, normally
numbering about 600 men.

^b Antiochus IV, king of Commagene ; Soaemus, king of
Emesa (B. ii. 500 f.).

^c The items supplied work out at not far short of this
figure. An exact computation is impossible owing to un-

legions were accompanied by eighteen cohorts [a] ;
five more cohorts with one squadron of cavalry came
to join them from Caesarea, and five squadrons of
cavalry from Syria. Of the twenty-three cohorts,
ten numbered each a thousand infantry, the remaining thirteen had each a strength of six hundred
infantry and a hundred and twenty cavalry. A
further considerable force of auxiliaries had been
mustered by the kings Antiochus, Agrippa, and
Soaemus,[b] each of whom furnished two thousand
unmounted bowmen and a thousand cavalry ; the
Arab Malchus sent a thousand cavalry and five
thousand infantry, mainly bowmen. Thus the total
strength of the forces, horse and foot, including the
contingents of the kings, amounted to sixty thousand,[c]
without counting the servants who followed in vast
numbers and may properly be included in the cate-
gory of combatants, whose military training they
shared ; for, taking part in peace time in all their
masters' manœuvres and in war time in their dangers,
they yielded to none but them in skill and prowess.

(v. 1) One cannot but admire the forethought Digression
shown in this particular by the Romans, in making on the
their servant class useful to them not only for the Roman
ministrations of ordinary life but also for war. If army.
one goes on to study the organization of their army [d]

certainty as to the strength of the squadrons (*alae*) of cavalry.
The legion=about 6120 men. If the *alae* are reckoned at
500 men each, the total is 55,720; if at 1000 men, it amounts
to 58,720.

[d] This remarkable chapter, a first-rate authority on the
Roman army in the first century, should be compared with
the passage which probably suggested it—the more detailed
digression of Polybius (vi. 19-42) on the army of three
centuries earlier.

25

ἀπίδοι, γνώσεται τὴν τοσήνδε ἡγεμονίαν αὐτοὺς
72 ἀρετῆς κτῆμα ἔχοντας, οὐ δῶρον τύχης. οὐ γὰρ
αὐτοῖς ἀρχὴ τῶν ὅπλων [ὁ] πόλεμος, οὐδ' ἐπὶ
μόνας τὰς χρείας τὼ χεῖρε κινοῦσιν ἐν εἰρήνῃ
προηργηκότες, ἀλλ' ὥσπερ συμπεφυκότες τοῖς
ὅπλοις οὐδέποτε τῆς ἀσκήσεως λαμβάνουσιν ἐκε-
73 χειρίαν οὐδὲ ἀναμένουσιν τοὺς καιρούς. αἱ μελέται
δ' αὐτοῖς οὐδὲν τῆς κατὰ ἀλήθειαν εὐτονίας
ἀποδέουσιν, ἀλλ' ἕκαστος ὁσημέραι στρατιώτης
πάσῃ προθυμίᾳ καθάπερ ἐν πολέμῳ γυμνάζεται.
74 διὸ κουφότατα τὰς μάχας διαφέρουσιν· οὔτε γὰρ
ἀταξία διασκίδνησιν αὐτοὺς ἀπὸ τῆς ἐν ἔθει συν-
τάξεως, οὔτε δέος ἐξίστησιν, οὔτε δαπανᾷ πόνος,
ἕπεται δὲ τὸ κρατεῖν ἀεὶ κατὰ τῶν οὐχ ὁμοίων
75 βέβαιον. καὶ οὐκ ἂν ἁμάρτοι τις εἰπὼν τὰς μὲν
μελέτας αὐτῶν χωρὶς αἵματος παρατάξεις, τὰς
76 παρατάξεις δὲ μεθ' αἵματος μελέτας. οὐδὲ γὰρ
ἐξ ἐπιδρομῆς εὐάλωτοι πολεμίοις· ὅπῃ δ' ἂν
ἐμβάλωσιν εἰς ἐχθρῶν γῆν, οὐ πρὶν ἅπτονται
77 μάχης ἢ τειχίσαι στρατόπεδον. τὸ δὲ οὐκ εἰκαῖον
οὐδὲ ἀνώμαλον ἐγείρουσιν, οὐδὲ πάντες ἢ ἀτάκτως
διαλαβόντες, ἀλλ' εἰ μὲν ἀνώμαλος ὢν τύχοι
χῶρος, ἐξομαλίζεται· διαμετρεῖται δὲ παρεμβολὴ
78 τετράγωνος αὐτοῖς. καὶ τεκτόνων πλῆθος ἕπεται
τῶν τε πρὸς τὴν δόμησιν ἐργαλείων.[1]
79 (2) Καὶ τὸ μὲν ἔνδον εἰς σκηνὰς διαλαμβά-

[1] τά τε . . . ἐργαλεῖα MVRC.

[a] Polybius, vi. 42, contrasts the practice of Greeks and

26

as a whole, it will be seen that this vast empire of
theirs has come to them as the prize of valour, and
not as a gift of fortune.

For their nation does not wait for the outbreak of Their
war to give men their first lesson in arms ; they do not training in
sit with folded hands in peace time only to put them peace time.
in motion in the hour of need. On the contrary, as
though they had been born with weapons in hand,
they never have a truce from training, never wait
for emergencies to arise. Moreover, their peace
manœuvres are no less strenuous than veritable
warfare ; each soldier daily throws all his energy into
his drill, as though he were in action. Hence that
perfect ease with which they sustain the shock of
battle : no confusion breaks their customary formation, no panic paralyses, no fatigue exhausts them ;
and as their opponents cannot match these qualities,
victory is the invariable and certain consequence.
Indeed, it would not be wrong to describe their
manœuvres as bloodless combats and their combats
as sanguinary manœuvres.

The Romans never lay themselves open to a sur- The camp :
prise attack ; for, whatever hostile territory they its
may invade, they engage in no battle until they have construc-
fortified their camp. This camp is not erected at tion.
random or unevenly ; they do not all work at once
or in disorderly parties ; if the ground is uneven, it
is first levelled ; [a] a site for the camp is then measured
out in the form of a square. For this purpose the
army is accompanied by a multitude of workmen and
of tools for building.

(2) The interior of the camp is divided into rows

Romans in constructing a camp ; the former follow the lie
of the ground and spare themselves the trouble of entrenching.

νουσιν, ἔξωθεν δ' ὁ κύκλος τείχους ὄψιν ἐπέχει,
80 πύργοις ἐξ ἴσου διαστήματος κεκοσμημένος. ἐπὶ
δὲ τῶν μεταπυργίων τούς τε ὀξυβελεῖς καὶ καταπέλτας καὶ λιθοβόλα καὶ πᾶν ἀφετήριον ὄργανον
81 τιθέασιν, πάντα πρὸς τὰς βολὰς ἕτοιμα. πύλαι
δὲ ἐνοικοδομοῦνται τέσσαρες καθ' ἕκαστον τοῦ
περιβόλου κλίμα, πρός τε εἰσόδους τῶν ὑποζυγίων
εὐμαρεῖς καὶ πρὸς τὰς ἐκδρομὰς αὐτῶν, εἰ κατ-
82 επείγοι, πλατεῖαι. ῥυμοτομοῦσι δ' εὐδιαθέτως εἴσω
τὸ στρατόπεδον, καὶ μέσας μὲν τὰς τῶν ἡγεμόνων
σκηνὰς τίθενται, μεσαίτατον δὲ τούτων τὸ στρατή-
83 γιον ναῷ παραπλήσιον· ὥσπερ δὲ ἐν σχεδίῳ πόλις
καὶ ἀγορά τις ἀποδείκνυται καὶ χειροτέχναις
χωρίον, θῶκοί τε λοχαγοῖς καὶ ταξιάρχοις, ὅπῃ
84 δικάζοιεν, εἴ τινες διαφέροιντο. τειχίζεται δὲ ὁ
περίβολος καὶ τὰ ἐν αὐτῷ πάντα θᾶττον ἐπινοίας
πλήθει καὶ ἐπιστήμῃ τῶν πονούντων· εἰ δ' ἐπείγοι,
καὶ τάφρος ἔξωθεν περιβάλλεται, βάθος τετρά-
πηχυς καὶ εὖρος ἴση.
85 (3) Φραξάμενοι δ' αὐλίζονται κατὰ συντάξεις
ἕκαστοι μεθ' ἡσυχίας τε καὶ κόσμου. πάντα δ'
αὐτοῖς καὶ τἆλλα μετ' εὐταξίας ἀνύεται καὶ ἀσφαλείας, ξυλεία τε καὶ ἐπισιτισμός, εἰ δέοιντο, καὶ
86 ὑδρεία κατὰ συντάξεις ἑκάστοις. οὐδὲ γὰρ δεῖπνον
ἢ ἄριστον, ὁπότε θελήσειαν, αὐτεξούσιον ἑκάστῳ,
πᾶσιν δ' ὁμοῦ, τούς τε ὕπνους αὐτοῖς καὶ τὰς
φυλακὰς καὶ τὰς ἐξεγέρσεις σάλπιγγες προ-

ᵃ ὀξυβελεῖς and καταπέλται, species of *catapultae*, mechanical
contrivances for discharging arrows by means of a wind-
lass ; λιθοβόλα, *ballistae*, for discharging stones with high
angle fire.

ᵇ The *praetorium*.

of tents. The exterior circuit presents the appearance of a wall and is furnished with towers at regular intervals; and on the spaces between the towers are placed " quick-firers," catapults, " stone-throwers," [a] and every variety of artillery engines, all ready for use. In this surrounding wall are set four gates, one on each side, spacious enough for beasts of burden to enter without difficulty and wide enough for sallies of troops in emergencies. The camp is intersected by streets symmetrically laid out; in the middle are the tents of the officers, and precisely in the centre the headquarters of the commander-in-chief,[b] resembling a small temple. Thus, as it were, an improvised city springs up,[c] with its market-place, its artisan quarter, its seats of judgement, where captains and colonels [d] adjudicate upon any differences which may arise. The outer wall and all the buildings within are completed quicker than thought, so numerous and skilled are the workmen. In case of need, the camp is further surrounded by a fosse, four cubits deep and of equal breadth.

(3) Once entrenched, the soldiers take up their quarters in their tents by companies, quietly and in good order. All their fatigue duties are performed with the same discipline, the same regard for security: the procuring of wood, food-supplies, and water, as required—each party has its allotted task. The hour for supper and breakfast is not left to individual discretion: all take their meals together. The hours for sleep, sentinel-duty, and rising, are announced

Daily routine of life in camp.

[c] *Cf.* Polyb. vi. 31 ὁ μὲν εἰς ἀγορὰν γίνεται τόπος ὁ δ' ἕτερος τῷ τε ταμιείῳ . . . πόλει παραπλησίαν ἔχει τὴν διάθεσιν.

[d] Perhaps centurions (λόχος = a century ii. 63) and tribunes (Reinach). But ταξίαρχοι appear to be distinguished from χιλίαρχοι in § 87 and in *A.* vii. 26.

σημαίνουσιν, οὐδ' ἔστιν ὅ τι γίνεται δίχα παρ-
87 αγγέλματος. ὑπὸ δὲ τὴν ἔω τὸ στρατιωτικὸν μὲν
ἐπὶ τοὺς ἑκατοντάρχας ἕκαστοι, πρὸς δὲ τοὺς
χιλιάρχους οὗτοι συνίασιν ἀσπασόμενοι, μεθ' ὧν
πρὸς τὸν ἡγεμόνα τῶν ὅλων οἱ ταξίαρχοι πάντες·
88 ὁ δ' αὐτοῖς τό τε ἐξ ἔθους σημεῖον καὶ τἆλλα
παραγγέλματα διαδίδωσιν[1] διαφέρειν εἰς τοὺς
ὑποτεταγμένους. ὃ δὴ κἀπὶ παρατάξεως πράτ-
τοντες ἐπιστρέφονταί [τε] ταχέως, ἵνα[2] δέοι, καὶ
πρὸς τὰς ἐφόδους αὐτοῖς[3] καὶ πρὸς τὰς ἀνακλήσεις
ὑποχωροῦσιν ἀθρόοι.

89 (4) Ἐξιέναι δὲ τοῦ στρατοπέδου δέον ὑπο-
σημαίνει μὲν ἡ σάλπιγξ, ἠρεμεῖ δ' οὐδείς, ἀλλ'
ἅμα νεύματι τὰς μὲν σκηνὰς ἀναιροῦσιν, πάντα δ'
90 ἐξαρτύονται πρὸς τὴν ἔξοδον. καὶ πάλιν αἱ
σάλπιγγες ὑποσημαίνουσιν παρεσκευάσθαι. οἱ δ'
ἐν τάχει τοῖς τε ὀρεῦσιν καὶ τοῖς ὑποζυγίοις
ἐπιθέντες τὴν ἀποσκευὴν ἑστᾶσιν ὥσπερ ἐφ'[4]
ὕσπληγος ἐξορμᾶν ἕτοιμοι, ὑποπιμπρᾶσίν τε ἤδη
τὴν παρεμβολήν, ὡς αὐτοῖς μὲν ὂν ῥάδιον ἐκεῖ[5]
πάλιν τειχίσασθαι, μὴ γένοιτο δ' ἐκεῖνό ποτε τοῖς
91 πολεμίοις χρήσιμον. καὶ τρίτον δ' ὁμοίως[6] αἱ
σάλπιγγες προσημαίνουσιν τὴν ἔξοδον, ἐπισπέρ-
χουσαι τοὺς δι' αἰτίαν τινὰ βραδύναντας, ὡς μή
92 τις ἀπολειφθείη [τῆς][7] τάξεως. ὅ τε κῆρυξ δεξιὸς

---

[1] PAM : διδωσιν the rest.
[2] RC = " where ": + εἰ the rest.
[3] Text doubtful. [4] ὑφ' P : ἀφ' Naber.
[5] om. Destinon (so apparently Lat.).
[6] Havercamp with one ms. : ὅμως the rest.
[7] ins. Bekker with one ms.

by the sound of the trumpet ; nothing is done without a word of command. At daybreak the rank and file report themselves to their respective centurions, the centurions go to salute the tribunes,[a] the tribunes with all the officers [b] then wait on the commander-in-chief, and he gives them, according to custom, the watchword and other orders to be communicated to the lower ranks. The same precision is maintained on the battle-field : the troops wheel smartly round in the requisite direction, and, whether advancing to the attack or retreating, all move as a unit at the word of command.

(4) When the camp is to be broken up, the trumpet sounds a first call ;[c] at that none remain idle : instantly, at this signal, they strike the tents and make all ready for departure. The trumpets sound a second call to prepare for the march : at once they pile their baggage on the mules and other beasts of burden and stand ready to start, like runners breasting the cord on the race-course. They then set fire to the encampment, both because they can easily construct another [on the spot], and to prevent the enemy from ever making use of it. A third time the trumpets give a similar signal for departure, to hasten the movements of stragglers, whatever the reason for their delay, and to ensure that none is out of his place in the ranks. Then the herald, standing on

Breaking camp: the army on the march.

[a] Cf. Polyb. vi. 36. 6 (at daybreak the inspectors of night-sentries report to the tribunes).

[b] ταξίαρχοι = either " officers " generally, including centurions and tribunes (Reinach), or perhaps " legates," i.e. commanders of the legions, for which, however, ἔπαρχος is used in § 310.

[c] Polybius, vi. 40, similarly describes three trumpet-calls before the march : (1) lower tents and collect baggage, (2) load beasts of burden, (3) march.

τῷ πολεμάρχῳ παραστάς, εἰ πρὸς πόλεμόν εἰσιν
ἕτοιμοι, τῇ πατρίῳ γλώσσῃ τρὶς ἀναπυνθάνεται.
κἀκεῖνοι τοσαυτάκις ἀντιβοῶσιν μέγα τι καὶ πρόθυμον, ἕτοιμοι λέγοντες εἶναι, φθάνουσιν δὲ τὸν
ἐπερωτῶντα, καί τινος ἀρηΐου πνεύματος ὑπο-
πιμπλάμενοι τῇ βοῇ συνεξαίρουσιν τὰς δεξιάς.

93   (5) Ἔπειτα προϊόντες ὁδεύουσιν ἡσυχῇ καὶ μετὰ
κόσμου πάντες, ὥσπερ ἐν πολέμῳ τὴν ἰδίαν τάξιν
ἕκαστος φυλάσσων, οἱ μὲν πεζοὶ θώραξιν [τε]
πεφραγμένοι καὶ κράνεσιν καὶ μαχαιροφοροῦντες
94   ἀμφοτέρωθεν. μακρότερον δ’ αὐτῶν τὸ λαιὸν
ξίφος πολλῷ· τὸ γὰρ κατὰ [τὸ]¹ δεξιὸν σπιθαμῆς
95   οὐ πλέον ἔχει τὸ μῆκος. φέρουσι δ’ οἱ μὲν περὶ
τὸν στρατηγὸν ἐπίλεκτοι πεζοὶ λόγχην καὶ ἀσπίδα,
ἡ δὲ λοιπὴ φάλαγξ ξυστόν τε καὶ θυρεὸν ἐπιμήκη,
πρὸς οἷς πρίονα καὶ κόφινον, ἄμην τε καὶ πέλεκυν,
πρὸς δὲ ἱμάντα καὶ δρέπανον καὶ ἅλυσιν, ἡμερῶν
τε τριῶν ἐφόδιον· ὡς ὀλίγον ἀποδεῖν τῶν ἀχθο-
96   φορούντων ὀρέων τὸν πεζόν. τοῖς δὲ ἱππεῦσιν
μάχαιρα μὲν ἐκ δεξιῶν μακρὰ καὶ κοντὸς ἐπι-
μήκης ἐν χειρί, θυρεὸς δὲ παρὰ πλευρὸν ἵππου
πλάγιος, καὶ κατὰ γωρυτοῦ παρήρτηνται τρεῖς ἢ
πλείους ἄκοντες, πλατεῖς μὲν αἰχμάς, οὐκ ἀπο-
δέοντες δὲ δοράτων μέγεθος· κράνη δὲ καὶ θώρακες
97   ὁμοίως τοῖς πεζοῖς ἅπασιν. οὐδενὶ δὲ ὅπλων
διαλλάττουσιν οἱ περὶ τὸν στρατηγὸν ἔκκριτοι
τῶν ἐν ταῖς ἴλαις ἱππέων. κλήρῳ δὲ τῶν ταγμάτων ἀεὶ τὸ λαχὸν ἡγεῖται.

¹ P: om. the rest.

ᵃ About 9 inches.   On the monuments this order is
reversed, the poniard (*pugio*) being on the left; similarly

the right of the war-lord, inquires three times in their native tongue whether they are ready for war. Three times they loudly and lustily shout in reply, " We are ready," some even anticipating the question; and, worked up to a kind of martial frenzy, they along with the shout raise their right arms in the air.

(5) Then they advance, all marching in silence and in good order, each man keeping his place in the ranks, as if in face of the enemy.

The infantry are armed with cuirass and helmet and carry a sword on either side ; that on the left is far the longer of the two, the dagger on the right being no longer than a span.[a] The picked infantry, forming the general's guard, carry a lance [b] and round shield,[c] the regiments of the line a javelin [d] and oblong buckler [e] ; the equipment of the latter further includes a saw, a basket, a pick and an axe, not to mention a strap, a bill-hook, a chain and three days' rations, so that an infantry man is almost as heavily laden as a pack-mule. *Arms and equipment of infantry*

The cavalry carry a large sword on their right side, a long pike in the hand, a buckler resting obliquely on the horse's flank, and in a quiver slung beside them three or more darts with broad points and as long as spears ; their helmets and cuirasses are the same as those worn by all the infantry. The select cavalry, forming the general's escort, are armed in precisely the same manner as the ordinary troopers. The legion which is to lead the column is always selected by lot.[f] *and of cavalry.*

Polybius, who omits the poniard, states that the sword is worn on the right (vi. 23. 6).
 [b] *Hasta.* 　　[c] *Parma.* 　　[d] *Pilum.* 　　[e] *Scutum.*
 [f] According to Polyb. vi. 40. 9 the order of march was governed by a daily rotation.

98 (6) Τοιαῦται μὲν οὖν αἱ Ῥωμαίων πορεῖαί τε
καὶ καταλύσεις, πρὸς δὲ ὅπλων διαφοραί, οὐδὲν
δὲ ἀπροβούλευτον ἐν ταῖς μάχαις οὐδὲ αὐτο-
σχέδιον, ἀλλὰ γνώμη μὲν ἀεὶ παντὸς ἔργου προάγει,
99 τοῖς δοχθεῖσι δ' ἔπεται τὰ ἔργα· παρ' ὃ καὶ
σφάλλονται μὲν ἥκιστα, κἂν πταίσωσι δέ, ῥᾳδίως
100 ἀναλαμβάνουσι τὰ σφάλματα. ἡγοῦνταί τε τῶν
ἀπὸ τύχης ἐπιτευγμάτων ἀμείνους τὰς ἐπὶ τοῖς
προβουλευθεῖσιν διαμαρτίας, ὡς τοῦ μὲν αὐτο-
μάτου καλοῦ δελεάζοντος εἰς ἀπρομήθειαν, τῆς
σκέψεως δέ, κἂν ἀτυχήσῃ ποτέ, πρὸς τὸ μὴ
101 αὖθις καλὴν ἐχούσης μελέτην· καὶ τῶν μὲν αὐτο-
μάτων ἀγαθῶν οὐ τὸν λαβόντα αἴτιον εἶναι, τῶν
δὲ παρὰ γνώμην προσπεσόντων σκυθρωπῶν παραμυθίαν τό γε προσηκόντως βεβουλεῦσθαι.
102 (7) Παρασκευάζουσι μὲν οὖν ἐν ταῖς μελέταις
τῶν ὅπλων οὐ τὰ σώματα μόνον ἀλλὰ καὶ τὰς
ψυχὰς ἀλκίμους, προσασκοῦνται δὲ καὶ τῷ φόβῳ.
103 οἵ τε γὰρ νόμοι παρ' αὐτοῖς οὐ λιποταξίου μόνον
ἀλλὰ καὶ ῥᾳστώνης ὀλίγης θανατικοί, οἵ τε
στρατηγοὶ τῶν νόμων φοβερώτεροι· ταῖς γὰρ πρὸς
τοὺς ἀγαθοὺς τιμαῖς ῥύονται τὸ[1] δοκεῖν ὠμοὶ
104 πρὸς τοὺς κολαζομένους. τοσοῦτον δ' αὐτῶν τὸ
πρὸς τοὺς ἡγεμόνας πειθήνιον, ὡς ἔν τε εἰρήνη
κόσμον εἶναι καὶ ἐπὶ παρατάξεως ἓν σῶμα τὴν
105 ὅλην στρατιάν. οὕτως αὐτῶν συναφεῖς[2] μὲν αἱ
τάξεις, εὔστροφοι δ' εἰσὶν αἱ περιαγωγαί, ὀξεῖαι
δ' ἀκοαὶ μὲν παραγγέλμασιν, ὄψεις δὲ σημείοις,
106 ἔργοις δὲ χεῖρες. ὅθεν δρᾶσαι μὲν ἀεὶ ταχεῖς,
βραδύτατοι δὲ παθεῖν εἰσιν, οὐδ' ἔστιν ὅπου στα-

[1] τοῦ Dindorf.
[2] L, cf. Lat. copulati: ἀσφαλεῖς or ἀφελεῖς the rest.

(6) Such is the routine of the Roman army on the Tactics. march and in camp, such are the various arms which they bear. In battle nothing is done unadvisedly or left to chance : consideration invariably precedes action, and action conforms to the decision reached. Consequently the Romans rarely err, and, if they do make a slip, easily repair their error. They consider, moreover, that a well-concerted plan, even if it ends in failure, is preferable to a happy stroke of fortune, because accidental success is a temptation to improvidence, whereas deliberation, though occasionally followed by misfortunes, teaches the useful lesson how to avoid their recurrence. They further reflect that one who profits by a happy accident can take no credit for it, while disasters which occur contrary to all calculations leave one at least the consolation that no proper precautions were neglected.

(7) By their military exercises the Romans instil Discipline. into their soldiers fortitude not only of body but also of soul ; fear, too, plays its part in their training. For they have laws which punish with death not merely desertion of the ranks, but even a slight neglect of duty ; and their generals are held in even greater awe than the laws. For the high honours with which they reward the brave prevent the offenders whom they punish from regarding themselves as treated cruelly.

This perfect discipline makes the army an orna- Rome owes ment of peace-time and in war welds the whole into its Empire
to its a single body ; so compact are their ranks, so alert efficient their movements in wheeling to right or left, so army. quick their ears for orders, their eyes for signals, their hands to act upon them. Prompt as they consequently ever are in action, none are slower than they

θέντες¹ ἢ πλήθους ἡσσήθησαν ἢ στρατηγημάτων
ἢ δυσχωρίας, ἀλλ' οὐδὲ τύχης· καὶ γὰρ ταύτης
107 αὐτοῖς τὸ κρατεῖν βεβαιότερον. οἷς οὖν βουλὴ
μὲν ἄρχει πράξεως,² ἔπεται δὲ τοῖς βεβουλευ-
μένοις στρατὸς οὕτω δραστήριος, τί θαυμαστόν,
εἰ πρὸς ἔω μὲν Εὐφράτης, ὠκεανὸς δὲ πρὸς
ἑσπέραν, μεσημβρινὸν δὲ Λιβύης τὸ πιότατον,
καὶ πρὸς ἄρκτον Ἴστρος τε καὶ Ῥῆνος τῆς
ἡγεμονίας ὅροι; δεόντως γὰρ ἄν τις εἴποι τὸ
κτῆμα τῶν κτησαμένων ἔλασσον.
108 (8) Ταῦτα μὲν οὖν διεξῆλθον οὐ Ῥωμαίους
ἐπαινέσαι προαιρούμενος τοσοῦτον, ὅσον εἴς τε
παραμυθίαν τῶν κεχειρωμένων καὶ εἰς ἀποτροπὴν
109 τῶν νεωτεριζόντων· εἴη δ' ἂν τοῖς ἀγνοοῦσιν τῶν
φιλοκαλούντων καὶ πρὸς ἐμπειρίας ἡ ἀγωγὴ τῆς
Ῥωμαίων στρατιᾶς. ἐπάνειμι δ' ὅθεν ἐπὶ ταῦτ'
ἐξέβην.

110 (vi. 1) Οὐεσπασιανὸς μὲν ἅμα τῷ παιδὶ Τίτῳ
διατρίβων τέως ἐν τῇ Πτολεμαΐδι συνέτασσεν τὰς
δυνάμεις, ὁ δὲ τὴν Γαλιλαίαν κατατρέχων Πλάκιδος ἐπεὶ πολὺ μὲν πλῆθος ἀνῃρήκει τῶν καταλαμβανομένων, τοῦτο δ' ἦν τὸ ἀσθενέστερον Γαλι-
111 λαίων καὶ ταῖς φυγαῖς³ ἐναποκάμνον, ὁρῶν δὲ
συμφεῦγον ἀεὶ τὸ μάχιμον εἰς τὰς ὑπὸ τοῦ Ἰωσή-

---

¹ PAL: συστάντες the rest.
² παρατάξεως PAL.
³ M (margin): φυλακαῖς or ψυχαῖς the rest.

ᵃ The motive here admitted is significant. As has been
said elsewhere (*Life*, Introd. p. xi), the *Jewish War*, "penned
in Vespasian's former palace by his pensioner, was probably
of the nature of a manifesto inspired by his imperial patrons

in succumbing to suffering, and never have they been
known in any predicament to be beaten by numbers,
by ruse, by difficulties of ground, or even by fortune ;
for they have more assurance of victory than
of fortune. Where counsel thus precedes active
operations, where the leaders' plan of campaign
is followed up by so efficient an army, no wonder
that the Empire has extended its boundaries
on the east to the Euphrates, on the west to the
ocean, on the south to the most fertile tracts of
Libya, on the north to the Ister and the Rhine. One
might say without exaggeration that, great as are
their possessions, the people that won them are
greater still.

(8) If I have dwelt at some length on this topic,
my intention was not so much to extol the Romans
as to console those whom they have vanquished and
to deter others who may be tempted to revolt.[a]
Perhaps, too, any cultured readers [b] who are un-
acquainted with the subject may profit by an account
of the organization of the Roman army. I will now
resume my narrative at the point where I digressed.

(vi. 1) Vespasian was detained for some time with
his son Titus at Ptolemais, consolidating his forces.
Meanwhile Placidus [c] was scouring Galilee and had
begun by killing large numbers of those who fell into
his hands, these being weak civilians who were exhausted by flight ; afterwards, observing that the
combatants always took refuge in the cities which

*Unsuccess-
ful attack of
Placidus on
Jotapata.*

and intended as a warning to the East of the futility of further
opposition." The danger of a rising of the Parthians or of
the Jews of Babylon (ii. 388 f.) was a constant menace.
[b] τῶν φιλοκαλούντων : cf. Polybius vi. 26. 12 τίς γὰρ οὕτως
ἐστὶν ἀπεοικὼς πρὸς τὰ καλὰ κτλ.　　　　　[c] § 59.

JOSEPHUS

που τειχισθείσας πόλεις ὥρμησεν ἐπὶ τὴν ὀχυρω-
τάτην αὐτῶν Ἰωταπάταν, οἰόμενος ἐξ ἐφόδου μὲν
αἱρήσειν ῥᾳδίως, μέγα δὲ κλέος αὐτῷ παρὰ τοῖς
ἡγεμόσιν κἀκείνοις ὄφελος εἰς τὰ λοιπὰ παρ-
έξειν· προσχωρήσειν γὰρ δέει τὰς ἄλλας πόλεις
112 τῆς καρτερωτάτης οἰχομένης.[1] πολύ γε μὴν δι-
ήμαρτεν τῆς ἐλπίδος· ἐπιόντα γὰρ αὐτὸν οἱ Ἰωτα-
πατηνοὶ προαισθόμενοι πρὸ τῆς πόλεως ἐκ-
δέχονται, καὶ τοῖς Ῥωμαίοις συρραγέντες ἀδοκήτοις
πολλοὶ καὶ πρὸς μάχην ἕτοιμοι, πρόθυμοί τε ὡς
ἂν ὑπὲρ κινδυνευούσης πατρίδος καὶ γυναικῶν καὶ
113 τέκνων, τρέπονται ταχέως. καὶ πολλοὺς μὲν
τιτρώσκουσι τῶν Ῥωμαίων, ἑπτὰ δὲ ἀναιροῦσιν
διὰ τὸ μήτε ἄτακτον αὐτῶν τὴν ὑποχώρησιν
γενέσθαι καὶ τὰς πληγὰς ἐπιπολαίους πεφραγ-
μένων πάντοθεν τῶν σωμάτων, τούς τε Ἰουδαίους
πόρρωθεν βάλλειν πλέον ἢ συμπλέκεσθαι θαρρεῖν
114 γυμνῆτας ὁπλίταις. ἔπεσον δὲ καὶ τῶν Ἰουδαίων
τρεῖς ἄνδρες καὶ ἐτρώθησαν ὀλίγοι. Πλάκιδος μὲν
οὖν τῆς ἐπὶ τὴν πόλιν ὁρμῆς ἀτονώτερος εὑρεθεὶς
φεύγει.
115 (2) Οὐεσπασιανὸς δὲ ὡρμημένος αὐτὸς ἐμβαλεῖν
εἰς τὴν Γαλιλαίαν ἐξελαύνει τῆς Πτολεμαΐδος
διατάξας τὴν στρατιὰν ὁδεύειν καθὰ Ῥωμαίοις
116 ἔθος. τοὺς μέν γε ψιλοὺς τῶν ἐπικούρων καὶ
τοξότας προάγειν ἐκέλευσεν, ὡς ἀνακόπτοιεν τὰς
ἐξαπιναίους τῶν πολεμίων ἐπιδρομὰς καὶ δι-
ερευνῷεν τὰς ὑπόπτους καὶ λοχᾶσθαι δυναμένας
ὕλας, οἷς εἵπετο καὶ Ῥωμαίων ὁπλιτικὴ μοῖρα,
117 πεζοί τε καὶ ἱππεῖς. τούτοις ἀφ' ἑκάστης ἑκατοντ-

[1] MVRC, cf. iv. 128: ἰχομένης PAL.

Josephus had fortified, he proceeded to attack the most formidable of them, Jotapata. He expected to have no difficulty in capturing it by a sudden assault, and thus to procure for himself a high reputation with his chiefs and for them a considerable advantage for the future campaign ; for, once the strongest town had fallen, terror would induce the rest to surrender. In this hope, however, he was greatly deceived. Forewarned of his approach, the people of Jotapata awaited his coming outside the town and burst unexpectedly upon the Romans. Being a large body, well prepared for battle, and kindled by the thought of the danger threatening their native city, their wives and their children, they quickly routed their opponents and wounded a large number of them. They killed no more than seven, because the Romans retired in good order and, their bodies being completely protected, received only superficial wounds, while their Jewish assailants, lightly equipped and opposed to heavy-armed regulars, kept their distance and did not venture to come to close quarters with them. The Jews on their side had three killed and a few wounded. Placidus, thus finding himself too feeble for an assault on the town, beat a retreat.

(2) But Vespasian, impatient to invade Galilee himself, now set out from Ptolemais, after drawing up his army for the march in the customary Roman order. The auxiliary light-armed troops and archers were sent in advance, to repel any sudden incursions of the enemy and to explore suspected woodland suited for the concealment of ambuscades. Next came a contingent of heavy-armed Roman soldiers, infantry and cavalry. They were followed by a detachment

Vespasian advances into Galilee. Order of his army on the march.

39

ἀρχίας ἠκολούθουν δέκα τήν τε ἑαυτῶν σκευὴν
118 καὶ τὰ μέτρα τῆς παρεμβολῆς φέροντες, καὶ μετ'
αὐτοὺς ὁδοποιοὶ τά τε σκολιὰ τῆς λεωφόρου
κατευθύνειν καὶ χθαμαλοῦν τὰ δύσβατα καὶ τὰς
ἐμποδίους ὕλας προανακόπτειν, ὡς μὴ ταλαιπω-
119 ροῖτο δυσποροῦν τὸ στράτευμα. κατόπιν δὲ τούτων τάς τε ἰδίας καὶ τὰς τῶν ὑπ' αὐτὸν ἡγεμόνων
ἔταξεν ἀποσκευὰς καὶ συχνοὺς ἐπὶ τούτοις πρὸς
120 ἀσφάλειαν τῶν ἱππέων. μεθ' οὓς αὐτὸς ἐξήλαυνεν
τούς τε ἐπιλέκτους τῶν πεζῶν καὶ ἱππέων καὶ
τοὺς λογχοφόρους ἔχων. εἵπετο δ' αὐτῷ τὸ ἴδιον
τοῦ τάγματος ἱππικόν· ἴδιοι γὰρ ἑκάστου τάγματος
121 εἴκοσι πρὸς τοῖς ἑκατὸν ἱππεῖς. τούτοις δ'
ἠκολούθουν οἱ τὰς ἑλεπόλεις φέροντες ὀρεῖς καὶ
122 τὰ λοιπὰ μηχανήματα. μετὰ τούτους ἡγεμόνες
τε καὶ σπειρῶν ἔπαρχοι σὺν χιλιάρχοις, ἐπιλέκτους
123 περὶ σφᾶς στρατιώτας ἔχοντες· ἔπειτα αἱ σημαῖαι
περιίσχουσαι τὸν ἀετόν, ὃς παντὸς ἄρχει Ῥωμαίοις τάγματος, βασιλεύς τε οἰωνῶν ἁπάντων
καὶ ἀλκιμώτατος ὤν· ὃ δὴ καὶ τῆς ἡγεμονίας
τεκμήριον αὐτοῖς καὶ κληδών, ἐφ' οὓς ἂν ἴωσιν,
124 τοῦ κρατήσειν δοκεῖ. τοῖς δὲ ἱεροῖς ἠκολούθουν
οἱ σαλπιγκταί, καὶ κατόπιν αὐτῶν ἡ φάλαγξ τὸ
στῖφος εἰς ἓξ πλατύνασα. τούτοις παρείπετό τις
ἑκατόνταρχος ἐξ ἔθους τὴν τάξιν ἐπισκοπούμενος.
125 τὸ δ' οἰκετικὸν ἑκάστου τάγματος ἅπαν τοῖς
πεζοῖς εἵπετο, τὰς ἀποσκευὰς τῶν στρατιωτῶν
ἐπὶ τοῖς ὀρεῦσιν καὶ τοῖς ὑποζυγίοις ἄγοντες·

composed of ten men from each century, carrying their own kit and the necessary instruments for marking out the camp ; after these came the pioneers to straighten sinuosities on the route, to level the rough places and to cut down obstructing woods, in order to spare the army the fatigues of a toilsome march. Behind these Vespasian posted his personal equipage and that of his lieutenants with a strong mounted escort to protect them. He himself rode behind with the pick of the infantry and cavalry and his guard of lancers. Then came the cavalry units of the legions ; for to each legion are attached a hundred and twenty horse. These were followed by the mules carrying the siege towers *a* and the other machines. Then came the legates, the prefects of the cohorts and the tribunes, with an escort of picked troops. Next the ensigns surrounding the eagle, which in the Roman army precedes every legion, because it is the king and the bravest of all the birds : it is regarded by them as the symbol of empire, and, whoever may be their adversaries, an omen of victory. These sacred emblems were followed by the trumpeters, and behind them came the solid column, marching six abreast. A centurion, according to custom, accompanied them *b* to superintend the order of the ranks. Behind the infantry the servants attached to each legion followed in a body, conducting the mules and other beasts of burden which carried the soldiers' kit. At the end of the

---

a For carrying battering-rams ; in iii. 230 the word ἐλέπολις seems to mean the battering-ram itself.

b Reinach thinks that a centurion for each legion must be intended.

126 κατόπιν δὲ πάντων τῶν ταγμάτων ὁ μίσθιος ὄχλος,
οἷς οὐραγοὶ πρὸς ἀσφάλειαν ἠκολούθουν πεζοί τε
καὶ ὁπλῖται καὶ τῶν ἱππέων συχνοί.

127 (3) Οὕτως ὁδεύσας Οὐεσπασιανὸς μετὰ τῆς
δυνάμεως εἰς τοὺς ὅρους ἀφικνεῖται τῆς Γαλιλαίας, ἔνθα καταστρατοπεδευσάμενος ὡρμημένους
εἰς πόλεμον τοὺς στρατιώτας κατεῖχεν, ἐπι-
δεικνύμενός τε τὴν στρατιὰν εἰς κατάπληξιν τοῖς
πολεμίοις καὶ μετανοίας καιρὸν διδούς, εἰ πρὸ
μάχης μεταβάλοιντο· ἅμα δὲ καὶ πρὸς πολιορκίαν
128 τῶν ἐρυμάτων ἐξηρτύετο. μετάνοιαν μὲν οὖν τῆς
ἀποστάσεως ὀφθεὶς ὁ στρατηγὸς πολλοῖς ἐνειρ-
129 γάσατο, κατάπληξιν δὲ πᾶσιν· οἱ μὲν γὰρ περὶ
τὸν Ἰώσηπον ἐστρατοπεδευκότες οὐκ ἄπωθεν τῆς
Σεπφώρεως [παρὰ πόλιν Γαρὶν καλουμένην],[1] ἐπεὶ
πλησιάζοντα τὸν πόλεμον ἤκουσαν ὅσον τε οὔπω
τοὺς Ῥωμαίους συμμίξοντας σφίσιν, οὐ μόνον
πρὸ μάχης, ἀλλὰ καὶ πρὶν ἰδεῖν τοὺς ἐχθροὺς
130 διασκίδνανται φυγῇ. καταλείπεται δ' ὁ Ἰώσηπος μετ' ὀλίγων, καὶ κατιδὼν ὡς οὔτε δέχεσθαι
τοὺς πολεμίους ἀρκετὴν ἔχοι[2] δύναμιν καὶ πε-
πτώκοι τὰ φρονήματα τῶν Ἰουδαίων ἄσμενοί τ'
ἄν, εἰ πιστεύοιντο, χωροῖεν οἱ πλείους ἐπὶ σπονδάς,
131 ἐδεδίει μὲν ἤδη περὶ παντὸς τοῦ πολέμου, τότε
δ' ὡς πορρωτάτω χωρίζεσθαι τῶν κινδύνων ἔκρι-

---

[1] om. PAL Lat.; perhaps a gloss from *Vita* 395, 412.
[2] ἔχει PM.

---

[a] Apparently the rest of the auxiliary cohorts, of whom a

42

column came the crowd of mercenaries,[a] and last of all for security a rearguard composed of light and heavy infantry and a considerable body of cavalry.

(3) Proceeding with his army in this order Vespasian reached the frontiers of Galilee. Here he established his camp and restrained the ardour of his soldiers, who were burning for the fray, being content to parade his forces before the enemy, with a view to intimidating them and giving time for reconsideration, if they wished, before an engagement, to desert their friends.[b] At the same time he made preparations for besieging the strongholds. The general's appearance on the scene in fact aroused in many regret for their revolt, and in all alarm. The troops under the command of Josephus, who were camping beside a town called Garis, not far from Sepphoris,[c] discovering that the war was upon them, and that they might at any moment be attacked by the Romans, dispersed and fled, not only before any engagement, but before they had even seen their foes. Josephus was left with a few companions ; he saw that he had not sufficient forces to await the enemy, that the Jews were crestfallen, and that the majority of them, if they could gain the enemy's confidence, would gladly capitulate. Already he had fears for the ultimate issue of the war ; for the moment he decided to remove as far as possible from

Josephus, deserted by his troops, retires to Tiberias.

portion only has been mentioned in § 116. Similarly, in Polyb. vi. 40. 6-8, "the left wing of the auxiliaries" bring up the rear ; if an enemy attack in the rear is expected the "picked auxiliaries" are transferred to that quarter from the van.

[b] Or, perhaps, "come to a better frame of mind."

[c] Twenty furlongs from Sepphoris (*Vita* 395, where Garis is called a village).

νεν, ἀναλαβών τε[1] τοὺς συμμείναντας εἰς Τιβεριάδα
καταφεύγει.

132 (vii. 1) Οὐεσπασιανὸς δὲ τῇ πόλει τῶν Γαβά-
ρων[2] ἐπελθὼν αἱρεῖ τε κατὰ πρώτην ἔφοδον αὐτήν,
133 μαχίμου πλήθους ἔρημον καταλαβών, καὶ παρελθὼν εἴσω πάντας ἡβηδὸν ἀναιρεῖ μηδεμιᾶς τῶν
Ῥωμαίων ἡλικίας ἔλεον ποιουμένων μίσει [τῷ]
πρὸς τὸ ἔθνος καὶ μνήμῃ τῆς κατὰ τὸν Κέστιον
134 αὐτῶν παρανομίας. ἐμπίμπρησιν δ᾽ οὐ μόνον αὐτὴν
τὴν πόλιν, ἀλλὰ καὶ τὰς πέριξ κώμας πάσας τε καὶ
πολίχνας, ἃς μὲν παντελῶς ἐκλελειμμένας, ἔστιν
δ᾽ ἃς αὐτὸς ἐξανδραποδιζόμενος.

135 (2) Ὁ δ᾽ Ἰώσηπος ἦν πρὸς ἀσφάλειαν εἵλετο
πόλιν αὐτὸς ἐνέπλησεν δέους καταφυγών· οἱ γὰρ[3]
ἀπὸ τῆς Τιβεριάδος οὐκ ἄν, εἰ μὴ πρὸς τὸ πᾶν
ἀπεγνώκει τὸν πόλεμον, τραπῆναί ποτε αὐτὸν
136 ᾤοντο. καὶ κατὰ τοῦτό γε οὐ διημάρτανον αὐτοῦ
τῆς γνώμης· ἑώρα μὲν γὰρ ποῖ ῥέψει τὰ Ἰουδαίων
τέλους, καὶ μίαν αὐτῶν ᾔδει σωτηρίαν, εἰ μετα-
137 βάλοιντο. αὐτὸς δὲ καίπερ συγγνωσθήσεσθαι παρὰ
Ῥωμαίοις προσδοκῶν, ὅμως τεθνάναι μᾶλλον
εἵλετο πολλάκις ἢ καταπροδοὺς τὴν πατρίδα καὶ
τὴν ἐμπιστευθεῖσαν αὐτῷ στρατηγίαν ὑβρίσας
138 εὐτυχεῖν παρ᾽ οἷς πολεμήσων ἐπέμφθη. γράφειν
οὖν τοῖς ἐν τέλει τῶν Ἱεροσολύμων διέγνω μετ᾽
ἀκριβείας τὰ πράγματα, ὡς μήτ᾽ ἐπὶ μεῖζον
ἐξάρας τὴν τῶν πολεμίων ἰσχὺν αὖθις εἰς δειλίαν
κακίζοιτο, μήτε ἐνδεέστερον ἀπαγγείλας κἂν μετα-

---

[1] Niese after Lat.: δὲ mss.: δὴ Bekker.
[2] Gfroerer: Γαδάρων or Γαδαρέων mss. Gadara was in
Decapolis and pro-Roman (B. iv. 413); Gabara was a
principal city of Galilee, due east of Ptolemais (Vita 123).
[3] From Lat.: δὲ mss.

the risk of a conflict.   Accordingly, with the remnant
of his troops, he took refuge in Tiberias.

(vii. 1) Vespasian's first objective was the city of *Vespasian*
Gabara, which he carried at the first assault, finding *captures*
it deprived of effective combatants.   Entering the *and*
destroys
city he slew all males who were of age, the Romans *Gabara.*
showing no mercy to old or young, so bitter was their
hatred of the nation and their memory of the affront
which had been done to Cestius.   Not content with
setting fire to the city, Vespasian burnt all the
villages and country towns in the neighbourhood ;
some he found completely deserted, in the others he
reduced the inhabitants to slavery.

(2) The arrival of Josephus filled with alarm the *Josephus*
city which he had chosen as his refuge, for the people *writes to*
Jerusalem
of Tiberias felt that he would never have fled, had *for*
he not abandoned all hope of success in the contest. *instruc-*
tions.
In this they correctly interpreted his opinion ; for
he foresaw the final catastrophe for which the
fortunes of the Jews were heading, and recognized
that their only hope of salvation lay in submission.
As for himself, although he might look for pardon
from the Romans, he would have preferred to suffer
a thousand deaths rather than betray his country
and disgracefully abandon the command which had
been entrusted to him, in order to seek his fortune
among those whom he had been commissioned to
fight.   He decided therefore to write to the authorities at Jerusalem an exact statement of the position
of affairs, neither exaggerating the strength of the
enemy, which might subsequently lead to his being
taunted with cowardice, nor underrating it, for fear

45

139 νοήσαντας ἴσως θρασύνειεν,[1] ἵνα τε ἢ σπονδὰς
αἱρούμενοι ταχέως ἀντιγράψωσιν, ἢ πολεμεῖν
ἐγνωκότες πρὸς Ῥωμαίους ἀξιόμαχον αὐτῷ πέμ-
140 ψωσι δύναμιν. ὁ μὲν οὖν ταῦτ' ἐπιστείλας πέμπει
διὰ τάχους ἐπὶ Ἱεροσολύμων τοὺς τὰ γράμματα
κομίζοντας.

141 (3) Οὐεσπασιανὸς δὲ ὡρμημένος ἐξαιρεῖν τὴν
Ἰωταπάταν, πέπυστο γὰρ εἰς αὐτὴν πλείστους
τῶν πολεμίων συμπεφευγέναι καὶ ἄλλως ὁρμητήριον ἰσχυρὸν οὖσαν αὐτῶν, πέμπει πεζούς τε καὶ
ἱππεῖς τοὺς προεξομαλιοῦντας τὴν ὁδὸν ὀρεινὴν
ὑπάρχουσαν καὶ πετρώδη, δύσβατον δὲ καὶ πεζοῖς,
142 ἱππεῦσιν δ' ἀμήχανον. οἱ μὲν οὖν τέσσαρσιν
ἡμέραις ἐξειργάσαντο καὶ πλατεῖαν ἤνοιξαν τῇ
στρατιᾷ λεωφόρον· τῇ πέμπτῃ δ' ὁ Ἰώσηπος,
αὕτη δ' ἦν Ἀρτεμισίου μηνὸς μία καὶ εἰκάς,
φθάνει παρελθὼν εἰς τὴν Ἰωταπάταν ἐκ τῆς
Τιβεριάδος καὶ πεπτωκότα τοῖς Ἰουδαίοις ἐγείρει
143 τὰ φρονήματα. Οὐεσπασιανῷ δέ τις εὐαγγελίζεται
τὴν μετάβασιν τοῦ ἀνδρὸς αὐτόμολος καὶ κατ-
ήπειγεν ἐπὶ τὴν πόλιν ὡς μετ' ἐκείνης αἱρήσοντα
πᾶσαν Ἰουδαίαν, εἰ λάβοι τὸν Ἰώσηπον ὑποχείριον.
144 ὁ δ' ἁρπάσας ὥσπερ μέγιστον εὐτύχημα τὴν
ἀγγελίαν καὶ προνοίᾳ θεοῦ τὸν συνετώτατον εἶναι
δοκοῦντα τῶν πολεμίων οἰόμενος εἰς εἱρκτὴν
αὐθαίρετον παρελθεῖν, εὐθέως μὲν σὺν χιλίοις

---

[1] LC: θρασύνοιεν the rest.

[a] The distance from Gabara to Jotapata seems to be

46

of encouraging them to hold out when possibly inclined to repent. If the magistrates intended to
negotiate, they were asked to reply to that effect
without delay ; if they decided to continue the war,
they should send him a force capable of coping with
the Romans. Having written a letter to this effect,
he sent it by express messengers to Jerusalem.

(3) Vespasian was impatient to make an end of
Jotapata, having heard that it was the refuge to
which most of the enemy had retired, and that it was,
moreover, their strong base ; he accordingly sent a
body of infantry and cavalry in advance to level the
road leading to it, a stony mountain track, difficult
for infantry and quite impracticable for mounted
troops.[a] In four days their task was completed and
a broad highway opened for the army. On the
fifth, which was the twenty-first[b] of the month
Artemisius, Josephus hurriedly left Tiberias and
entered Jotapata, his arrival raising the dejected
spirits of the Jews. A deserter brought to Vespasian
the welcome intelligence of the general's movement,
and urged him to hasten to attack the city, because
its fall, could he but secure Josephus, would amount
to the capture of all Judaea. Vespasian caught at
this information as a godsend, regarding it as by
God's providential ordering that the man who was
reputed to be the most sagacious of his enemies had
thus deliberately entered a prison ; he instantly

Josephus
enters
Jotapata :
Vespasian
invests it.

May-June
A.D. 67.

slightly underestimated in *Vita* 234 as " about 40 *stades* " ;
it is six miles due south.

[b] There is some doubt about this figure, which it is difficult
to reconcile with the statement that Jotapata was taken on
the first of Panemus (§ 339) after a siege of forty-seven days
(§ 316). The 21st of Artemisius, according to Niese's calculation, was the 8th of June, A.D. 67.

ἱππεῦσιν πέμπει Πλάκιδον καὶ δεκαδάρχην Αἰ-
βούτιον, ἄνδρα τῶν ἐπισήμων κατὰ χεῖρα καὶ
σύνεσιν, περικατασχεῖν κελεύσας τὴν πόλιν, ὡς
μὴ λάθοι διαδρὰς ὁ Ἰώσηπος.
145 (4) Αὐτὸς δὲ μετὰ μίαν ἡμέραν ἀναλαβὼν
πᾶσαν τὴν δύναμιν εἵπετο καὶ μέχρι δείλης
146 ὀδεύσας πρὸς τὴν Ἰωταπάταν ἀφικνεῖται. ἀναλαβὼν δὲ τὴν στρατιὰν εἰς τὸ προσάρκτιον αὐτῆς
μέρος ἔν τινι λόφῳ στρατοπεδεύεται διέχοντι
σταδίους ἑπτὰ τῆς πόλεως, πειρώμενος ὡς μάλιστα τοῖς πολεμίοις εὐσύνοπτος εἶναι πρὸς ἔκ-
147 πληξιν· ἣ καὶ παραχρῆμα τοσαύτη τοὺς Ἰουδαίους
κατέσχεν, ὡς μηδένα τοῦ τείχους τολμῆσαι προ-
148 ελθεῖν. Ῥωμαῖοι δ' εὐθὺς μὲν ἀπώκνησαν προσ-
βαλεῖν, δι' ὅλης ὡδευκότες ἡμέρας, διπλῇ δὲ τῇ
φάλαγγι κυκλοῦνται τὴν πόλιν καὶ τρίτην ἔξωθεν
περιστᾶσιν τὴν ἵππον, πάσας ἀποφράσσοντες
149 αὐτοῖς τὰς ἐξόδους. τοῦτ' ἐν ἀπογνώσει σωτηρίας παρώξυνε τοὺς Ἰουδαίους πρὸς τόλμαν· οὐδὲν
γὰρ ἀνάγκης ἐν πολέμῳ μαχιμώτερον.
150 (5) Γενομένης δὲ μεθ' ἡμέραν προσβολῆς τὸ
μὲν πρῶτον Ἰουδαῖοι κατὰ χώραν μένοντες
ἀντεῖχον, ἀντικρὺ τῶν Ῥωμαίων ἐστρατοπεδευ-
151 κότες[1] πρὸ τοῦ τείχους· ὡς δὲ Οὐεσπασιανὸς
τούτοις μὲν τοὺς τοξότας καὶ σφενδονήτας καὶ
πᾶν τὸ τῶν ἐκηβόλων πλῆθος ἐπιστήσας ἐπέτρεψεν βάλλειν, αὐτὸς δὲ μετὰ τῶν πεζῶν εἰς τὸ

[1] The Lat. translates ἐστρατοπεδευκότων.

---

[a] Aebutius, in the service of Agrippa, had at an early
stage of the war been entrusted with the oversight of the

48

dispatched Placidus and the decurion Aebutius,[a] a
man of marked energy and ability, with a thousand
horse, with orders to invest the town and prevent
Josephus from escaping secretly.

(4) Vespasian followed them the next day with all
his army and, marching until evening, arrived before
Jotapata. Leading his troops up to the north side
of the city he encamped on a hill seven furlongs
distant from it, seeking a position as conspicuous as
possible to the enemy in order to intimidate them.
In fact the spectacle had such an instantaneous effect
on the Jews that none ventured outside the walls.
The Romans, after their full day's march, were not
prepared to make an immediate attack, but they
surrounded the city with a double cordon of infantry,
and posted outside these a third line of cavalry,
blocking all means of exit. This manœuvre, cutting
off hope of escape, stimulated the Jews to deeds of
gallantry ; for nothing in war so rouses the martial
spirit as necessity.

(5) Next day an attack was made. At first those First
of the Jews who were encamped opposite the Romans fighting at
Jotapata.
outside the walls [b] merely held their ground against
the enemy ; but when Vespasian brought up his
archers, slingers, and all his other marksmen in full
force and gave orders to shoot down these opponents,
while he himself with the infantry pushed up the

Great Plain and had an encounter with Josephus (*Vita*
114 ff.) ; his previous acquaintance with Josephus doubtless
accounts for his selection on this occasion.

[b] The Jews may well have had a camp *extra muros* in the
early days of the siege ; this must have been rapidly driven
in as we hear no more of it. The Latin has, " the Jews
merely held their ground opposite the Romans who were
encamped outside the walls."

πρόσαντες ἀνεώθει[1] καθ᾽ ὃ τὸ τεῖχος ἦν εὐάλωτον,
δείσας ὁ Ἰώσηπος περὶ τῇ πόλει προπηδᾷ καὶ
152 σὺν αὐτῷ πᾶν τὸ τῶν Ἰουδαίων πλῆθος. συμ-
πεσόντες δὲ τοῖς Ῥωμαίοις ἀθρόοι τοῦ μὲν τείχους
ἀνέστειλαν αὐτούς, πολλὰ δ᾽ ἐπεδείκνυντο χειρῶν
ἔργα καὶ τόλμης. οὐκ ἐλάσσω[2] γε μὴν ὧν ἔδρων
153 ἀντέπασχον· ὅσον γὰρ αὐτοὺς ἡ τῆς σωτηρίας
ἀπόγνωσις, τοσοῦτο τοὺς Ῥωμαίους αἰδὼς παρ-
εκρότει, καὶ τοὺς μὲν ἐμπειρία μετ᾽ ἀλκῆς, τοὺς
δὲ θράσος ὥπλιζε τῷ θυμῷ στρατηγουμένους.
154 παραταξάμενοι δὲ δι᾽ ὅλης ἡμέρας νυκτὶ δια-
λύονται, τρώσαντες μὲν πλείστους Ῥωμαίων,
δεκατρεῖς δ᾽ ἀνελόντες· αὐτῶν δ᾽ ἔπεσον μὲν
δεκαεπτά, τραυματίαι δ᾽ ἐγένοντο ἑξακόσιοι.
155 (6) Τῇ δ᾽ ὑστεραίᾳ [ἡμέρᾳ] πάλιν προσβάλ-
λουσι τοῖς Ῥωμαίοις ἐπεξελθόντες καὶ πολὺ καρτερώτερον ἀντιπαρετάξαντο, θαρραλεώτεροι μὲν ἐκ
τοῦ παρὰ λόγον ἀντισχεῖν τῇ προτέρᾳ[3] γεγενημένοι,
χρώμενοι δὲ καὶ τοῖς Ῥωμαίοις μαχιμωτέροις·
156 ὑπὸ γὰρ αἰδοῦς εἰς ὀργὴν ἐξεκαίοντο, τὸ μὴ
157 ταχέως νικᾶν ἧτταν ἡγούμενοι. καὶ μέχρι πέμπτης
ἡμέρας προσβολαὶ μὲν ἐγίνοντο τῶν Ῥωμαίων
ἀδιάλειπτοι, ἐκδρομαὶ δὲ τῶν Ἰωταπατηνῶν καὶ
τειχομαχίαι καρτερώτεραι, καὶ οὔτε Ἰουδαῖοι τὴν
τῶν πολεμίων ἰσχὺν κατωρρώδουν οὔτε Ῥωμαῖοι
πρὸς τὸ τῆς πόλεως δυσάλωτον ἀπέκαμνον.
158 (7) Ἔστιν δ᾽ Ἰωταπάτα πλὴν ὀλίγου πᾶσα

---

[1] conj. with Naber: ἀνώθει (sic) mss.: ἀνωθεῖ Niese.
[2] ἔλασσον PL. [3] προτεραίᾳ Niese.

[a] The phrase θράσος ὁπλίζειν comes from Soph. El. 995 f.,
a play of which there are other reminiscences in Josephus;
cf. ψυχῆς ἀφειδεῖν B. iii. 212, Soph. El. 980.

slope at the point where the wall offered little difficulty, Josephus, alarmed for the fate of the town, made a sally with the whole multitude of the Jews. Falling in a body upon the Romans they drove them from the ramparts and performed many signal feats of prowess and daring. However, they suffered as much loss as they inflicted, for if the Jews were emboldened by despair, the Romans were no less roused by shame; on the one side were skilled experience and strength, the other had recklessness for its armour,[a] and passion for its leader. The battle lasted all day, and night alone parted the combatants. Of the Romans very many were wounded and thirteen killed. The Jewish casualties were seventeen killed and six hundred wounded.

(6) On the following day, when the Romans returned to the attack, the Jews made a fresh sally and offered a much more stubborn resistance, from the confidence inspired by their unexpectedly successful resistance on the previous day. But the Romans on their side proved more resolute opponents, being enflamed to fury by shame and regarding a lack of instant victory as tantamount to defeat. So for five days the Romans incessantly renewed their assaults, and the garrison of Jotapata their sallies and their yet more stubborn defence from the ramparts, the Jews undaunted by their enemy's strength, the Romans undeterred by the difficulties which their objective presented.

(7) The town of Jotapata [b] is almost entirely built Site of Jotapata.

[b] Modern *Jefat*, Talmudic Jodaphath (according to the Mishna it was an old town, walled since the time of Joshua); in the hills to the north of the plain of Asochis, midway between Gabara (N.) and Sepphoris (S.).

κρημνός, ἐκ μὲν τῶν ἄλλων μερῶν πάντοθεν
φάραγξιν ἀπείροις ἀπότομος, ὡς τῶν κατιδεῖν
πειρωμένων τὰς ὄψεις προεξασθενεῖν τοῦ βάθους,
ἀπὸ βορέου δὲ προσιτὴ μόνον, καθ' ὃ λήγοντι
159 τῷ ὄρει πλαγίως[1] προσέκτισται.[2] καὶ τοῦτο δ' ὁ
Ἰώσηπος ἐμπεριειλήφει τειχίζων τὴν πόλιν, ὡς
ἀκατάληπτον εἶναι πολεμίοις τὴν ὑπὲρ αὐτῆς
160 ἀκρώρειαν. κυκλόθεν δ' ἄλλοις ὄρεσιν καλυπτο-
μένη, πρὶν εἰσαφίκοιτό τις εἰς αὐτήν, παντελῶς
ἀόρατος ἦν. εἶχε μὲν οὖν οὕτως ὀχυρότητος
Ἰωταπάτη.

161 (8) Οὐεσπασιανὸς δὲ τῇ τε φύσει τοῦ χωρίου
καὶ ταῖς τόλμαις τῶν Ἰουδαίων ἀντιφιλονεικῶν
ἔγνω καρτερώτερον ἅπτεσθαι τῆς πολιορκίας, καὶ
προσκαλεσάμενος τοὺς ὑπ' αὐτὸν ἡγεμόνας ἐβου-
162 λεύετο περὶ τῆς προσβολῆς. δόξαν δὲ χῶσαι τὸ
προσιτὸν τοῦ τείχους, ἐπὶ συγκομιδὴν ὕλης
ἐκπέμπει πᾶν τὸ στράτευμα, καὶ κοπέντων τῶν
περὶ τὴν πόλιν ὀρῶν, συναλισθείσης τε ἅμα τοῖς
163 ξύλοις ἀπείρου χερμάδος, οἱ μὲν πρὸς ἀλεωρὰν
τῶν ὕπερθεν ἀφιεμένων βελῶν γέρρα διατείναντες
ὑπὲρ χαρακωμάτων ἔχουν ὑπ' αὐτοῖς, οὐδὲν ἢ
μικρὰ βλαπτόμενοι ταῖς ἀπὸ τοῦ τείχους βολαῖς,
164 οἱ δὲ τοὺς πλησίον ὄχθους ἀνασπῶντες γῆν αὐτοῖς
ἀδιαλείπτως προσέφερον, καὶ τριχῇ διῃρημένων
165 ἀργὸς ἦν οὐδείς. οἱ δὲ Ἰουδαῖοι πέτρας τε
μεγάλας ἀπὸ τῶν τειχῶν τοῖς σκεπάσμασιν αὐτῶν
ἐπηφίεσαν καὶ πᾶν εἶδος βελῶν· ἦν δὲ καὶ μὴ
διικνουμένων πολὺς ὁ ψόφος καὶ φοβερὸς ἐμπόδιον
τοῖς ἐργαζομένοις.

[1] ML: πλαγίῳ the rest.
[2] προσεκτείνεται P*ALM: for text cf. B. v. 148.

on precipitous cliffs, being surrounded on three sides
by ravines so deep that sight fails in the attempt to
fathom the abyss. On the north side alone, where
the town has straggled sideways up a descending
spur of the mountains, is it accessible. But this
quarter, too, Josephus, when he fortified the city,
had enclosed within his wall, in order to prevent the
enemy from occupying the ridge which commanded it.
Concealed by other mountains surrounding it, the
town was quite invisible until one came right up to
it. Such was the strong position of Jotapata.

(8) Vespasian, pitting his strength against the
nature of the ground and the determination of the
Jews, resolved to press the siege more vigorously ;
he accordingly summoned his principal officers to
deliberate with him on the plan of attack. It was
decided to erect earthworks against the accessible
portion of the wall, whereupon the whole army was
sent out to procure the necessary materials. The
mountain forests surrounding the town were stripped,
and, besides timber, enormous masses of stones were
collected. Then one party of soldiers spread screens
of hurdles over palisades, as a cover from missiles
from above, and thus protected constructed the earthworks, suffering little or no injury from their assailants
on the ramparts ; while others pulled to pieces the
adjacent mounds and kept their comrades constantly
supplied with earth. With this triple division of
labour not a man was idle. The Jews, meanwhile,
launched from the walls great boulders upon the
enemy's shelters with all sorts of projectiles, the
crash of which, even when they failed to penetrate,
was so loud [a] and terrific as to impede the workers.

The siege begun.

---

[a] Or " continuous."

166 (9) Οὐεσπασιανὸς δὲ ἐν κύκλῳ τὰς ἀφετηρίους
μηχανὰς ἐπιστήσας, τὰ πάντα δ' ἦν ἑκατὸν ἑξήκοντα ὄργανα, βάλλειν ἐκέλευσεν τοὺς ἐπὶ τοῦ
167 τείχους. ὁμοῦ δ' οἵ τε καταπέλται τὰς λόγχας
ἀνερροίζουν καὶ ταλαντιαῖοι λίθοι μέγεθος ἐκ τῶν
πετροβόλων ἐβάλλοντο, πῦρ τε καὶ πλῆθος ἀθρόων
οἰστῶν, ἅπερ οὐ μόνον τὸ τεῖχος ἀνεπίβατον τοῖς
Ἰουδαίοις ἐποίησεν, ἀλλὰ καὶ τὴν ἐντὸς ὅσης
168 ἐφικνεῖτο χώρας· καὶ γὰρ καὶ τὸ τῶν Ἀράβων
τοξοτῶν πλῆθος ἀκοντισταί τε καὶ σφενδονῆται
169 πάντες ἅμα τοῖς μηχανήμασιν ἔβαλλον. οὐ μὴν
εἰργόμενοι τῆς καθύπερθεν ἀμύνης ἠρέμουν· ἐκτρέχοντες γὰρ λῃστρικώτερον κατὰ λόχους περιέσπων
τε τῶν ἐργαζομένων τὰς σκέπας καὶ τοὺς γυμνου-
μένους ἔπαιον, καὶ καθ' ὃ παρείκοιεν ἐκεῖνοι
διερρίπτουν τε τὸ χῶμα καὶ τὰ χαρακώματα σὺν
170 τοῖς γέρροις ἐνεπίμπρασαν, μέχρι συνεὶς Οὐεσπασιανὸς τὴν διαίρεσιν τῶν ἔργων αἰτίαν εἶναι τῆς
βλάβης, τὰ γὰρ διαστήματα τοῖς Ἰουδαίοις προσβολῆς παρεῖχεν τόπον, ἑνοῖ τὰ σκεπάσματα, καὶ
συναφθείσης ἅμα αὐτοῖς τῆς δυνάμεως ἀνείρχθησαν
αἱ τῶν Ἰουδαίων παραδύσεις.
171 (10) Ἐγειρομένου δὲ τοῦ χώματος ἤδη καὶ ταῖς
ἐπάλξεσιν ὅσον οὔπω πλησιάζοντος, δεινὸν ὁ
Ἰώσηπος νομίσας εἰ μηδὲν ἀντιμηχανήσαιτο τῇ
πόλει σωτήριον, συναθροίζει τέκτονας καὶ τὸ τεῖχος
172 ἐκέλευσεν ὑψοῦν. τῶν δ' ἀδύνατον εἶναι φαμένων
οἰκοδομεῖν τοσούτοις βέλεσι βαλλομένους, σκέπην
173 αὐτοῖς ἐπινοεῖ τοιάνδε· δρυφάκτους πῆξασθαι

ᵃ Vegetius ii. 25 reckons 55 catapults to a legion in his
time (end of 4th century); this would give 165 of these
engines to Vespasian's army of 3 legions (Reinach).

(9) Vespasian now had his artillery engines—
numbering in all one hundred and sixty [a]—brought
into position round the spot and gave orders to fire
upon the defenders on the wall. In one tremendous
volley the catapults sent lances hurtling through the
air, the stone-projectors discharged blocks of the
weight of a talent,[b] fire-brands flew, and there was a
hail of arrows, with the effect not only of driving the
Jews from the ramparts, but of rendering untenable
all the space behind them which came within range
of the missiles. For the artillery fire was reinforced
by a simultaneous volley from a host of Arab archers,
javelin-men, and slingers. Though checked in their
defence of the ramparts, the Jews did not remain
inactive. Parties of them sallied out in guerilla
fashion, stripped off the enemy's shelters and assailed
the workmen thus exposed ; and, wherever the latter
fell back, they demolished the earthworks and set fire
to the palisades and hurdles. At length Vespasian,
on tracing the cause of this injury to the separation
of the earthworks (as the intervals afforded the Jews
a loophole for attack) united the various shelters and
simultaneously closed up his troops, with the result
that further Jewish incursions were repressed.

(10) The embankment was now rising and almost
on a level with the battlements, when Josephus,
thinking it shameful if he could not devise some
counter-measures to save the town, summoned
masons and directed them to increase the height of
the wall. On their protesting that building was impossible under such a hail of missiles, he invented the
following protection for them. Palisades were, by his

Counter-
manœuvres :
Josephus
heightens
the walls.

---

[b] About three quarters of a hundredweight, if the Attic
commercial standard is followed.

κελεύσας ἐμπετάσαι τε βύρσας νεοδόρους βοῶν,
ὡς ἀναδέχοιντο μὲν τοὺς ἀπὸ τῶν πετροβόλων
λίθους κολπούμεναι, περιολισθάνοι δ' ἀπ' αὐτῶν
[καὶ] τὰ λοιπὰ βέλη καὶ τὸ πῦρ ὑπὸ τῆς ἰκμάδος
174 εἴργοιτο, προανίστησιν τῶν τεκτόνων. ὑφ' οἷς
ἀσφαλῶς ἐργαζόμενοι δι' ἡμέρας τε καὶ νυκτὸς
τὸ τεῖχος ἤγειραν εἰς εἴκοσι πήχεις τὸ ὕψος, καὶ
συχνοὺς μὲν πύργους ἐνῳκοδόμησαν αὐτῷ, καρ-
175 τερὰν δὲ ἔπαλξιν ἐφηρμόσαντο. τοῦτο τοῖς Ῥωμαίοις ἤδη τῆς πόλεως ἐντὸς οἰομένοις εἶναι
πολλὴν ἐποίησεν ἀθυμίαν, καὶ πρός τε τὴν ἐπίνοιαν
τοῦ Ἰωσήπου καὶ τὸ παράστημα τῶν ἐπὶ τῆς
πόλεως κατεπλάγησαν.

176   (11) Οὐεσπασιανὸς δὲ καὶ πρὸς τὸ πανοῦργον
τοῦ στρατηγήματος καὶ πρὸς τὰς τόλμας παρ-
177 ωξύνετο τῶν Ἰωταπατηνῶν· πάλιν γὰρ ἀναθαρσή-
σαντες ἐπὶ τῷ τειχισμῷ τοῖς Ῥωμαίοις ἐπεξέθεον,
καὶ καθ' ἡμέραν ἐγίνοντο συμπλοκαὶ κατὰ λόχους
ἐπίνοιά τε ληστρικὴ πᾶσα καὶ τῶν προστυχόντων
178 ἁρπαγαὶ καὶ τῶν ἄλλων ἔργων πυρπολήσεις, ἕως
Οὐεσπασιανὸς ἀναπαύσας τὴν στρατιὰν μάχης
διέγνω προσκαθεζόμενος σπάνει τῶν ἐπιτηδείων
179 αἱρεῖν τὴν πόλιν· ἢ γὰρ ἀναγκαζομένους ταῖς
ἀπορίαις ἱκετεύσειν αὐτὸν ἢ μέχρι παντὸς ἀπαυθα-
180 δισαμένους διαφθαρήσεσθαι λιμῷ· πολύ τε ῥᾷσιν
αὐτοῖς ἠξίου χρήσεσθαι κατὰ τὴν μάχην, εἰ δια-
λιπὼν αὖθις ἐκτετρυχωμένοις ἐπιπέσοι. φρουρεῖν
δὴ πάσας αὐτῶν ἐκέλευσεν τὰς ἐξόδους.

181   (12) Τοῖς δὲ σίτου μὲν πλῆθος ἦν ἔνδον καὶ τῶν

ᵃ Reinach quotes Vegetius iv. 15, showing that this method
of defence was known to the Romans.

56

orders, fixed to the wall, and over these were spread
hides of oxen that had just been flayed, to catch in
their folds the stones hurled by the engines, while
the other projectiles would glance off their surface
and their moisture would extinguish the flaming
brands.[a] Under this screen the builders, working in
security day and night, raised the wall to a height of
twenty cubits, erected numerous towers and crowned
the whole with a stout parapet. At this spectacle
the Romans, who imagined themselves already
masters of the town, were greatly disheartened; the
ingenuity of Josephus and the perseverance of the
inhabitants astounded them.

(11) Vespasian was no less provoked both at the
cleverness of this stratagem and at the audacity of
the people of Jotapata; for, emboldened by their new
fortification, they recommenced their sallies against
the Romans. Every day parties of them came into
conflict with the besiegers, employing all the ruses of
guerilla warfare, pillaging whatever fell in their way
and setting fire to the rest[b] of the Roman works.
This continued until Vespasian, ordering his troops
to cease fighting, resolved to resort to a blockade and
to starve the city into surrender: the defenders, he
reckoned, would either be reduced by their privations
to sue for mercy or, if they remained obdurate to the
last, would perish of hunger. Moreover, if it came to
a battle, he counted on obtaining a far easier victory,
if, after an interval, he renewed his attack upon
exhausted opponents. He accordingly gave orders to
keep a strict guard on all the exits from the city.

(12) The besieged had abundance of corn and of

The siege converted into a blockade.

---

[b] *i.e.* apparently other than the embankments which had
been protected by the method described in § 170 (Reinach).

JOSEPHUS

ἄλλων πλὴν ἁλὸς ἁπάντων, ἔνδεια δ' ὕδατος ὡς ἂν
πηγῆς μὲν οὐκ οὔσης κατὰ τὴν πόλιν, τῷ δ'
ὀμβρίῳ διαρκουμένων τῶν ἐν αὐτῇ· σπάνιον δ' εἴ
182 ποτε τὸ κλίμα¹ θέρους ὕεται. καὶ κατὰ ταύτην
τὴν ὥραν πολιορκουμένων ἀθυμία δεινὴ πρὸς τὴν
τοῦ δίψους ἐπίνοιαν ἦν, ἀσχαλλόντων ἤδη ὡς
183 καθάπαν ἐπιλελοιπότος ὕδατος· ὁ γὰρ Ἰώσηπος
τήν τε πόλιν ὁρῶν τῶν ἄλλων ἐπιτηδείων εὔπορον
καὶ τὰ φρονήματα γενναῖα τῶν ἀνδρῶν, βουλόμενός
τε παρ' ἐλπίδα τοῖς Ῥωμαίοις ἐκτεῖναι τὴν πολιορκίαν, μέτρῳ τὸ ποτὸν αὐτοῖς διένειμεν [εὐθέως].²
184 οἱ δὲ τὸ ταμιεύεσθαι χαλεπώτερον ἐνδείας ὑπελάμβανον, καὶ τὸ μὴ αὐτεξούσιον αὐτῶν πλέον ἐκίνει
τὴν ὄρεξιν, καὶ καθάπερ εἰς ἔσχατον ἤδη δίψους
προήκοντες ἀπέκαμνον. διακείμενοι δ' οὕτως οὐκ
185 ἐλάνθανον τοὺς Ῥωμαίους· ἀπὸ γὰρ τοῦ κατάντους
ἑώρων αὐτοὺς ὑπὲρ τὸ τεῖχος ἐφ' ἕνα συρρέοντας
τόπον καὶ μετρουμένους τὸ ὕδωρ, ἐφ' ὃν καὶ τοῖς
ὀξυβελέσιν ἐξικνούμενοι πολλοὺς ἀνῄρουν.
186 (13) Καὶ Οὐεσπασιανὸς μὲν οὐκ εἰς μακρὰν τῶν
ἐκδοχείων κενωθέντων ἤλπιζεν ὑπὸ τῆς ἀνάγκης
187 αὐτῷ παραδοθήσεσθαι τὴν πόλιν· ὁ δὲ Ἰώσηπος
κλάσαι τὴν ἐλπίδα ταύτην αὐτῷ προαιρούμενος
ἐμβρέξαι κελεύει πλείστους τὰ ἱμάτια καὶ κατα-
κρεμάσαι περὶ τὰς ἐπάλξεις, ὥστε περιρρεῖσθαι
188 πᾶν ἐξαπίνης τὸ τεῖχος. πρὸς τοῦτ' ἀθυμία τῶν
Ῥωμαίων καὶ κατάπληξις ἦν θεασαμένων εἰς
χλεύην τοσοῦτον παραναλίσκοντας ὕδατος οὓς οὐδὲ
ποτὸν ἔχειν ὑπελάμβανον, ὥστε καὶ τὸν στρατηγὸν
ἀπογνόντα τὴν δι' ἐνδείας ἅλωσιν τρέπεσθαι πάλιν

¹ +τοῦτο Hudson with one ms. (Lat. illo tractu).
² διένειμεν εὐθέως PA: διένεμεν εὐθέως L: διένεμεν the rest.
58

all other necessaries, salt excepted, but they lacked Lack of
water, because, there being no springs within the water: the
town, the inhabitants were dependent on rain-water ; system.
but in this region rain rarely, if ever, falls in summer,
which was precisely the season at which they were
besieged. The mere idea of thirst filled them with
dire despondency, and already they were chafing, as
though water had entirely failed. For Josephus,
seeing the abundance of the city's other supplies and
the courageous spirit of its defenders, and desirous
to prolong the siege beyond the expectation of the
Romans, had from the first put them on water
rations. This control system appeared to them
harder than actual want ; the constraint of their
liberty only increased their craving and they became
as limp as though they had already reached the last
extremity of thirst. The Romans were not ignorant
of their plight : from the slopes above they could
see over the wall the Jews flocking to one place and
having their water doled out to them, and, directing
their catapults [a] upon the spot, killed numbers of
them.

(13) Vespasian expected that the water in the
cisterns would ere long be exhausted and the city
reduced to capitulate. To crush this hope, Josephus
had a number of dripping garments hung round the
battlements, with the result that the whole wall was
suddenly seen streaming with water. The Romans
were filled with dismay and consternation at the
spectacle of all this water being wasted as a jest by
those who they supposed had not even enough to
drink. The general himself, despairing of reducing
the place by famine, reverted to armed measures and

[a] Greek " quick-firers " (§ 80).

JOSEPHUS

189 πρὸς ὅπλα καὶ βίαν. ὃ δὴ τοῖς Ἰουδαίοις δι᾽
ἐπιθυμίας ἦν· ἀπεγνωκότες γὰρ ἑαυτοὺς καὶ τὴν
πόλιν πρὸ λιμοῦ καὶ δίψης τὸν ἐν πολέμῳ θάνατον
ᾑροῦντο.

190 (14) Ὁ μέντοι γε Ἰώσηπος πρὸς τῷδε τῷ
στρατηγήματι καὶ ἕτερον ἐπενόησεν εἰς περιουσίαν
191 αὐτῷ· διά τινος χαράδρας δυσβάτου καὶ διὰ τοῦθ᾽
ὑπὸ τῶν φυλάκων ἀμελουμένης κατὰ τὰ πρὸς δύσιν
μέρη τῆς φάραγγος ἐκπέμπων τινὰς γράμματά τε
πρὸς οὓς ἠβούλετο τῶν ἔξω Ἰουδαίων διεπέμψατο
καὶ παρ᾽ αὐτῶν ἐλάμβανεν, παντός τε ἐπιτηδείου
τῶν ἀνὰ τὴν πόλιν ἐπιλελοιπότων εὐπόρησεν,
192 ἕρπειν τὰ πολλὰ παρὰ τὰς φυλακὰς κελεύσας τοῖς
ἐξιοῦσιν καὶ τὰ νῶτα καλύπτειν νάκεσιν, ὡς εἰ
καὶ κατίδοι τις αὐτοὺς νύκτωρ, φαντασίαν παρ-
έχοιεν κυνῶν, μέχρι συναισθόμενοι τὴν ἐπίνοιαν
οἱ φρουροὶ περιίσχουσιν τὴν χαράδραν.

193 (15) Καὶ τόθ᾽ ὁ Ἰώσηπος μὲν τὴν πόλιν οὐκ
εἰς μακρὰν ὁρῶν ἀνθέξειν, ἐν ἀπόρῳ δὲ τὴν ἑαυτοῦ[1]
σωτηρίαν εἰ μένοι, δρασμὸν ἅμα τοῖς δυνατοῖς
ἐβουλεύετο. συναισθόμενοι δὲ τὸ πλῆθος καὶ
περιχυθὲν αὐτῷ κατηντιβόλουν μὴ σφᾶς περιιδεῖν
194 ἐπ᾽ αὐτῷ μόνῳ κειμένους· εἶναι γὰρ τῇ πόλει καὶ
σωτηρίας μὲν ἐλπὶς παραμένων,[2] παντὸς ἀγω-
νισομένου δι᾽ αὐτὸν προθύμως, κἂν ἁλῶσιν δέ,
195 παραμυθίαν. πρέπειν δ᾽ αὐτῷ μήτε φυγεῖν τοὺς
ἐχθροὺς μήτ᾽ ἐγκαταλιπεῖν τοὺς φίλους μήτ᾽ ἀπο-
πηδᾶν ὥσπερ χειμαζομένης νεώς, εἰς ἣν ἐν γαλήνῃ
196 παρῆλθεν· ἐπιβαπτίσειν γὰρ αὐτοῖς τὴν πόλιν,

_____
[1] ἑαυτῶν PA.
[2] Text uncertain: Herwerden reads ἐλπίδα παραμένοντα.

60

force. That was just what the Jews desired; for, having given up all hope for themselves and the city, they preferred death in battle to perishing of hunger and thirst.

(14) After this stratagem, Josephus devised yet another to procure himself supplies in abundance. There was, leading down to the ravine on the west side, a gully so difficult to traverse that it had been neglected by the enemy's outposts; by this route Josephus succeeded in sending letters, by some of his men, to Jews outside the city with whom he wished to communicate, and receiving replies from them; by the same means he stocked the town with all necessaries when its supplies began to fail. The messengers sent out had general orders to creep past the sentries on all fours and to wear fleeces on their backs, in order that, if they were seen at night, they might be taken for dogs. However, the guards eventually detected the ruse and blocked the gully. *A neglected gully used to obtain supplies.*

(15) Josephus, now recognizing that the city could not long hold out and that his own life would be endangered if he remained there, took counsel with the principal citizens about the means of flight. The people discovered his intention and crowded round him, imploring him not to abandon them, as they depended on him alone. If he remained, they urged, he would be their one hope of the town being saved, as everyone, because he was with them, would put his heart into the struggle; were capture in store for them, even then he would be their one consolation. Moreover, it would be unworthy of him to fly from his foes, to desert his friends, to leap in the storm from the vessel on which he had embarked in a calm. For his departure would wreck *Josephus contemplates flight.*

JOSEPHUS

μηδενὸς ἔτι τοῖς πολεμίοις τολμῶντος ἀνθίστασθαι,
δι' ὃν ἂν θαρσοῖεν οἰχομένου.

197 (16) Ὁ δὲ Ἰώσηπος τὸ καθ' αὑτὸν ἀσφαλὲς
ὑποστελλόμενος ὑπὲρ αὐτῶν ἔφασκεν ποιεῖσθαι
198 τὴν ἔξοδον· μένων μὲν γὰρ εἴσω οὔτ' ἂν ὠφελῆσαί
τι μέγα σωζομένους, κἂν ἁλίσκωνται, συναπολεῖσθαι περιττῶς, ἐκδὺς δὲ τῆς πολιορκίας ἔξωθεν
199 αὐτοὺς ὠφελήσειν μέγιστα· τούς τε γὰρ ἐκ τῆς
χώρας Γαλιλαίους συναθροίσειν ᾗ τάχος καὶ Ῥωμαίους ἑτέρῳ πολέμῳ τῆς πόλεως αὐτῶν ἀντι-
200 περισπάσειν. οὐχ ὁρᾶν δέ, τί παρακαθεζόμενος
αὐτοῖς χρήσιμος ⟨ἂν⟩[1] εἴη νῦν, πλὴν εἰ μὴ Ῥωμαίους παροξύνων μᾶλλον ἐπὶ τὴν πολιορκίαν, οὓς
περὶ πλείστου ποιεῖσθαι λαβεῖν αὐτόν· εἰ δ' ἐκ-
δράντα πύθοιντο, πολὺ τῆς ἐπὶ τὴν πόλιν ὁρμῆς
201 ἀνήσειν. οὐκ ἔπειθεν δὲ τούτοις,[2] ἀλλὰ μᾶλλον
ἐξέκαυσεν τὸ πλῆθος αὐτοῦ περιέχεσθαι· παιδία
γοῦν καὶ γέροντες καὶ γύναια μετὰ νηπίων ὀδυρό-
μενα προσέπιπτον αὐτῷ καὶ τοῖς ποσὶν ἐμπλεκό-
202 μενοι πάντες εἴχοντο, καὶ μετὰ κωκυτῶν κοινωνὸν
σφίσι τῆς τύχης μένειν ἱκέτευον, οὐ φθόνῳ τῆς
ἐκείνου σωτηρίας, ἔμοιγε δοκεῖν, ἀλλ' ἐλπίδι τῆς
ἑαυτῶν· οὐδὲν γὰρ ἠξίουν πείσεσθαι δεινὸν Ἰωσήπου μένοντος.

203 (17) Ὁ δὲ πειθομένῳ μὲν ἱκετηρίαν ταῦτα
νομίσας, βιαζομένῳ δὲ φρουράν, πολὺ δ' αὐτοῦ

---

[1] ins. Niese.　　[2] L Lat.: τούτους or αὐτοὺς the rest.

---

[a] εἴχοντο καὶ μετὰ κωκυτῶν : a reminiscence of Hom. Il.
xxii. 408 (the mourning over Hector) ἀμφὶ δὲ λαοὶ κωκυτῷ τ'
εἴχοντο καὶ οἰμωγῇ κατὰ ἄστυ. There is a similar scene in
Vita 210 ff.

the town, as none would have the heart to resist
the enemy any longer, when he whose presence
would have given them courage was gone.

(16) Josephus, suppressing any allusion to his own ^{His}
safety, assured them that it was in their own interests ^{intention is prevented.}
that he had contemplated departure ; for his presence
in the town could not materially assist them if they
were saved, and if they were taken what end would
be served by his perishing with them ? Were he,
on the contrary, once clear of the siege, he could from
outside render them the greatest service, for he
would promptly muster the Galilaeans from the
country and, by creating a diversion elsewhere, draw
off the Romans from their city. He failed to see how
his presence at their side could assist them in present
circumstances, or have any other effect except to
spur the Romans to press the siege more vigorously
than ever, as they attached so much importance to
his capture ; whereas, if they heard that he had fled,
they would considerably relax the ferocity of their
attack. Unmoved, however, by these words, the
multitude only clung to him more ardently : children,
old men, women with infants in their arms, all threw
themselves weeping before him ; they embraced
and held him by his feet, they implored him with
sobs [a] to stay and share their fortune. All this they
did, I cannot but think, not because they grudged
him his chance of safety, but because they thought
of their own ; for, with Josephus on the spot, they
were convinced that no disaster could befall them.

(17) Josephus suspected that this insistence would
not go beyond supplication if he yielded, but meant
that watch would be kept upon him if he opposed
their wishes. Moreover, his determination to leave

τῆς εἰς τὴν ἀπόλειψιν ὁρμῆς καὶ ὁ τῶν ὀδυρομένων
204 ἔκλασεν οἶκτος, μένειν τε ἔγνω, καὶ τὴν κοινὴν τῆς
πόλεως ἀπόγνωσιν ὁπλισάμενος, '' νῦν καιρός,''
εἰπών, '' ἄρχεσθαι μάχης, ὅτ᾽ ἐλπὶς οὐκ ἔστι
σωτηρίας· καλὸν εὔκλειαν ἀντικαταλλαξάμενον τοῦ
βίου καὶ δράσαντά τι γενναῖον εἰς μνήμην ὀψιγενῶν
205 πεσεῖν,'' ἐπ᾽ ἔργα τρέπεται. καὶ προελθὼν μετὰ
τῶν μαχιμωτάτων διεσκίδα τε τοὺς φρουροὺς καὶ
μέχρι τοῦ στρατοπέδου τῶν Ῥωμαίων κατέτρεχεν,
καὶ τὰς μὲν ἐπὶ τῶν χωμάτων δέρρεις, αἷς ὑπ-
εσκήνουν, διέσπα, τοῖς δὲ ἔργοις ἐνέβαλλεν πῦρ.
206 τῇ θ᾽ ἑξῆς ὁμοίως καὶ τῇ τρίτῃ καὶ ἐπὶ συχνὰς
ἡμέρας καὶ νύκτας πολεμῶν οὐκ ἔκαμνεν.
207 (18) Οὐεσπασιανὸς δὲ τῶν¹ Ῥωμαίων κακου-
μένων ταῖς ἐκδρομαῖς, τρέπεσθαί τε γὰρ ὑπὸ
Ἰουδαίων ᾐδοῦντο καὶ τραπέντων ἐπιδιώκειν
βάρει τῶν ὅπλων ἦσαν βραδεῖς, οἵ τε Ἰουδαῖοι
πρίν τι παθεῖν ἀεὶ δρῶντες ἀνέφευγον εἰς τὴν
208 πόλιν, τοῖς μὲν ὁπλίταις τὰς ὁρμὰς αὐτῶν ἐκκλίνειν ἐκέλευσεν καὶ μὴ συμπλέκεσθαι θανατῶσιν
209 ἀνθρώποις· οὐδὲν γὰρ ἀλκιμώτερον εἶναι τῆς
ἀπογνώσεως, περισβέννυσθαι δὲ αὐτῶν τὰς ὁρμὰς
210 σκοπῶν ἀπορουμένας, ὥσπερ ὕλης τὸ πῦρ· προσήκειν γε μὴν καὶ Ῥωμαίοις μετ᾽ ἀσφαλείας καὶ
τὸ νικᾶν, ὡς ἂν οὐκ ἐξ ἀνάγκης πολεμοῦσιν, ἀλλὰ
211 προσκτωμένοις. τοῖς δὲ τῶν Ἀράβων τοξόταις
καὶ τοῖς ἀπὸ τῆς Συρίας σφενδονήταις καὶ λιθο-
βόλοις τὰ πολλὰ τοὺς Ἰουδαίους ἀνέστελλεν·
ἠρέμει δ᾽ οὐδὲ τῶν ἀφετηρίων ὀργάνων τὸ πλῆθος.
212 οἱ δὲ τούτοις μὲν εἶκον κακούμενοι, τῶν δὲ πόρρω

---

¹ +τε mss.: om. Lat.

them was greatly shaken by compassion for their distress. He therefore decided to remain, and, making the universal despair of the city into a weapon for himself,[a] " Now is the time," he exclaimed, " to begin the combat, when all hope of deliverance is past. Fine is it to sacrifice life for renown and by some glorious exploit to ensure in falling the memory of posterity ! " Suiting his action to his words, he sallied out with his bravest warriors, dispersed the guards, and penetrating to the Romans' camp, tore up the tents of skin under which they were sheltered on the embankment, and set fire to the works. This he repeated the next day, and the day after that, and for a series of days and nights indefatigably continued the fight.

Jewish sallies.

(18) The Romans suffered from these sallies, for they were ashamed to fly before Jews, and when they put the latter to flight the weight of their arms impeded them in the pursuit, while the Jews always did some mischief before the enemy could retaliate, and then took refuge in the town. In view of this, Vespasian ordered his legionaries to shun these attacks and not to be drawn into an engagement with men who were bent on death. " Nothing," he said, " is more redoubtable than despair, and their impetuosity, deprived of an objective, will be extinguished, like fire for lack of fuel. Besides, it becomes even Romans to think of safety as well as victory, since they make war not from necessity, but to increase their empire." Thenceforth he relied mainly on his Arab archers and the Syrian slingers and stone-throwers to repel the Jewish assaults ; the greater part of his artillery was also constantly in action. Severely handled by the engines, the Jews

---

[a] *Cf.* § 153 note.

βαλλομένων ἐνδοτέρω γινόμενοι προσέκειντο τοῖς
Ῥωμαίοις χαλεποὶ καὶ ψυχῆς καὶ σώματος ἀφει
δοῦντες ἐμάχοντο, ἐκ διαδοχῆς ἑκάτεροι τὸ κε
κμηκὸς ἑαυτῶν ἀναλαμβάνοντες.

213 (19) Οὐεσπασιανὸς δὲ ἡγούμενος τῷ μήκει τοῦ
χρόνου καὶ ταῖς ἐκδρομαῖς ἀντιπολιορκεῖσθαι, τῶν
χωμάτων ἤδη τοῖς τείχεσι πελαζόντων προσάγειν
214 ἔγνω τὸν κριόν. ὁ δ' ἐστὶν ὑπερμεγέθης δοκὸς
ἱστῷ νεὼς παραπλήσιος· ἐστόμωται δὲ παχεῖ
σιδήρῳ κατ' ἄκρον εἰς κριοῦ προτομήν, ἀφ' οὗ
215 καὶ καλεῖται, τετυπωμένω. καταιωρεῖται δὲ κά
λοις μέσος ὥσπερ ἀπὸ πλάστιγγος ἑτέρας δοκοῦ,
σταυροῖς ἑκατέρωθεν ἑδραίοις ὑπεστηριγμένης.
216 ἀνωθούμενος δὲ ὑπὸ πλήθους ἀνδρῶν εἰς τὸ κατό
πιν, τῶν αὐτῶν ἀθρόως πάλιν εἰς τοὔμπροσθεν ἐπι
βρισάντων τύπτει τὰ τείχη τῷ προανέχοντι σιδήρῳ.
217 καὶ οὐδεὶς οὕτως καρτερὸς πύργος ἢ περίβολος
πλατύς, ὃς κἂν τὰς πρώτας πληγὰς ἐνέγκη[1] κατ
218 ίσχυσεν[2] τῆς ἐπιμονῆς. ἐπὶ ταύτην τὴν πεῖραν ὁ
στρατηγὸς τῶν Ῥωμαίων μετέβαινεν βίᾳ τὴν
πόλιν ἑλεῖν σπεύδων, ὡς τὸ προσκαθέζεσθαι
219 βλαβερὸν ἦν Ἰουδαίων οὐκ ἠρεμούντων. οἱ μὲν
οὖν τούς τε καταπέλτας καὶ τὰ λοιπὰ τῶν ἀφε
τηρίων, ὡς ἐξικνοῖτο τῶν ἐπὶ τοῦ τείχους κω
λύειν πειρωμένων, ἔγγιον προσαγαγόντες ἔβαλλον·
ὁμοίως δὲ συνήγγιζον οἱ τοξόται καὶ σφενδονῆται.
220 διὰ δὲ ταῦτα μηδενὸς τῶν περιβόλων ἐπιβῆναι
τολμῶντος, προσῆγον ἕτεροι τὸν κριὸν γέρροις
τε διηνεκέσι καὶ καθύπερθεν πεφραγμένον δέρρει

---

[1] Niese: ἐνεγκεῖν or ἐνέγκαι MSS.   [2] κατισχύσει VRC.

[a] Cf. Soph. El. 980 ψυχῆς ἀφειδήσαντε with note on § 153.

gave way, but once past the reach of their adversaries' long-range projectiles they flung themselves
furiously on the Romans and fought desperately,
prodigal of life and limb,[a] one party after another
relieving their exhausted comrades.

(19) The length of the siege and the sallies of the The
enemy made Vespasian feel that the position was battering-
reversed and himself the besieged ; so, now that the ram applied.
earthworks were approaching the ramparts, he decided to bring up the " ram." This is an immense
beam, like the mast of a ship, reinforced at its extremity with a mass of iron in the form of a ram's
head, whence the machine takes its name. It is
suspended at its middle point by ropes, like the
beam of a balance, to another beam which is supported at either end by posts fixed in the ground. A
large body of men first draw the ram backward and
then, all pushing together with all their weight,
heave it forward so that it batters the wall with the
projecting iron. And there is no tower so strong,
no wall so thick, as, even though it sustain the initial
impact, to withstand the repeated assaults of this
engine. Such was the expedient to which the Roman
general had recourse, being impatient to carry the
city by storm, as the long blockade, coupled with the
activity of the Jews, was proving injurious. The
Romans now brought forward the catapults and the
rest of their artillery within range of the Jews on the
ramparts who were endeavouring to beat them off, and
put these engines into action ; the archers and slingers
simultaneously advanced. While the fire of these
troops would not permit any to venture on the ramparts, another party brought up the ram, protected
by a long line of hurdles, over which was a covering

πρός τε αὐτῶν καὶ τοῦ μηχανήματος ἀσφάλειαν.
221 καὶ κατὰ τὴν πρώτην πληγὴν διεσείσθη μὲν τὸ
τεῖχος, κραυγὴ δὲ μεγίστη παρὰ τῶν ἔνδον ἤρθη
καθάπερ ἑαλωκότων ἤδη.

222 (20) Πολλάκις δὲ εἰς τὸν αὐτὸν παίοντος[1] τόπον
ὁ Ἰώσηπος ὁρῶν ὅσον οὔπω καταρριφθησόμενον
τὸ τεῖχος, σοφίζεται πρὸς[2] ὀλίγον τὴν βίαν τοῦ
223 μηχανήματος. σάκκους ἀχύρων πληρώσαντας ἐκέλευσεν καθιμᾶν καθ᾽ ὃ φερόμενον ἀεὶ τὸν κριὸν
ὁρῶεν, ὡς πλάζοιτό τε ἡ ἐμβολὴ καὶ δεχόμενοι
224 τὰς πληγὰς ἐκκενοῖεν τῇ χαυνότητι. τοῦτο πλείστην διατριβὴν παρέσχεν τοῖς Ῥωμαίοις, καθ᾽ ὃ
μὲν τρέποιεν τὴν μηχανὴν ἀντιπαραγόντων τοὺς
σάκκους τῶν ὕπερθεν, ὑποβαλλόντων τε[3] ταῖς ἐμβολαῖς, ὡς μηδὲν κατ᾽ ἀντιτυπίαν βλάπτεσθαι τὸ
225 τεῖχος· ἕως ἀντεπινοήσαντες κοντοὺς οἱ Ῥωμαῖοι
μακροὺς καὶ δρέπανα δήσαντες ἐπ᾽ ἄκρων τοὺς
226 σάκκους ἀπέτεμνον. ἐνεργοῦ δὲ οὕτω τῆς ἑλε-
πόλεως γενομένης καὶ τοῦ τείχους, νεοπαγὲς γὰρ
ἦν, ἐνδιδόντος ἤδη, τὸ λοιπὸν ἐπὶ τὴν ἐκ πυρὸς
227 ἄμυναν οἱ περὶ τὸν Ἰώσηπον ὥρμησαν. ἁψάμενοι
δὲ ὅσον αὔης εἶχον ὕλης τριχόθεν ἐπεκθέουσιν,
καὶ τά τε μηχανήματα καὶ τὰ γέρρα καὶ τὰ
228 χώματα τῶν Ῥωμαίων ὑπεπίμπρασαν. οἱ δὲ
κακῶς ἐπεβοήθουν, πρός τε τὴν τόλμαν αὐτῶν
καταπεπληγότες καὶ ὑπὸ τῆς φλογὸς τὰς ἀμύνας

---

[1] Niese: παίοντες, παίοντα(ς) or παίονται MSS.
[2] κατ᾽ PA.   [3] Niese: δὲ MSS.

---

[a] Sacks of rags (*centones*) were used by the Romans
(Veget. iv. 23, quoted by Reinach).   [b] Or " continually."
[c] The ἑλέπολις, here used for the ram, was originally the

of skin for the greater security of themselves and of their engine. At the first blow the wall was shaken and a piercing cry arose from the interior of the town as though it had already been taken.

(20) Josephus, seeing that under the repeated blows constantly directed upon the same spot the wall was on the verge of collapsing, devised a method of paralysing for a while the force of the machine. He directed that sacks filled with chaff [a] should be let down by ropes at the place which the ram was seen from time to time [b] to be battering, with the object of deflecting the head and deadening the force of the blow by the soft cushion which received it. This seriously retarded the Romans, for, wherever they turned their engine, those above retorted by opposing their sacks beneath the strokes, and so the wall suffered no injury from the impact ; until the Romans invented a counter-device of long poles to the ends of which were attached scythes, with which they cut the cords supporting the sacks. The engine [c] having thus recovered its efficacy, and the newly built wall already showing signs of giving way, Josephus and his comrades, as a last resort, had recourse to fire. Snatching up [d] all the dry wood which they could find, they rushed out from three quarters of the town and set fire to the engines, wicker shelters, and props of the enemy's earth-works. The Romans did little to save them, stupefied by their opponents' audacity and outstripped by the

Counter devices of the besieged : they set fire to the Roman engines.

name given to a movable tower, invented by Demetrius, with several stories for the carriage of artillery and troops (cf. § 121).

[d] ἀψάμενοι: cf. ἀράμενοι πῦρ πάλιν, § 234. The meaning " kindle " (so Reinach) is usually expressed by the *active* ἅπτειν, though the middle is used for " set fire to " (a building), *B.* v. 287 τῶν ἔργων ἥπτετο τὸ πῦρ.

φθανόμενοι· ξηρᾶς γὰρ ὕλης, πρὸς δὲ ἀσφάλτου
τε καὶ πίσσης, ἔτι δὲ θείου, διίπτατο τὸ πῦρ
ἐπινοίας τάχιον, καὶ τὰ πολλῷ καμάτῳ πεπονη-
μένα τοῖς Ῥωμαίοις ἐπὶ μιᾶς ὥρας ἐνέμετο.

229 (21) Ἔνθα καὶ ἀνήρ τις ἐξεφάνη Ἰουδαίων
λόγου καὶ μνήμης ἄξιος· Σαμαίου[1] μὲν παῖς ἦν,
Ἐλεάζαρος δ' ἐκαλεῖτο, Σαβὰ[2] δὲ πατρὶς αὐτῷ
230 τῆς Γαλιλαίας· οὗτος ὑπερμεγέθη[3] πέτραν ἀρά-
μενος ἀφίησιν ἀπὸ τοῦ τείχους ἐπὶ τὴν ἑλέπολιν
μετὰ τοσαύτης βίας, ὥστε ἀπορρῆξαι τὴν κεφαλὴν
τοῦ μηχανήματος, ἣν καὶ καταπηδήσας ἐκ μέσων
αἴρεται τῶν πολεμίων καὶ μετὰ πολλῆς ἀδείας
231 ἐπὶ τὸ τεῖχος ἔφερεν. σκοπὸς δὲ πᾶσιν τοῖς
ἐχθροῖς γενόμενος καὶ γυμνῷ τῷ σώματι τὰς
πληγὰς δεξάμενος πέντε μὲν διαπείρεται βέλεσιν,
232 πρὸς οὐδὲν δὲ τούτων ἐπιστραφείς, ὅτε τὸ τεῖχος
ἀνέβη καὶ περίοπτος πᾶσιν τῆς εὐτολμίας ἔστη,
τότε ἰλυσπώμενος ὑπὸ τῶν τραυμάτων μετὰ τοῦ
233 κριοῦ κατέπεσεν. ἄριστοι μετ' αὐτὸν ἐφάνησαν
ἀδελφοὶ δύο Νετείρας καὶ Φίλιππος, ἀπὸ Ῥούμας
κώμης, Γαλιλαῖοι καὶ αὐτοί, [οἳ][4] προπηδῶσι μὲν
εἰς τοὺς ἀπὸ τοῦ δεκάτου τάγματος, τοσούτῳ δὲ
ῥοίζῳ καὶ βίᾳ τοῖς Ῥωμαίοις συνέπεσον, ὡς δι-
αρρῆξαί τε τὰς τάξεις καὶ τρέψασθαι καθ' οὓς ἐφ-
ορμήσειαν ἅπαντας.

234 (22) Μετὰ τούτους ὅ τε Ἰώσηπος καὶ τὸ
λοιπὸν πλῆθος ἀράμενοι πῦρ πάλιν τὰ μηχανήματα καὶ τὰς ὑποδύσεις ἅμα τοῖς ἔργοις ὑφῆψαν
τοῦ τε πέμπτου καὶ τοῦ δεκάτου τραπέντος τάγ-

---

[1] Σαμίου PAL.
[2] So or Σαβαὰ or Σαὰβ the mss.: Niese suggests Γάβα, a
known town of Galilee.

flames in their efforts to rescue them; for fed by dry
tinder, with the addition of bitumen, pitch, and
sulphur, the fire flew in all directions quicker than
thought, and works which had cost the Romans such
severe labour were consumed in a single hour.

(21) On this occasion one Jew who made his mark Jewish
deserves record and remembrance; his name was heroes.
Eleazar, son of Sameas, a native of Saba in Galilee.
Lifting an enormous stone, he hurled it from the wall
at the ram with such force that he broke off its head;
then, leaping down, he carried off this trophy from
the midst of the enemy and bore it with perfect
composure to the foot of the ramparts. Now become
a target for all his foes, and receiving their hits in his
defenceless body, he was pierced by five arrows.
But, without a thought for these, he scaled the wall
and there stood conspicuous to all the admirers of his
bravery; then, writhing under his wounds, he fell
headlong with the ram's head in his hands. Next
to him those who most distinguished themselves
were two brothers, Netiras and Philip, also Galilaeans, from the village of Ruma[a]: dashing out
against the lines of the tenth legion, they charged
the Romans with such impetuosity and force that
they broke their ranks and put to flight all whom
they encountered.

(22) Following in the wake of these men, Josephus
and the rest of the people, with fire-brands in their
hands, again sallied out and set fire to the machines,
shelters and earthworks of the fifth legion and of

[a] Modern *Rumah*, a few miles from Jotapata on the south
of the Plain of Asochis.

---

[3] οὗτος ὑπερμεγέθη M (Lat.): ὑπερμεγέθη δὲ or ὑπερμεγέθη
the rest.   [4] ins. M Lat.: om. the rest.

ματος, οἱ λοιποὶ δὲ φθάσαντες καὶ τὰ ὄργανα καὶ
235 πᾶσαν ὕλην κατέχωσαν. περὶ δὲ δείλην πάλιν
ἀναστήσαντες προσῆγον τὸν κριὸν ᾗ προπεπονήκει
236 τυπτόμενον τὸ τεῖχος. ἔνθα τις τῶν ἀμυνομέ-
νων ἀπ' αὐτοῦ βάλλει τὸν Οὐεσπασιανὸν βέλει
κατὰ τὸν ταρσὸν τοῦ ποδὸς καὶ τιτρώσκει μὲν
ἐπιπολαίως, προεκλύσαντος τὸ βληθὲν τοῦ διαστήματος, μέγιστον δὲ θόρυβον ἐνεποίησεν τοῖς
237 Ῥωμαίοις· πρὸς γὰρ τὸ αἷμα ταραχθέντων τῶν
πλησίον φήμη διὰ παντὸς ἐπήει τοῦ στρατοῦ, καὶ
τῆς πολιορκίας οἱ πλείους ἀφέμενοι μετ' ἐκπλή-
238 ξεως καὶ δέους ἐπὶ τὸν στρατηγὸν συνέθεον. πρὸ
δὲ πάντων Τίτος δείσας περὶ τῷ πατρὶ παρῆν,
ὡς τὸ πλῆθος καὶ τῇ πρὸς τὸν ἡγούμενον εὐνοίᾳ
καὶ τῇ τοῦ παιδὸς ἀγωνίᾳ συγχυθῆναι. ῥᾷστα
μέντοι τόν τε υἱὸν ὁ πατὴρ δεδιότα καὶ τὴν στρα-
239 τιὰν ἔπαυσεν τοῦ θορύβου· τῶν γὰρ ἀλγηδόνων
ἐπάνω γενόμενος καὶ πᾶσιν τοῖς ἐπτοημένοις δι'
αὐτὸν ὀφθῆναι σπουδάσας χαλεπώτερον Ἰουδαίοις
ἐπήγειρε[1] τὸν πόλεμον· ἕκαστος γὰρ ὡς τιμωρὸς
τοῦ στρατηγοῦ προκινδυνεύειν ἤθελεν, καὶ βοῇ
παρακροτοῦντες ἀλλήλους ἐπὶ τὸ τεῖχος ὥρμων.
240 (23) Οἱ δὲ περὶ τὸν Ἰώσηπον, καίπερ ἐπ'
ἀλλήλοις πίπτοντες ὑπὸ τῶν καταπελτικῶν καὶ
τῶν πετροβόλων, ὅμως οὐκ ἀπετρέποντο τοῦ
τείχους, ἀλλὰ πυρὶ καὶ σιδήρῳ καὶ πέτροις τοὺς
ὑπὸ[2] τὰ γέρρα τὸν κριὸν ἐπιβρίθοντας ἔβαλλον.

---

[1] ἐπῆρεν PA; for text cf. B. v. 98.
[2] Destinon, Holwerda: ἐπὶ MSS.

a § 233.

the tenth which had been routed[a]; the other
legions hastily buried their machinery and all com-
bustible materials. Towards evening the Romans
re-erected the ram and brought it up to the spot
where the wall had been weakened by its previous
blows. At this moment, one of the defenders of *Vespasian*
the ramparts hit Vespasian with an arrow in the sole *wounded.*
of the foot. The wound was slight, the distance
having broken the force of the missile, but the incident created a vast commotion among the Romans :
the sight of blood alarmed those immediately surrounding Vespasian, the news at once spread through
the whole army, and most of the soldiers, abandoning
the siege, came running towards their general in
consternation and terror. The first on the spot was
Titus, with grave fears for his father, so that the
troops were doubly agitated, both by their affection
for their chief and by the sight of his son's anguish.
However, Vespasian found little difficulty in allaying
both the fears of his son and the tumult of the army.
Mastering his pain, he hastened to show himself to
all who had trembled for his life, and so roused them
to fight the Jews more fiercely than ever. Each
wished to be the first to brave danger in avenging
his general, and, with shouts of mutual encouragement, they rushed for the ramparts.

(23) Josephus and his men, though falling one *Fierce night*
upon another under the hail of missiles from the *assault of*
catapults and stone-projectors, still were not driven *the Romans.*
from the battlements, but with fire, iron,[b] and stones
continued to assail the soldiers who, under cover of
their wicker shelters, were propelling the ram. How-

---

[b] Usually = " sword-blade " ; here probably iron arrow-
heads are meant (Hom. *Il.* iv. 123).

241 καὶ ἤνυον μὲν οὐδὲν ἢ μικρόν, αὐτοὶ δ' ἀδιαλείπτως ἔπιπτον ὑπὸ μὴ βλεπομένων καθορώ-
242 μενοι· αὐτοί τε γὰρ ὑπὸ τῆς σφετέρας περι-
λαμπόμενοι φλογὸς σκοπὸς ἦσαν τοῖς πολεμίοις
εὐσύνοπτος, ὥσπερ ἐν ἡμέρᾳ, καὶ τῶν ὀργάνων
πόρρωθεν μὴ βλεπομένων δυσφύλακτον ἦν τὸ
243 βαλλόμενον. ἡ γοῦν[1] τῶν ὀξυβελῶν καὶ κατα-
πελτῶν βία πολλοὺς ἅμα διήλαυνεν, καὶ τῶν ὑπὸ
τῆς μηχανῆς ἀφιεμένων πετρῶν ὁ ῥοῖζος ἐπάλξεις
τε ἀπέσυρεν καὶ γωνίας ἀπέθρυπτε πύργων.
244 ἀνδρῶν μὲν γὰρ ⟨οὐδὲν⟩[2] οὕτως ἰσχυρὸν στῖφος,
ὃ μὴ μέχρις ἐσχάτης στρώννυται φάλαγγος βίᾳ
245 τε καὶ μεγέθει τοῦ λίθου. μάθοι δ' ἄν τις τὴν
τοῦ μηχανήματος ἀλκὴν ἐκ τῶν ἐπὶ τῆσδε τῆς
νυκτὸς γενομένων· πληγεὶς γάρ τις ἀπ' αὐτοῦ
τῶν περὶ τὸν Ἰώσηπον ἑστώτων ἀνὰ τὸ τεῖχος
ἀπαράσσεται τὴν κεφαλὴν ὑπὸ τῆς πέτρας, καὶ
τὸ κρανίον ἀπὸ τριῶν ἐσφενδονήθη σταδίων.
246 γυναικός τε μεθ' ἡμέραν ἐγκύμονος πληγείσης
τὴν γαστέρα, προῄει δὲ νέον ἐξ οἰκίας, ἐξέσεισεν
ἐφ' ἡμιστάδιον τὸ βρέφος· τοσαύτη ἦν ἡ τοῦ
247 λιθοβόλου βία. τῶν οὖν ὀργάνων φοβερώτερος ὁ
248 ῥοῖζος, τῶν δὲ βαλλομένων ἦν ὁ ψόφος. ἐπ-
άλληλοι δὲ ἐκτύπουν οἱ νεκροὶ κατὰ τοῦ τείχους
ῥιπτόμενοι, καὶ δεινὴ μὲν ἔνδοθεν κραυγὴ γυναικῶν
ἠγείρετο, συνήχουν δ' ἔξωθεν οἰμωγαὶ φονευο-
249 μένων. αἵματι δ' ἐρρεῖτο πᾶς ὁ πρὸ τῆς μάχης

---

[1] Niese: τε οὖν mss.
[2] Niese: om. PA*L: A² has οὐδενὶ, the other mss. ins. οὐκ
ἦν before or after οὕτως.

---

[a] § 80.
[b] i.e. the λιθοβόλον, Lat. ballista, § 80 ; Reinach identifies

ever, their efforts had little or no effect, and they
were incessantly falling, because the enemy saw them
without being seen ; for, with the glare of their own
lights all round them, they formed as conspicuous a
mark for the enemy as in broad daylight, while they
found difficulty in avoiding the projectiles from the
engines which they could not see in the distance.
Thus the missiles from the "quick-firers"[a] and
catapults came with such force as to strike down
whole files, and the whizzing stones hurled by the
engine[b] carried away the battlements and broke off
the angles of the towers. Indeed, there is no body
of troops, however strong, which the force and mass
of these stones cannot lay low to the last rank. Some
incidents of that night will give an idea of the power
of this engine. One of the men standing on the wall
beside Josephus had his head carried away by a stone,
and his skull was shot, as from a sling, to a distance
of three furlongs ; a woman with child was struck on
the belly just as she was leaving her house at daybreak, and the babe in her womb was flung half a
furlong away.[c] So mighty was the force of these
stone-projectors. More alarming even than the
engines was their whirring drone, more frightful than
the missiles the crash.[d] Then there was the thud of
the dead falling one after another from the wall.
Fearful shrieks from the women within the town
mingled with the moans of the dying victims without. The whole surrounding area in front of the fight-

Examples of
the force of
the Roman
engines.

the "engine" as the *onager*, another form of stone-projector,
but apparently not invented till later.

  [c] Josephus is prone to exaggeration.

  [d] It seems unnecessary to correct φοβερώτερος to φοβερὸς
or φοβερώτατος with Reinach, who renders "Terrible aussi
était le sifflement des machines et le fracas de leur ravage."

περίβολος, καὶ προσβατὸν ὑπὸ πτωμάτων τὸ
250 τεῖχος ἐγίνετο. φοβερωτέραν δ' ἐποίουν τὴν βοὴν
περιηχοῦντα τὰ ὄρη, καὶ οὐδὲν ἐπ' ἐκείνης τῆς
νυκτὸς οὔτε εἰς ἀκοῆς οὔτε εἰς ὄψεως κατάπληξιν
251 ἀπελείπετο. πλεῖστοι μέν γε τῶν ἐπὶ τῆς Ἰωταπάτης ἀγωνιζόμενοι γενναίως ἔπεσον, πλεῖστοι δ'
ἐγένοντο τραυματίαι, καὶ μόλις περὶ τὴν ἑωθινὴν
φυλακὴν ἐνδίδωσι τοῖς μηχανήμασι τὸ τεῖχος
252 ἀδιαλείπτως τυπτόμενον· οἱ δὲ φραξάμενοι τοῖς
σώμασι καὶ τοῖς ὅπλοις τὸ καταρριφθὲν ἀντ-
ωχύρωσαν, πρὶν βληθῆναι τὰς ἐπιβατηρίους ὑπὸ τῶν
Ῥωμαίων μηχανάς.
253   (24) Ὑπὸ δὲ τὴν ἕω Οὐεσπασιανὸς ἐπὶ τὴν
κατάληψιν τῆς πόλεως συνῆγεν τὴν στρατιάν,
ὀλίγον ἀπὸ τοῦ νυκτερινοῦ πόνου διαναπαύσας.
254 βουλόμενος δ' ἀπὸ τῶν καταρριφθέντων περι-
σπάσαι τοὺς εἴργοντας, τοὺς μὲν γενναιοτάτους
τῶν ἱππέων ἀποβήσας [τῶν ἵππων]¹ τριχῇ διέταξεν
κατὰ τὰ πεπτωκότα τοῦ τείχους, πάντοθεν πεφραγμένους τοῖς ὅπλοις καὶ τοὺς κοντοὺς προΐσχοντας,
ὡς ὁπότε τὰς ἐπιβατηρίους βάλλοιεν μηχανὰς
255 κατάρχοιντο τῆς εἰσόδου· κατόπιν δὲ αὐτῶν ἔταξεν
τοῦ πεζοῦ τὸ ἀκμαιότατον, τὸ δὲ λοιπὸν ἱππικὸν
ἀντιπαρεξέτεινεν τῷ τείχει κατὰ πᾶσαν τὴν ὀρεινὴν
πρὸς τὸ μηδένα τῶν ἀναφευγόντων ἐκ τῆς ἁλώσεως
256 διαλαθεῖν. κατόπιν δὲ τούτων περιέστησεν τοὺς
τοξότας ἔχειν κελεύσας ἕτοιμα τὰ βέλη πρὸς
ἄφεσιν, ὁμοίως δὲ καὶ σφενδονήτας καὶ τοὺς ἐπὶ
257 τῶν μηχανημάτων, ἑτέρους δὲ κλίμακας ἀραμένους
προσφέρειν ἐπάνω τοῖς ἀκεραίοις τείχεσιν, ἵν' οἱ

¹ om. as gloss Destinon; cf. iii. 449.

ing line ran with blood, and the piles of corpses formed
a path to the summit of the wall. The echo from
the mountains around added to the horrible din; in
short nothing that can terrify ear or eye was wanting
on that dreadful night. Multitudes of the defenders
of Jotapata fell in valiant fight, multitudes were
wounded; and not till towards the hour of the
morning watch did the wall, after incessant battering, A breach in
succumb to the machines. The besieged, however, the wall.
blocking the breach with their persons and their
weapons, threw up a makeshift defence before the
Romans could lay the gangways for the escalade.

(24) Vespasian, having allowed his troops a brief Prepara-
respite after the fatigues of the night, reassembled escalade.
them soon after daybreak for the final assault. His
object was to draw off the defenders from the breach.
With this intention, he ordered the bravest of his
cavalry to dismount and marshalled them in three
divisions [a] opposite the ruined portions of the wall;
protected by armour from head to foot and with
lances couched, they were to be the first to enter the
town the moment the gangways were laid; behind
these he placed the flower of the infantry. (The rest
of the cavalry were deployed all along the mountain
side facing the ramparts, to prevent the escape of a
single fugitive when the town was taken.[b]) Further
in the rear he posted the archers in a semicircle,
with directions to have their arrows ready to shoot,
along with the slingers and the artillery, under similar
orders. Other parties were then told off to bring up
ladders and plant them against the wall where it was

[a] Or " three deep."
[b] As Reinach suggests, § 255 appears to be a parenthesis,
and § 256 follows, in the order of battle, immediately after
§ 254.

JOSEPHUS

μὲν τούτους κωλύειν πειρώμενοι καταλίποιεν τὴν
ἐπὶ τοῖς καταρριφθεῖσιν φυλακήν, οἱ λοιποὶ δ᾽
ὑπ᾽ ἀθρόων βιαζόμενοι τῶν βελῶν εἴξωσιν τῆς
εἰσόδου.

258 (25) Ἰώσηπος δὲ συνιεὶς[1] τὴν ἐπίνοιαν ἐπὶ μὲν
τοῦ μένοντος τείχους σὺν τοῖς κεκμηκόσιν ἵστησι
τοὺς γηραιοὺς ὡς μηδὲν ταύτῃ βλαβησομένους,
εἰς δὲ τὰ παρερρωγότα[2] τοῦ τείχους τοὺς δυνα-
τωτάτους καὶ πρὸ πάντων ἀνὰ ἓξ ἄνδρας, μεθ᾽
ὧν καὶ αὐτὸς εἰς τὸ προκινδυνεύειν ἐκληρώσατο.
259 ἐκέλευσέν τε πρὸς μὲν τὸν ἀλαλαγμὸν τῶν ταγμάτων ἀποφράξαι τὰς ἀκοάς, ὡς ἂν μὴ καταπλαγεῖεν,
πρὸς δὲ τὸ πλῆθος τῶν βελῶν συνοκλάσαντας
καλύψασθαι καθύπερθεν τοῖς θυρεοῖς, ὑποχωρῆσαί
τε πρὸς ὀλίγον,[3] ἕως τὰς φαρέτρας κενώσωσιν οἱ
260 τοξόται· βαλλόντων δὲ τὰς ἐπιβατηρίους μηχανὰς
αὐτοὺς προπηδᾶν καὶ διὰ τῶν ἰδίων ὀργάνων
ἀπαντᾶν τοῖς πολεμίοις, ἀγωνίζεσθαί τε ἕκαστον
οὐχ ὡς ὑπὲρ σωθησομένης, ἀλλ᾽ ὡς ὑπὲρ ἀπ-
261 ολωλυίας ἤδη τῆς πατρίδος ἀμυνόμενον, λαμβάνειν
τε πρὸ ὀφθαλμῶν σφαγησομένους γέροντας καὶ
τέκνα καὶ γυναῖκας ἀναιρεθησομένας[4] ὑπὸ τῶν
ἐχθρῶν ὅσον οὐδέπω, καὶ τὸν ἐπὶ ταῖς μελλούσαις
συμφοραῖς θυμὸν προαλίσαντας ἐναφεῖναι τοῖς δρά-
σουσιν αὐτάς.
262 (26) Ἔταξεν μὲν οὖν οὕτως ἑκάτερον· τὸ δ᾽
ἀργὸν ἀπὸ τῆς πόλεως πλῆθος, γύναια καὶ παῖδες,

---

[1] συνιεὶς MVRC. [2] κατερρωγότα PAML.
[3] πρὸς ὀλίγον] κατ᾽ ὀλίγον "little by little" L Lat. (perhaps rightly).
[4] εὐρεθησομένους (-μένας) P(AL): capi Lat.

still intact, in order that some of the besieged, in the attempt to repel them, might be induced to abandon the defence of the breach, and the remainder, overwhelmed by a hail of missiles, be forced to give way.

(25) Josephus, penetrating this design, entrusted the protection of the intact portions of the wall to the fatigued and older men, expecting that there they would come to no harm ; but he placed at the breach the most vigorous of his men, and at the head of each group six men,[a] drawn by lot, among whom he himself drew for his place [b] to bear the brunt of the battle. He instructed his men, when the legions raised their war-cry, to stop their ears, so as not to be frightened ; when the volley of missiles came, to crouch down and cover their bodies with their bucklers, and to fall back for a while, until the archers had emptied their quivers ; but, the instant the gangways were laid, to spring on to them themselves and confront the enemy by means of his own instruments.[c] " Let each man fight," he continued, " not as the saviour of his native place, but as its avenger, as though it were lost already. Let him picture to himself the butchery of the old men, the fate of the children and women at the hands of the foe, momentarily impending. Let the anticipation of these threatened calamities arouse his concentrated fury, and let him vent it upon the would-be perpetrators."

(26) Such was the disposition of his two divisions. But when the crowd of non-combatant townsfolk,

Josephus's disposition of his troops.

[a] Meaning a little doubtful. These leaders are the πρόμαχοι mentioned in § 270.

[b] Cf. § 263 (ᾗ ἔλαχεν).

[c] "The engineer hoist with his own petard " (*Hamlet*, III. iv.).

ὡς ἐθεάσαντο τριπλῇ μὲν φάλαγγι τὴν πόλιν
ἐζωσμένην, οὐδὲν γὰρ εἰς τὴν μάχην μετακεκίνητο
τῶν πάλαι φυλακῶν, πρὸς δὲ τοῖς βεβλημένοις
τείχεσιν τοὺς πολεμίους ξιφήρεις καὶ τὴν καθύπερθεν ὀρεινὴν λαμπομένην ὅπλοις, τά τε βέλη
τοῖς τοξόταις ὑπερανέχοντα¹ τῶν Ἀράβων, ὕστα-
τόν τινα κωκυτὸν ἁλώσεως συνήχησαν, ὡς οὐκ
ἀπειλουμένων ἔτι τῶν κακῶν ἀλλ' ἤδη παρόντων.
263 ὁ δὲ Ἰώσηπος τὰς μὲν γυναῖκας, ὡς μὴ θηλύνοιεν
οἴκτῳ τὰς ὁρμὰς τῶν σφετέρων, κατακλείει ταῖς
οἰκίαις μετ' ἀπειλῆς ἡσυχάζειν κελεύσας· αὐτὸς
264 δὲ ἐπὶ τῶν ἐρειφθέντων ᾗ ἔλαχεν παρῄει. τοῖς
μὲν οὖν καθ' ἕτερα προσφέρουσι τὰς κλίμακας οὐ
προσεῖχεν, ἀπεκαραδόκει δὲ τὴν ὁρμὴν τῶν βελῶν.
265 (27) Ὁμοῦ δ' οἵ τε σαλπικταὶ τῶν ταγμάτων
ἁπάντων συνήχησαν καὶ δεινὸν ἐπηλάλαξεν ἡ
στρατιά, καὶ πάντοθεν ἀφιεμένων ἀπὸ συνθήματος
266 τῶν βελῶν τὸ φῶς ὑπετέμνετο. μεμνημένοι γε
μὴν τῶν τοῦ Ἰωσήπου προσταγμάτων οἱ σὺν
αὐτῷ τάς τε ἀκοὰς πρὸς τὴν βοὴν καὶ τὰ σώματα
267 πρὸς τὰς ἀφέσεις ἐφράξαντο, καὶ βαλλόντων τὰς
μηχανὰς ἐπεξέδραμον δι' αὐτῶν πρὶν ἐπιβῆναι τοὺς
268 βάλλοντας, συμπλεκόμενοί τε² τοῖς ἀνιοῦσιν παν-
τοῖα καὶ χειρῶν ἔργα καὶ ψυχῆς ἐναπεδείκνυντο,
πειρώμενοι παρὰ τὰς ἐσχάτας συμφορὰς μὴ χεί-
ρους φαίνεσθαι τῶν ἐν ἀκινδύνῳ τῷ κατὰ σφᾶς
269 ἀνδριζομένων· ὥστε οὐ πρότερον ἀπερρήγνυντο
270 τῶν Ῥωμαίων πρὶν ἢ πεσεῖν ἢ διαφθεῖραι. ὡς
δ' οἱ μὲν ἔκαμον διηνεκῶς ἀμυνόμενοι καὶ τοὺς

---

¹ conj.: ἐπανέχοντα mss.　　　　² γε μὴν LVRC.

ª § 148.

women and children, beheld the city encircled by a
triple cordon of troops—for the Romans had not
shifted for the battle any of the guards which they
had posted at the outset,[a]—when they saw, moreover,
at the foot of the ruined walls the enemy sword in
hand, and above them the mountain-side gleaming
with arms and higher still the arrows of the Arab
archers pointed at the town, they shrieked aloud,
a last shriek, as it were, at their capture, as though
the catastrophe were no longer imminent but already
upon them. Josephus, fearing that the wailing of
the women might unman the combatants, had them
shut up in their houses, ordering them with threats
to hold their peace. He then took up his allotted
position at the breach, and, regardless of the ladders
which were being brought up elsewhere, breathlessly
awaited the hail of arrows.

(27) And now the trumpeters of all the legions
simultaneously sounded, the troops raised a terrific
shout, and at a given signal arrows poured from
all quarters, intercepting the light. Mindful of
the injunctions of Josephus, his comrades screened
their ears from the shout and their bodies from the
volleys ; and, as the planks were laid, they dashed
out across them, before those who had laid them
could set foot on them. In the ensuing hand-to-
hand fight with their mounting enemy, they displayed all manner of feats of strength and gallantry,
endeavouring in the depth of calamity to prove
themselves not inferior to men who, without the
same interests at stake, were so courageous. None
relaxed his struggle with a Roman until he had killed
him or perished. But whereas the Jews, now becoming exhausted by the incessant combat, had none

Hand-to-
hand fight
on the
gangways.

81

προμάχους ἀμείβειν οὐκ ἔχοντες, τὸ κεκμηκὸς
δὲ τῶν Ῥωμαίων ἀκραιφνεῖς διεδέχοντο καὶ
ταχέως ἀντὶ τῶν ἀποβιασθέντων ἐπέβαινον ἕτεροι,
παρακελευσάμενοί τε ἀλλήλοις καὶ πλευρὰν μὲν
ἑνώσαντες, τοῖς δὲ θυρεοῖς καθύπερθεν φραξάμενοι στῖφος ἄρρηκτον ἐγένοντο, καὶ καθάπερ ἑνὶ
σώματι πάσῃ τῇ φάλαγγι τοὺς Ἰουδαίους ἀνωθοῦντες ἤδη τοῦ τείχους ἐπέβαινον.

271 (28) Ὁ δὲ Ἰώσηπος ἐν ταῖς ἀμηχανίαις σύμβουλον λαβὼν τὴν ἀνάγκην, ἥ δ᾽ ἐστὶν δεινὴ πρὸς
ἐπίνοιαν, ὅταν αὐτὴν ἀπόγνωσις ἐρεθίζῃ, ζέον
272 ἔλαιον ἐκέλευσεν καταχεῖν τῶν συνησπικότων. οἱ
δ᾽, ὡς παρεσκευασμένον ἔχοντες, μετὰ τάχους
πολλοὶ καὶ πολὺ πάντοθεν τῶν Ῥωμαίων κατέχεον
συνεπαφιέντες καὶ τὰ ἀγγεῖα βρασσόμενα τῇ θέρμῃ·
273 τοῦτο καιομένων τῶν Ῥωμαίων διεσκέδασεν τὴν
τάξιν, καὶ μετὰ δεινῶν ἀλγηδόνων ἀπεκυλινδοῦντο
274 τοῦ τείχους· ῥᾷστα μὲν γὰρ τὸ ἔλαιον ἀπὸ κορυφῆς
μέχρι ποδῶν ὑπὸ τὰς πανοπλίας διέρρει τοῦ σώματος ὅλου, καὶ τὴν σάρκα φλογὸς οὐδὲν ἔλασσον
ἐπεβόσκετο, θερμαινόμενόν τε φύσει ταχέως καὶ
275 ψυχόμενον βραδέως διὰ τὴν πιότητα. τοῖς δὲ
θώραξιν καὶ τοῖς κράνεσιν ἐνδεδεμένων ἀπαλλαγὴ
τῆς καύσεως οὐκ ἦν, πηδῶντες δὲ καὶ συνει-
λούμενοι ταῖς ἀλγηδόσιν ἀπὸ τῶν γεφυρωμάτων
ἔπιπτον· οἱ δὲ τραπέντες εἰς τοὺς σφετέρους πρόσω
βιαζομένους εὐχείρωτοι τοῖς κατόπιν τιτρώσκουσιν
ἦσαν.

276 (29) Ἐπέλειπεν[1] δ᾽ οὔτε Ῥωμαίους ἐν ταῖς
κακοπραγίαις ἰσχὺς οὔτε τοὺς Ἰουδαίους σύνεσις,

¹ ἐπέλιπεν PA.

_____

ᵃ See § 258.

to replace their foremost champions,[a] in the Roman ranks the exhausted men were relieved by fresh troops, and when one party was driven back another instantly took its place ; the assailants cheered each other on, and, side linked to side, with their bucklers protecting them above, they formed an invulnerable column,[b] which with its united mass, like one solid body, pushed the Jews before them and was even now mounting the ramparts.

(28) In this critical situation, Josephus, taking counsel from necessity,—ready as she is in invention when stimulated by despair,—ordered boiling oil to be poured upon this roof of close-locked shields. His men had it ready, and at once from all quarters deluged the Romans with large quantities, flinging after it the vessels, still scalding hot. This broke their formation ; the Romans, burning and in excruciating agony, rolled headlong from the ramparts. For the oil instantaneously penetrated beneath their armour from head to foot, spreading over the whole surface of their bodies and devouring the flesh with the fierceness of a flame, this liquid being, from its nature, quick in absorbing heat and, from its fatty properties, slow in cooling. Encumbered with their cuirasses and their helmets, the victims had no escape from the scalding fluid : leaping and writhing in anguish, they dropped from the scaling-bridges. Those who turned to fly were blocked by their comrades pressing forward to the assault and became an easy mark for Jewish assailants in their rear.

(29) But, in the midst of these trials, the Romans showed no lack of fortitude, nor yet the Jews of

Scalding oil poured on the Romans.

---

[b] The *testudo* formation (*cf. B.* ii. 537).

ἀλλ' οἱ μὲν καίπερ οἰκτρὰ πάσχοντας ὁρῶντες
τοὺς καταχυθέντας ὅμως εἰς τοὺς καταχέοντας
ἐφέροντο, τὸν πρὸ αὑτοῦ κακίζων ἕκαστος ὡς
277 ἐμπόδιον ὄντα τῆς ῥύμης[1]· οἱ δὲ Ἰουδαῖοι δόλῳ
δευτέρῳ τὰς προσβάσεις[2] αὐτῶν ἐπέσφαλλον τῆλιν
ἐφθὴν ὑποχέοντες[3] ταῖς σανίσιν, ἧς[4] ἐπολισθάνοντες
278 ὑπεσύροντο. καὶ οὔτε τῶν τρεπομένων οὔτε τῶν
προσβαινόντων[5] τις ὀρθὸς ἔμενεν, ἀλλ' οἱ μὲν ἐπ'
αὐτῶν ὑπτιαζόμενοι τῶν ἐπιβατηρίων μηχανῶν
συνεπατοῦντο, πολλοὶ δ' ἐπὶ τὸ χῶμα κατέπιπτον.
279 ἐπαίοντο δ' ὑπὸ τῶν Ἰουδαίων οἱ πεσόντες·
ἐσφαλμένων γὰρ τῶν Ῥωμαίων οὗτοι, τῆς κατὰ
χεῖρα συμπλοκῆς ἐλευθερωθέντες, εἰς τὰς βολὰς
280 εὐστόχουν.[6] πολλὰ δὲ κακουμένους ἐν τῇ προσβολῇ
τοὺς στρατιώτας ὁ στρατηγὸς περὶ δείλην ἀνεκάλει.
281 ἔπεσον δὲ τούτων μὲν οὐκ ὀλίγοι καὶ πλείους
ἐτρώθησαν, τῶν δ' ἀπὸ τῆς Ἰωταπάτης ἀπέθανον
μὲν ἓξ ἄνδρες, τραυματίαι δ' ὑπὲρ τριακοσίους
282 ἀνεκομίσθησαν. εἰκάδι μὲν Δαισίου μηνὸς ἡ
παράταξις ἦν.

283 (30) Οὐεσπασιανὸς δὲ ἐπὶ τοῖς συμβεβηκόσι τὴν
στρατιὰν παραμυθούμενος, ὡς θυμουμένους ἑώρα
284 καὶ οὐ προτροπῆς ἀλλ' ἔργων δεομένους, προσ-
υψῶσαι μὲν τὰ χώματα, πύργους δὲ τρεῖς,
πεντήκοντα ποδῶν τὸ ὕψος ἕκαστον, κατασκευάσαι
κελεύσας πάντοθεν σιδήρῳ κεκαλυμμένους, ὡς
ἑδραῖοί τε εἶεν ὑπὸ βρίθους καὶ δυσάλωτοι πυρί,
285 τῶν χωμάτων ἐπέστησεν, συνεπιβήσας αὐτοῖς

---

[1] Destinon (cf. A. vii. 289 φερόμενος μετὰ ῥύμης) : ῥώμης mss.
[2] προβάσεις PAML.
[3] ἐπιχέοντες Hudson with one ms.
[4] αἷς MVRC.   [5] προβαινόντων PAL.
[6] εὐσχόλουν " had leisure to take good aim " LVRC.

resourcefulness. The former, though they saw their comrades in tortures from the drenching oil, none the less rushed on against those who poured it, each cursing the man in front of him for impeding the charge. The Jews, on their side, invented a second ruse to trip their assailants, by pouring over the gangway-planks boiled fenugreek [a], on which the Romans slipped and stumbled backward. Whether attempting to retreat or to advance, not a man could remain erect : some collapsed on their backs on the gangways and were crushed under foot, many fell off on to the earthworks, where they were pierced by the arrows of the Jews ; for, in consequence of this prostration of the Romans, the defenders, relieved from hand-to-hand fighting, showed good marksmanship. After severe losses sustained in this assault the troops, towards evening, were called off by the general. The Romans had many dead and more wounded. The defenders of Jotapata lost only six dead, but upwards of three hundred wounded were brought back to the town. This combat took place on the twentieth of the month Daesius.

Another Jewish ruse.

The assault repulsed.

June-July [b] A.D. 67.

(30) Vespasian at first sought to console his troops for their recent experiences. But when he found them in sullen mood and calling, not for encouragement, but for action, he ordered them to raise the height of the embankments and to construct three towers, each fifty feet high, entirely covered with sheet-iron, both to ensure their stability by their weight and to render them fire-proof. He then had these erected on the earth-works and mounted upon

Vespasian raises and fortifies his earth-works.

[a] *Foenum Graecum* ; Reinach remarks that this plant would be in flower precisely at this season (June-July).
[b] 8 July (Niese's reckoning).

ἀκοντιστάς τε καὶ τοξότας καὶ τῶν ἀφετηρίων
ὀργάνων τὰ κουφότερα, πρὸς δὲ τοὺς ῥωμα-
286 λεωτάτους σφενδονήτας· οἳ μὴ καθορώμενοι διὰ
τὸ ὕψος καὶ τὰ θωράκια τῶν πύργων εἰς καθ-
287 ορωμένους τοὺς ἐπὶ τοῦ τείχους ἔβαλλον. οἱ δὲ
μήτε κατὰ κόρσης φερομένων τῶν βελῶν ἐκκλίνειν
ῥᾳδίως δυνάμενοι μήτε τοὺς ἀφανεῖς ἀμύνεσθαι,
καὶ τὸ μὲν ὕψος τῶν πύργων δυσέφικτον ὁρῶντες
ἐκ χειρὸς βέλει, πυρὶ δὲ τὸν περὶ αὐτοῖς σίδηρον
ἀνάλωτον, ἔφευγον ἀπὸ τοῦ τείχους καὶ προσ-
288 βάλλειν πειρωμένοις ἐπεξέθεον. καὶ οἱ μὲν ἐπὶ
τῆς Ἰωταπάτης ἀντεῖχον οὕτως, ἀναιρούμενοί τε
καθ᾽ ἡμέραν πολλοὶ καὶ μηδὲν ἀντικακοῦν τοὺς
πολεμίους, ὅτι μὴ μετὰ κινδύνων ἀνείργειν ἔχοντες.
289 (31) Κατὰ δὲ τὰς αὐτὰς ἡμέρας Οὐεσπασιανὸς
ἐπί τινα τῶν τῆς Ἰωταπάτης ἀστυγειτόνων πόλιν,
Ἰαφα καλεῖται, νεωτερίζουσαν καὶ τῶν Ἰωταπατηνῶν παρὰ δόξαν ἀντεχόντων ἐπαιρομένην,
Τραϊανὸν ὄντα τοῦ δεκάτου τάγματος ἡγεμόνα
ἐκπέμπει παραδοὺς αὐτῷ χιλίους μὲν ἱππεῖς,
290 πεζοὺς δὲ δισχιλίους. ὁ δὲ τὴν μὲν πόλιν δυσάλωτον καταλαβών, πρὸς γὰρ τῷ φύσει καρτερὰ
τυγχάνειν οὖσα καὶ διπλῷ περιβόλῳ τετείχιστο, προ-
απηντηκότας δὲ τοὺς ἐξ αὐτῆς ἑτοίμους εἰς μάχην
ἰδὼν συμβάλλει καὶ πρὸς ὀλίγον ἀντισχόντας
291 ἐδίωκεν. συμφυγόντων δὲ εἰς τὸ πρῶτον τεῖχος
οἱ Ῥωμαῖοι κατὰ πόδας προσκείμενοι συνεισ-
292 έπεσον. ὁρμήσαντας δὲ πάλιν εἰς τὸ δεύτερον

---

[a] The father of the future emperor of that name.
[b] Japhia of the O.T. (Joshua xix. 12), modern *Yafa*, some
ten miles south of Jotapata and two miles south-west of

them, besides the lighter artillery, the javelin-men, archers, and the most robust of the slingers. These troops, being screened from view by the height of the towers and their breastworks, opened fire on the besieged who were plainly visible to them on the wall. The Jews, finding no means of avoiding the projectiles directed at their heads or of avenging themselves on an invisible foe, seeing these lofty towers inaccessible to missiles thrown by hand and protected against fire by their iron casing, abandoned the wall and made sallies against any who attempted to renew the escalade. Thus did Jotapata continue to hold out ; day by day many of its defenders fell ; powerless to retaliate on the enemy, they could only hold them at bay at peril of their lives.

(31) In the course of these days Vespasian dispatched Trajan,[a] the commander of the tenth legion, with a thousand horse and two thousand foot, against a town in the vicinity of Jotapata, called Japha,[b] which had revolted, encouraged by the surprising resistance of their neighbours at Jotapata. Trajan found a city presenting formidable difficulties, for in addition to its naturally strong situation, it was protected by a double ring of walls. However, its inhabitants ventured to advance to meet him, prepared, as he saw, for action ; he charged them and, after a brief resistance, routed them and started in pursuit. They burst into the first enclosure, whither the Romans, following hard on their heels, penetrated with them. But when the fugitives rushed on to the

Capture of Japha by Trajan and Titus.

Nazareth, here called a " city," but elsewhere described as " the largest village in Galilee," *Vita* 230 ; at one time the headquarters of Josephus (*ib.* 270).

τεῖχος ἀποκλείουσιν τῆς πόλεως οἱ σφέτεροι, δεί-
293 σαντες μὴ συνεισβάλωσιν οἱ πολέμιοι. θεὸς δ᾽
ἦν ἄρα ὁ Ῥωμαίοις τὰ Γαλιλαίων πάθη χαριζόμενος, ὃς καὶ τότε τὸν τῆς πόλεως λαὸν αὔτανδρον,
χερσὶν οἰκείαις ἐκκλεισθέντα, πρὸς ἀπώλειαν ἔκ-
294 δοτον φονῶσιν ἐχθροῖς παρέστησεν. ἐμπίπτοντες
γὰρ ἀθρόοι ταῖς πύλαις καὶ πολλὰ τοὺς ἐπ᾽ αὐτῶν ὀνομαστὶ καλοῦντες ἐν μέσαις ἀπεσφάττον-
295 το ταῖς ἱκεσίαις. καὶ τὸ μὲν πρῶτον αὐτοῖς
τεῖχος οἱ πολέμιοι, τὸ δεύτερον δ᾽ ἔκλεισαν οἱ
296 σφέτεροι· μέσοι δὲ τοῖν δυοῖν κατειλούμενοι περιβόλων βύζην,¹ πολλοὶ μὲν τοῖς ἀλλήλων, πολλοὶ
δὲ τοῖς ἰδίοις περιεπείροντο ξίφεσιν, ἄπειροι δὲ
ὑπὸ Ῥωμαίων ἔπιπτον οὐδὲ ὅσον εἰς ἄμυναν
ἀναθαρροῦντες· πρὸς γὰρ τῷ καταπεπλῆχθαι τοὺς
πολεμίους τὰς ψυχὰς αὐτῶν ἔκλασεν ἡ τῶν οἰκείων
297 προδοσία. πέρας ἔθνησκον οὐ Ῥωμαίοις ἀλλὰ τοῖς
ἰδίοις² καταρώμενοι, μέχρι πάντες ἀπώλοντο μύριοι
298 καὶ δισχίλιοι τὸν ἀριθμὸν ὄντες. κενὴν δὲ μαχίμων
λογιζόμενος εἶναι τὴν πόλιν ὁ Τραϊανός, εἰ δὲ
καί τινες ἔνδον εἶεν, οἰόμενος μηδὲν αὐτοὺς τολμή-
σειν ὑπὸ δέους, ἀνετίθει τῷ στρατηγῷ τὴν ἅλωσιν,
καὶ στείλας ἀγγέλους πρὸς Οὐεσπασιανὸν ᾐτεῖτο
πέμψαι τὸν υἱὸν αὐτοῦ³ Τίτον ἐπιθήσοντα τῇ νίκῃ
299 τέλος. ὁ δὲ συμβαλὼν ὑπολείπεσθαί τινα πόνον
μετὰ στρατιᾶς τὸν υἱὸν ἐπιπέμπει πεντακοσίων
300 μὲν ἱππέων, χιλίων δὲ πεζῶν. ὁ δὲ πρὸς τὴν
πόλιν ἐλθὼν διὰ τάχους καὶ διατάξας τὴν στρατιὰν

---

¹ om. PL: the word recurs in B. vi. 326.
² οἰκείοις P.
³ C: ἑαυτοῦ VR, suum Lat.: αὐτῷ the rest.

ᵃ Cf. the message of Joab to David at the siege of Rabbah

second wall, their own fellow-citizens shut them out,
for fear of the enemy forcing their way in at the
same time. God, and no other, it was who made a
present to the Romans of the wretched Galilaeans ;
it was He who now caused the population of the town
to be excluded by the hands of their own people and
delivered them to their murderous foes, to be exterminated to a man. Vainly did the swarming
crowds batter the gates and implore the sentinels by
their names to let them in : while their supplications
were on their lips they were butchered. The first
wall was closed to them by the enemy, the second by
their friends. Cooped up and huddled together
between the two ramparts, they fell, many impaled
on their comrades' swords, many on their own, while
prodigious numbers were slain by the Romans, without even having the heart to defend themselves ; for
to their terror of the enemy was added the perfidy
of their friends, and that broke their spirit. Cursing,
in their dying moments, not the Romans but their
own people, in the end they all perished, to the
number of twelve thousand. Trajan, judging that
the city was bereft of combatants or that any who
still remained within would be paralysed by fear,
decided to reserve for his chief the credit of capturing
the place. He accordingly dispatched a message to
Vespasian, requesting him to send his son Titus to
complete the victory.[a] The general, conjecturing
that some work still remained to be done, sent with
his son reinforcements consisting of five hundred
cavalry and a thousand infantry. Titus rapidly
marched to the city, drew up his troops for battle,

of Ammon, 2 Sam. xii. 26 ff. ; this courtesy was common to
Jews and Romans.

ἐπὶ μὲν τοῦ λαιοῦ κέρως τὸν Τραϊανὸν ἵστησιν,
αὐτὸς δὲ τὸ δεξιὸν ἔχων ἐξηγεῖτο πρὸς τὴν πολι-
301 ορκίαν. τῶν δὲ στρατιωτῶν κλίμακας πάντοθεν
τῷ τείχει προσφερόντων πρὸς ὀλίγον οἱ Γαλιλαῖοι
καθύπερθεν ἀμυνάμενοι[1] λείπουσιν τὸν περίβολον,
302 ἐπιπηδήσαντες δ' οἱ περὶ τὸν Τίτον τῆς μὲν
πόλεως ἐκράτησαν ταχέως, πρὸς δὲ τοὺς ἔνδον
αὐτοῖς συστραφέντας καρτερὰ μάχη συρρήγνυται·
303 καὶ γὰρ ἐν τοῖς στενωποῖς οἱ δυνατοὶ προσέπιπτον
καὶ ἀπὸ τῶν οἰκιῶν αἱ γυναῖκες ἔβαλλον πᾶν τὸ
304 προστυχὸν αὐταῖς. καὶ μέχρι μὲν ἐξ ὡρῶν ἀντεῖχον
μαχόμενοι, δαπανηθέντων δὲ τῶν μαχίμων τὸ
λοιπὸν πλῆθος ἔν τε τοῖς ὑπαίθροις καὶ κατὰ τὰς
οἰκίας ἀπεσφάττοντο, νέοι τε ὁμοῦ καὶ γέροντες·
οὐδὲν γὰρ ἄρρεν ὑπελείφθη δίχα νηπίων, ἃ μετὰ
305 γυναικῶν ἐξηνδραποδίσαντο. τῶν μὲν οὖν ἀν-
αιρεθέντων ἀνά τε τὴν πόλιν κἀπὶ τῆς προτέρας
παρατάξεως ἀριθμὸς μύριοι πρὸς τοῖς πεντακισχιλίοις ἦν, τὰ δ' αἰχμάλωτα δισχίλια ἑκατὸν
306 καὶ τριάκοντα. τοῦτο συνέβη τὸ πάθος Γαλιλαίοις
πέμπτῃ καὶ εἰκάδι Δαισίου μηνός.
307 (32) Ἔμειναν δὲ οὐδὲ Σαμαρεῖς ἀπείρατοι συμ-
φορῶν· ἀθροισθέντες γὰρ ἐπὶ τὸ Γαριζεὶν καλούμενον ὄρος, ὅπερ αὐτοῖς ἐστιν ἅγιον, κατὰ χώραν
μὲν ἔμενον, πολέμου δ' εἶχον ἀπειλὴν ἥ τε σύνοδος
308 αὐτῶν καὶ τὰ φρονήματα. καὶ οὐδὲ τοῖς γειτνιῶσι
κακοῖς ἐσωφρονίζοντο, πρὸς δὲ τὰς Ῥωμαίων
εὐπραγίας ἐν ἀλογίστῳ τὴν κατὰ σφᾶς ἀσθένειαν[2]

---

[1] Destinon: ἀμυνόμενοι MSS.
[2] PA: τῇ κατὰ σφᾶς ἀσθενείᾳ the rest; text doubtful.

posting Trajan on the left wing, and himself taking command of the right, and led them to the assault. As the soldiers were bringing up ladders to every portion of the wall, the Galilaeans, after a brief defence from that quarter, abandoned it; the troops of Titus thereupon scaled the ramparts and were instantly masters of the town. But within the walls, where the inhabitants had rallied to meet them, a desperate struggle ensued: the able-bodied fell upon the Romans in the narrow alleys, while from the houses the women pelted them with whatever missiles came to hand. For six hours the contest was maintained; the more efficient combatants were at length exterminated, and the rest of the population was then massacred in the open or in their houses, young and old alike. For no males were spared, except infants; these, along with the women, the Romans sold as slaves. The slain, whether in the city or in the previous action, amounted in all to fifteen thousand; the captives numbered two thousand one hundred and thirty. This disaster befell the Galilaeans on the twenty-fifth of the month Daesius.[a]

(32) The Samaritans, too, did not escape their share of calamity. Assembling on their sacred mountain called Garizim, they did not move from the spot, but this mustering of the clan and their determined attitude contained a menace of war. They had learnt nothing from their neighbours' calamities; the successes of the Romans only made them ridiculously conceited of their own feebleness, and they were

Massacre of the Samaritans on Mt. Gerizim by Cerealius.

[a] 13 July, A.D. 67 (according to Niese's reckoning).

ᾤδουν καὶ μετέωροι πρὸς ταραχὴν ὑπῆρχον.
309 ἐδόκει δὲ Οὐεσπασιανῷ φθάσαι τὸ κίνημα καὶ τὰς
ὁρμὰς αὐτῶν ὑποτέμνεσθαι· καὶ γὰρ εἰ[1] φρουραῖς
ἡ Σαμαρεῖτις ὅλη διείληπτο, τό γε[2] πλῆθος τῶν
310 ἐληλυθότων καὶ ἡ σύνταξις ἦν φοβερά. Κερεάλιον
οὖν ἔπαρχον ὄντα τοῦ πέμπτου τάγματος μεθ'
ἑξακοσίων ἱππέων καὶ πεζῶν τρισχιλίων πέμπει.
311 τούτῳ προσβαίνειν μὲν τὸ ὄρος καὶ συνάπτειν
μάχην οὐκ ἀσφαλὲς ἔδοξεν πολλῶν καθύπερθεν
τῶν πολεμίων ὄντων, κυκλωσάμενος δὲ τῇ δυνάμει
πᾶσαν τὴν ὑπόρειον δι' ὅλης αὐτοὺς ἐφρούρει τῆς
312 ἡμέρας. συνέβη δὲ ὕδατος ἀπορουμένων τῶν
Σαμαρέων ἐκφλεγῆναι τότε καὶ καῦμα δεινόν·
ὥρα δ' ἦν θέρους καὶ τῶν ἐπιτηδείων τὸ πλῆθος
313 ἀπαράσκευον· ὡς τινὰς[3] μὲν αὐθημερὸν ὑπὸ[4]
τοῦ δίψους ἀποθανεῖν, πολλοὺς δὲ τῆς τοιαύτης
ἀπωλείας τὸ δουλεύειν προαιρουμένους Ῥωμαίοις
314 προσφυγεῖν. ἐξ ὧν συνεὶς ὁ Κερεάλιος καὶ τοὺς
ἔτι συμμένοντας ὑπὸ τῶν δεινῶν κατεαγότας
ἐπαναβαίνει τῷ ὄρει, καὶ τὴν δύναμιν ἐν κύκλῳ
περιστήσας τοῖς πολεμίοις τὸ μὲν πρῶτον ἐπὶ
δεξιὰς προυκαλεῖτο καὶ σώζεσθαι παρεκάλει, δια-
315 βεβαιούμενος ἀσφάλειαν τὰ ὅπλα ῥίψασιν. ὡς δ'
οὐκ ἔπειθεν, προσπεσὼν ἀπέκτεινεν πάντας, χιλίους
ἑξακοσίους ἐπὶ μυρίοις ὄντας· ἑβδόμη καὶ εἰκάδι
Δαισίου μηνὸς ἐπράχθη. καὶ τοιαύταις μὲν συμφοραῖς Σαμαρεῖται ἐχρήσαντο.
316   (33) Τῶν δ' ἀνὰ τὰ Ἰωτάπατα καρτερούντων

---

[1] M (Lat. etsi): om. PA: ἀεὶ the rest.
[2] M (Lat. tamen): τε the rest.
[3] τοὺς P.   [4] Bekker: ἀπὸ mss.

eagerly contemplating the prospect of revolt.[a]
Vespasian accordingly decided to anticipate the
movement and to curb their ardour ; for, although
the whole district of Samaria was already occupied
by garrisons, this large assemblage and their con-
federacy gave ground for alarm. He therefore
dispatched to the spot Cerealius,[b] commander of the
fifth legion, with a force of six hundred cavalry and
three thousand infantry. This officer, considering it
hazardous to ascend the mountain and engage in
battle, as the enemy were in such strength on the
summit, confined himself to surrounding the entire
base of Garizim with his troops and kept strict guard
during the whole day. The Samaritans happened
to be short of water just at the period of a terrific
heat-wave ; it was the height of summer and the
multitude had not laid in provisions. The result was
that several died of thirst that very day, while many
others, preferring slavery to such a fate, deserted to
the Romans. Cerealius, concluding therefrom that
the rest, who still held together, were broken down by
their sufferings, now ascended the mountain and,
having disposed his troops in a circle round the
enemy, began by inviting them to treat, exhorting
them to save their lives and assuring them of security
if they laid down their arms. These overtures
proving ineffectual, he attacked and slew them to a
man, eleven thousand six hundred in all ; this was on
the twenty-seventh of the month Daesius.[c] Such was
the catastrophe which overtook the Samaritans.

(33) Meanwhile the defenders of Jotapata were

The fall of
Jotapata.

---

[a] The historian's animus against the Samaritans appears
elsewhere, notably in *A.* ix. 290 f.

[b] Sextus Cerealis Vettulenus.   [c] 15 July, A.D. 67 (Niese).

καὶ παρ' ἐλπίδα τοῖς δεινοῖς ἀντεχόντων τεσ-
σαρακοστῇ μὲν ἡμέρᾳ καὶ ἑβδόμῃ τὰ χώματα
317 τῶν Ῥωμαίων ὑπερήρθη τὸ τεῖχος, αὐτομολεῖ δέ
τις πρὸς τὸν Οὐεσπασιανὸν τῆς αὐτῆς ἡμέρας τήν
τε ὀλιγότητα τῶν ἐπὶ τῆς πόλεως ἐξαγγέλλων καὶ
318 τὴν ἀσθένειαν, καὶ ὡς ἀγρυπνίᾳ διηνεκεῖ καὶ
μάχαις ἐπαλλήλοις δεδαπανημένοι δυνατοὶ μὲν
εἶεν οὐδὲ βιαζομένους ἔτι φέρειν, καὶ δόλῳ δ' ἂν
319 ἁλοῖεν, εἴ τις ἐπιθοῖτο· περὶ γὰρ τὴν ἐσχάτην
φυλακήν, καθ' ἣν ἄνεσίν τε τῶν δεινῶν ἐδόκουν
ἔχειν καὶ καθάπτεται μάλιστα κεκοπωμένων ἑω-
θινὸς ὕπνος, καταδαρθάνειν ἔφασκεν τοὺς φύλακας,
συνεβούλευέν τε κατὰ ταύτην τὴν ὥραν ἐπελθεῖν.
320 τῷ δ' ἦν μὲν δι' ὑπονοίας ὁ αὐτόμολος, τό τε
πρὸς ἀλλήλους πιστὸν εἰδότι τῶν Ἰουδαίων καὶ
321 τὴν πρὸς τὰς κολάσεις ὑπεροψίαν, ἐπειδὴ καὶ
πρότερον ληφθείς τις τῶν ἀπὸ τῆς Ἰωταπάτης
πρὸς πᾶσαν αἰκίαν βασάνων ἀντέσχεν καὶ μηδὲν
διὰ πυρὸς ἐξερευνῶσι τοῖς πολεμίοις περὶ τῶν
ἔνδον εἰπὼν ἀνεσταυρώθη τοῦ θανάτου κατα-
322 μειδιῶν· τά γε μὴν εἰκότα πιστὸν ἐποίει τὸν
προδότην, καὶ τάχα μὲν ἀληθεύειν ἐκεῖνον, μηδὲν
δ' αὐτὸς ἐξ ἐνέδρας πείσεσθαι μέγα προσδοκῶν,
τὸν μὲν φυλάσσειν ἐκέλευσεν, ἐπὶ δὲ τὴν κατάληψιν τῆς πόλεως παρεσκεύαζε τὴν στρατιάν.
323 (34) Κατὰ δὲ τὴν μηνυθεῖσαν ὥραν ᾔεσαν ἡσυχῇ
324 πρὸς τὸ τεῖχος. καὶ πρῶτος ἐπιβαίνει Τίτος σὺν
ἑνὶ τῶν χιλιάρχων Δομετίῳ Σαβίνῳ, τῶν ἀπὸ
τοῦ πέμπτου καὶ δεκάτου τάγματος ὀλίγους ἄγων·

---

[a] The writer possibly has a more famous siege in mind,
that of Troy; cf. " tempus erat quo prima quies mortalibus
aegris incipit," Virg. Aen. ii. 268, and just before "inuadunt

still holding out and beyond all expectation bearing up under their miseries, when on the forty-seventh day of the siege the earthworks of the Romans over-topped the wall. That same day a deserter reported to Vespasian the reduced numbers and strength of the defence, and that, worn out with perpetual watching and continuous fighting, they would be unable longer to resist a vigorous assault and might be taken by stratagem, if the attempt were made. He stated that about the last watch of the night—an hour when they expected some respite from their sufferings and when jaded men easily succumb to morning slumber [a] —the sentinels used to drop asleep ; and that was the hour when he advised the Romans to attack. Vespasian, knowing the Jews' loyalty to each other and their indifference to chastisement, regarded the deserter with suspicion. For on a former occasion a man of Jotapata who had been taken prisoner had held out under every variety of torture, and, without betraying to the enemy a word about the state of the town, even under the ordeal of fire, was finally crucified, meeting death with a smile. However, the probability of his account lent credit to the traitor ; and so, thinking that the man might be speaking the truth, and that, even if his story were a trap, no serious risk would be run by acting upon it, Vespasian ordered him into custody and made ready his army for the capture of the city.

(34) At the hour named they advanced in silence to the walls. The first to mount them was Titus, with one of the tribunes, Domitius Sabinus, followed by a few men of the fifteenth legion. They cut down

urbem somno uinoque sepultam ; caeduntur uigiles " 265 f. with § 325 (ἀποσφάξαντες δὲ τοὺς φύλακας εἰσίασιν εἰς τὴν πόλιν) and § 327 (ὕπνῳ διαλέλυντο).

325 ἀποσφάξαντες δὲ τοὺς φύλακας εἰσίασιν εἰς τὴν
πόλιν. μεθ' οὓς Σέξτος τις Καλουάριος χιλιάρχης
καὶ Πλάκιδος τοὺς ὑπὸ σφίσι τεταγμένους εἰσῆγον.
326 κατειλημμένης δὲ τῆς ἄκρας καὶ τῶν πολεμίων
ἐν μέσῳ στρεφομένων, ἤδη δὲ καὶ ἡμέρας οὔσης,
ὅμως οὔπω τῆς ἁλώσεως τοῖς κρατουμένοις αἴ-
327 σθησις ἦν· καμάτῳ τε γὰρ οἱ πολλοὶ καὶ ὕπνῳ
διαλέλυντο, καὶ τῶν διανισταμένων ὁμίχλη τὰς
ὄψεις ἀπήμβλυνεν πολλὴ κατὰ τύχην τότε τῇ
328 πόλει περιχυθεῖσα, μέχρι πάσης τῆς στρατιᾶς
εἰσπεσούσης πρὸς μόνην τὴν τῶν κακῶν αἴσθησιν
ἐξανέστησαν καὶ τὴν ἅλωσιν ἐπίστευον ἀναιρού-
329 μενοι. Ῥωμαίους δὲ κατὰ μνήμην ὧν ἐκ[1] τῆς
πολιορκίας ἔπαθον οὔτε φειδὼς εἰσῄει τινὸς οὔτ'
ἔλεος, ἀλλ' εἰς τὸ κάταντες[2] ἀπὸ τῆς ἄκρας τὸν
330 λεὼν συνωθοῦντες ἐφόνευον. ἔνθα καὶ τοὺς ἔτι
μάχεσθαι δυναμένους ἡ δυσχωρία τὴν ἄμυναν
ἀφείλετο· θλιβόμενοι γὰρ ἐν τοῖς στενωποῖς καὶ
κατὰ τοῦ πρανοῦς ὑπολισθάνοντες ῥέοντι κατ'
331 ἄκρας ἐκαλύπτοντο τῷ πολέμῳ. τοῦτο πολλοὺς
καὶ τῶν περὶ τὸν Ἰώσηπον ἐπιλέκτων ἐπ' αὐτο-
χειρίαν παρώξυνεν· κατιδόντες γὰρ ὡς οὐδένα
τῶν Ῥωμαίων ἀνελεῖν δύνανται, τό γε πεσεῖν
αὐτοὺς[3] ὑπὸ Ῥωμαίων προέλαβον καὶ συναθροισθέντες ἐπὶ τὰ καταλήγοντα τῆς πόλεως σφᾶς
αὐτοὺς ἀνεῖλον.
332 (35) Ὅσοι γε μὴν ὑπὸ πρώτην τῆς καταλήψεως
αἴσθησιν τῶν φυλάκων διαφυγεῖν ἔφθασαν ἀνα-
βάντες εἴς τινα τῶν προσαρκτίων πύργων μέχρι
μέν τινος ἀπημύναντο, περισχεθέντες δὲ πλήθει

---

[1] ἐπὶ Niese : the inferior mss. have περὶ (τὴν πολιορκίαν).
[2] + ἅπαντες PAML.   [3] Text doubtful.

the sentries and entered the city. Behind them came Sextus Calvarius, a tribune, and Placidus with the troops under their command. The citadel had actually been taken, the enemy was ranging through the heart of the town, and it was now broad daylight, before the vanquished inhabitants were aware of the capture. Most of them were worn out with fatigue and asleep, and if any awoke, a thick mist, which happened at the time to envelop the city, obscured their vision. At length, when the whole army had poured in, they started up, but only to realize their calamity; the blade at their throat brought home to them that Jotapata was taken.

The Romans, remembering what they had borne during the siege, showed no quarter or pity for any, but thrust the people down the steep slope from the citadel in a general massacre. Even those still able to fight here found themselves deprived of the means of defence by the difficulties of the ground : crushed in the narrow alleys and slipping down the declivity, they were engulfed in the wave of carnage that streamed from the citadel. The situation even drove many of Josephus's picked men to suicide ; seeing themselves powerless to kill a single Roman, they could at least forestall death at Roman hands, and, retiring in a body to the outskirts of the town, they there put an end to themselves.

(35) Those soldiers of the guard who, the moment it was known that the town was taken, had succeeded in escaping, took refuge in one of the northern [a] towers, where for some time they held their own ; but, being surrounded by large numbers of the

---

[a] The Romans had entered from the north (§§ 158, 162).

τῶν πολεμίων ὀψὲ παρεῖσαν τὰς δεξιὰς καὶ τοῖς
333 ἐφεστῶσιν τὴν σφαγὴν εὔθυμοι παρέσχον. ἀναί-
μακτον δ᾽ ἂν ἦν αὐχῆσαι Ῥωμαίοις τὸ τέλος τῆς
πολιορκίας, εἰ μὴ κατὰ τὴν ἅλωσιν εἰς ἔπεσέν
τις· ἑκατοντάρχης ἦν Ἀντώνιος, θνήσκει δ᾽ ἐξ
334 ἐνέδρας. τῶν γὰρ εἰς τὰ σπήλαιά τις συμ-
πεφευγότων, πολλοὶ δ᾽ οὗτοι πλῆθος ἦσαν, ἱκετεύει
τὸν Ἀντώνιον ὀρέξαι δεξιὰν αὐτῷ, πίστιν τε
335 σωτηρίας καὶ βοήθειαν πρὸς ἄνοδον· ὁ δ᾽ ἀ-
φυλάκτως ὤρεγε τὴν χεῖρα, καὶ φθάσας αὐτὸν
ἐκεῖνος νύττει κάτωθεν ὑπὸ[1] τὸν βουβῶνα δόρατι
καὶ παραχρῆμα διεργάζεται.
336 (36) Κατ᾽ ἐκείνην μὲν οὖν τὴν ἡμέραν τὸ
φανερὸν πλῆθος ἀνεῖλον οἱ Ῥωμαῖοι, ταῖς δ᾽
ἐπιούσαις ἀνερευνώμενοι τὰς καταδύσεις τοὺς ἐν
τοῖς ὑπονόμοις καὶ τοῖς σπηλαίοις ἐπεξῇεσαν καὶ
διὰ πάσης ἐχώρουν ἡλικίας πλὴν νηπίων καὶ
337 γυναικῶν. καὶ τὰ μὲν αἰχμάλωτα χίλια πρὸς τοῖς
διακοσίοις συνήχθη, νεκροὶ δὲ κατὰ τὴν ἅλωσιν
καὶ τὰς πρότερον μάχας συνηριθμήθησαν τετρα-
338 κισμύριοι. Οὐεσπασιανὸς δὲ τήν τε πόλιν κατα-
σκάψαι κελεύει καὶ τὰ φρούρια πάντα προσεμ-
339 πίπρησιν αὐτῆς. Ἰωτάπατα μὲν οὖν οὕτως ἑάλω
τρισκαιδεκάτῳ τῆς Νέρωνος ἡγεμονίας ἔτει Πανέμου νουμηνίᾳ.
340 (viii. 1) Ῥωμαῖοι δὲ τὸν Ἰώσηπον ἀναζητοῦν-
τες κατά τε ὀργὴν σφετέραν καὶ σφόδρα τοῦ
στρατηγοῦ φιλοτιμουμένου, μεγίστη γὰρ ἦν μοῖρα
τοῦ πολέμου ληφθείς, τούς τε νεκροὺς διηρεύνων

[1] ἐπὶ PAL.

enemy, they at length surrendered and cheerfully extended their throats to their assailants. The Romans might have boasted that this last phase of the siege had cost them no loss of life, had not one of them, the centurion Antonius, fallen when the town was captured. He was killed by treachery. One of the many fugitives who had taken refuge in the caverns besought Antonius to extend his hand to him, as a pledge of protection and to assist him to rise ; the centurion incautiously complied, whereupon the Jew from below instantly stabbed him with his spear beneath the groin, and killed him on the spot.

(36) On that day the Romans massacred all who showed themselves ; on the ensuing days they searched the hiding-places and wreaked their vengeance on those who had sought refuge in subterranean vaults and caverns, sparing none, whatever their age, save infants and women. The prisoners thus collected were twelve hundred ; the total number of the dead, whether killed in the final assault or in the previous combats, was computed at forty thousand. Vespasian ordered the city to be razed and had all its forts burnt to the ground. Thus was Jotapata taken in the thirteenth year of the principate of Nero, on the new moon of Panemus.[a]

(viii. 1) A search for Josephus was then instituted by the Romans, to satisfy both their own resentment and the keen desire of their general, who considered that the issue of the war depended largely on his capture. So the bodies of the slain and the men in

Josephus, in hiding in a cave,

---

[a] 20 July, A.D. 67 (Niese).

JOSEPHUS

341 καὶ τοὺς ἀποκρύφους.¹ ὁ δὲ² τῆς πόλεως ἁλι-
σκομένης, δαιμονίῳ τινὶ συνεργίᾳ χρησάμενος,
μέσον μὲν ἑαυτὸν ἐκκλέπτει τῶν πολεμίων, καθ-
άλλεται δὲ εἴς τινα βαθὺν λάκκον, ᾧ πλατὺ σπήλαιον
342 διέζευκτο κατὰ πλευρὰν τοῖς ἄνωθεν ἀόρατον. ἔνθα
τεσσαράκοντα μὲν τῶν ἐπισήμων ἄνδρας καταλαμβάνει λανθάνοντας, παρασκευὴν δ᾽ ἐπιτηδείων
343 οὐκ ὀλίγαις ἡμέραις διαρκεῖν δυναμένην. μεθ᾽
ἡμέραν μὲν οὖν ὑπεστέλλετο τῶν πολεμίων πάντα
διειληφότων, νυκτὸς δ᾽ ἀνιὼν ἐζήτει δρασμοῦ
διάδυσιν καὶ τὰς φυλακὰς κατεσκέπτετο. φρουρουμένων δὲ πάντοθεν πάντων δι᾽ αὐτόν, ὡς λαθεῖν
344 οὐκ ἦν, αὖθις εἰς τὸ σπήλαιον κατήει. δύο μὲν
οὖν ἡμέραις διαλανθάνει, τῇ δὲ τρίτῃ γυναικὸς
ἁλούσης τῶν ἅμα αὐτοῖς μηνύεται, καὶ Οὐεσπασιανὸς αὐτίκα μετὰ σπουδῆς πέμπει δύο χιλιάρχους, Παυλῖνον καὶ Γαλλικανόν, δεξιάς τε τῷ
Ἰωσήπῳ δοῦναι κελεύσας καὶ προτρεψομένους
ἀνελθεῖν.

345 (2) Ἀφικόμενοι γοῦν παρεκάλουν οὗτοι τὸν
ἄνδρα καὶ πίστεις περὶ σωτηρίας ἐδίδοσαν, οὐ
346 μὴν ἔπειθον· ἐκ γὰρ ὧν εἰκὸς ἦν τοσαῦτα δράσαντα
παθεῖν, οὐκ ἐκ τοῦ φύσει τῶν παρακαλούντων
ἥμερου τὰς ὑποψίας συνέλεγεν, ἐδεδίει τε ὡς
ἐπὶ τιμωρίαν προκαλουμένους, ἕως Οὐεσπασιανὸς
τρίτον ἐπιπέμπει χιλίαρχον Νικάνορα, γνώριμον

¹ + τῆς πόλεως μυχούς MVRC, " the secret recesses of the
city." ² + ἄρτι MVRC.

ᵃ Probably, as Reinach suggests, a relative of M. Valerius
Paulinus, a friend of Vespasian, and in A.D. 69 governor of
Gallia Narbonensis (Tac. *Hist.* iii. 43).

hiding were closely examined. But Josephus, when
the city was on the point of being taken, aided by
some divine providence, had succeeded in stealing
away from the midst of the enemy and plunged into
a deep pit, giving access on one side to a broad
cavern, invisible to those above. There he found
forty persons of distinction in hiding, with a supply
of provisions sufficient to last for a considerable time.
During the day he lay hid, as the enemy were in
occupation of every quarter of the town, but at night
he would come up and look for some loophole for
escape and reconnoitre the sentries ; but, finding
every spot guarded on his account and no means of
eluding detection, he descended again into the cave.
So for two days he continued in hiding. On the is discovered
third, his secret was betrayed by a woman of the by the
party, who was captured ; whereupon Vespasian at invited to
once eagerly sent two tribunes, Paulinus [a] and surrender.
Gallicanus, with orders to offer Josephus security
and to urge him to come up.

(2) On reaching the spot they pressed him to do His parley
so and pledged themselves for his safety, but failed Roman
to persuade him. His suspicions were based not on officers.
the humane character of the envoys, but on the
consciousness of all he had done and the feeling that
he must suffer proportionately. The presentiment
that he was being summoned to punishment per-
sisted, until Vespasian sent a third messenger, the
tribune Nicanor,[b] an old acquaintance and friend of

[b] A friend of Titus, who was afterwards wounded while
endeavouring, in company with Josephus, to parley with the
Jews of Jerusalem, by whom he was known, *B.* v. 261. It
has been suggested that he may have served under Agrippa
and so become acquainted with Josephus (Kohout).

101

347 τῷ Ἰωσήπῳ καὶ συνήθη πάλαι. παρελθὼν δ᾽
οὗτος τό τε φύσει Ῥωμαίων χρηστὸν πρὸς οὓς
ἂν ἅπαξ ἕλωσι διεξήει, καὶ ὡς δι᾽ ἀρετὴν αὐτὸς
θαυμάζοιτο μᾶλλον ἢ μισοῖτο πρὸς τῶν ἡγεμόνων,
348 σπουδάζειν τε τὸν στρατηγὸν οὐκ ἐπὶ τιμωρίαν
ἀναγαγεῖν αὐτόν, ἐνεῖναι γὰρ ταύτην καὶ παρὰ
μὴ προϊόντος λαβεῖν, ἀλλὰ σῶσαι προαιρούμενον
349 ἄνδρα γενναῖον. προσετίθει δ᾽ ὡς οὔτ᾽ ἂν Οὐεσπασιανὸς ἐνεδρεύων φίλον ἔπεμπεν, ἵνα τοῦ
κακίστου πράγματος προστήσηται τὸ κάλλιστον,
ἀπιστίας φιλίαν, οὐδ᾽ ἂν αὐτὸς ἀπατήσων ἄνδρα
φίλον ὑπήκουσεν ἐλθεῖν.

350 (3) Ἐνδοιάζοντος δὲ τοῦ Ἰωσήπου καὶ πρὸς
τὸν Νικάνορα, τὸ μὲν στρατιωτικὸν ὑπ᾽ ὀργῆς
ἐκκαίειν τὸ σπήλαιον ὥρμητο, κατεῖχεν δ᾽ αὐτοὺς
ὁ πολέμαρχος ζωγρῆσαι τὸν ἄνδρα φιλοτιμούμενος.
351 ὡς δ᾽ ὅ τε Νικάνωρ προσέκειτο λιπαρῶν καὶ τὰς
ἀπειλὰς τοῦ πολεμίου πλήθους ὁ Ἰώσηπος ἔμαθεν,
ἀνάμνησις αὐτὸν τῶν διὰ νυκτὸς ὀνείρων εἰσέρχεται,
δι᾽ ὧν ὁ θεὸς τάς τε μελλούσας αὐτῷ συμφορὰς
προεσήμανεν Ἰουδαίων καὶ τὰ περὶ τοὺς Ῥωμαίων
352 βασιλεῖς ἐσόμενα. ἦν δὲ καὶ περὶ κρίσεις ὀνείρων
ἱκανὸς συμβαλεῖν τὰ ἀμφιβόλως ὑπὸ τοῦ θείου
λεγόμενα· τῶν γε μὴν ἱερῶν βίβλων οὐκ ἠγνόει
τὰς προφητείας ὡς ἂν αὐτός τε ὢν ἱερεὺς καὶ
353 ἱερέων ἔγγονος. ὧν ἐπὶ τῆς τότε ὥρας ἔνθους
γενόμενος καὶ τὰ φρικώδη τῶν προσφάτων
ὀνείρων σπάσας φαντάσματα προσφέρει τῷ θεῷ
354 λεληθυῖαν εὐχήν, καὶ " ἐπειδὴ τὸ Ἰουδαίων," ἔφη,

---

[a] Cf. " Romane, memento . . . parcere subiectis," Virg.
Aen. vi. 851 ff.

[b] Did he claim kinship with his namesake, the patriarch

Josephus. He, on his arrival, dwelt on the innate generosity of the Romans to those whom they had once subdued,[a] assuring him that his valour made him an object rather of admiration, than of hatred, to the commanding officers, and that the general was anxious to bring him up from his retreat, not for punishment—that he could inflict though he refused to come forth—but from a desire to save a brave man. He added that Vespasian, had he intended to entrap him, would never have sent him one of his friends, thus using the fairest of virtues, friendship, as a cloak for the foulest of crimes, perfidy ; nor would he himself have consented to come in order to deceive a friend.

(3) While Josephus was still hesitating, even after Nicanor's assurances, the soldiers in their rage attempted to set fire to the cave, but were restrained by their commander, who was anxious to take the Jewish general alive. But as Nicanor was urgently pressing his proposals and Josephus overheard the threats of the hostile crowd, suddenly there came back into his mind those nightly dreams, in which God had foretold to him the impending fate of the Jews and the destinies of the Roman sovereigns. He was an interpreter of dreams and skilled in divining the meaning of ambiguous utterances of the Deity ;[b] a priest himself and of priestly descent, he was not ignorant of the prophecies in the sacred books. At that hour he was inspired to read their meaning, and, recalling the dreadful images of his recent dreams, he offered up a silent prayer to God. " Since it pleases thee," so it ran, " who didst create

Joseph ? For his interest in dreams *cf. B.* ii. 112-116 ; he tells us of another dream at a crisis in his life, *Vita* 208 ff.

" φῦλον κλάσαι[1] δοκεῖ σοι τῷ κτίσαντι, μετέβη
δὲ πρὸς Ῥωμαίους ἡ τύχη πᾶσα, καὶ τὴν ἐμὴν
ψυχὴν ἐπελέξω τὰ μέλλοντα εἰπεῖν, δίδωμι μὲν
Ῥωμαίοις τὰς χεῖρας ἑκὼν καὶ ζῶ, μαρτύρομαι
δὲ ὡς οὐ προδότης, ἀλλὰ σὸς ἄπειμι διάκονος."
355 (4) Ταῦτ' εἰπὼν ἐνεδίδου τῷ Νικάνορι. καὶ
τῶν Ἰουδαίων οἱ συγκαταφυγόντες ὡς τὸν Ἰώσηπον συνίεσαν εἴκοντα τοῖς παρακαλοῦσιν, ἀθρόοι
356 περιστάντες, " ἦ μεγάλα γ' ἂν στενάξειαν,"
ἐβόων, " οἱ πάτριοι νόμοι, καὶ κατηφήσαι[2] θεὸς
Ἰουδαίοις ὁ κτίσας ψυχὰς θανάτου καταφρονούσας.
357 φιλοζωεῖς,[3] Ἰώσηπε, καὶ φῶς ὑπομένεις ὁρᾶν
δοῦλος; ὡς ταχέως ἐπελάθου σαυτοῦ. πόσους
358 ὑπὲρ ἐλευθερίας ἀποθνήσκειν ἔπεισας. ψευδῆ μὲν
ἄρα δόξαν ἀνδρείας, ψευδῆ δὲ καὶ συνέσεως εἶχες,
εἴ γε σωτηρίαν μὲν ἔχειν ἐλπίζεις παρ' οἷς οὕτως
ἐπολέμησας, σώζεσθαι δ' ὑπ' ἐκείνων, κἂν ᾖ
359 βέβαιον, θέλεις. ἀλλ' εἰ καὶ σοὶ λήθην σεαυτοῦ
κατέχεεν ἡ Ῥωμαίων τύχη, προνοητέον ἡμῖν τοῦ
πατρίου κλέους. χρήσομέν σοι δεξιὰν καὶ ξίφος·
σὺ δ' ἂν μὲν ἑκὼν θνήσκῃς, Ἰουδαίων στρατηγός,
360 ἂν δ' ἄκων, προδότης τεθνήξῃ." ταῦθ' ἅμα
λέγοντες ἐπανετείναντο τὰ ξίφη καὶ διηπείλουν
ἀναιρήσειν αὐτόν, εἰ τοῖς Ῥωμαίοις ἐνδιδοίη.[4]
361 (5) Δείσας δὲ τὴν ἔφοδον ὁ Ἰώσηπος καὶ προδοσίαν ἡγούμενος εἶναι τῶν τοῦ θεοῦ προσταγμάτων, εἰ προαποθάνοι τῆς διαγγελίας, ἤρχετο
362 πρὸς αὐτοὺς φιλοσοφεῖν ἐπὶ τῆς ἀνάγκης· " τί

[1] A Leyden ms. quoted by Naber: κολάσαι PAML:
ὀκλάσαι the rest (followed by Niese and Naber), "that it
should sink into the dust."
[2] καὶ κατηφήσαι MVRC: οὓς κατέφησεν the rest.

the Jewish nation, to break thy work, since fortune
has wholly passed to the Romans, and since thou
hast made choice of my spirit to announce the things
that are to come, I willingly surrender to the Romans His
and consent to live ; but I take thee to witness that surrender
I go, not as a traitor, but as thy minister." intention to

(4) With these words he was about to surrender is opposed
to Nicanor. But when the Jews who shared his companions
retreat understood that Josephus was yielding to who
entreaty, they came round him in a body, crying out, to kill him.
" Ah ! well might the laws of our fathers groan aloud
and God Himself hide His face for grief—God who
implanted in Jewish breasts souls that scorn death !
Is life so dear to you, Josephus, that you can endure
to see the light in slavery ? How soon have you
forgotten yourself ! How many have you persuaded
to die for liberty ! False, then, was that reputation
for bravery, false that fame for sagacity, if you can
hope for pardon from those whom you have fought
so bitterly, or, supposing that they grant it, can deign
to accept your life at their hands. Nay, if the fortune
of the Romans has cast over you some strange forget-
fulness of yourself, the care of our country's honour
devolves on *us*. We will lend you a right hand and
a sword. If you meet death willingly, you will
have died as general of the Jews ; if unwillingly, as
a traitor." With these words they pointed their
swords at him and threatened to kill him if he
surrendered to the Romans.

(5) Josephus, fearing an assault, and holding that Josephus
it would be a betrayal of God's commands, should he them on
die before delivering his message, proceeded, in this the crime
emergency, to reason philosophically with them. of suicide.

---

[3] + ὦ P.   [4] ἐνδιδοίη Dindorf : ἐνδιδώη MSS.

γὰρ τοσοῦτον," ἔφη, "σφῶν αὐτῶν, ἑταῖροι,
φονῶμεν; ἢ τί τὰ φίλτατα διαστασιάζομεν, σῶμα
363 καὶ ψυχήν; ἠλλάχθαι¹ τις ἐμέ φησιν. ἀλλ'
οἴδασιν Ῥωμαῖοι τοῦτό γε. [καὶ] καλὸν ἐν
πολέμῳ θνήσκειν, ἀλλὰ πολέμου νόμῳ, τουτέστιν
364 ὑπὸ τῶν κρατούντων. εἰ μὲν οὖν τὸν Ῥωμαίων
ἀποστρέφομαι σίδηρον, ἄξιος ἀληθῶς εἰμι τοὐμοῦ
ξίφους καὶ χειρὸς τῆς ἐμῆς· εἰ δ' ἐκείνους εἰσέρχεται φειδὼ πολεμίου, πόσῳ δικαιότερον ἂν ἡμᾶς
ἡμῶν αὐτῶν εἰσέλθοι; καὶ γὰρ ἠλίθιον ταῦτα
δρᾶν σφᾶς αὐτούς, περὶ ὧν πρὸς ἐκείνους δι-
365 ιστάμεθα. καλὸν γὰρ ὑπὲρ τῆς ἐλευθερίας ἀπο-
θνήσκειν· φημὶ κἀγώ, μαχομένους μέντοι, καὶ ὑπὸ
τῶν ἀφαιρουμένων αὐτήν. νῦν δ' οὔτ' εἰς μάχην
ἀντιάζουσιν ἡμῖν οὔτ' ἀναιροῦσιν ἡμᾶς· δειλὸς
δὲ ὁμοίως ὅ τε μὴ βουλόμενος θνήσκειν ὅταν δέῃ
366 καὶ ὁ βουλόμενος, ὅταν μὴ δέῃ. τί δὲ καὶ δεδοικό-
τες πρὸς Ῥωμαίους οὐκ ἄνιμεν; ἆρ' οὐχὶ θάνατον;
367 εἶθ' ὃν δεδοίκαμεν ἐκ τῶν ἐχθρῶν ὑποπτευόμενον,
ἑαυτοῖς βέβαιον ἐπιστήσομεν; ἀλλὰ δουλείαν,
368 ἐρεῖ τις. πάνυ γοῦν νῦν ἐσμεν ἐλεύθεροι. γενναῖον γὰρ ἀνελεῖν ἑαυτόν, φήσει τις. οὔ μὲν οὖν,
ἀλλ' ἀγενέστατον, ὡς ἔγωγε καὶ κυβερνήτην ἡγοῦ-
μαι δειλότατον, ὅστις χειμῶνα δεδοικὼς πρὸ τῆς
369 θυέλλης ἐβάπτισεν ἑκὼν τὸ σκάφος. ἀλλὰ μὴν ἡ
αὐτοχειρία καὶ τῆς κοινῆς ἁπάντων ζῴων φύσεως
ἀλλότριον καὶ πρὸς τὸν κτίσαντα θεὸν ἡμᾶς ἐστιν
370 ἀσέβεια. τῶν μέν γε ζῴων οὐδέν ἐστιν ὃ θνήσκει
μετὰ προνοίας ἢ δι' αὐτοῦ· φύσεως γὰρ νόμος

¹ διηλλάχθαι PAML

106

"Why, comrades," said he, "this thirst for our
own blood? Why set asunder such fond companions
as soul and body? One says that I am changed:
well, the Romans know the truth about that. Another
says, 'It is honourable to die in war': yes, but
according to the law of war, that is to say by the
hand of the conqueror. Were I now flinching from
the sword of the Romans, I should assuredly deserve
to perish by my own sword and my own hand; but
if they are moved to spare an enemy, how much
stronger reason have we to spare ourselves? It
would surely be folly to inflict on ourselves treatment
which we seek to avoid by our quarrel with them.
'It is honourable to die for liberty,' says another:
I concur, but on condition that one dies fighting, by
the hands of those who would rob us of it. But now
they are neither coming to fight us nor to take our
lives. It is equally cowardly not to wish to die when
one ought to do so, and to wish to die when one ought
not. What is it we fear that prevents us from sur-
rendering to the Romans? Is it not death? And
shall we then inflict upon ourselves certain death, to
avoid an uncertain death, which we fear, at the hands
of our foes? 'No, it is slavery we fear,' I shall be
told. Much liberty we enjoy at present! 'It is noble
to destroy oneself,' another will say. Not so, I retort,
but most ignoble; in my opinion there could be no
more arrant coward than the pilot who, for fear of a
tempest, deliberately sinks his ship before the storm.

"No; suicide is alike repugnant to that nature
which all creatures share, and an act of impiety
towards God who created us. Among the animals
there is not one that deliberately seeks death or kills
itself; so firmly rooted in all is nature's law—the

107

ἰσχυρὸς ἐν ἅπασιν τὸ ζῆν ἐθέλειν· διὰ τοῦτο καὶ
τοὺς φανερῶς ἀφαιρουμένους ἡμᾶς τούτου πολεμίους ἡγούμεθα καὶ τοὺς ἐξ ἐνέδρας τιμωρούμεθα.
371 τὸν δὲ θεὸν οὐκ οἴεσθε ἀγανακτεῖν, ὅταν ἄνθρωπος
αὐτοῦ τὸ δῶρον ὑβρίζῃ; καὶ γὰρ εἰλήφαμεν παρ᾽
ἐκείνου τὸ εἶναι καὶ τὸ μηκέτι εἶναι πάλιν ἐκείνῳ
372 διδῶμεν.¹ τὰ μέν γε σώματα θνητὰ πᾶσιν καὶ ἐκ
φθαρτῆς ὕλης δεδημιούργηται, ψυχὴ δὲ ἀθάνατος
ἀεὶ καὶ θεοῦ μοῖρα τοῖς σώμασιν ἐνοικίζεται· εἶτ᾽
ἐὰν μὲν ἀφανίσῃ τις ἀνθρώπου παρακαταθήκην ἢ
διαθῆται κακῶς, πονηρὸς εἶναι δοκεῖ καὶ ἄπιστος,
εἰ δέ τις τοῦ σφετέρου σώματος ἐκβάλλει τὴν
παρακαταθήκην τοῦ θεοῦ, λεληθέναι δοκεῖ τὸν
373 ἀδικούμενον; καὶ κολάζειν μὲν τοὺς ἀποδράντας
οἰκέτας δίκαιον νενόμισται, κἂν πονηροὺς κατα-
λείπωσι δεσπότας, αὐτοὶ δὲ κάλλιστον δεσπότην
ἀποδιδράσκοντες τὸν θεὸν οὐ δοκοῦμεν ἀσεβεῖν;
374 ἆρ᾽ οὐκ ἴστε, ὅτι τῶν μὲν ἐξιόντων τοῦ βίου κατὰ
τὸν τῆς φύσεως νόμον καὶ τὸ ληφθὲν παρὰ τοῦ
θεοῦ χρέος ἐκτινύντων, ὅταν ὁ δοὺς κομίσασθαι
θέλῃ, κλέος μὲν αἰώνιον, οἶκοι δὲ καὶ γενεαὶ βέ-
βαιοι, καθαραὶ δὲ καὶ ἐπήκοοι μένουσιν αἱ ψυχαί,
χῶρον οὐράνιον² λαχοῦσαι τὸν ἁγιώτατον, ἔνθεν
ἐκ περιτροπῆς αἰώνων ἁγνοῖς πάλιν ἀντενοικί-
375 ζονται σώμασιν· ὅσοις δὲ καθ᾽ ἑαυτῶν ἐμάνησαν
αἱ χεῖρες, τούτων ᾅδης μὲν δέχεται τὰς ψυχὰς
σκοτεινότερος, ὁ δὲ τούτων πατὴρ θεὸς εἰς ἐγ-

---

¹ Niese: διδόαμεν, δίδομεν or δίδωμεν (sic) mss.
² P: οὐρανοῦ the rest.

108

will to live. That is why we account as enemies
those who would openly take our lives and punish as
assassins those who clandestinely attempt to do so.
And God—think you not that He is indignant when
man treats His gift with scorn? For it is from Him
that we have received our being, and it is to Him
that we should leave the decision to take it away.
All of us, it is true, have mortal bodies, composed of
perishable matter, but the soul lives for ever, im-
mortal : it is a portion of the Deity housed in our
bodies. If, then, one who makes away with or mis-
applies a deposit entrusted to him by a fellow-man
is reckoned a perjured villain, how can he who casts
out from his own body the deposit which God has
placed there, hope to elude Him whom he has thus
wronged? It is considered right to punish a fugitive
slave, even though the master he leaves be a
scoundrel ; and shall we fly from the best of masters,
from God Himself, and not be deemed impious?
Know you not that they who depart this life in
accordance with the law of nature and repay the loan
which they received from God, when He who lent is
pleased to reclaim it, win eternal renown ; that their
houses and families are secure ; that their souls,
remaining spotless and obedient, are allotted the
most holy place in heaven, whence, in the revolution
of the ages, they return to find in chaste bodies a
new habitation? [a] But as for those who have laid
mad hands upon themselves, the darker regions of
the nether world receive their souls, and God, their

---

[a] With this passage cf. *Ap.* ii. 218 " . . to those who observe
the laws and, if they must needs die for them, willingly meet
death, God has granted a renewed existence and in the
revolution (of the ages) the gift of a better life."

γόνους τιμωρεῖται †τοὺς τῶν πατέρων ὑβριστάς†.[1]
376 διὰ τοῦτο μεμίσηται παρὰ θεῷ τοῦτο καὶ παρὰ
377 τῷ σοφωτάτῳ κολάζεται νομοθέτῃ· τοὺς γοῦν
ἀναιροῦντας ἑαυτοὺς παρὰ μὲν ἡμῖν μέχρις ἡλίου
δύσεως ἀτάφους ἐκρίπτειν ἔκριναν, καίτοι καὶ
378 πολεμίους θάπτειν θεμιτὸν ἡγούμενοι, παρ' ἑτέροις
δὲ καὶ τὰς δεξιὰς τῶν τοιούτων νεκρῶν ἀποκόπτειν ἐκέλευσαν, αἷς ἐστρατεύσαντο καθ' ἑαυτῶν,
ἡγούμενοι, καθάπερ τὸ σῶμα τῆς ψυχῆς ἀλλότριον,
379 οὕτως καὶ τὴν χεῖρα τοῦ σώματος. καλὸν οὖν,
ἑταῖροι, δίκαια φρονεῖν καὶ μὴ ταῖς ἀνθρωπίναις
συμφοραῖς προσθεῖναι τὴν εἰς τὸν κτίσαντα ἡμᾶς
380 δυσσέβειαν. εἰ σῴζεσθαι δοκεῖ, σῳζώμεθα· καὶ
γὰρ οὐκ ἄδοξος ἡ σωτηρία παρ' οἷς διὰ τοσούτων
ἔργων ἐπεδειξάμεθα τὰς ἀρετάς· εἰ τεθνάναι, καλὸν
381 ὑπὸ τῶν ἑλόντων. οὐ μεταβήσομαι δ' ἐγὼ εἰς τὴν
τῶν πολεμίων τάξιν, ἵν' ἐμαυτοῦ προδότης γένω-
μαι· καὶ γὰρ ἂν εἴην πολὺ τῶν αὐτομολούντων
πρὸς τοὺς πολεμίους ἠλιθιώτερος, εἴ γ' ἐκεῖνοι
μὲν ἐπὶ σωτηρίᾳ τοῦτο πράττουσιν, ἐγὼ δ' ἐπὶ
382 ἀπωλείᾳ, καί γε τῇ ἐμαυτοῦ. τὴν μέντοι Ῥωμαίων ἐνέδραν εὔχομαι· μετὰ γὰρ δεξιὰν ἀναιρούμενος ὑπ' αὐτῶν εὔθυμος τεθνήξομαι, τὴν
τῶν ψευσαμένων ἀπιστίαν νίκης μείζονι ἀποφέρων
παραμυθίαν.''

---

[1] Text corrupt: I suggest τὰς τῶν πατέρων ὕβρεις; the text
may have arisen out of an erroneous τοὺς corrected in the
margin to τάς.

[a] Josephus apparently refers to some Rabbinical tradition ;
the Pentateuch is silent on the subject of suicide. For the
burial at sunset of the hanged criminal see Deut. xxi. 22 f.,
and of the slain enemy, Joshua viii. 29, x. 27.

[b] Such was the Athenian custom, as appears from Aeschines,

father, visits upon their posterity the outrageous acts
of the parents. That is why this crime, so hateful to
God, is punished also by the sagest of legislators.
With us it is ordained that the body of a suicide
should be exposed unburied until sunset, although it
is thought right to bury even our enemies slain in
war.[a] In other nations the law requires that a
suicide's right hand, with which he made war on
himself, should be cut off, holding that, as the body
was unnaturally severed from the soul, so the hand
should be severed from the body.[b]

"We shall do well then, comrades, to listen to
reason and not to add to our human calamities the
crime of impiety towards our creator. If our lives
are offered us, let us live : there is nothing dishonour-
able in accepting this offer from those who have had
so many proofs of our valour ; if they think fit to
kill us, death at the hands of our conquerors is
honourable. But, for my part, I shall never pass over
to the enemy's ranks, to prove a traitor to myself ;
I should indeed then be far more senseless than
deserters who go over to the enemy for safety,
whereas I should be going to destruction—my own
destruction.[c] I pray, however, that the Romans
may prove faithless ; if, after pledging their word,
they put me to death, I shall die content, for I shall
carry with me the consolation, better than a victory,
that their triumph has been sullied by perjury."

Cont. Ctesiph. 244 (quoted by Reinach) ἐάν τις αὐτὸν
διαχρήσηται, τὴν χεῖρα τὴν τοῦτο πράξασαν χωρὶς τοῦ σώματος
θάπτομεν. For this piece of erudition, comparable to other
instances in the *Contra Apionem*, Josephus is doubtless
indebted to his Greek assistants (*Ap.* i. 50).

[c] "The consciousness of such treachery would be my ruin,"
seems to be the meaning.

JOSEPHUS

383 (6) Ὁ μὲν οὖν Ἰώσηπος πολλὰ τοιαῦτα πρὸς
384 ἀποτροπὴν τῆς αὐτοχειρίας ἔλεγεν· οἱ δὲ πεφραγ-
μένας ἀπογνώσει τὰς ἀκοὰς ἔχοντες, ὡς ἂν πάλαι
καθοσιώσαντες ἑαυτοὺς τῷ θανάτῳ, παρωξύνοντο
πρὸς αὐτόν, καὶ προστρέχων ἄλλος ἄλλοθεν
ξιφήρεις ἐκάκιζόν τε εἰς ἀνανδρίαν καὶ ὡς ἕκαστος
385 αὐτίκα πλήξων δῆλος ἦν. ὁ δὲ τὸν μὲν ὀνομαστὶ
καλῶν, τῷ δὲ στρατηγικώτερον ἐμβλέπων, τοῦ δὲ
δρασσόμενος τῆς δεξιᾶς, ὃν δὲ δεήσει δυσωπῶν,
καὶ ποικίλοις διαιρούμενος πάθεσιν ἐπὶ τῆς ἀνάγκης εἶργεν ἀπὸ τῆς σφαγῆς πάντων τὸν σίδηρον,
ὥσπερ τὰ κυκλωθέντα τῶν θηρίων ἀεὶ πρὸς τὸν
386 καθαπτόμενον ἀντιστρεφόμενος. τῶν δὲ καὶ παρὰ
τὰς ἐσχάτας συμφορὰς ἔτι τὸν στρατηγὸν αἰδου-
μένων παρελύοντο μὲν αἱ δεξιαί, περιωλίσθανεν
δὲ τὰ ξίφη, καὶ πολλοὶ τὰς ῥομφαίας ἐπιφέροντες
αὐτομάτως παρεῖσαν.[1]

387 (7) Ὁ δ' ἐν ταῖς ἀμηχανίαις οὐκ ἠπόρησεν
ἐπινοίας, ἀλλὰ πιστεύων τῷ κηδεμόνι θεῷ τὴν
388 σωτηρίαν παραβάλλεται, καὶ '' ἐπεὶ δέδοκται τὸ
θνήσκειν,'' ἔφη, '' φέρε κλήρῳ τὰς ἀλλήλων σφαγὰς
ἐπιτρέψωμεν, ὁ λαχὼν δ' ὑπὸ τοῦ μετ' αὐτὸν
389 πιπτέτω, καὶ διοδεύσει πάντων οὕτως ἡ τύχη,
μηδ' ἐπὶ τῆς ἰδίας κείσθω δεξιᾶς ἕκαστος· ἄδικον
γὰρ οἰχομένων τινὰ τῶν ἄλλων μετανοήσαντα
σωθῆναι.'' πιστὸς [δ'] ἔδοξεν ταῦτα εἰπὼν καὶ
390 συνεκληροῦτο πείσας. ἑτοίμην δ' ὁ λαχὼν τῷ μεθ'
αὐτὸν παρεῖχεν τὴν σφαγήν, ὡς αὐτίκα τεθνη-
ξομένου καὶ τοῦ στρατηγοῦ· ζωῆς γὰρ ἡδίω τὸν
391 μετὰ τοῦ Ἰωσήπου θάνατον ἡγοῦντο. κατα-

[1] παρείθησαν '' were paralysed '' MVRC.

(6) By these and many similar arguments Josephus sought to deter his companions from suicide. But desperation stopped their ears, for they had long since devoted themselves to death ; they were, therefore, infuriated at him, and ran at him from this side and that, sword in hand, upbraiding him as a coward, each one seeming on the point of striking him. But he, addressing one by name, fixing his general's eye of command upon another, clasping the hand of a third, shaming a fourth by entreaty, and torn by all manner of emotions at this critical moment, succeeded in warding off from his throat the blades of all, turning like a wild beast surrounded by the hunters to face his successive assailants. Even in his extremity, they still held their general in reverence ; their hands were powerless, their swords glanced aside, and many, in the act of thrusting at him, spontaneously dropped their weapons.

(7) But, in his straits, his resource did not forsake him. Trusting to God's protection, he put his life to the hazard, and said : " Since we are resolved to die, come, let us leave the lot to decide the order in which we are to kill ourselves ; let him who draws the first lot fall by the hand of him who comes next ; fortune will thus take her course through the whole number, and we shall be spared from taking our lives with our own hands. For it would be unjust that, when the rest were gone, any should repent and escape." This proposal inspired confidence ; his advice was taken, and he drew lots with the rest. Each man thus selected presented his throat to his neighbour, in the assurance that his general was forthwith to share his fate ; for sweeter to them than life was the thought of death with Josephus. He,

Josephus, in peril of his life,

proposes drawing lots.

His companions kill each other and he escapes.

113

JOSEPHUS

λείπεται δ' οὗτος, εἴτε ὑπὸ τύχης χρὴ λέγειν, εἴτε[1]
ὑπὸ θεοῦ προνοίας, σὺν ἑτέρῳ, καὶ σπουδάζων
μήθ' ὑπὸ τοῦ κλήρου καταδικασθῆναι μήτε, εἰ
τελευταῖος λείποιτο, μιᾶναι τὴν δεξιὰν ὁμοφύλῳ
φόνῳ πείθει κἀκεῖνον ἐπὶ πίστει ζῆν.

392 (8) Ὁ μὲν οὖν οὕτως τόν τε Ῥωμαίων καὶ τὸν
οἰκεῖον[2] διαφυγὼν πόλεμον ἐπὶ Οὐεσπασιανὸν
393 ἤγετο ὑπὸ τοῦ Νικάνορος. οἱ δὲ Ῥωμαῖοι πάντες
ἐπὶ θέαν αὐτοῦ συνέτρεχον, καὶ τοῦ πλήθους
συνθλιβομένου περὶ τῷ στρατηγῷ θόρυβος ἦν
ποικίλος, τῶν μὲν γεγηθότων ἐπὶ τῷ ληφθέντι,
τῶν δ' ἀπειλούντων, τῶν δ' ἐγγύθεν ἰδεῖν βιαζο-
394 μένων. καὶ οἱ μὲν πόρρωθεν κολάζειν ἐβόων τὸν
πολέμιον, τοὺς[3] δὲ πλησίον ἀνάμνησις αὐτοῦ τῶν
395 ἔργων εἰσῄει καὶ πρὸς τὴν μεταβολὴν θάμβος, τῶν
τε ἡγεμόνων οὐδεὶς ἦν ὅς, εἰ καὶ πρότερον ὠργί-
ζετο, τότε πρὸς τὴν ὄψιν οὐκ ἐνέδωκεν αὐτοῦ.
396 μάλιστα δὲ τὸν Τίτον ἐξαιρέτως[4] τό τε καρτερικὸν
ἐν ταῖς συμφοραῖς ᾕρει τοῦ Ἰωσήπου καὶ πρὸς
τὴν ἡλικίαν ἔλεος, ἀναμιμνησκομένῳ τε τὸν[5] πάλαι
μαχόμενον καὶ τὸν ἐν χερσὶν ἐχθρῶν ἄρτι κείμενον
ὁρῶντι παρῆν [δὲ][6] νοεῖν, ὅσον δύναται τύχη, καὶ
ὡς ὀξεῖα μὲν πολέμου ῥοπή, τῶν δ' ἀνθρωπίνων
397 οὐδὲν βέβαιον· παρὸ καὶ τότε συνδιέθηκεν μὲν
πλείστους ἑαυτῷ καὶ πρὸς οἶκτον τοῦ Ἰωσήπου,
πλείστη δ' αὐτῷ καὶ παρὰ τῷ πατρὶ μοῖρα σω-

---

[1] εἴτε ὑπὸ τύχης χρὴ λέγειν, εἴτε om. PAL.
[2] τὸν οἰκεῖον L: τῶν οἰκείων most mss.: τὸν τῶν οἰκείων Naber.
[3] MC: τῶν the rest.
[4] ἐξ ἀρετῆς LVRC and in the margin of PA.
[5] + οὐ VRC, mistaking the use, frequent in Josephus, of πάλαι = " formerly," " recently."
[6] om. Lat.

114

however (should one say by fortune or by the providence of God?), was left alone with one other; and, anxious neither to be condemned by the lot nor, should he be left to the last, to stain his hand with the blood of a fellow-countryman, he persuaded this man also, under a pledge, to remain alive.[a]

(8) Having thus survived both the war with the Romans and that with his own friends, Josephus was brought by Nicanor into Vespasian's presence. The Romans all flocked to see him, and from the multitude crowding around the general arose a hubbub of discordant voices: some exulting at his capture, some threatening, some pushing forward to obtain a nearer view. The more distant spectators clamoured for the punishment of their enemy, but those close beside him recalled his exploits and marvelled at such a reversal of fortune. Of the officers there was not one who, whatever his past resentment, did not then relent at the sight of him. Titus in particular was specially touched by the fortitude of Josephus under misfortunes and by pity for his youth.[b] As he recalled the combatant of yesterday and saw him now a prisoner in his enemy's hands, he was led to reflect on the power of fortune, the quick vicissitudes of war, and the general instability of human affairs. So he brought over many Romans at the time to share his compassion for Josephus, and his pleading with his father was the

Josephus before Vespasian.

---

[a] The historian's veracity in this narrative is not above suspicion; his inconsistency in other autobiographical passages, doubly reported, does not inspire confidence. That his companions would have tolerated the rhetorical speech on suicide is incredible.

[b] Josephus, born in A.D. 37 (*Vita* 5), was now thirty years old.

398 τηρίας ἐγένετο. ὁ μέντοι Οὐεσπασιανὸς φρουρεῖν
αὐτὸν μετὰ πάσης ἀσφαλείας προσέταττεν ὡς
ἀναπέμψων αὐτίκα Νέρωνι.

399 (9) Τοῦτο ἀκούσας ὁ Ἰώσηπος μόνῳ τι διαλεχθῆναι θέλειν ἔλεγεν αὐτῷ. μεταστησαμένου δ᾽
ἐκείνου πλὴν τοῦ παιδὸς Τίτου καὶ δυοῖν φίλων

400 τοὺς ἄλλους ἅπαντας " σὺ μέν," εἶπεν, " Οὐεσπασιανέ, νομίζεις αἰχμάλωτον αὐτὸ μόνον εἰλη-
φέναι τὸν Ἰώσηπον, ἐγὼ δ᾽ ἄγγελος ἥκω σοι
μειζόνων· μὴ γὰρ ὑπὸ θεοῦ προπεμπόμενος ᾔδειν
τὸν Ἰουδαίων νόμον, καὶ πῶς στρατηγοῖς ἀπο-

401 θνῄσκειν πρέπει. Νέρωνί με πέμπεις; τί γάρ; * *[1]
οἱ μετὰ Νέρωνα μέχρι σοῦ διάδοχοι μενοῦσιν; σὺ
Καῖσαρ, Οὐεσπασιανέ, καὶ αὐτοκράτωρ, σὺ καὶ

402 παῖς ὁ σὸς οὗτος. δέσμει δέ με νῦν ἀσφαλέστερον
καὶ τήρει σεαυτῷ· δεσπότης μὲν γὰρ οὐ μόνον
ἐμοῦ σύ, Καῖσαρ, ἀλλὰ καὶ γῆς καὶ θαλάττης καὶ
παντὸς ἀνθρώπων γένους, ἐγὼ δ᾽ ἐπὶ τιμωρίαν
δέομαι φρουρᾶς μείζονος, εἰ κατασχεδιάζω[2] καὶ

403 θεοῦ." ταῦτ᾽ εἰπόντος παραχρῆμα μὲν Οὐεσπασιανὸς ἀπιστεῖν ἐδόκει καὶ τὸν Ἰώσηπον ὑπ-

404 ελάμβανεν ταῦτα περὶ σωτηρίας πανουργεῖν, κατὰ
μικρὸν δὲ εἰς πίστιν ὑπήγετο, τοῦ θεοῦ δι-
εγείροντος αὐτὸν εἰς τὴν ἡγεμονίαν ἤδη καὶ
τὰ σκῆπτρα δι᾽ ἑτέρων σημείων προδεικνύντος.

405 ἀτρεκῆ δὲ τὸν Ἰώσηπον καὶ ἐν ἄλλοις κατ-

---

[1] A mention of Nero's impending death seems to have
dropped out.

[2] κατασχεδιάσω PAML Suid.

[a] For the sending of prisoners of importance to be tried by
the Emperor cf. B. ii. 243 f. (Cumanus the procurator and
the leading rebels), Vita 408 f. (Philip ben Jacimus), and in
the N.T the case of S. Paul (at his own appeal).

main influence in saving the prisoner's life. Vespasian, however, ordered him to be guarded with every precaution, intending shortly to send him to Nero.[a]

(9) On hearing this, Josephus expressed a desire for a private interview with him. Vespasian having ordered all to withdraw except his son Titus and two of his friends, the prisoner thus addressed him : " You imagine, Vespasian, that in the person of Josephus you have taken a mere captive ; but I come to you as a messenger of greater destinies. Had I not been sent on this errand by God, I knew the law of the Jews and how it becomes a general to die. To Nero do you send me ? Why then ? Think you that [Nero and] those who before your accession succeed him will continue ? You will be Caesar, Vespasian, you will be emperor, you and your son here. Bind me then yet more securely in chains and keep me for yourself ; for you, Caesar, are master not of me only, but of land and sea and the whole human race. For myself, I ask to be punished by stricter custody, if I have dared to trifle with the words of God." To this speech Vespasian, at the moment, seemed to attach little credit, supposing it to be a trick of Josephus to save his life. Gradually, however, he was led to believe it, for God was already rousing in him thoughts of empire and by other tokens foreshadowing the throne.[b] He found, moreover, that Josephus had

He predicts Vespasian's accession as Emperor,

---

[b] These omens and oracles are mentioned by Tacitus, *Hist.* i. 10 (" ostentis ac responsis destinatum Vespasiano liberisque eius imperium "), ii. 1 (" praesaga responsa "), and in other passages cited by Reinach. The widespread belief that " persons proceeding from Judaea were to become masters of the world," is reported in almost identical terms by Tacitus (*Hist.* v. 13) and Suetonius (*Vesp.* 4).

JOSEPHUS

ἐλάμβανεν· τῶν γὰρ τοῖς ἀπορρήτοις παρατυχόντων
φίλων [ὁ] ἕτερος θαυμάζειν ἔφη πῶς οὔτε τοῖς ἐπὶ
τῶν Ἰωταπάτων περὶ ἁλώσεως οὔθ᾽ ἑαυτῷ προ-
μαντεύσαιτο αἰχμαλωσίαν, εἰ μὴ ταῦτα λῆρος εἴη
406 διακρουομένου τὰς ἐπ᾽ αὐτὸν ὀργάς. ὁ δὲ Ἰώσηπος καὶ τοῖς Ἰωταπατηνοῖς ὅτι μετὰ τεσσαρακοστὴν
ἑβδόμην ἡμέραν ἁλώσονται προειπεῖν ἔφη, καὶ
407 ὅτι πρὸς Ῥωμαίων αὐτὸς ζωγρηθήσεται. ταῦτα
παρὰ τῶν αἰχμαλώτων κατ᾽ ἰδίαν ὁ Οὐεσπασιανὸς
ἐκπυθόμενος ὡς εὕρισκεν ἀληθῆ, οὕτω πιστεύειν[1]
408 περὶ τῶν κατ᾽ αὐτὸν ἦρκτο. φρουρᾶς μὲν οὖν
καὶ δεσμῶν οὐκ ἀνίει τὸν Ἰώσηπον, ἐδωρεῖτο
δ᾽ ἐσθῆτι καὶ τοῖς ἄλλοις κειμηλίοις, φιλοφρονού-
μενός τε καὶ περιέπων διετέλει τὰ πολλὰ Τίτου
τῇ τιμῇ συνεργοῦντος.

409 (ix. 1) Τετάρτῃ δὲ Πανέμου μηνὸς ἀναζεύξας
εἰς Πτολεμαΐδα κἀκεῖθεν εἰς τὴν παράλιον ἀφικνεῖται Καισάρειαν, μεγίστην τῆς τε Ἰουδαίας
πόλιν καὶ τὸ πλέον[2] ὑφ᾽ Ἑλλήνων οἰκουμένην.
410 ἐδέχοντο δὲ καὶ τὴν στρατιὰν καὶ τὸν στρατηγὸν
μετὰ πάσης εὐφημίας καὶ φιλοφροσύνης οἱ ἐπι-

---

[1] + καὶ Niese. [2] πλεῖστον PAML.

---

[a] The fact of this prediction of Josephus to Vespasian is
confirmed by Suet. *Vesp.* 5 "unus ex nobilibus captiuis
Iosepus, cum coiceretur in uincula, constantissime asseue-
rauit fore ut ab eodem breui solueretur, uerum iam impera-

118

proved a veracious prophet in other matters. For
one of the two friends in attendance at the private
interview remarked : " If these words are not a
nonsensical invention of the prisoner to avert the
storm which he has raised, I am surprised that
Josephus neither predicted the fall of Jotapata to
its inhabitants nor his own captivity." To this
Josephus replied that he had foretold to the people
of Jotapata that their city would be captured after
forty-seven days and that he himself would be taken
alive by the Romans. Vespasian, having privately ^{and is}
questioned the prisoners on these statements and ^{consider-}
found them true, then began to credit those con- ^{ately treated}
cerning himself. While he did not release Josephus ^{prisoner.}
from his custody or chains, he presented him with
raiment and other precious gifts, and continued to
treat him with kindness and solicitude, being warmly
supported by Titus in these courtesies.[a]

(ix. 1) On the fourth of the month of Panemus,[b] ^{Vespasian}
Vespasian led off his troops to Ptolemais and from ^{quarters}
there to Caesarea-on-sea, one of the largest cities ^{in Caesarea}
of Judaea with a population consisting chiefly of ^{and}
Greeks.[c] The inhabitants received the army and ^{Scythopolis.}
its general with blessings and congratulations of

tore," and by Dio Cassius (epitome, lxvi. 1) who instead
of *breui* (" shortly ") writes more precisely μετ᾽ ἐνιαυτόν.
Reinach, who quotes these passages, refers also to the
curious Rabbinic attribution of this prophecy to Johanan
ben Zakkai, on the occasion of his escape from the siege of
Jerusalem.

[b] 23 July A.D. 67 (Niese's reckoning).

[c] Notwithstanding its predominant Greek population the
city from the time of its refoundation by Herod the Great
" always continued united with Judaea " (Schürer).

χώριοι, καὶ κατ᾿ εὔνοιαν μὲν τὴν πρὸς ῾Ρωμαίους,
τὸ δὲ πλέον ἔχθει τῶν κατεστραμμένων· διὸ καὶ
τὸν Ἰώσηπον ἀθρόοι καταβοῶντες ἠξίουν κολάζειν.

411 Οὐεσπασιανὸς δὲ τὴν [μὲν] περὶ τούτου δέησιν
ὡς ὑπ᾿ ἀκρίτου γινομένην πλήθους ἐξέλυσεν

412 ἡσυχίᾳ· τῶν δὲ ταγμάτων τὰ μὲν δύο χειμε-
ρίσοντα ἐκάθισεν ἐπὶ τῆς Καισαρείας, ἐπιτήδειον
ὁρῶν τὴν πόλιν, τὸ δέκατον δὲ καὶ πέμπτον εἰς
Σκυθόπολιν, ὡς μὴ θλίβοι παντὶ τῷ στρατῷ τὴν

413 Καισάρειαν. ἀλεεινὴ δ᾿ ἦν κἀκείνη χειμῶνος
ὥρᾳ, καθ᾿ ὅσον πνιγώδης θέρους ὑπὸ καυμάτων,
πεδιὰς οὖσα καὶ παράλιος.

414 (2) Ἐν δὲ τούτῳ συναθροισθέντες οἵ τε κατὰ
στάσιν ἐκπίπτοντες τῶν πόλεων[1] καὶ οἱ δια-
φυγόντες ἐκ τῶν κατεστραμμένων, πλῆθος οὐκ
ὀλίγον, ἀνακτίζουσιν Ἰόππην ὁρμητήριον σφίσιν,

415 ἐρημωθεῖσαν ὑπὸ Κεστίου πρότερον, καὶ τῆς
χώρας ἐκπεπολεμωμένης ἀνειργόμενοι μεταβαίνειν

416 ἔγνωσαν εἰς τὴν θάλασσαν. πηξάμενοί τε πειρα-
τικὰ σκάφη πλεῖστα τόν τε Συρίας καὶ Φοινίκης
καὶ τὸν ἐπ᾿ Αἰγύπτου πόρον ἐλῄστευον, ἄπλωτά

417 τε πᾶσιν ἐποίουν τὰ τῇδε πελάγη. Οὐεσπασιανὸς
δὲ ὡς ἔγνω τὴν σύνταξιν αὐτῶν, πέμπει πεζούς
τε καὶ ἱππεῖς ἐπὶ τὴν Ἰόππην, οἳ νύκτωρ ὡς ἀ-

418 φύλακτον εἰσέρχονται τὴν πόλιν. οἱ δ᾿ ἐν αὐτῇ
προῄσθοντο μὲν τὴν εἰσβολὴν καὶ καταδείσαντες
τοῦ μὲν εἴργειν τοὺς ῾Ρωμαίους ἀπετρέποντο,

---

[1] V : πολεμίων the rest.

---

[a] The 5th and 10th (§ 65).
[b] Bethshan, thirty-five miles due east of Caesarea.

every description, prompted partly by goodwill towards the Romans, but mainly by hatred of the vanquished. This feeling showed itself in a loud and universal demand for the punishment of Josephus; but Vespasian by his silence quashed this petition emanating from an incompetent crowd. Of his three legions he established two [a] in winter quarters at Caesarea, finding the city suitable for the purpose ; the fifteenth legion he sent to Scythopolis,[b] in order not to burden Caesarea with his whole army. The climate of the last-named city is, like Scythopolis,[c] as genial in winter as it is suffocatingly hot in summer, from its situation in the plain and on the coast.

(2) Meanwhile, the Jews who had been driven by sedition from the towns and the refugees, whose homes had been destroyed, had united their not inconsiderable forces, and, to provide themselves with a base, rebuilt Joppa, recently devastated by Cestius [d] ; and then, finding themselves cut off from the country, which had passed into the enemy's hands, they resolved to take to the sea. They accordingly built themselves a fleet of piratical ships and made raids on the traffic along the coast of Syria and Phoenicia and the route to Egypt, rendering navigation in those seas quite impossible. Vespasian, on learning of this gang, dispatched to Joppa a body of infantry and cavalry, who entered the city by night, finding it unguarded. The inhabitants had received news of the coming attack, but in their alarm made no attempt to

The pirates of Joppa are pursued by the Romans

---

[c] κἀκείνη : Reinach, referring the pronoun to Scythopolis, is reduced to correcting παράλιος to παραποτάμιος.

[d] B. ii. 507 f.

συμφυγόντες δ' εἰς τὰς ναῦς ἐξωτέρω βέλους διενυκτέρευσαν.

419 (3) Ἀλιμένου δ' οὔσης φύσει τῆς Ἰόππης, αἰγιαλῷ γὰρ ἐπιλήγει τραχεῖ καὶ τὸ μὲν ἄλλο πᾶν ὀρθίῳ, βραχὺ δὲ συννεύοντι κατὰ τὰς κεραίας
420 ἑκατέρωθεν· αἱ δέ εἰσιν κρημνοὶ βαθεῖς καὶ προύχουσαι σπιλάδες εἰς τὸ πέλαγος, ἔνθα καὶ τῶν Ἀνδρομέδας δεσμῶν ἔτι δεικνύμενοι τύποι πι-
421 στοῦνται τὴν ἀρχαιότητα τοῦ μύθου, τύπτων δὲ τὸν αἰγιαλὸν ἐναντίος βορέας καὶ πρὸς ταῖς δεχομέναις πέτραις ὑψηλὸν ἀνακόπτων[1] τὸ κῦμα σφαλερώτερον ἐρημίας τὸν ὅρμον ἀπεργάζεται·
422 κατὰ τοῦτον σαλεύουσιν τοῖς ἀπὸ τῆς Ἰόππης ὑπὸ τὴν ἕω πνεῦμα βίαιον ἐπιπίπτει· μελαμβόριον
423 ὑπὸ τῶν ταύτῃ πλοϊζομένων καλεῖται· καὶ τὰς μὲν ἀλλήλαις τῶν νεῶν αὐτόθι συνήραξεν, τὰς δὲ πρὸς ταῖς πέτραις, πολλὰς δὲ πρὸς ἀντίον κῦμα βιαζομένας εἰς τὸ πέλαγος, τόν τε γὰρ αἰγιαλὸν ὄντα πετρώδη καὶ τοὺς ἐπ' αὐτοῦ πολεμίους ἐδεδοίκεσαν, μετέωρος ὑπεραρθεὶς ὁ κλύδων ἐβά-
424 πτιζεν. ἦν δ' οὔτε φυγῆς τόπος οὔτε μένουσιν σωτηρία, βίᾳ μὲν ἀνέμου τῆς θαλάσσης ἐξωθουμένοις, Ῥωμαίων δὲ τῆς πόλεως. καὶ πολλὴ μὲν οἰμωγὴ συρρηγνυμένων ἐγίνετο τῶν σκαφῶν,
425 πολὺς δ' ἀγνυμένων ὁ ψόφος. καὶ τοῦ πλήθους οἱ μὲν ὑπὸ τῶν κυμάτων καλυπτόμενοι διεφθεί-

---

[1] ἀναπέμπων P*A*L.

[a] The localization of this legend at Joppa is widely attested. Reinach quotes Pliny, *Nat. Hist.* v. 69 (marks of the chains shown on a projecting rock), Strabo xvi. 2. 28 (ἐνταῦθα μυθεύουσί τινες τὴν Ἀνδρομέδαν ἐκτεθῆναι τῷ κήτει), Pausanias iv. 35. 9 (a blood-red spring where Perseus washed himself after slaying the monster), Jerome, *In Jon.* i.

oppose the Romans and sought refuge in their ships, where they passed the night out of bowshot.

(3) Nature has not provided Joppa with a port. *and destroyed by a storm at sea.* It terminates in a rugged shore, which runs for nearly its whole length in a straight line, but is slightly curved at its two extremities in crescent fashion ; these horns consist of steep cliffs and reefs jutting far out into the deep ; here are still shown the impressions of Andromeda's chains, to attest the antiquity of that legend.[a] The north wind, beating full upon the coast, dashes the waves high against the face of the rocks and renders this roadstead more perilous to sailors than the watery waste.[b] It was here that the people of Joppa were tossing, when, towards dawn, a furious blast burst upon them, the wind called by navigators in those parts the " Black Norther." Some of the ships were dashed to pieces against each other on the spot, others were shattered upon the rocks. Many from dread of this rock-strewn coast and the enemy that occupied it, strove to gain the open sea in the teeth of the gale, and foundered among the towering billows. There was neither means of flight, nor hope of safety if they remained where they were : the fury of the wind repelled them from the sea, that of the Romans from the town. Piercing were the shrieks as the vessels collided, terrific the crash as they broke up. Of the crews who perished, some were engulfed in the waves, many crushed by the

(the holes through which had passed the rings of the chains were still shown in his day). *Cf.* G. A. Smith, *Hist. Geog. of Holy Land,* 163 f.

[b] Literally " than a desert " ; I adopt the late Dr. R. Traill's happy paraphrase, and see no reason to suspect the text.

ροντο, πολλοὶ δὲ τοῖς ναυαγίοις ἐμπλεκόμενοι·
τινὲς δ' ὡς κουφοτέρῳ τὴν θάλατταν ἔφθανον τῷ
426 σιδήρῳ σφᾶς αὐτοὺς ἀναιροῦντες. τό γε μὴν
πλεῖστον ὑπὸ τῶν κυμάτων ἐκφερόμενον περι-
εξαίνετο ταῖς ἀπορρῶξιν, ὡς αἱμαχθῆναι μὲν ἐπὶ
πλεῖστον τὸ πέλαγος, πληρωθῆναι δὲ νεκρῶν τὴν
παράλιον· καὶ γὰρ τοὺς ἐπὶ τὸν αἰγιαλὸν ἐκ-
φερομένους ἐφεστῶτες οἱ Ῥωμαῖοι διέφθειρον.
427 ἀριθμὸς [δὲ] τῶν ἐκβρασθέντων σωμάτων τετρακισχίλιοι πρὸς τοῖς διακοσίοις ἦν. Ῥωμαῖοι δὲ
λαβόντες ἀμαχητὶ τὴν πόλιν κατασκάπτουσιν.
428   (4) Ἰόππη μὲν οὖν ἐν ὀλίγῳ χρόνῳ δεύτερον ὑπὸ
429 Ῥωμαίοις ἑάλω. Οὐεσπασιανὸς δ' ὡς μὴ πάλιν
οἱ πειραταὶ συναλισθεῖεν εἰς αὐτήν, στρατόπεδόν
τε ἐπὶ τῆς ἀκροπόλεως ἐγείρει καὶ τὸ ἱππικὸν ἐν
430 αὐτῷ καταλείπει μετὰ πεζῶν ὀλίγων, ἵν' οὗτοι μὲν
κατὰ χώραν μένοντες φρουρῶσι τὸ στρατόπεδον,
οἱ δ' ἱππεῖς προνομεύωσι τὴν πέριξ καὶ τὰς
περιοίκους κώμας τε καὶ πολίχνας ἐξαιρῶσιν τῆς
431 Ἰόππης. οἱ μὲν οὖν κατὰ τὰ προσταχθέντα τὴν
χώραν κατατρέχοντες καθ' ἡμέραν ἔτεμνόν τε καὶ
ἠρήμουν ἅπασαν.
432   (5) Ὡς δὲ εἰς τὰ Ἱεροσόλυμα τὸ κατὰ τὴν
Ἰωταπάτην πάθος ἠγγέλη, τὸ μὲν πρῶτον ἠπί-
στουν οἱ πολλοὶ καὶ διὰ τὸ μέγεθος τῆς συμφορᾶς
καὶ διὰ τὸ μηδένα τῶν λεγομένων αὐτόπτην
433 παρεῖναι· διεσώθη γὰρ οὐδὲ ἄγγελος, ἀλλ' αὐτο-
μάτη[1] διεκήρυσσεν φήμη τὴν ἅλωσιν, οἰκείᾳ φύσει
434 τῶν σκυθρωποτέρων. κατ' ὀλίγον δὲ διὰ τῶν
προσχώρων ὥδευε τἀληθὲς καὶ παρὰ πᾶσιν ἀμφι-

[1] αὐτοματὶ PA.

124

wreckage from which they could not extricate themselves ; others, regarding the sword as a lighter evil than the sea, anticipated drowning by suicide. The majority, however, were swept to shore by the waves and their bodies hurled and mangled against the cliffs. A wide area of sea was red with their blood, and the coast was covered with corpses ; for the Romans, lining the beach, massacred those who were cast up. The number of bodies. washed up amounted to four thousand two hundred. The Romans took the town without opposition and razed it to the ground.

(4) Thus was Joppa, after a brief interval, for the second time [a] captured by the Romans. Vespasian, in order to prevent the pirates from congregating there again, established a camp on the acropolis and left in it the cavalry with a small body of infantry. The latter were to remain on the spot and guard the camp, the cavalry to ravage the neighbourhood and destroy the villages and small towns around Joppa. In obedience to these orders, they daily scoured the country, pillaging and reducing it to an utter desert.

(5) When the news of the fate of Jotapata reached Jerusalem, it was received at first with general incredulity, both because of the magnitude of the calamity and because no eyewitness had come to confirm the report. In fact, not a man had escaped to tell the tale ; rumour, with its natural propensity to black tidings,[b] spontaneously spread the news of the city's fall. Little by little, however, the truth made its way from place to place, and was soon

---

[a] ii. 507 f.

[b] *Cf.* the description of " Fama " in Virg. *Aen.* iv. 173 ff., especially 190, " facta atque infecta canebat," with " facts embroidered by fiction " in Josephus.

JOSEPHUS

βολίας ἦν ἤδη βεβαιότερον· προσεσχεδιάζετό γε
μὴν τοῖς πεπραγμένοις καὶ τὰ μὴ γενόμενα,
τεθνεὼς γὰρ ἐπὶ τῆς ἁλώσεως καὶ ὁ Ἰώσηπος
435 ἠγγέλλετο. τοῦτο μεγίστου τὰ Ἱεροσόλυμα πέν-
θους ἐπλήρωσεν· κατὰ μέν γε οἴκους καὶ κατὰ
συγγενείας οἷς προσήκων ἕκαστος ἦν τῶν ἀπολω-
436 λότων ἐθρηνεῖτο, τὸ δ᾽ ἐπὶ τῷ στρατηγῷ πένθος
ἐδημεύθη, καὶ οἱ μὲν ξένους, οἱ δὲ συγγενεῖς, οἱ
δὲ φίλους [οἱ δὲ ἀδελφοὺς]¹ ἐθρήνουν, τὸν Ἰώ-
437 σηπον δὲ πάντες· ὡς ἐπὶ τριακοστὴν μὲν ἡμέραν
μὴ διαλιπεῖν τὰς ὀλοφύρσεις ἐν τῇ πόλει, πλείστους δὲ μισθοῦσθαι τοὺς αὐλητάς, οἳ θρήνων
αὐτοῖς ἐξῆρχον.
438 (6) Ὡς δὲ τἀληθῆ διεκαλύπτετο τῷ χρόνῳ καὶ
τὰ μὲν κατὰ τὴν Ἰωταπάτην ὥσπερ εἶχεν, ἐσχεδια-
σμένον δὲ τὸ κατὰ τὸν Ἰώσηπον πάθος εὑρίσκετο,
ζῆν δ᾽ αὐτὸν ἔγνωσαν καὶ παρὰ Ῥωμαίοις ὄντα
καὶ πρὸς τῶν ἡγεμόνων πλέον ἢ κατ᾽ αἰχμαλώτου
τύχην περιέπεσθαι, τοσοῦτον ὀργῆς ἐπὶ ζῶντος
ὅσον εὐνοίας ἐπὶ τεθνάναι δοκοῦντος πρότερον
439 ἀνελάμβανον. καὶ παρ᾽ οἷς μὲν εἰς ἀνανδρίαν,
παρ᾽ οἷς δ᾽ εἰς προδοσίαν ἐκακίζετο, πλήρης τε
ἀγανακτήσεως ἦν καὶ τῶν κατ᾽ αὐτοῦ βλασφημιῶν
440 ἡ πόλις. παρωξύνοντο δὲ ταῖς πληγαῖς καὶ προσ-
εξεκαίοντο ταῖς κακοπραγίαις· τό γε μὴν πταίειν,
ὃ γίνεται τοῖς εὖ φρονοῦσιν ἀσφαλείας καὶ τῶν
ὁμοίων φυλακῆς αἴτιον, ἐκείνοις κέντρον ἑτέρων
ἐγίνετο συμφορῶν, καὶ τὸ τέλος ἀεὶ τῶν κακῶν

¹ om. PA.

———

ᵃ Or " guest-friend."
ᵇ The period, as Reinach remarks, of the mourning for
126

regarded by all as established beyond doubt. But
the facts were embroidered by fiction ; thus Josephus
himself was reported to have fallen when the city
was taken. This intelligence filled Jerusalem with
the profoundest grief ; whereas in each household
and family there was mourning of the relatives for
their own lost ones, the lamentation for the commander was national. While some mourned for a
host,[a] others for a relative, some for a friend, others
for a brother, all alike wept for Josephus. Thus for
thirty days [b] the lamentations never ceased in the
city, and many of the mourners hired flute-players [c]
to accompany their funeral dirges.

(6) But when time revealed the truth and all that
had really happened at Jotapata, when the death
of Josephus was found to be a fiction, and it became
known that he was alive and in Roman hands and
being treated by the commanding officers with a
respect beyond the common lot of a prisoner, the
demonstrations of wrath at his being still alive were
as loud as the former expressions of affection when
he was believed to be dead. Some abused him as
a coward, others as a traitor, and throughout the city
there was general indignation, and curses were
heaped upon his devoted head. The citizens were,
moreover, exasperated by their reverses, and their
misfortunes only added fuel to the flames. A defeat,
which with the wise induces precaution and care to
provide against similar misadventures, only goaded
them to further disasters ; and the end of one
calamity was always the beginning of the next.

Outcry against Josephus.

men such as Moses (Deut. xxxiv. 8) and Aaron (Numb. xx.
29). The normal period was seven days (Ecclus. xxii. 12).
  [c] Such funeral flute-players are mentioned in Matt. ix. 23.

441 αὖθις ἀρχή· μᾶλλον γοῦν ὥρμων ἐπὶ τοὺς Ῥωμαίους ὡς καὶ Ἰώσηπον ἐν αὐτοῖς ἀμυνούμενοι.
442 τοὺς μὲν οὖν ἐπὶ τῶν Ἱεροσολύμων τοιοῦτοι
θόρυβοι κατεῖχον.

443   (7) Οὐεσπασιανὸς δὲ καθ᾽ ἱστορίαν τῆς Ἀγρίππα βασιλείας, ἐνῆγεν γὰρ βασιλεὺς αὐτόν,[1] ἅμα
[δὲ] καὶ δεξιώσασθαι τὸν ἡγεμόνα σὺν τῇ στρατιᾷ τῷ κατὰ τὸν οἶκον ὄλβῳ προαιρούμενος καὶ
καταστεῖλαι δι᾽ αὐτῶν τὰ νοσοῦντα τῆς ἀρχῆς,
ἄρας ἀπὸ τῆς παράλου Καισαρείας εἰς τὴν Φι-
444 λίππου καλουμένην μεταβαίνει Καισάρειαν. ἔνθα
μέχρι μὲν ἡμερῶν εἴκοσι τὴν στρατιὰν διαναπαύων
καὶ αὐτὸς ἐν εὐωχίαις ἦν, ἀποδιδοὺς τῷ θεῷ
445 χαριστήρια τῶν κατωρθωμένων. ὡς δ᾽ αὐτῷ
Τιβεριὰς μὲν νεωτερίζειν, ἀφεστάναι δ᾽ ἠγγέλλοντο
Ταριχαῖαι, μοῖρα δὲ τῆς Ἀγρίππα βασιλείας ἦσαν
ἀμφότεραι, πάντοθεν τοὺς Ἰουδαίους καταστρέ-
φεσθαι διεγνωκὼς τὴν ἐπὶ τούτους[2] στρατείαν
εὔκαιρον ἡγεῖτο καὶ δι᾽ Ἀγρίππαν, ὡς εἰς ξενίας
446 ἀμοιβὴν σωφρονίσων αὐτῷ τὰς πόλεις. πέμπει
δὴ τὸν υἱὸν Τίτον εἰς Καισάρειαν μετάξοντα τὴν
ἐκεῖθεν στρατιὰν εἰς Σκυθόπολιν· ἡ δ᾽ ἐστὶν
μεγίστη τῆς Δεκαπόλεως καὶ γείτων τῆς Τιβε-
447 ριάδος. ἔνθα καὶ αὐτὸς παραγενόμενος ἐκδέχεται
τὸν υἱόν, καὶ μετὰ τριῶν ταγμάτων προελθὼν
στρατοπεδεύεται μὲν ἀπὸ τριάκοντα τῆς Τιβεριάδος σταδίων κατά τινα σταθμὸν εὐσύνοπτον τοῖς
448 νεωτερίζουσιν· Σενναβρὶς ὀνομάζεται. πέμπει δὲ[3]

---

[1] PA: αὐτός the rest.
[2] Niese: τούτου or τούτοις mss.   [3] δὴ PAL.

---

[a] Or rather a part of them (§ 446).   [b] ii. 168.

They were now animated with greater fury against
the Romans by the thought that, in having their
revenge on them, they would also be avenged on
Josephus. Such was the state of agitation prevailing
in Jerusalem.

(7) Vespasian, however, had gone to visit Agrippa's
kingdom, to which the king had invited him with the
double object of entertaining the general and his
troops [a] with all the wealth of his royal household
and of quelling, by their aid, the disorders within
his realm. Leaving Caesarea-on-sea, Vespasian,
accordingly repaired to the other Caesarea called
Caesarea Philippi.[b] There for twenty days he rested
his troops, while he was being fêted himself and
rendering thankofferings to God for the successes
which he had obtained. But when he learnt that
Tiberias was disaffected and Tarichaeae already in
revolt—both cities formed part of Agrippa's realm—
he thought that now was the time to march against
these rebels, in pursuance of his fixed intention of
crushing the Jews wherever they rose, and also to
oblige Agrippa and to repay his hospitality by
recalling these cities of his to their allegiance. He
accordingly sent his son Titus to Caesarea to fetch
the troops quartered there and march them to
Scythopolis, the largest city of Decapolis and in the
neighbourhood of Tiberias.[c] Thither he proceeded
himself to receive his son, and then, advancing with
three legions, encamped thirty furlongs from Tiberias
at a station, well within view of the rebels, called
Sennabris.[d] From there he sent the decurion

Vespasian as
Agrippa's
guest at
Caesarea
Philippi.

Tiberias,
attempting
revolution,

---

[c] Scythopolis is some twenty miles south of Tiberias.
[d] Modern *Sinn en-Nabrah*, on the south-west side of the
Lake of Gennesareth, near Tarichaeae.

δεκαδάρχην Οὐαλεριανὸν σὺν ἱππεῦσιν πεντήκοντα διαλεχθησόμενον εἰρηνικὰ τοῖς κατὰ τὴν
πόλιν καὶ προτρεψόμενον ἐπὶ πίστεις· ἀκηκόει
γάρ, ὡς ἐπιθυμοίη μὲν εἰρήνης ὁ δῆμος, κατα-
στασιάζοιτο δ' ὑπὸ τινῶν πολεμεῖν βιαζομένων,
449 προσελάσας δ' Οὐαλεριανὸς ἐπεὶ πλησίον ἦν τοῦ
τείχους, αὐτός τε καταβαίνει καὶ τοὺς σὺν αὐτῷ
τῶν ἱππέων ἀπέβησεν, ὡς μὴ δοκοῖεν ἀκροβολι-
ζόμενοι παρεῖναι. καὶ πρὶν εἰς λόγους ἐλθεῖν
ἐπεκθέουσιν αὐτῷ τῶν στασιαστῶν οἱ δυνατώ-
450 τατοι μεθ' ὅπλων. ἐξηγεῖτο δ' αὐτῶν Ἰησοῦς τις
ὄνομα, παῖς Σαφάτου,[1] τοῦ λῃστρικοῦ στίφους ὁ
451 κορυφαιότατος. Οὐαλεριανὸς δὲ οὔτε παρὰ τὰς
ἐντολὰς τοῦ στρατηγοῦ συμβαλεῖν ἀσφαλὲς ἡγούμενος, εἰ καὶ τὸ νικᾶν εἴη βέβαιον, καὶ σφαλερὸν
τὸ μάχεσθαι πολλοῖς μετ' ὀλίγων ἀπαρασκευάστοις
452 τε πρὸς ἑτοίμους, καὶ ἄλλως ἐκπλαγεὶς τὴν
ἀδόκητον τῶν Ἰουδαίων τόλμαν, φεύγει πεζός,
ἕτεροί τε ὁμοίως πέντε τοὺς ἵππους ἀπέλιπον, οὓς
οἱ περὶ τὸν Ἰησοῦν ἀπήγαγον εἰς τὴν πόλιν γεγηθότες ὡς μάχῃ ληφθέντας, οὐκ ἐνέδρα.
453 (8) Τοῦτο καταδείσαντες οἱ γηραιοὶ τοῦ δήμου
καὶ προύχειν δοκοῦντες φεύγουσι μὲν εἰς τὸ τῶν
454 Ῥωμαίων στρατόπεδον, ἐπαγόμενοι δὲ τὸν βασιλέα
προσπίπτουσιν ἱκέται Οὐεσπασιανῷ, μὴ σφᾶς
περιιδεῖν δεόμενοι, μηδὲ τὴν ὀλίγων ἀπόνοιαν
455 ἡγήσασθαι τῆς πόλεως ὅλης, φείσασθαι δὲ τοῦ
δήμου Ῥωμαίοις φίλα φρονοῦντος ἀεί, καὶ τοὺς
αἰτίους τιμωρήσασθαι τῆς ἀποστάσεως, ὑφ' ὧν
αὐτοὶ φρουρηθῆναι μέχρι νῦν, ἐπὶ δεξιὰς ἐπ-

[1] MC (cf. ii. 599, Vita 66, 134, where he is called son of
Σαπφίας): most mss. have Τούφα.

Valerianus with fifty horsemen to make peaceful proposals to the townsfolk and to urge them to treat ; for he had heard that the people in general desired peace, but were overruled and being driven to hostilities by some seditious individuals. Valerianus advanced on horseback and, on approaching the wall, dismounted and directed his troop to do the same, to prevent any suspicion that they had come to skirmish. But before any parley had taken place, the principal promoters of the rising dashed out in arms to meet him, headed by a certain Jesus,[a] son of Saphat, the ringleader of this band of brigands. Valerianus thought it both imprudent to fight them in defiance of his general's orders, however certain of victory, and, moreover, dangerous with a small and unprepared force to face a large army equipped for battle. In short, he was taken aback by the unexpected daring of the Jews, and fled on foot, five of his companions likewise abandoning their horses. The troops of Jesus brought back these steeds in triumph to the town, as jubilant as if they had taken them in battle and not by a surprise attack.

(8) Dreading the consequences of this incident, is reduced to sub-mission, the elders and the more respected of the citizens fled to the Roman camp and, after obtaining the king's support, threw themselves as suppliants at Vespasian's feet, entreating him not to disregard them nor to impute to the whole city the madness of a few ; let him spare a people who had always shown themselves friendly to the Romans and punish the authors of the revolt, under whose power they themselves had been kept to this day, long as they

---

[a] Chief magistrate of Tiberias, *B.* ii. 599.

456 εἰγόμενοι πάλαι. ταύταις ἐνεδίδου ταῖς ἱκεσίαις ὁ
στρατηγός, καίτοι διὰ τὴν ἁρπαγὴν τῶν ἵππων
ἐφ' ὅλην ὠργισμένος τὴν πόλιν· καὶ γὰρ ἀγωνιῶντα
457 περὶ αὐτῆς τὸν Ἀγρίππαν ἑώρα. λαβόντων δὲ
τούτων τῷ δήμῳ¹ δεξιὰς οἱ περὶ τὸν Ἰησοῦν
οὐκέτ' ἀσφαλὲς ἡγούμενοι μένειν ἐπὶ τῆς Τιβε-
458 ριάδος εἰς Ταριχαίας ἀποδιδράσκουσιν. καὶ μεθ'
ἡμέραν Οὐεσπασιανὸς σὺν ἱππεῦσιν προπέμπει
πρὸς τὴν ἀκρώρειαν Τραϊανὸν ἀποπειραθῆναι τοῦ
459 πλήθους, εἰ πάντες εἰρηνικὰ φρονοῖεν. ὡς δ'
ἔγνω τὸν δῆμον ὁμοφρονοῦντα τοῖς ἱκέταις, ἀναλαβὼν τὴν δύναμιν ᾔει πρὸς τὴν πόλιν. οἱ δὲ τάς
τε πύλας ἀνοίγουσιν αὐτῷ καὶ μετ' εὐφημιῶν
ὑπήντων σωτῆρα καὶ εὐεργέτην ἀνακαλοῦντες.
460 τῆς δὲ στρατιᾶς τριβομένης περὶ τὴν τῶν εἰσόδων
στενότητα παραρρῆξαι τοῦ κατὰ μεσημβρίαν τείχους Οὐεσπασιανὸς κελεύσας πλατύνει τὴν εἰσβολὴν
461 αὐτοῖς. ἁρπαγῆς μέντοι καὶ ὕβρεως ἀπέχεσθαι παρ-
ήγγειλεν, τῷ βασιλεῖ χαριζόμενος, τῶν τε τειχῶν
διὰ τοῦτον ἐφείσατο, συμμενεῖν πρὸς τὸ λοιπὸν
ἐγγυωμένου τοὺς ἐν αὐτοῖς, καὶ πολλὰ κεκακωμέ-
νην τὴν πόλιν ἐκ τῆς στάσεως ἀνελάμβανεν.
462 (x. 1) Ἔπειτα προελθὼν αὐτῆς τε μεταξὺ καὶ
Ταριχαιῶν στρατοπεδεύεται, τειχίζει τε τὴν παρ-
εμβολὴν ὀχυρωτέραν, ὑφορώμενος ἐκεῖ πολέμου

¹ VR Lat.: τοῦ δήμου the rest.

ᵃ The meaning must surely be " to proceed along the
ridge " (shown in Smith and Bartholomew's Map of Galilee
on the west of the lake) *and to enter the town.*
ᵇ Ordinarily identified with the modern *Kerak* at the
south-west corner of the lake (*cf.* Pliny, *Hist. Nat.* v. 71 " a
132

had been anxious to sue for terms. The general,
though indignant at the whole city on account of
the capture of the horses, none the less yielded
to these entreaties, because he saw that Agrippa
was seriously concerned for the town. The delegates
thus secured terms on behalf of their fellow-citizens,
whereupon Jesus and his party, thinking themselves
no longer safe at Tiberias, fled to Tarichaeae. The
next day Vespasian sent forward Trajan to [a] the
ridge of the hill to discover whether the whole
multitude were peaceably disposed. Having assured
himself that the people were of one mind with
the petitioners, he then advanced with his army
to the city. The population opened their gates to
him and went out to meet him with acclamations,
hailing him as saviour and benefactor. As the troops
were incommoded by the narrowness of the entrances,
Vespasian ordered part of the south wall to be thrown
down and so opened a broad passage for his soldiers.
However, as a compliment to the king, he strictly
forbade any pillage or violence, and for the same
reason spared the walls, after receiving from Agrippa
a guarantee for the future fidelity of the inhabitants.
He thus brought new life to a city which had sorely
suffered from the effects of sedition.

and spared
for
Agrippa's
sake.

(x. 1) Vespasian, then continuing his march,
pitched his camp between Tiberias and Tarichaeae,[b]
fortifying it with more than ordinary care, in anticipa-

Vespasian
advances
upon
Tarichaeae,
the centre
of
revolution.

meridie Tarichea"). Reinach, however, with others, argues
from the word προελθών, and the previous line of march
from south to north, that Tarichaeae lay to the *north* of
Tiberias. The ordinary identification is supported by the
fact that Vespasian's camp was at Ammathus (" warm
baths,"*·B.* iv. 11), undoubtedly the modern *Hammam* south
of Tiberias.

463 τριβὴν αὐτῷ γενησομένην· συνέρρει γὰρ εἰς τὰς
Ταριχαίας πᾶν τὸ νεωτερίζον, τῇ τε τῆς πόλεως
ὀχυρότητι καὶ τῇ λίμνῃ πεποιθότες, ἣ καλεῖται
464 Γεννησὰρ πρὸς τῶν ἐπιχωρίων. ἡ μὲν γὰρ πόλις,
ὥσπερ ἡ Τιβεριὰς ὑπώρειος οὖσα, καθὰ μὴ τῇ
λίμνῃ προσεκλύζετο πάντοθεν ὑπὸ τοῦ Ἰωσήπου
τετείχιστο καρτερῶς, ἔλασσον μέντοι τῆς Τιβε-
465 ριάδος· τὸν μὲν γὰρ ἐκεῖ περίβολον ἐν ἀρχῇ τῆς
ἀποστάσεως δαψιλείᾳ χρημάτων καὶ δυνάμεως
ἐκρατύνατο, Ταριχαῖαι δ' αὐτοῦ τὰ λείψανα τῆς
466 φιλοτιμίας μετέλαβον. σκάφη δ' ἦν αὐτοῖς ἐπὶ
τῆς λίμνης παρεσκευασμένα πολλὰ πρός τε τὸ
συμφεύγειν ἐπὶ γῆς ἡττωμένους, κἂν εἰ δέοι δια-
467 ναυμαχεῖν ἐξηρτυμένα. περιβαλλομένων δὲ τῶν
Ῥωμαίων τὸ στρατόπεδον οἱ περὶ τὸν Ἰησοῦν
οὔτε πρὸς τὸ πλῆθος οὔτε πρὸς τὴν εὐταξίαν
468 τῶν πολεμίων ὑποδείσαντες προθέουσιν, καὶ πρὸς
τὴν πρώτην ἔφοδον τῶν τειχοποιῶν σκεδασθέντων
ὀλίγα τῆς δομήσεως σπαράξαντες, ὡς ἑώρων τοὺς
ὁπλίτας ἀθροιζομένους, πρίν τι παθεῖν εἰς τοὺς
σφετέρους ἀνέφευγον· ἐπιδιώξαντες δὲ Ῥωμαῖοι
469 συνελαύνουσιν αὐτοὺς εἰς τὰ σκάφη. καὶ οἱ μὲν
ἀναχθέντες εἰς ὅσον ἐξικνεῖσθαι τῶν Ῥωμαίων
βάλλοντες δύναιντο τάς τε ἀγκύρας ἔβαλλον καὶ
πυκνώσαντες ὥσπερ φάλαγγα τὰς ναῦς ἐπαλλήλους
470 τοῖς ἐπὶ γῆς πολεμίοις διεναυμάχουν. Οὐεσπασιανὸς δὲ τὸ πολὺ πλῆθος αὐτῶν ἠθροισμένον
ἀκούων ἐν τῷ πρὸ τῆς πόλεως πεδίῳ πέμπει τὸν
υἱὸν σὺν ἱππεῦσιν ἑξακοσίοις ἐπιλέκτοις.

---

[a] This flatly contradicts *Vita* 156, where it is said that the
people of Tiberias pressed Josephus to build walls for their
city " *having heard that Tarichaeae had already been fortified.*"

tion of prolonged hostilities. For the whole body of revolutionaries was flocking into Taricheae, relying upon the strength of the place and its proximity to the lake, which the native inhabitants call Gennesar. The city, built like Tiberias at the foot of the hills, had in fact been completely surrounded by Josephus, except on the side washed by the lake, with solid ramparts, though not so strong as those at Tiberias; for the fortifications there had been built by him at the outbreak of the revolt in the plenitude of his resources and his power, whereas Taricheae only obtained the leavings of his bounty.[a] The inhabitants, moreover, had ready on the lake a considerable fleet, to serve as a refuge if they were defeated on land, and equipped for naval combat, if required for that purpose. While the Romans were intrenching their camp, Jesus and his companions, undeterred by the strength and orderly discipline of the enemy, made a sally, and at the first onset dispersed the workmen and pulled down a portion of the structure. However, when they saw the legionaries mustering, they hastily fell back upon their own party, before sustaining any loss; the Romans pursued and drove them to their ships. Putting out into the lake just far enough to leave the Romans within bowshot, they then cast anchor and, closing up their vessels one against another like an army in line of battle, they kept up as it were a sea-fight with their enemy on shore. However, Vespasian, hearing that the main body of the Jews was assembled in the plain outside the town, sent thither his son with six hundred picked cavalry.

JOSEPHUS

471 (2) Ὁ δ᾽ ὑπέρογκον εὑρὼν τὴν τῶν πολεμίων
πληθὺν πρὸς μὲν τὸν πατέρα πέμπει, πλείονος
δυνάμεως αὐτῷ δεῖν λέγων, αὐτὸς δὲ τοὺς μὲν
πλείους τῶν ἱππέων ὡρμημένους ὁρῶν καὶ πρὶν
ἀφικέσθαι βοήθειαν, ἔστιν δ᾽ οὓς ἡσυχῇ πρὸς τὸ
πλῆθος τῶν Ἰουδαίων καταπεπληγότας, ἐν ἐπηκόῳ
472 στὰς [ἔλεξεν ὧδε]¹· " ἄνδρες," ἔφη, " Ῥωμαῖοι,
καλὸν γὰρ ἐν ἀρχῇ τῶν λόγων ὑπομνῆσαι τοῦ
γένους ὑμᾶς, ἵν᾽ εἰδῆτε, τίνες ὄντες² πρὸς τίνας
473 μάχεσθαι μέλλομεν. τὰς μέν γε ἡμετέρας χεῖρας
οὐδὲν εἰς τοῦτο τῶν ἐπὶ τῆς οἰκουμένης δια-
πέφευγεν, Ἰουδαῖοι δέ, ἵν᾽ εἴπωμεν καὶ ὑπὲρ αὐτῶν,
μέχρι νῦν οὐ κοπιῶσιν ἡττώμενοι. καὶ δεινόν,
ἐκείνων ἑστώτων ἐν ταῖς κακοπραγίαις, ἡμᾶς τοῖς
474 εὐτυχήμασιν ἐγκάμνειν. προθυμίας μὲν εἰς τὸ
φανερὸν ὑμᾶς εὖ ἔχοντας χαίρω βλέπων, δέδοικα
δὲ μή τινι τῶν πολεμίων τὸ πλῆθος κατάπληξιν
475 λεληθυῖαν ἐνεργάσηται. λογισάσθω δὴ πάλιν οἷος
πρὸς οἵους παρατάξεται, καὶ διότι Ἰουδαῖοι μέν,
εἰ καὶ σφόδρα τολμηταὶ καὶ θανάτου κατα-
φρονοῦντες, ἀλλ᾽ ἀσύντακτοί τε καὶ πολέμων
ἄπειροι καὶ ὄχλος ἂν ἄλλως, οὐ στρατιὰ λέγοιντο·
τὰ δὲ τῆς ἡμετέρας ἐμπειρίας καὶ τάξεως τί δεῖ
καὶ λέγειν; ἐπὶ τοῦτο μέντοι γε μόνοι καὶ κατ᾽
εἰρήνην ἀσκούμεθα τοῖς ὅπλοις, ἵν᾽ ἐν πολέμῳ
476 μὴ πρὸς τὸ ἀντίπαλον ἀριθμῶμεν ἑαυτούς. ἐπεὶ
τίς ὄνησις τῆς διηνεκοῦς στρατείας, ἂν ἴσοι πρὸς
477 ἀστρατεύτους ἀντιτασσώμεθα; λογίζεσθε δὲ ὅτι
καὶ πρὸς γυμνῆτας ὁπλῖται καὶ ἱππεῖς πρὸς πε-

¹ PA: om. the rest.   ² +καὶ mss.: om. Bekker.
136

(2) Titus, finding the enemy in prodigious strength, sent word to his father that he required more troops. For his own part, observing that, although most of his cavalry were burning for action without waiting for the arrival of the reinforcements, there were others who betrayed secret dismay at this immense number of Jews, he took up a position where he was audible to all and spoke as follows :

"Romans—it is well at the outset of my address to remind you of the name of your race, that you may bear in mind who you are and whom we have to fight. Our hands to this hour no nation in the habitable world has succeeded in escaping ; though the Jews, to give them their due, so far staunchly refuse to accept defeat. If they in their disasters still stand fast, would it not be disgraceful for our courage to flag in the full tide of success ? I rejoice to see in your faces such admirable ardour ; but I fear that the multitude of our enemies may have inspired some of you with a lurking alarm. Let such an one reflect once more who he is and against whom he is going into battle. Let him remember that the Jews, however dauntless and reckless of life they may be, are yet undisciplined and unskilled in war and deserve to be called a mere rabble, rather than an army. Of our experience and our discipline is there any need to speak ? If, alone of all nations, we exercise ourselves in arms in peace-time, it is for this very object, that in war-time we need not contrast our numbers with those of our opponents. What would be the use of this perpetual training, if we must be equal in numbers to an untrained foe before we face them ? Consider again that you will contend in full armour against men that have scarcely

Titus before Tarichaeae addresses his troops.

137

ζοὺς καὶ στρατηγούμενοι πρὸς ἀστρατηγήτους δι-
αγωνίζεσθε, καὶ ὡς ὑμᾶς μὲν ταῦτα πολλαπλασίους
ποιεῖ τὰ πλεονεκτήματα, πολὺ δὲ τοῦ τῶν πολε-
478 μίων ἀριθμοῦ παραιρεῖται τὰ ἐλαττώματα. κατ-
ορθοῖ δὲ τοὺς πολέμους οὐ πλῆθος ἀνθρώπων, κἂν
ᾖ μάχιμον,[1] ἀνδρεία δέ, κἂν ἐν ὀλίγοις· οἱ μέν γε[2]
καὶ τάξασθαι[3] ῥᾴδιοι καὶ προσαμύνειν ἑαυτοῖς, αἱ
δ᾽ ὑπέρογκοι δυνάμεις ὑφ᾽ ἑαυτῶν βλάπτονται
479 πλέον ἢ τῶν πολεμίων. Ἰουδαίων μὲν οὖν τόλμα
καὶ θράσος ἡγεῖται καὶ ἀπόνοια,[4] πάθη κατὰ μὲν
τὰς εὐπραγίας εὔτονα, σβεννύμενα δ᾽ ἐν ἐλαχίστοις
σφάλμασιν· ἡμῶν δ᾽ ἀρετὴ καὶ εὐπείθεια καὶ τὸ
γενναῖον, ὃ κἂν τοῖς [ἄλλοις][5] εὐτυχήμασιν ἀκμάζει
κἂν τοῖς πταίσμασιν μέχρι τέλους οὐ σφάλλεται.
480 καὶ ὑπὲρ μειζόνων δὲ ἢ Ἰουδαῖοι διαγωνιεῖσθε·
καὶ γὰρ εἰ περὶ ἐλευθερίας καὶ πατρίδων ἐκείνοις
ὁ πόλεμος κινδυνεύεται, τί μεῖζον ἡμῖν εὐδοξίας
καὶ τοῦ μὴ δοκεῖν μετὰ τὴν τῆς οἰκουμένης ἡγε-
481 μονίαν ἐν ἀντιπάλῳ τὰ Ἰουδαίων τίθεσθαι; σκε-
πτέον δ᾽ ὅτι καὶ παθεῖν μὲν οὐδὲν ἀνήκεστον ἡμῖν
φόβος· πολλοὶ γὰρ οἱ βοηθήσοντες καὶ πλησίον·
ἁρπάσαι δὲ τὴν νίκην δυνάμεθα, καὶ χρὴ τοὺς ὑπὸ
τοῦ πατρὸς πεμπομένους ἡμῖν συμμάχους φθάνειν,
ἵν᾽ ἀκοινώνητόν τε ᾖ τὸ κατόρθωμα καὶ μεῖζον.
482 νομίζω δ᾽ ἔγωγε ἐπὶ τῆσδε τῆς ὥρας καὶ τὸν
πατέρα τὸν ἐμὸν κρίνεσθαι κἀμὲ καὶ ὑμᾶς, εἰ τῶν
μὲν προκατωρθωμένων ἄξιος ἐκεῖνος, ἐγὼ δ᾽
ἐκείνου παῖς, στρατιῶται δ᾽ ὑμεῖς ἐμοῦ· καὶ γὰρ
ἐκείνῳ τὸ νικᾶν ἔθος, κἀγὼ πρὸς αὐτὸν ὑπο-

---

[1] ἀμήχανον Destinon, " however huge," but this sense is
unparalleled in Josephus.
[2] μὲν γὰρ ML.   [3] παρατάξασθαι MVRC.

any, that you are cavalry against infantry, that you have generals and they have none ; these advantages greatly multiply your effective strength, as the enemy's disadvantages greatly detract from his. Wars are not won by numbers, however efficient the soldiers, but by courage, however few the men : small forces are easily manœuvred and brought up to each other's support, whereas unwieldy armies do themselves more injury than they receive from the enemy. The Jews are led on by audacity, temerity and despair, emotions which are bracing in the flush of success but are damped by the slightest check ; we, by valour, discipline, and a heroism which, though doubtless seen to perfection when favoured by fortune, in adversity also holds on to the last. Again, you will contend for a higher cause than the Jews ; for, though they face war for liberty and country in jeopardy, what higher motive could there be for us than glory and the determination, after having dominated the world, not to let the Jews be regarded as a match for ourselves ? Nor should you forget that we have no irretrievable disaster to fear. Our supports are numerous and at hand ; yet we can snatch a victory, and we ought to anticipate the arrival of the reinforcements now on their way from my father. Our triumph will be more glorious if unshared. For myself, I believe that in this hour my father and I and you are all on our trial ; it will be seen whether he is really worthy of his past successes, whether I am worthy to be his son, and you to be my soldiers. Victory to him is habitual ; how

---

⁴ ἀπόνοια] + καὶ PA : ἀπονοίας (omitting preceding καὶ) the rest.   ⁵ om. LVR.

483 στρέφειν οὐκ ἂν ὑπομείναιμι λειφθείς. ὑμεῖς δὲ
πῶς οὐκ ἂν αἰσχύνοισθε προκινδυνεύοντος ἡγεμό-
νος ἡττώμενοι; προκινδυνεύσω γάρ, εὖ ἴστε, καὶ
484 πρῶτος εἰς τοὺς πολεμίους ἐμβαλῶ. μὴ λείπεσθε
δ᾿ ὑμεῖς ἐμοῦ πεπεισμένοι τὴν ἐμὴν ὁρμὴν παρα-
κροτεῖσθαι θεῷ συμμάχῳ, καὶ προγινώσκετε
σαφῶς, ὅτι τῆς ἔξω μάχης πλέον τι κατορθώ-
σομεν."

485 (3) Ταῦτα τοῦ Τίτου διεξιόντος προθυμία δαιμόνιος ἐμπίπτει τοῖς ἀνδράσιν, καὶ προσγενομένου
πρὶν συμβαλεῖν Τραϊανοῦ μετὰ τετρακοσίων ἱππέων ἤσχαλλον ὡς μειουμένης τῆς νίκης αὐτοῖς
486 διὰ τὴν κοινωνίαν. ἔπεμψεν δὲ Οὐεσπασιανὸς καὶ
᾿Αντώνιον Σίλωνα σὺν δισχιλίοις τοξόταις, κελεύσας καταλαβόντας τὸ ἀντικρὺ τῆς πόλεως ὄρος
487 τοὺς ἐπὶ τοῦ τείχους ἀνείργειν. καὶ οἱ μέν, ὡς
προσετέτακτο, τοὺς ταύτῃ πειρωμένους ἐκβοηθεῖν
περιέσχον, ὁ δὲ Τίτος πρῶτος τὸν ἵππον ἤλαυνεν
εἰς τοὺς πολεμίους καὶ σὺν κραυγῇ μετ᾿ αὐτὸν οἱ
λοιποὶ παρεκτείναντες ἑαυτοὺς εἰς ὅσον ἐπεῖχον
οἱ πολέμιοι τὸ πεδίον, παρὸ καὶ πολὺ πλείους
488 ἔδοξαν. οἱ δὲ ᾿Ιουδαῖοι, καίτοι τήν τε ὁρμὴν καὶ
τὴν εὐταξίαν αὐτῶν καταπλαγέντες, πρὸς ὀλίγον
μὲν ἀντέσχον ταῖς ἐμβολαῖς, νυσσόμενοι δὲ τοῖς
κοντοῖς καὶ τῷ ῥοίζῳ τῶν ἱππέων ἀνατρεπόμενοι
489 συνεπατοῦντο. πολλῶν δὲ πανταχοῦ φονευομένων
διασκίδνανται καὶ πρὸς τὴν πόλιν ὡς ἕκαστος
490 εἶχεν τάχους ἔφευγον. Τίτος δὲ τοὺς μὲν κατόπιν
προσκείμενος ἀνῄρει, τῶν δὲ διεκπαίων ἀθρόων,
οὓς δὲ φθάνων κατὰ στόμα διήλαυνεν, πολλοὺς

---

could I dare return to him if defeated [a] ? And you, surely you would be ashamed to be surpassed when your chief leads the way to danger. For lead I will, be sure of it, and will charge the enemy at your head. Do you then not fail me, have confidence that God is on my side and supports my ardour, and be assured that, beyond mere victory in this battle outside the walls, we shall achieve some further success."

(3) As Titus thus harangued them a supernatural frenzy took possession of his men, and when, before the engagement, Trajan joined them with four hundred cavalry, they chafed as though these partners had come to detract from their own credit for the victory. Vespasian at the same time sent Antonius Silo with two thousand archers to occupy the hill opposite the town and beat off the enemy on the ramparts ; these troops, in accordance with their instructions, prevented any attempts from that quarter to assist the Jewish army outside. Titus now led the charge, spurring his horse against the enemy ; behind him, with loud shouts, came his men, deploying across the plain so as to cover the whole of the enemy's front, thereby materially increasing their apparent strength. The Jews, though dismayed by the impetuosity and good order of this attack, for a while sustained the Roman charges ; but pierced by the lances and overthrown by the rush of cavalry they fell and were trampled under foot. When the plain on all sides was covered with corpses, they dispersed and fled to the city, as fast as each man's legs could carry him. Titus, hotly pursuing, now cut down the laggards in the rear, now made lanes through their bunched masses ; here rode ahead of them and charged them in front, there

Defeat of the Jewish army outside the town.

141

δὲ συνηλοία περὶ ἀλλήλοις πεσόντας ἐμπηδῶν,
491 πᾶσιν δὲ τὰς πρὸς τὸ τεῖχος φυγὰς ὑπετέμνετο
καὶ πρὸς τὸ πεδίον ἀπέστρεφεν, ἕως τῷ πλήθει
βιασάμενοι καὶ διεκπεσόντες¹ εἰς τὴν πόλιν συν-
έφευγον.

492 (4) Ἐκδέχεται δὲ αὐτοὺς πάλιν στάσις εἴσω
χαλεπή. τοῖς μὲν γὰρ ἐπιχωρίοις διά τε τὰς
κτήσεις καὶ τὴν πόλιν οὐκ ἐδόκει πολεμεῖν ἀπ᾽
493 ἀρχῆς, καὶ τότε διὰ τὴν ἧτταν πλέον· ὁ δ᾽ ἔπηλυς
πολὺς ὢν πλεῖον ἐβιάζετο, καὶ διωργισμένων ἐπ᾽
ἀλλήλοις κραυγή τε ἦν καὶ θόρυβος ὡς ὅσον οὔπω
494 φερομένων εἰς ὅπλα. κατακούσας δὲ τῆς ταραχῆς
Τίτος, οὐ γὰρ ἦν ἄπωθεν τοῦ τείχους, "οὗτος
ἦν ὁ καιρός," ἐκβοᾷ, καὶ " τί, συστρατιῶται,
μέλλομεν ἐκδιδόντος ἡμῖν Ἰουδαίους θεοῦ; δέ-
495 ξασθε τὴν νίκην. οὐκ ἀκούετε βοῆς; στασιά-
ζουσιν οἱ τὰς χεῖρας ἡμῶν διαφυγόντες.² ἔχομεν
τὴν πόλιν, ἐὰν ταχύνωμεν· δεῖ δὲ πόνου πρὸς
τῷ τάχει καὶ λήματος· οὐδὲν γὰρ τῶν μεγάλων
496 φιλεῖ δίχα κινδύνου κατορθοῦσθαι. φθάνειν δ᾽ οὐ
μόνον χρὴ τὴν τῶν πολεμίων ὁμόνοιαν, οὓς
ἀνάγκη διαλλάξει ταχέως, ἀλλὰ καὶ τὴν τῶν
ἡμετέρων βοήθειαν, ἵνα πρὸς τῷ νικῆσαι τοσοῦτον
πλῆθος ὀλίγοι καὶ τὴν πόλιν ἕλωμεν μόνοι."

¹ PA: διεκπαίσαντες L (improbable repetition of verb already used).
² διεκφυγόντες P (for text cf. § 473).

ᵃ Probably, as suggested by Reinach, the incident recorded in Suet. *Tit.* 4 took place on this occasion : " Taricheas et Gamalam (the latter was really taken by Vespasian, iv. 4 ff.) . . . in potestatem redegit, equo quadam acie sub feminibus amisso alteroque inscenso, cuius rector circa se dimicans occubuerat."

dashed into groups which had fallen foul of each other and trampled them to pieces. For all, in short, he sought to intercept retreat to the walls and to head them off into the plain, until at length, by superior numbers, they succeeded in forcing a way through and flinging themselves into the town.[a]

(4) But there a new and terrible contention awaited them. The indigenous population, intent on their property and their city, had from the first disapproved of the war, and after this defeat were now more opposed to it than ever. But the crowd from outside, a numerous body, were only the more determined to hold them to it. There were mutual angry recriminations, shouts and uproar; the two parties seemed on the point of coming to blows. From his position not far from the wall, Titus overheard this commotion. " Now is the time," he cried ; " why tarry, comrades, when God himself delivers the Jews into our hands ? Hail the victory that is given you. Do you not hear that clamour ? They are at strife with each other—those men who have just slipped through our hands. The town is ours if we are quick. But besides haste we need effort and resolution ; great successes never come without risks.[b] We must not wait till concord is re-established among our enemies : necessity will reconcile them all too soon. But neither let us wait for assistance from our friends : after defeating such a multitude with our small force, let us have the further honour of taking the city unaided."

[b] A reminiscence of Soph. *Electra* 945 ὅρα πόνου τοι χωρὶς οὐδὲν εὐτυχεῖ, similarly paraphrased elsewhere (*B.* v. 501 δίχα πόνου κατορθοῦν τι τῶν μεγάλων οὐδενὶ ῥᾴδιον, *cf. A.* iii. 58 τῷ πονεῖν . . πάντα ληπτά). We have already had other phrases drawn from the same context (*B.* iii. 153, 212).

497　(5) Ταῦθ' ἅμα λέγων ἐπὶ τὸν ἵππον ἀναπηδᾷ
καὶ καθηγεῖται πρὸς τὴν λίμνην, δι' ἧς ἐλάσας
πρῶτος εἰς τὴν πόλιν εἰσέρχεται καὶ μετ' αὐτὸν
498 οἱ λοιποί. δέος δὲ πρὸς τὴν τόλμαν αὐτοῦ τοῖς
ἐπὶ τῶν τειχῶν ἐνέπεσεν, καὶ μάχεσθαι μὲν ἢ
διακωλύειν οὐδεὶς ὑπέμεινεν, λιπόντες δὲ τὴν
φρουρὰν οἱ μὲν περὶ τὸν Ἰησοῦν διὰ τῆς χώρας
499 ἔφευγον, οἱ δ' ἐπὶ τὴν λίμνην καταθέοντες ὑπ-
αντιάζουσιν τοῖς πολεμίοις περιέπιπτον· ἐκτείνοντο
δ' οἱ μὲν ἐπιβαίνοντες τῶν σκαφῶν, οἱ δὲ τοῖς
500 ἀναχθεῖσιν προσνεῖν[1] πειρώμενοι. πολὺς δὲ τῶν
κατὰ τὴν πόλιν ἦν φόνος, τῶν μὲν ἐπηλύδων ὅσοι
μὴ διαφυγεῖν ἔφθασαν ἀντιτασσομένων, ἀμαχητὶ
δὲ τῶν ἐπιχωρίων· κατὰ γὰρ ἐλπίδα δεξιᾶς καὶ
τὸ συνειδὸς τοῦ μὴ βεβουλεῦσθαι[2] πολεμεῖν μάχης
501 ἀπετρέποντο, μέχρι Τίτος τοὺς μὲν αἰτίους ἀνελών,
οἰκτείρας δὲ τοὺς ἐπιχωρίους ἀνεπαύσατο φόνου.[3]
502 καὶ οἱ μὲν εἰς τὴν λίμνην καταφυγόντες ἐπεὶ τὴν
πόλιν εἶδον ἑαλωκυῖαν, ὡς πορρωτάτω τῶν πολεμίων ἀνήχθησαν.

503　(6) Τίτος δ' ἐκπέμψας τινὰ τῶν ἱππέων εὐ-
504 αγγελίζεται τῷ πατρὶ τὸ ἔργον. ὁ δ', ὡς εἰκός,
ὑπερησθεὶς τῇ τε τοῦ παιδὸς ἀρετῇ καὶ τῷ κατορθώματι, μεγίστη γὰρ ἐδόκει καθῃρῆσθαι μοῖρα
τοῦ πολέμου, τότε μὲν ἐλθὼν περισχόντας τὴν
πόλιν φρουρεῖν ἐκέλευσεν, ὡς μὴ διαλάθοι τις ἐξ
505 αὐτῆς, καὶ κτείνειν προσέταξεν[4]**, τῇ δ' ὑστεραίᾳ

---

[1] Destinon from Lat. natando assequi: προσμένειν L: προσπίπτειν most MSS.
[2] βεβουλῆσθαι R　　[3] Hudson from Lat.: πόνου MSS.
[4] P: ἐκέλευσεν the rest; there is apparently a lacuna.

144

(5) As he spoke he leapt on his horse, led his troops to the lake, rode through the water ^a and was the first to enter the town, followed by his men. Terror-struck at his audacity, none of the defenders on the ramparts ventured to fight or to resist him ; all abandoned their posts and fled, the partisans of Jesus across country, the others down to the lake. The latter ran into the arms of the enemy advancing to meet them ; some were killed while boarding their boats, others endeavouring to swim out to their companions, who had previously gained the open water.^b In the town itself there was great slaughter, without discrimination between the strangers who had not succeeded in escaping and now made some resistance, and the residents who offered none, their hope of pardon and their consciousness of having discountenanced the war leading them to lay down their arms. At length, Titus, after the real culprits had been slain, took pity on the natives of the place and stopped the massacre. Those who had taken refuge on the lake, seeing the city taken, sailed off and kept as far as possible out of range of the enemy.

(6) Titus dispatched a trooper to convey the gratifying news of this achievement to his father. Vespasian, as was to be expected, was highly delighted at his son's valour and at the success of his enterprise, which seemed like the termination of a serious portion of the war. Repairing instantly to the spot he gave orders to keep a strict guard round the city, to prevent any from escaping, and to kill ⟨any who attempted to do so⟩. The next day he

Vespasian
prepares
rafts to
pursue the
fugitives.

---

^a The town was unwalled on the side facing the lake (§ 464).
^b § 469.

πρὸς τὴν λίμνην καταβὰς σχεδίας ἐκέλευσεν
πήσσειν[1] ἐπὶ τοὺς καταπεφευγότας· αἱ δ' ἐγίνοντο
ταχέως ἀφθονίᾳ τε ὕλης καὶ πλήθει τεχνιτῶν.

506 (7) Ἡ δὲ λίμνη Γεννησὰρ μὲν ἀπὸ τῆς προσ-
εχοῦς χώρας καλεῖται, σταδίων δ' εὖρος οὖσα
τεσσαράκοντα καὶ πρὸς τούτοις ἑτέρων ἑκατὸν
τὸ μῆκος, γλυκεῖά τε ὅμως ἐστὶ καὶ ποτιμωτάτη·
507 καὶ γὰρ τῆς ἐλώδους παχύτητος ἔχει τὸ νᾶμα
λεπτότερον, καθαρά τ' ἐστὶν πάντοθεν αἰγιαλοῖς
ἐπιλήγουσα καὶ ψάμμῳ, πρὸς δὲ εὔκρατος ἀρύ-
σασθαι, ποταμοῦ μὲν ἢ κρήνης προσηνεστέρα,
ψυχροτέρα δὲ ἢ κατὰ λίμνης διάχυσιν ἀεὶ μένουσα.
508 τὸ μέν γε ὕδωρ οὐκ ἀπᾴδει χιόνος ἐξαιθριασθέν,
ὅπερ θέρους νυκτὸς ποιεῖν ἔθος τοῖς ἐπιχωρίοις,
γένη δ' ἰχθύων ἐν αὐτῇ διάφορα πρὸς τοὺς ἀλ-
509 λαχοῦ γεῦσίν τε καὶ ἰδέαν. μέση δ' ὑπὸ τοῦ
Ἰορδάνου τέμνεται. καὶ δοκεῖ μὲν Ἰορδάνου
πηγὴ τὸ Πάνειον, φέρεται δ' ὑπὸ γῆν εἰς τοῦτο
510 κρυπτῶς ἐκ τῆς καλουμένης Φιάλης· ἡ δ' ἐστὶν
ἀνιόντων εἰς τὴν Τραχωνῖτιν ἀπὸ σταδίων ἑκατὸν
εἴκοσι Καισαρείας, τῆς ὁδοῦ κατὰ τὸ δεξιὸν μέρος
511 οὐκ ἄπωθεν. ἐκ μὲν οὖν τῆς περιφερείας ἐτύμως[2]
Φιάλη καλεῖται τροχοειδὴς οὖσα λίμνη, μένει δ'

---

[1] + ὡς P.   [2] Hudson after Lat.: ἑτοίμως MSS.

---

[a] i.e. about 16 miles long by 4½ broad; the Greek *stade*,
rendered "furlong", = 606¾ English feet. The real measure-
ments on a modern map are about 12½ miles by 7 miles (at
its broadest part). Josephus possibly intends to give the
average breadth (the breadth at Tiberias is about 5 miles);
but the length is, anyhow, overstated, and there is no authority
for regarding (with Reinach) the words πρὸς τούτοις ἑτέρων
as interpolated, thus reducing it to 100 *stades* (=about 11½
miles).

descended to the lake and gave directions for the construction of rafts for the pursuit of the fugitives. With an abundance of wood and of workmen, the flotilla was soon ready.

(7) The lake of Gennesar takes its name from the adjacent territory. It is forty furlongs broad and a hundred and forty long.[a] Notwithstanding its extent, its water is sweet to the taste and excellent to drink : clearer than marsh water with its thick sediment, it is perfectly pure, the lake everywhere ending in pebbly or sandy beaches. Moreover, when drawn it has an agreeable temperature, more pleasant than that of river or spring water, yet invariably cooler than the great expanse of the lake would lead one to expect. It becomes as cold as snow when one has exposed it to the air, as the people of the country are in the habit of doing during the summer nights. The lake contains species of fish different, both in taste and appearance, from those found elsewhere. The Jordan runs through the middle of the lake. This river has its apparent source at Panion[b]; in reality it rises in the pool called Phiale from which it passes by an unseen subterranean channel to Panion. Phiale will be found at a distance of a hundred and twenty furlongs from Caesarea (Philippi), on the right of and not far from the road ascending to Trachonitis ; the pool derives its name Phiale[c] from its circular form ;

Marginal notes: Description of the lake of Gennesareth. The Jordan and its source

---

[b] " Pan's grotto " (cf. B. i. 404 ff.), in the neighbourhood of which Philip the Tetrarch built Paneas (Caesarea Philippi, *Banias*), B. ii. 168.

[c] Meaning " saucer." The pool is probably the modern *Birket Ram*, some four miles south-east of Caesarea Philippi; but the possibility of any connexion between this pool and Panion is denied by modern geographers (Reinach).

ἐπὶ χείλους αὐτῆς ἀεὶ τὸ ὕδωρ μήθ' ὑπονοστοῦν
512 μήθ' ὑπερχεόμενον. ἀγνοούμενος δὲ τέως ὁ Ἰορδάνης ἐντεῦθεν ἄρχεσθαι διὰ τοῦ τετραρχήσαντος
513 Τραχωνιτῶν ἠλέγχθη Φιλίππου· βαλὼν γὰρ οὗτος
εἰς τὴν Φιάλην ἄχυρα κατὰ τὸ Πάνειον, ἔνθεν
ἐδόκουν οἱ παλαιοὶ γεννᾶσθαι τὸν ποταμόν, εὗρεν
514 ἀνενεχθέντα. τοῦ μὲν οὖν Πανείου τὸ φυσικὸν
κάλλος ὑπὸ τῆς βασιλικῆς προσεξήσκηται πολυ-
τελείας, τῷ[1] Ἀγρίππα πλούτῳ κεκοσμημένον·
515 ἀρχόμενος δὲ φανεροῦ ῥεύματος ὁ Ἰορδάνης ἀπὸ
τοῦδε τοῦ ἄντρου κόπτει μὲν τὰ τῆς Σεμε-
χωνίτιδος λίμνης ἕλη καὶ τέλματα, διαμείψας δ'
ἑτέρους ἑκατὸν εἴκοσι σταδίους μετὰ πόλιν Ἰουλιάδα διεκπαίει τὴν Γεννησὰρ μέσην, ἔπειτα πολλὴν ἀναμετρούμενος ἐρημίαν εἰς τὴν Ἀσφαλτῖτιν
ἔξεισι λίμνην.
516 (8) Παρατείνει δὲ τὴν Γεννησὰρ ὁμώνυμος
χώρα, θαυμαστὴ φύσιν τε καὶ κάλλος· οὔτε γὰρ
αὐτή τι φυτὸν ἀρνεῖται διὰ τὴν πιότητα, καὶ πᾶν
πεφυτεύκασιν οἱ νεμόμενοι, τοῦ δ' ἀέρος τὸ
517 εὔκρατον ἁρμόζει καὶ τοῖς διαφόροις. καρύαι μέν
γε, φυτῶν τὸ χειμεριώτατον, ἄπειροι τεθήλασιν,
ἔνθα φοίνικες, οἳ καύματι τρέφονται, συκαῖ δὲ
καὶ ἐλαῖαι πλησίον τούτων, αἷς μαλθακώτερος
518 ἀὴρ ἀποδέδεικται. φιλοτιμίαν ἄν τις εἴποι τῆς
φύσεως βιασαμένης εἰς ἓν συναγαγεῖν τὰ μάχιμα,
καὶ τῶν ὡρῶν ἀγαθὴν ἔριν, ἑκάστης ὥσπερ ἀντι-

---

[1] Bekker: τὸν (or τῶν) mss. with subsequent πλοῦτον in most.

---

[a] Modern *Baheiret el Huleh* (perhaps the "waters of Merom" of Josh. xi. 5).

the water always fills the basin to the brim without ever subsiding or overflowing. It was for long unknown that this was the true source of the Jordan, but the fact was proved by Philip, tetrarch of Trachonitis : he had chaff thrown into the pool of Phiale and found it cast up at Panion, where the ancients believed that the stream had its origin. The natural beauties of Panion have been enhanced by royal munificence, the place having been embellished by Agrippa at great expense. After issuing from this grotto the Jordan, whose course is now visible, intersects the marshes and lagoons of Lake Semechonitis,[a] then traverses another hundred and twenty furlongs, and below the town of Julias [b] cuts across the Lake of Gennesar, from which, after meandering through a long desert region, it ends by falling into the Lake Asphaltitis.[c]

(8) Skirting the lake of Gennesar, and also bearing that name, lies a region whose natural properties and beauty are very remarkable.[d] There is not a plant which its fertile soil refuses to produce, and its cultivators in fact grow every species ; the air is so well-tempered that it suits the most opposite varieties. The walnut, a tree which delights in the most wintry climate, here grows luxuriantly, beside palm-trees, which thrive on heat, and figs and olives, which require a milder atmosphere. One might say that nature had taken pride in thus assembling, by a *tour de force*, the most discordant species in a single spot, and that, by a happy rivalry, each of the seasons wished to claim this region for her own.

The fertile district of Gennesareth.

[b] B. ii. 168. [c] The Dead Sea.
[d] The plain of Gennesaret (*el Ghuweir*) on the north-west of the lake between Capernaum and Magdala.

ποιουμένης τοῦ χωρίου· καὶ γὰρ οὐ μόνον τρέφει
παρὰ δόξαν τὰς διαφόρους ὀπώρας, ἀλλὰ καὶ
519 διαφυλάσσει. τὰ μέν γε βασιλικώτατα, σταφυλήν
τε καὶ σῦκον, δέκα μησὶν ἀδιαλείπτως χορηγεῖ,
τοὺς δὲ λοιποὺς καρποὺς δι' ἔτους ὅλου περιγηρά-
σκοντας ἑαυτοῖς[1]· πρὸς γὰρ τῇ τῶν ἀέρων εὐκρασίᾳ
καὶ πηγῇ διάρδεται γονιμωτάτῃ, Καφαρναοὺμ
520 αὐτὴν οἱ ἐπιχώριοι καλοῦσιν. ταύτην φλέβα τοῦ
Νείλου τινὲς ἔδοξαν, ἐπεὶ γεννᾷ τῷ κατὰ τὴν
521 Ἀλεξανδρέων λίμνην κορακίνῳ παραπλήσιον. μῆκος δὲ τοῦ χωρίου παρατείνει κατὰ τὸν αἰγιαλὸν
τῆς ὁμωνύμου λίμνης ἐπὶ σταδίους τριάκοντα
καὶ εὖρος εἴκοσι. ταῦτα μὲν [οὖν] οὕτως φύσεως
ἔχει.
522 (9) Οὐεσπασιανὸς δ', ἐπεὶ παρεσκευάσθησαν αἱ
σχεδίαι, τῆς δυνάμεως ἐπιβήσας ὅσον ᾤετο τοῖς
κατὰ τὴν λίμνην ἀνταρκέσειν ἐπανήγετο. τοῖς
δὲ συνελαυνομένοις οὔτ' ἐπὶ γῆν διαφεύγειν ἦν
ἐκπεπολεμωμένων πάντων οὔτ' ἐξ ἴσου δια-
523 ναυμαχεῖν· τά τε γὰρ σκάφη μικρὰ ὄντα καὶ
ληστρικὰ πρὸς τὰς σχεδίας ἦν ἀσθενῆ, καὶ καθ'
ἕκαστον ἐμπλέοντες ὀλίγοι πρὸς ἀθρόους ἐφ-
εστῶτας τοὺς Ῥωμαίους ἐγγίζειν ἐδεδοίκεισαν.
524 ὅμως δ' οὖν ἐκπεριπλέοντες τὰς σχεδίας, ἔστιν δ'
ὅπου καὶ πλησιάζοντες, πόρρωθεν τοὺς Ῥωμαίους
ἔβαλλον λίθοις καὶ παραξύοντες ἐγγύθεν ἔπαιον.

---

[1] L: om. Lat.: αὐτοῖς the rest: text doubtful.

For not only has the country this surprising merit of producing such diverse fruits, but it also preserves them : for ten months without intermission it supplies those kings of fruits, the grape and the fig ; the rest mature on the trees the whole year round. Besides being favoured by its genial air, the country is watered by a highly fertilizing spring, called by the inhabitants Capharnaum [a] ; some have imagined this to be a branch of the Nile, from its producing a fish resembling the *coracin* found in the lake of Alexandria.[b] This region extends along the border of the lake which bears its name for a length of thirty furlongs and inland to a depth of twenty. Such is the nature of this district.

(9) Vespasian, when his rafts were ready, put on board as many troops as he considered necessary to cope with the fugitives on the lake and launched his flotilla. The Jews, thus rounded up, could neither escape to land, where all were in arms against them, nor sustain a naval combat on equal terms. For their skiffs, being small and built for piracy, were no match for the rafts, and each was manned by no more than a handful of men who were afraid to close with the dense ranks of their Roman assailants. However, they hovered round the rafts, occasionally even approaching them, now flinging stones from a distance at the Romans, now scraping alongside and attacking them at close

Naval battle on the lake : destruction of the Jewish fleet.

been identified either with *Khan Minyeh* (more probable) or with *Tell Hum*, farther north. The latter is a waterless site (G. A. Smith) ; above the former rises a copious spring which communicates by a canal with the plain.

[b] The Lake Mareotis. The *coracin*, so called from its raven-black colour, seems to have resembled an eel ; Martial, xiii. 85, calls it " princeps Niliaci macelli."

525 ἐκακοῦντο δ' αὐτοὶ πλέον κατ' ἀμφότερα· ταῖς τε
γὰρ χερμάσιν οὐδὲν δρῶντες ὅτι μὴ κτύπον ἐπάλληλον, εἰς γὰρ πεφραγμένους ἔβαλλον, ἐφικτοὶ
τοῖς Ῥωμαίων ἐγίνοντο βέλεσιν, καὶ πλησιάζειν
τολμῶντες πρὶν δρᾶσαί τι παθεῖν ἔφθανον καὶ
526 σὺν αὐτοῖς ἐβαπτίζοντο τοῖς σκάφεσιν. τῶν δὲ
διεκπαίειν πειρωμένων πολλοὺς μὲν ἐφικνούμενοι
κοντοῖς διέπειρον, οὓς δὲ ξιφήρεις ἐπιπηδῶντες
εἰς τὰ σκάφη, τινὰς δὲ συντρεχούσαις ταῖς σχε-
δίαις ἐναποληφθέντας μέσους εἷλον[1] ἅμα ταῖς
527 ἁλιάσιν. τῶν δὲ βαπτισθέντων τοὺς ἀνανεύοντας
[ἢ] βέλος ἔφθανεν ἢ σχεδία κατελάμβανεν, καὶ
προσβαίνειν ὑπ' ἀμηχανίας εἰς τοὺς ἐχθροὺς
πειρωμένων ἢ κεφαλὰς ἢ χεῖρας ἀπέκοπτον οἱ
528 Ῥωμαῖοι. πολλή τε ἦν αὐτῶν καὶ ποικίλη φθορὰ
πανταχοῦ, μέχρι τραπέντες εἰς γῆν ἐξεώσθησαν
οἱ λοιποὶ κεκυκλωμένων αὐτοῖς τῶν ἁλιάδων.
529 ἐκχεόμενοι[2] δὲ πολλοὶ μὲν ἐν αὐτῇ κατηκοντίζοντο
τῇ λίμνῃ, πολλοὺς δ' ἐκπηδήσαντας οἱ Ῥωμαῖοι
διέφθειραν ἐπὶ γῆς. ἦν δ' ἰδεῖν κεκραμένην μὲν
αἵματι, πεπληρωμένην δὲ νεκρῶν τὴν λίμνην
530 ἅπασαν· διεσώθη γὰρ οὐδείς. δεινὴ δὲ ταῖς ἑξῆς
ἡμέραις περιεῖχε τὴν χώραν ὀδμή τε καὶ ὄψις· οἱ
μὲν γὰρ αἰγιαλοὶ ναυαγίων ἅμα καὶ διοιδούντων
ἔγεμον σωμάτων, ἐκκαιόμενοι δὲ καὶ μυδῶντες οἱ
νεκροὶ τὸν ἀέρα διέφθειρον, ὡς μὴ μόνον οἰκτρὸν
Ἰουδαίοις γενέσθαι τὸ πάθος, ἀλλὰ καὶ διὰ μίσους
531 τοῖς δράσασιν ἐλθεῖν. τοῦτο μὲν ἐκείνης τῆς
ναυμαχίας τὸ τέλος, ἀπέθανον δὲ σὺν τοῖς ἐπὶ

---

[1] MVRC Lat.: ἦλθον PA: (συν)ηλόων Destinon.
[2] PAL Lat. (cf. B. vii. 69, 101): ἐκκλειόμενοι the rest.

range. But in both these manœuvres they sustained
greater injury themselves : their stones produced
nothing but a continuous rattle in striking men well
protected by armour, while they were themselves
exposed to the arrows of the Romans ; on the other
hand, when they ventured to approach, before they
had time to do anything they instantly came to
grief and were sent to the bottom with their skiffs.
If they tried to break through the line, the Romans
could reach them with their lances and transfixed
numbers of them, or leaping upon the barks passed
their swords through their bodies ; sometimes the
rafts closed in and caught their enemies between
them, capturing men and vessels. When any who
had been sunk rose to the surface, an arrow quickly
reached or a raft overtook them ; if in their despair
they sought to board the enemy's fleet, the Romans
cut off their heads or their hands. Thus perished
these wretches on all sides in countless numbers and
countless manners, until the survivors were routed
and forced to the shore, their vessels surrounded by
the enemy. As they streamed forth from them
many were speared in the water ; many sprang on
land, where they were slain by the Romans. One
could see the whole lake red with blood and covered
with corpses, for not a man escaped. During the
following days the district reeked with a dreadful
stench and presented a spectacle equally horrible.
The beaches were strewn with wrecks and swollen
carcases : these corpses, scorched and clammy in
decay, so polluted the atmosphere that the catastrophe
which plunged the Jews in mourning inspired even
its authors with disgust. Such was the issue of this
naval engagement. The dead, including those who

τῆς πόλεως πρότερον πεσοῦσιν ἑξακισχίλιοι ἑπτα-
κόσιοι.[1]

532 (10) Οὐεσπασιανὸς δὲ μετὰ τὴν μάχην καθίζει
μὲν ἐπὶ βήματος ἐν Ταριχαίαις, διακρίνων δ' ἀπὸ
τῶν ἐπιχωρίων τὸν ἔπηλυν λεών, κατάρξαι γὰρ
οὗτος ἐδόκει πολέμου, μετὰ τῶν ἡγεμόνων εἰ χρὴ
533 καὶ τούτους σώζειν ἐσκέπτετο. φαμένων δὲ τούτων βλαβερὰν ἔσεσθαι τὴν ἄφεσιν αὐτῶν, οὐ γὰρ
ἠρεμήσειν ἀπολυθέντας ἀνθρώπους ἐστερημένους
μὲν τῶν πατρίδων, βιάζεσθαι δὲ καὶ πρὸς οὓς
534 ἂν καταφύγωσιν πολεμεῖν δυναμένους, Οὐεσπασιανὸς ὡς μὲν οὔτ' ἄξιοι σωτηρίας εἶεν καὶ[2]
διαφεύξονται κατὰ τῶν ἀφέντων[3] ἐγίνωσκεν, τὸν
535 δὲ τρόπον αὐτῶν τῆς ἀναιρέσεως διενοεῖτο. καὶ
γὰρ αὐτόθι κτείνων ἐκπολεμώσειν ὑφεωρᾶτο τοὺς
ἐπιχωρίους, οὐ γὰρ ἀνέξεσθαι φονευομένων ἱκετῶν
τοσούτων παρ' αὐτοῖς, καὶ μετὰ πίστεις ἐπιθέσθαι
536 προελθοῦσιν οὐχ ὑπέμενεν. ἐξενίκων δ' οἱ φίλοι
μηδὲν εἶναι κατὰ 'Ιουδαίων ἀσεβὲς λέγοντες καὶ
χρῆναι τὸ συμφέρον αἱρεῖσθαι πρὸ τοῦ πρέποντος,
537 ὅταν ᾖ μὴ δυνατὸν ἄμφω. κατανεύσας οὖν αὐτοῖς
ἄδειαν ἀμφίβολον ἐπέτρεψεν ἐξιέναι διὰ μόνης
538 τῆς ἐπὶ Τιβεριάδα φερούσης ὁδοῦ. τῶν δὲ ταχέως
πιστευσάντων οἷς ἤθελον καὶ μετὰ φανερῶν ⟨ὡς⟩[4]
ἐν ἀσφαλεῖ τῶν χρημάτων ᾗπερ ἐπετράπη χω-

---

[1] PA Heg.: πεντακόσιοι the rest.
[2] R: κἂν or καὶ εἰ the rest.
[3] + ὁπλίζευθαι M.   [4] ins. Destinon, Niese.

---

[a] This naval engagement was, it seems, commemorated
in the triumphal procession at Rome by the " numerous
ships " which accompanied it (B. vii. 147). Reinach refers

fell in the previous defence of the town, numbered
six thousand seven hundred.[a]

(10) After the battle Vespasian took his seat on
his tribunal at Tarichaeae, and separating the native
population from the crowd of immigrants who had
evidently given the signal for hostilities, consulted
with his lieutenants whether the lives of the latter
also should be spared. All unanimously declared
that their liberation would be pernicious ; once let
loose, these expatriated men would never keep quiet,
and would, moreover, be capable of forcing into
revolt those with whom they sought refuge.
Vespasian recognized that they were undeserving
of pardon and that they would only abuse their
liberty to the detriment of their liberators, but he
asked himself how he could make away with them :
if he killed them on the spot, he suspected that he
would bitterly alienate the residents, who would
not tolerate the massacre in their city of all these
refugees who had sued for mercy ; on the other
hand, he could not bring himself to let them go,
and then, after pledging his word, to fall upon them.
However, in the end his friends overcame his scruples
by telling him that against Jews there could be no
question of impiety, and that he ought to prefer
expediency to propriety when the two were in-
compatible. Vespasian accordingly granted these
aliens an amnesty in equivocal terms, but permitted
them to quit the city by only one route, that leading
to Tiberias. Prompt to believe what they earnestly
desired, the wretches set out in complete confidence,
carrying their effects without any disguise, in the

Fate of the
rebels
congregated
at
Tarichaeae.

to bronzes of Vespasian and his sons bearing the legend
VICTORIA NAVALIS.

ρούντων, διαλαμβάνουσιν μὲν οἱ ῾Ρωμαῖοι τὴν
μέχρι Τιβεριάδος πᾶσαν, ὡς μή τις ἀποκλίνειεν,
539 συγκλείουσι δ᾽ αὐτοὺς εἰς τὴν πόλιν. καὶ Οὐεσπασιανὸς ἐπελθὼν ἵστησι πάντας ἐν τῷ σταδίῳ,
καὶ γηραιοὺς μὲν ἅμα τοῖς ἀχρήστοις διακοσίους
540 ἐπὶ χιλίοις ὄντας ἀνελεῖν ἐκέλευσεν, τῶν δὲ νέων
ἐπιλέξας τοὺς ἰσχυροτάτους ἑξακισχιλίους ἔπεμψεν εἰς τὸν ἰσθμὸν Νέρωνι, καὶ τὸ λοιπὸν πλῆθος
εἰς τρισμυρίους καὶ τετρακοσίους ὄντας πιπράσκει
541 χωρὶς τῶν ᾽Αγρίππᾳ χαρισθέντων· τοὺς γὰρ ἐκ
τῆς τούτου βασιλείας ἐπέτρεψεν αὐτῷ ποιεῖν εἴ
τι¹ βούλοιτο· πιπράσκει δὲ καὶ τούτους ὁ βασιλεύς.
542 ὁ μέντοι γε ἄλλος ὄχλος Τραχωνῖται καὶ Γαυ-
λανῖται καὶ ῾Ιππηνοὶ καὶ ἐκ τῆς Γαδαρίτιδος τὸ
πλέον ὡς² στασιασταὶ καὶ φυγάδες καὶ οἷς τὰ
τῆς εἰρήνης³ ὀνείδη τὸν πόλεμον προυξένει. ἑάλωσαν [δὲ] Γορπιαίου μηνὸς ὀγδόῃ.

¹ εἴ τι] ὅ τι VRC.
² ἦσαν Havercamp with one ms.
³ τῆς εἰρήνης] ἐν εἰρήνῃ PAML.

ᵃ i.e. of Corinth, to be employed on the work of the canal,

prescribed direction. The Romans, meanwhile, lined the whole road to Tiberias, to prevent any deviation from it, and on their arrival shut them into that town. Vespasian followed in due course and had them all removed to the stadium. He then gave orders for the execution of the old and unserviceable, to the number of twelve hundred ; from the youths he selected six thousand of the most robust and sent them to Nero at the isthmus.[a] The rest of the multitude, numbering thirty thousand four hundred, he sold, excepting those of whom he made a present to Agrippa, namely the former subjects of his realm ; these Vespasian permitted him to deal with at his discretion, and the king in his turn sold them. The remainder of this mob consisted, for the most part, of people from Trachonitis, Gaulanitis, Hippos, and Gadara, a crowd of seditious individuals and fugitives, to whom their infamous careers in peace-time gave war its attractions. Their capture took place on the eighth of the month Gorpiaeus.[b]

for which Nero himself had recently dug the first sod (Suet. *Nero*, 19).

[b] 26 September A.D. 67 (Niese's reckoning).

ΒΙΒΛΙΟΝ Δ'

1 (i. 1) Ὅσοι δὲ μετὰ τὴν Ἰωταπάτων ἅλωσιν
Γαλιλαῖοι Ῥωμαίων ἀφεστήκεσαν, οὗτοι τῶν ἐν
Ταριχαίαις ἡττηθέντων προσεχώρουν, καὶ παρ-
έλαβον πάντα Ῥωμαῖοι τὰ φρούρια καὶ τὰς πόλεις
πλὴν Γισχάλων καὶ τῶν τὸ Ἰταβύριον ὄρος
2 κατειληφότων. συνέστη δὲ τούτοις καὶ Γάμαλα
πόλις Ταριχαιῶν ἄντικρυς ὑπὲρ τὴν λίμνην κειμένη.
τῆς δ' Ἀγρίππα λήξεως αὕτη τε ἦν καὶ Σωγάνη
καὶ Σελεύκεια, καὶ αἱ μὲν ἐκ τῆς Γαυλανίτιδος
ἀμφότεραι· τοῦ γὰρ ἄνω καλουμένου Γαυλανᾶ
μέρος ἦν ἡ Σωγάνη, τοῦ κάτω δ' ἡ Γάμαλα·
3 Σελεύκεια δὲ πρὸς τῇ Σεμεχωνιτῶν λίμνῃ. ταύτῃ
τριάκοντα μὲν εὖρος, ἑξήκοντα δὲ μῆκος στάδιοι·

ᵃ Usually identified with *Kul'at el Hoṣn*, close to the E.
side of the lake, opposite Tiberias ; by others with *Dschamle*,
a day's journey E. of the lake, Schürer, *G.J.V.*³ i. 615 f.
At the opening of the war it kept its allegiance to Rome,
under the influence of Agrippa's officer Philip, *Vita* 46-61 ;
afterwards it joined the insurgents.

BOOK IV

(i. 1) Such Galilaeans as after the fall of Jotapata still remained in revolt from Rome now, on the reduction of Tarichaeae, surrendered ; and the Romans
received the submission of all the fortresses and
towns except Gischala and the force which had
occupied Mount Tabor.   Gamala *a* was also in league
with these rebels, a city situated on the other side
of the lake, opposite Tarichaeae.   Gamala formed
part of the territory allotted to Agrippa, like Sogane
and Seleucia *b* ;   Gamala and Sogane were both in
Gaulanitis, the latter belonging to what is known as
Upper, the former to Lower, Gaulan ;   Seleucia was
near the lake Semechonitis.*c*   That lake is thirty
furlongs in breadth and sixty in length ;   but its

*Most of
Galilee
surrenders :
places still
in revolt.*

b Sogane (in Gaulan, unidentified ;   distinct from S. in
Galilee) and Seleucia (*Selukiyeh*, N.E. of Bethsaida Julias)
are mentioned together in *Vita* 187, *B.* ii. 574, as places
fortified by Josephus.
   c *Baheiret el Huleh*, the little lake N. of Gennesaret ;   *B.*
iii. 515.   Its length as here given (60 " stades " = nearly
7 miles) must include part of the northern marshes ;   the
dimensions on the modern map are 4 miles by 3 (at its
broadest part).

159

διατείνει δ' αὐτῆς τὰ ἔλη μέχρι Δάφνης[1] χωρίου
τά τε ἄλλα τρυφεροῦ καὶ πηγὰς ἔχοντος, αἳ
τρέφουσαι τὸν μικρὸν καλούμενον Ἰόρδανον[2] ὑπὸ
τὸν τῆς χρυσῆς βοὸς νεὼν προπέμπουσι τῷ μεγάλῳ.
4 τοὺς μὲν οὖν ἐπὶ Σωγάνης καὶ Σελευκείας[3] ὑπὸ[4]
τὴν ἀρχὴν τῆς ἀποστάσεως δεξιαῖς Ἀγρίππας
προσηγάγετο, Γάμαλα δ' οὐ προσεχώρει πεποιθυῖα
5 τῇ δυσχωρίᾳ πλέον τῶν Ἰωταπάτων. τραχὺς
γὰρ αὐχὴν ἀφ' ὑψηλοῦ κατατείνων ὄρους μέσον
ἐπαίρει τένοντα, μηκύνεται δ' ἐκ τῆς ὑπεροχῆς
εἰς τοὔμπροσθεν ἐκκλίνων ὅσον κατόπιν, ὡς
εἰκάζεσθαι καμήλῳ τὸ σχῆμα, παρ' ἣν ὠνόμασται,
τὸ τρανὸν τῆς κλήσεως οὐκ ἐξακριβούντων τῶν
6 ἐπιχωρίων. κατὰ πλευρὰ[5] μὲν δὴ καὶ πρόσωπον
εἰς φάραγγας ἀβάτους περισχίζεται, τὸ κατ'
οὐρὰν δ' ὀλίγον ἀναφεύγει τὰς[6] δυσχωρίας, ὅθεν
ἀπήρτηται τοῦ ὄρους· καὶ τοῦτο δ' ἐπικαρσίᾳ
παρακόψαντες τάφρῳ δύσβατον οἱ ἐπιχώριοι κατ-
7 εσκεύασαν. πρὸς ὀρθίῳ δὲ τῇ λαγόνι δεδομη-
μέναι πεπύκνωντο δεινῶς ἐπ' ἀλλήλαις αἱ οἰκίαι,
κρημνιζομένη τε ἡ πόλις ἐοικυῖα κατέτρεχεν εἰς
8 ἑαυτὴν ἀπὸ τῆς ὀξύτητος. καὶ πρὸς μεσημβρίαν
μὲν ἔκλινεν, ὁ νότιος δ' αὐτῆς ὄχθος εἰς ἄπειρον
ὕψος ἀνατείνων ἄκρα τῆς πόλεως ἦν, ἀτείχιστος

---

[1] Δάφης Reland; cf. A. viii. 226.
[2] PA (as in A. vii. 210 +): Ἰορδάνην the rest.
[3] Niese: ἐπὶ Σωγάνην κ. Σελεύκειαν MSS.
[4] L: ἐπὶ PA: παρὰ the rest.
[5] A Lat.: πλευρὰν the rest.
[6] Niese: τῆς MSS.

---

[a] Probably *Khurbet Dufna*, a little S. of Dan (Laish), the
source of one tributary of the Jordan.

marshes extend as far as Daphne,[a] a delightful spot with springs which feed the so-called little Jordan, beneath the temple of the golden cow,[b] and speed it on its way to the greater river.[c]   Now Sogane and Seleucia had quite early in the revolt been induced by Agrippa to come to terms ; but Gamala refused to surrender, relying even more confidently than Jotapata upon the natural difficulties of its position. From a lofty mountain there descends a rugged spur rising in the middle to a hump, the declivity from the summit of which is of the same length before as behind, so that in form the ridge resembles a camel ; whence it derives its name, the natives pronouncing the sharp sound of that word inaccurately.[d]   Its sides and face are cleft all round by inaccessible ravines, but at the tail end, where it hangs on to the mountain, it is somewhat easier of approach ; but this quarter also the inhabitants, by cutting a trench across it, had rendered difficult of access.   The houses were built against the steep mountain flank and astonishingly huddled together, one on top of the other, and this perpendicular site gave the city the appearance of being suspended in air and falling headlong upon itself.   It faced south, and its southern eminence, rising to an immense height, formed the citadel ;

GAMALA, description of.

[b] One of the two golden calves erected by Jeroboam at Dan and Bethel respectively (1 Kings xii. 29, Jos. *A.* viii. 226).

[c] The eastern stream descending from Caesarea Philippi, *Banias.*

[d] *i.e.* they slurred the sharp (lit. "clear") K into Γ, calling it Gamala, not Kamala.   The remark is made purely from the *Greek* point of view ; " camel " both in Hebrew (*Gāmāl*) and in Aramaic (*Gamlā'*) has initial G.

161

[ὁ]¹ δὲ ὑπ᾽² αὐτῆς³ κρημνὸς εἰς τὴν βαθυτάτην
κατατείνων φάραγγα· πηγὴ δ᾽ ἐντὸς τοῦ τείχους,
ἐφ᾽ ἣν τὸ ἄστυ κατέληγεν.

9   (2) Οὕτως οὖσαν φύσει δυσμήχανον⁴ τὴν πόλιν
τειχίζων ὁ Ἰώσηπος ἐποίησεν ὀχυρωτέραν ὑπο-
10 νόμοις τε καὶ διώρυξιν. οἱ δ᾽ ἐν αὐτῇ φύσει μὲν
τοῦ χωρίου θαρραλεώτεροι τῶν κατὰ τὴν Ἰωταπάτην ἦσαν, πολὺ δ᾽ ἐλάττους μάχιμοι, καὶ τῷ
τόπῳ πεποιθότες οὐδὲ πλείονας ὑπελάμβανον·
πεπλήρωτο γὰρ ἡ πόλις διὰ τὴν ὀχυρότητα
συμφυγόντων· παρὸ καὶ τοῖς ὑπ᾽ Ἀγρίππα προ-
πεμφθεῖσιν ἐπὶ τὴν πολιορκίαν ἀντεῖχεν ἐπὶ
μῆνας ἑπτά.

11   (3) Οὐεσπασιανὸς δ᾽ ἄρας ἀπὸ τῆς Ἀμμαθοῦς,
ἔνθα πρὸ τῆς Τιβεριάδος ἐστρατοπεδεύκει· μεθ-
ερμηνευομένη δ᾽ Ἀμμαθοῦς θερμὰ λέγοιτ᾽ ἄν,
ἔστι γὰρ ἐν αὐτῇ πηγὴ θερμῶν ὑδάτων πρὸς
ἄκεσιν ἐπιτηδείων· ἀφικνεῖται πρὸς τὴν Γάμαλαν.
12 καὶ πᾶσαν μὲν κυκλώσασθαι φυλακῇ τὴν πόλιν
οὐχ οἷός τε ἦν οὕτως διακειμένην, πρὸς δὲ τοῖς
δυνατοῖς φρουροὺς καθίστησι καὶ τὸ ὑπερκείμενον
13 ὄρος καταλαμβάνεται. τειχισαμένων δὲ ὥσπερ
ἔθος τῶν ταγμάτων ὑπὲρ αὐτοῦ στρατόπεδα
χωμάτων ἤρχετο κατ᾽ οὐράν, καὶ τὸ μὲν κατ᾽
ἀνατολὰς αὐτῷ μέρος, ᾗπερ ὁ ἀνωτάτω τῆς
πόλεως πύργος ἦν, ἔχου⁵ τὸ πέμπτον καὶ δέκατον
τάγμα, τὸ πέμπτον δὲ ⟨τὰ⟩ κατὰ μέσην ἐξειργά-

¹ ins. PAL.
² Niese: ὑπὲρ mss., περὶ Destinon perhaps rightly (cf. § 74).
³ αὐτὴν L.
⁴ δύσμαχον C and perhaps Lat.
⁵ Destinon: ἐφ᾽ οὗ mss. The text of the next line is
uncertain: I follow Niese, who inserts the bracketed τὰ.

below this an unwalled precipice descended to the deepest of the ravines. There was a spring within the walls at the confines of the town.

(2) This city, which nature had rendered so impregnable, Josephus had fortified with walls [a] and secured still further by mines and trenches. Its occupants felt greater confidence in the nature of their site than did those of Jotapata, though far inferior to them in the number of combatants ; indeed such trust had they in their position that they would admit no more. For the city was packed with fugitives owing to the strength of its defences, which had enabled it to hold out for seven months against the force [b] previously sent by Agrippa to besiege it.

(3) Vespasian now broke up the camp which he had pitched in front of Tiberias at Ammathus [c] (this name may be interpreted as " warm baths," being derived from a spring of warm water within the city possessing curative properties) and proceeded to Gamala. Finding the complete investment of a city in such a situation impossible, he posted sentries wherever this was practicable and occupied the mountain that overhung it. The legions having, according to custom, fortified their camps on these heights, Vespasian commenced the erection of earthworks at the tail end ; those on the east of the ridge, over against the point where stood the highest tower in the town, were raised by the fifteenth legion, those opposite the centre of the city were undertaken by

Vespasian besieges Gamala.

[a] B. ii. 574.

[b] Under Aequus Modius, *Vita* 114.

[c] *Hammam*, between Tiberias (N.) and Tarichaeae (S.) ; cf. B. iii. 462, and for the warm baths *A.* xviii. 36.

ζετο τὴν πόλιν, τὰς δὲ διώρυγας ἀνεπλήρου καὶ
14 τὰς φάραγγας τὸ δέκατον. κἂν τούτῳ προσελθόντα
τοῖς τείχεσιν Ἀγρίππαν τὸν βασιλέα καὶ περὶ
παραδόσεως τοῖς ἐφεστῶσι πειρώμενον διαλέγεσθαι
βάλλει τις τῶν σφενδονητῶν κατὰ τὸν δεξιὸν
15 ἀγκῶνα λίθῳ. καὶ ὁ μὲν ὑπὸ τῶν οἰκείων θᾶττον
περιεσχέθη, Ῥωμαίους δ᾽ ἐπήγειρεν εἰς τὴν
πολιορκίαν ὀργή τε περὶ τοῦ βασιλέως καὶ περὶ
16 σφῶν αὐτῶν δέος· οὐ γὰρ ἀπολείψειν ὠμότητος
ὑπερβολὴν κατ᾽ ἀλλοφύλων καὶ πολεμίων τοὺς
πρὸς ὁμόφυλον καὶ τῶν συμφερόντων αὐτοῖς
σύμβουλον οὕτως ἀγριωθέντας.

17   (4) Συντελεσθέντων οὖν τῶν χωμάτων θᾶττον
πλήθει χειρῶν καὶ τῶν πραττομένων ἔθει προσῆγον
18 τὰς μηχανάς. οἱ δὲ περὶ τὸν Χάρητα καὶ Ἰώσηπον,[1] οὗτοι γὰρ ἦσαν τῶν κατὰ τὴν πόλιν
δυνατώτατοι, καίπερ καταπεπληγότας τοὺς ὁ-
πλίτας τάττουσιν, ἐπειδὴ μέχρι πολλοῦ πρὸς τὴν
πολιορκίαν ἀνθέξειν οὐχ ὑπελάμβανον, ὕδατι καὶ
19 τοῖς ἄλλοις ἐπιτηδείοις μὴ διαρκούμενοι. παρα-
κροτήσαντες δ᾽ ὅμως ἐξήγαγον ἐπὶ τὸ τεῖχος,
καὶ πρὸς ὀλίγον μὲν ἀπημύναντο τοὺς προσάγοντας
τὰς μηχανάς, βαλλόμενοι δὲ τοῖς καταπελτικοῖς
καὶ τοῖς πετροβόλοις ἀνεχώρουν εἰς τὴν πόλιν.
20 καὶ προσαγόντες[2] οἱ Ῥωμαῖοι τριχόθεν τοὺς
κριοὺς διασείουσι μὲν τὸ τεῖχος, ὑπὲρ δὲ τῶν
ἐρειφθέντων εἰσχεόμενοι μετὰ πολλοῦ σαλπίγγων
ἤχου καὶ κτύπου τῶν ὅπλων αὐτοί τ᾽ ἐπαλαλάζοντες
21 συνερρήγνυντο τοῖς κατὰ τὴν πόλιν. οἱ δὲ τέως
μὲν κατὰ τὰς πρώτας εἰσόδους ἐνιστάμενοι
προσωτέρω χωρεῖν ἐκώλυον καὶ καρτερῶς τοὺς

---

[1] Ἰώσην L[1]; cf. § 66.   [2] M : προσάγοντες the rest.

the fifth, while the tenth legion was employed in filling up the trenches [a] and ravines. During these operations King Agrippa, who had approached the ramparts and was endeavouring to parley with the defenders about capitulation, was struck on the right elbow with a stone by one of the slingers. He was at once surrounded by his troops, but the Romans were thus stimulated to press the siege alike by resentment on the king's behalf and by concern for themselves, convinced that men who could so savagely attack a fellow-countryman, while advising them for their welfare, would shrink from no excess of cruelty towards aliens and enemies.

Agrippa wounded.

(4) With such a multitude of hands accustomed to the task, the earthworks were rapidly completed and the engines brought into position. Chares and Joseph, the most prominent leaders in the town, drew up their troops, though the men were dispirited by the thought that they could not long withstand a siege owing to a deficiency of water and other necessaries. Their generals, however, encouraged them and led them out to the ramparts, where for a while they kept at bay those who were bringing up the engines, but the fire of the catapults and stone-projectors drove them back into the town. The Romans then applying the battering-rams at three different quarters broke through the wall, and pouring through the breach with loud trumpet-blasts, clash of arms, and the soldiers' battle-cries, engaged the defenders of the town. The latter, when the first Romans entered, for a time held their ground, arrested their further advance and stubbornly re-

Romans enter Gamala with disastrous results.

---

[a] Previously dug by Josephus, § 9.

22 Ῥωμαίους ἀνεῖργον· βιαζόμενοι δὲ ὑπὸ πολλῶν
καὶ πάντοθεν τρέπονται πρὸς τὰ ὑψηλὰ τῆς
πόλεως καὶ προσκειμένοις τοῖς πολεμίοις ἐξ
ὑποστροφῆς ἐπιπεσόντες συνώθουν εἰς τὸ κάταντες
καὶ τῇ στενότητι καὶ δυσχωρίᾳ θλιβομένους ἀν-
23 ήρουν. οἱ δὲ μήτε τοὺς κατὰ κορυφὴν ἀμύνασθαι
δυνάμενοι μήτε διεκπαίειν τῶν σφετέρων πρόσω
βιαζομένων ἐπὶ τὰς οἰκίας τῶν πολεμίων, πρός-
24 γειοι γὰρ ἦσαν, ἀνέφευγον. αἱ δὲ ταχέως κατηρεί-
ποντο πληρούμεναι καὶ τὸ βάρος μὴ στέγουσαι,
κατέσειε δὲ πολλὰς μία τῶν ὑπ' αὐτῆς[1] πεσοῦσα
25 καὶ πάλιν ἐκεῖναι τὰς ὑπ' αὐτάς. τοῦτο πλείστους
διέφθειρε τῶν Ῥωμαίων· ὑπὸ γὰρ ἀμηχανίας
καίτοι συνιζανούσας ὁρῶντες ἐπεπήδων ταῖς
στέγαις, καὶ πολλοὶ μὲν κατεχώννυντο τοῖς
ἐρειπίοις, πολλοὶ δ' ὑποφεύγοντες μέρη[2] τοῦ
σώματος κατελαμβάνοντο, πλείστους δ' ὁ κονιορτὸς
26 ἄγχων ἀνῄρει. συνεργίαν θεοῦ τοῦτο Γαμαλεῖς
ὑπελάμβανον καὶ τῆς κατὰ σφᾶς ἀμελοῦντες
βλάβης ἐπέκειντο, πρός τε τὰ τέγη τοὺς πολεμίους
ἀνωθοῦντες [καί τοι][3] κατολισθάνοντας ἐν ὀξέσι
τοῖς στενωποῖς καὶ ἀεὶ τοὺς πίπτοντας ὕπερθεν
27 βάλλοντες ἔκτεινον. καὶ τὰ μὲν ἐρείπια χερμάδων
πλέα ἦν[4] αὐτοῖς, σίδηρον δὲ παρεῖχον οἱ τῶν
πολεμίων νεκροί· παρασπῶντες γὰρ τὰ τῶν
πεσόντων ξίφη κατὰ τῶν δυσθανατώντων[5] ἐχρῶντο.
28 πολλοὶ δ' ἀπὸ πιπτόντων ἤδη τῶν δωμάτων σφᾶς

---

[1] V[2]: the other mss. have αὐτήν, αὐτοῖς, or αὐτῶν.
[2] μέρει Dindorf with one ms.
[3] Bracketed by Niese: the text is doubtful and the Lat.
suggests that some words have fallen out.
[4] πλέα ἦν] πλῆθος L Lat.
[5] δυσθανατούντων PA.

pulsed them ; then, overpowered by numbers pouring in on all sides, they fled to the upper parts of the town, where, rounding upon the pursuing enemy, they thrust them down the slopes and slew them while impeded by the narrowness and difficulties of the ground. The Romans, unable either to repel the enemy above them or to force their way back through their comrades pressing forward behind, took refuge on the roofs of the enemy's houses, which came close to the ground.[a] These, being crowded with soldiers and unequal to the weight, soon fell in ; one house in its fall brought down several others beneath it and these again carried away those lower down. This disaster was the ruin of multitudes of Romans ; for, having nowhere to turn, although they saw the houses subsiding, they continued to leap on to the roofs. Many were buried by the ruins, many in trying to escape from under them were pinned down by some portion of their persons, and still more died of suffocation from the dust. Seeing in this the interposition of divine providence, the men of Gamala pressed their attack regardless of their own casualties; they forced the enemy, stumbling in the steep alleys, up on to the roofs and with a continual fire from above slew any who fell. The debris supplied them with boulders in abundance and the enemy's dead with blades ; for they wrested the swords from the fallen and used them to dispatch any still struggling in death. Many flung themselves from the houses when in the act of collapsing and died from the fall.

[a] The "perpendicular" nature of the site (such as that of Clovelly or Rocca di Papa) has to be remembered, § 7; the roof at the end higher up the slope would be $\pi\rho\delta\sigma\gamma\epsilon\iota\sigma s$, while its other end would be well above the ground.

29 αὐτοὺς βάλλοντες ἔθνησκον. ἦν δ' οὐδὲ τραπέντων
ἡ φυγὴ ῥᾴδιος· κατὰ γὰρ ἄγνοιαν τῶν ὁδῶν καὶ
παχύτητα τοῦ κονιορτοῦ μηδὲ ἀλλήλους ἐπι-
γινώσκοντες ἀνειλοῦντο καὶ περὶ σφᾶς ἔπιπτον.

30 (5) Οἱ μὲν οὖν μόλις εὑρίσκοντες τὰς ἐξόδους
31 ἀνεχώρησαν ἐκ τῆς πόλεως· Οὐεσπασιανὸς δ'
ἀεὶ προσμένων τοῖς πονουμένοις, δεινὸν γάρ τι
πάθος αὐτὸν εἰσῄει κατερειπομένην ὁρῶντα περὶ
τῷ στρατῷ τὴν πόλιν, ἐν λήθῃ τοῦ καθ' αὑτὸν
ἀσφαλοῦς γενόμενος λανθάνει κατὰ μικρὸν ἀνωτάτω τῆς πόλεως προελθών, ἔνθα μέσοις ἐγκατα-
λείπεται τοῖς κινδύνοις μετ' ὀλίγων παντελῶς·
32 οὐδὲ γὰρ ὁ παῖς αὐτῷ Τίτος τότε συμπαρῆν,
τηνικαῦτα πρὸς Μουκιανὸν εἰς Συρίαν ἀπεσταλ-
33 μένος. τραπῆναι μὲν οὖν οὐκέτ'[1] ἀσφαλὲς οὔτε
πρέπον ἡγήσατο, μνησθεὶς δὲ τῶν ἀπὸ νεότητος
αὐτῷ πεπονημένων καὶ τῆς ἰδίας ἀρετῆς, ὥσπερ
ἔνθους γενόμενος, συνασπίζει μὲν τοὺς ἀμ' αὐτῷ
34 τά τε σώματα καὶ τὰς πανοπλίας, ἐνυφίσταται
δὲ κατὰ κορυφὴν ἐπιρρέοντα τὸν πόλεμον καὶ
οὔτε ἀνδρῶν πλῆθος οὔτε βελῶν ὑποπτήξας
ἐπέμενε, μέχρι δαιμόνιον τὸ παράστημα τῆς
ψυχῆς συννοήσαντες οἱ πολέμιοι ταῖς ὁρμαῖς
35 ἐνέδοσαν. ἀτονώτερον δὲ προσκειμένων αὐτὸς
ὑπὸ πόδα ἀνεχώρει, νῶτα μὴ δεικνὺς ἕως ἔξω
36 τοῦ τείχους ἐγένετο. πλεῖστοι μὲν οὖν Ῥωμαίων
κατὰ ταύτην ἔπεσον τὴν μάχην, ἐν οἷς ὁ δεκαδ-
άρχης Λιβούτιος, ἀνὴρ οὐ μόνον ἐφ' ἧς ἔπεσε
παρατάξεως, ἀλλὰ πανταχοῦ καὶ πρότερον γεν-
ναιότατος φανεὶς καὶ πλεῖστα κακὰ Ἰουδαίους

---

[1] PAL: οὔτε the rest.

Even those who fled found flight no easy matter; since through their ignorance of the roads and the dense clouds of dust they failed to recognize their comrades and in their bewilderment fell foul of each other.

(5) Thus, with difficulty discovering the outlets, these fugitives beat a retreat from the town. Meanwhile Vespasian, always keeping close to his distressed troops, being deeply affected by the sight of the city falling in ruins about his army, had, forgetful of his own safety, gradually and unconsciously advanced to the highest quarters of the town. Here he found himself left in the thick of danger with a mere handful of followers : even his son Titus was not with him on this occasion, having been just sent off to Syria to Mucianus.[a] Thinking it now neither safe nor honourable to turn, and mindful of the hardships which he had borne from his youth and his innate valour, he, like one inspired, linked his comrades together, with shields enveloping both body and armour, and stemmed the tide of war that streamed upon him from above ; and so, undaunted by the multitude either of men or missiles, he stood his ground, until the enemy, impressed by such supernatural intrepidity, relaxed their ardour. Being now less hard pressed, he retreated step by step, not turning his back until he was outside the walls. In this engagement multitudes of Romans fell, including the decurion Aebutius, a man who had shown the utmost gallantry and inflicted the severest losses on the Jews, not only in the action in which he perished,

Vespasian's perilous position.

---

[a] Governor (*legatus*) of Syria, and subsequently one of the strongest supporters of Vespasian's claims to the empire.

37 ἐργασάμενος. ἑκατοντάρχης δέ τις, Γάλλος ὀνό-
ματι, μετὰ στρατιωτῶν δέκα περισχεθεὶς ἐν τῇ
38 ταραχῇ κατέδυ μὲν εἴς τινος οἰκίαν, τῶν δ' ἐν αὐτῇ
διαλαλούντων παρὰ δεῖπνον ὅσα κατὰ τῶν Ῥωμαίων ἢ περὶ σφῶν ὁ δῆμος ἐβουλεύετο κατ-
ακροασάμενος, ἦν δ' αὐτός τε καὶ οἱ σὺν αὐτῷ
Σύροι, νύκτωρ ἐπανίσταται καὶ πάντας ἀποσφάξας
μετὰ τῶν στρατιωτῶν εἰς τοὺς Ῥωμαίους διασώζεται.
39 (6) Οὐεσπασιανὸς δ' ἀθυμοῦσαν τὴν στρατιὰν
ἀγνοίᾳ[1] πταισμάτων καὶ διότι τέως οὐδαμοῦ
τηλικαύτῃ συμφορᾷ κέχρηντο, τό γε μὴν πλέον
αἰδουμένους ἐπὶ τῷ τὸν στρατηγὸν μόνον τοῖς
40 κινδύνοις ἐγκαταλιπεῖν, παρεμυθεῖτο, περὶ μὲν
τοῦ καθ' αὑτὸν ὑποστελλόμενος, ὡς μηδὲ τὴν
ἀρχὴν μέμφεσθαι δοκοίη, δεῖν δὲ τὰ κοινὰ
λέγων ἀνδρείως φέρειν, τὴν τοῦ πολέμου φύσιν
ἐννοοῦντας, ὡς οὐδαμοῦ τὸ νικᾶν ἀναιμωτὶ
περιγίνεται, παλίμπους δ' ἡ τύχη παρίσταται.[2]
41 τοσαύτας μέντοι μυριάδας Ἰουδαίων ἀνελόντας
αὐτοὺς ὀλίγην τῷ δαίμονι δεδωκέναι συμβολήν.
42 εἶναι δ' ὥσπερ ἀπειροκάλων τὸ λίαν ἐπαίρεσθαι
ταῖς εὐπραγίαις, οὕτως ἀνάνδρων τὸ καταπτήσσειν
ἐν τοῖς πταίσμασιν· "ὀξεῖα γὰρ ἐν ἀμφοτέροις
ἡ μεταβολή, κἀκεῖνος ἄριστος ὁ κἀν τοῖς εὐτυχήμασιν νήφων, ἵνα μένῃ καὶ δι' εὐθυμίας ἀνα-

[1] Destinon : ἀνοία mss. (cf. Vita 167 for similar confusion):
ἐννοίᾳ, "at the thought of," Bos.

[2] παλίμπους κτλ. Niese (and so apparently the first hand
of L): δαπανᾷ δ' ἡ τύχη τι καὶ παρίσταται PAM[1]: ἡ γὰρ
παλίμπους τύχη περιίσταται VRCM[2].

[a] Aebutius had skirmishes with Josephus in Galilee early
in the war, Vita 115-120, and as "a man of marked energy

but on all previous occasions.[a] One centurion, named
Gallus, being cut off with ten of his men in the fray,
crept into a private house, where he—a Syrian like
his companions—overheard the inmates discussing at
supper the citizens' plans of attack on the Romans
and of self-defence ; during the night he arose and
fell upon them, slew them all, and with his men
made his way safely back to the Roman camp.

(6) Vespasian, seeing his army despondent owing
to their ignorance of reverses and because they had
nowhere so far met with such a disaster, and still
more ashamed of themselves for leaving their general
to face danger alone, proceeded to console them.
Refraining from any mention of himself, for fear of
appearing to cast the slightest reflection upon them,
he said that they ought manfully to bear misfortunes
which were common to all, reflecting on the nature
of war, which never grants a bloodless victory, and
how Fortune flits back again to one's side.[b] "After
all," he continued, " you have slain myriads of
Jews, but yourselves have paid but a trifling
contribution to the deity.[c] As it is a mark
of vulgarity to be over-elated by success, so is it
unmanly to be downcast in adversity ; for the transi-
tion from one to the other is rapid, and the best
soldier is he who meets good fortune with sobriety,
to the end that he may still remain cheerful when

Vespasian
consoles
his troops.

and ability " was selected for special duty at the outset of
the siege of Jotapata, *B.* iii. 144.
 [b] The rare word παλίμπους ("with returning foot " or
" retrograde ") occurs, together with another word, δυσύποιστος,
only attested elsewhere in Jos. *A.* xv. 208, in an epigram of
Meleager of Gadara (*Anth. Pal.* v. 163), from which
Josephus or his συνεργός not improbably borrowed it.
 [c] *i.e.* the god of war (or Fortune), who demands blood.

JOSEPHUS

43 παλαίων τὰ σφάλματα. τὰ μέντοι συμβεβηκότα
νῦν οὔτε μαλακισθέντων ἡμῶν¹ οὔτε παρὰ τὴν
τῶν Ἰουδαίων ἀρετὴν γέγονεν, ἀλλὰ κἀκείνοις τοῦ
πλεονεκτῆσαι καὶ τοῦ διαμαρτεῖν ἡμῖν αἴτιον ἡ
44 δυσχωρία. καθ' ἢν ἄν² τις ὑμῶν μέμψαιτο τῆς
ὁρμῆς τὸ ἀταμίευτον· ἀναφυγόντων γὰρ ἐπὶ τὰ
ὑψηλὰ τῶν πολεμίων αὐτοὺς ὑποστέλλειν ἐχρῆν,
καὶ μὴ κατὰ κορυφὴν ἱσταμένοις τοῖς κινδύνοις
ἕπεσθαι, κρατοῦντας δὲ τῆς κάτω πόλεως κατ'
ὀλίγον προκαλεῖσθαι τοὺς ἀναφεύγοντας εἰς ἀσφαλῆ
καὶ ἑδραίαν μάχην. νυνὶ δὲ ἀκρατῶς ἐπὶ τὴν
45 νίκην ἐπειγόμενοι τῆς ἀσφαλείας ἠμελήσατε. τὸ δ'
ἀπερίσκεπτον ἐν πολέμῳ καὶ τῆς ὁρμῆς μανιῶδες
οὐ πρὸς Ῥωμαίων, οἳ πάντα ἐμπειρίᾳ καὶ τάξει
κατορθοῦμεν, ἀλλὰ βαρβαρικόν, καὶ ᾧ μάλιστα
46 Ἰουδαῖοι κρατοῦνται. χρὴ τοίνυν ἐπὶ τὴν αὐτῶν
ἀρετὴν ἀναδραμεῖν καὶ θυμοῦσθαι μᾶλλον ἢ
47 προσαθυμεῖν τῷ παρ' ἀξίαν πταίσματι. τὴν δ'
ἀρίστην ἕκαστος ἐκ τῆς ἰδίας χειρὸς ἐπιζητείτω
παραμυθίαν· οὕτω γὰρ τοῖς τε ἀπολωλόσι τι-
48 μωρήσεσθε καὶ τοὺς ἀνελόντας ἀμυνεῖσθε. πειρά-
σομαι δ' ἐγώ, καθάπερ νῦν, ἐπὶ πάσης μάχης
προάγειν τε ὑμῶν εἰς τοὺς πολεμίους καὶ τελευταῖος ἀποχωρεῖν.''

49 (7) Ὁ μὲν οὖν τοιαῦτα λέγων τὴν στρατιὰν
ἀνελάμβανεν, τοῖς δὲ Γαμαλεῦσιν πρὸς ὀλίγον
μὲν θαρρῆσαι τῷ κατορθώματι παρέστη παρα-
50 λόγως τε συμβάντι καὶ μεγάλως, λογιζόμενοι δ'
ὕστερον ἀφηρῆσθαι σφᾶς αὐτοὺς καὶ δεξιᾶς
ἐλπίδας, τό τε μὴ δύνασθαι διαφεύγειν ἐννοοῦντες,

¹ L Lat.: ὑμῶν the rest.
² L: ἄγαν the rest: γ' ἂν Destinon.

172

contending with reverses. What has now happened, to be sure, is attributable neither to any weakness on our part nor to the valour of the Jews ; the one cause of their superiority and of our failure was the difficulty of the ground. In view of that, fault might be found with your inordinate ardour ; for when the enemy fled to the higher ground, you should have restrained yourselves and not by pursuit exposed yourselves to the perils impending over your heads. Instead, having mastered the lower town, you should gradually have lured the fugitives to a safe combat on firm ground ; whereas, through your intemperate eagerness for victory, you neglected your own safety. But incautiousness in war and mad impetuosity are alien to us Romans, who owe all our success to skill and discipline : they are a barbarian fault and one to which the Jews mainly owe their defeats. It behoves us therefore to fall back upon our native valour and to be moved rather to wrath than to despondency by this unworthy reverse. But the best consolation should be sought by each man in his own right hand : for so you will avenge the dead and punish those who slew them. For my part, it shall be my endeavour, as in this so in every engagement, to face the enemy at your head and to be the last to retire."

(7) By such words as these he reanimated his troops. The people of Gamala, on their side, derived a momentary confidence from their unlooked for and signal success ; but when they subsequently reflected that they had deprived themselves of all hope of terms, and thought of the impossibility of escape (for

ἤδη γὰρ ἐπέλιπε τἀπιτήδεια, δεινῶς ἠθύμουν καὶ
51 ταῖς ψυχαῖς ἀναπεπτώκεσαν. οὐ μὴν εἰς τὸ
δυνατὸν ἠμέλουν σωτηρίας, ἀλλὰ καὶ τὰ παρ-
αρρηχθέντα[1] τοῦ τείχους οἱ γενναιότατοι καὶ τὰ
μένοντα περισχόντες ἐφύλασσον οἱ λοιποί. τῶν δὲ
52 Ῥωμαίων ἐπιρρωννύντων[2] τὰ χώματα καὶ πάλιν
πειρωμένων προσβολῆς οἱ πολλοὶ διεδίδρασκον
ἐκ τῆς πόλεως κατά τε δυσβάτων φαράγγων,
ᾗπερ οὐκ ἔκειντο φυλακαί, καὶ διὰ τῶν ὑπονόμων.
53 ὅσοι γε μὴν δέει τοῦ ληφθῆναι παρέμενον, [ἐν]
ἐνδείᾳ διεφθείροντο· πανταχόθεν γὰρ τροφὴ τοῖς
μάχεσθαι δυναμένοις συνηθροίζετο.

54   (8) Καὶ οἱ μὲν ἐν τοιούτοις πάθεσι διεκαρτέρουν,
Οὐεσπασιανὸς δὲ πάρεργον ἐποιεῖτο τῆς πολιορκίας
τοὺς τὸ Ἰταβύριον κατειληφότας ὄρος, ὅ ἐστι
55 τοῦ μεγάλου πεδίου καὶ Σκυθοπόλεως μέσον· οὗ
τὸ μὲν ὕψος ἐπὶ τριάκοντα σταδίους ἀνίσχει,
μόλις προσβατὸν κατὰ τὸ προσάρκτιον κλίμα,
πεδίον δ᾽ ἐστὶν ἡ κορυφὴ σταδίων ἓξ καὶ εἴκοσι,
56 πᾶν τετειχισμένον. ἤγειρε δὲ τοσοῦτον ὄντα τὸν
περίβολον ὁ Ἰώσηπος ἐν τεσσαράκοντα ἡμέραις
τῇ τε ἄλλῃ χορηγούμενος ὕλῃ κάτωθεν καὶ
ὕδατι· καὶ γὰρ τοῖς ἐποίκοις μόνον ἦν ὄμβριον.
57 πολλοῦ οὖν πλήθους ἐπὶ τούτου συνειλεγμένου[3]

[1] Herwerden: περιρρηχθέντα mss.
[2] ἐπιχωννύντων MVRC.
[3] πολλῆς οὖν πληθύος ἐπὶ τοῦ τόπου συνειλεγμένης Niese,
avoiding the double hiatus.

---

[a] § 9.
[b] If " the Great Plain " means here, as usual, the plain of
Esdraelon, the description above is inaccurate, as Mt. Tabor
lies well to the N. of a line drawn through that plain, and its

their supplies had already failed them), they became
sorely dejected and lost heart. Nevertheless, they
did not neglect to take what precautions they could
to protect themselves : the bravest guarded the
breaches, the rest manned what still remained of the
wall. But when the Romans proceeded to strengthen
their earthworks and to attempt a fresh assault, the
people began to run from the town, down trackless
ravines, where no sentries were posted, or through
the underground passages ^a ; while all who stayed
behind from fear of being caught were perishing
from hunger, as every quarter had been ransacked
for provisions for those capable of bearing arms.

(8) While the people of Gamala under such straits
were still holding out, Vespasian undertook, as a
minor diversion from the siege, the reduction of the
occupants of Mount Tabor. This lies midway be-
tween the Great Plain and Scythopolis,^b and rises to
a height of thirty furlongs,^c being almost inaccessible
on its northern face ; the summit is a table-land
twenty-six furlongs ^c long, entirely surrounded by a
wall. This extensive rampart was erected in forty
days by Josephus,^d who was supplied from below
with all materials, including water, the inhabitants
depending solely on rain. To this spot, on which a
vast multitude had assembled, Vespasian dispatched

continuation, the valley of Jezreel, to Scythopolis. If the
plain of Asochis (described as " the great plain in which my
quarters lay " in *Vita* 207) is meant, the description is
approximately correct.

^c These figures are absurdly inaccurate ; the summit is
only 1843 feet above the Plain of Esdraelon (1312 ft. from
the base), the platform on the summit is 3000 ft. long and
1300 ft. at its greatest breadth (*Encycl. Bibl. s.v.*).

^d Tabor is mentioned in a list of places fortified by him in
Vita 188.

Οὐεσπασιανὸς Πλάκιδον σὺν ἱππεῦσιν ἑξακοσίοις
58 πέμπει. τούτῳ τὸ μὲν προσβαίνειν ἀμήχανον ἦν,
ἐλπίδι δὲ δεξιῶν καὶ παρακλήσει[1] πρὸς εἰρήνην
59 τοὺς πολλοὺς προεκαλεῖτο.[2] κατῄεσαν δὲ ἀντ-
επιβουλεύοντες· ὅ τε γὰρ Πλάκιδος ὡμίλει πραό-
τερον σπουδάζων αὐτοὺς ἐν τῷ πεδίῳ λαβεῖν,
κἀκεῖνοι κατῄεσαν ὡς πειθόμενοι δῆθεν, ἵν᾽
60 ἀφυλάκτῳ προσπέσωσιν. ἐνίκα μέντοι τὸ Πλακίδου πανοῦργον· ἀρξαμένων γὰρ τῶν Ἰουδαίων
μάχης φυγὴν ὑποκρίνεται καὶ διώκοντας ἑλκύσας
ἐπὶ πολὺ τοῦ πεδίου τοὺς ἱππεῖς ἐπιστρέφει,
τρεψάμενος δὲ πλείστους μὲν αὐτῶν ἀναιρεῖ,
τὸ δὲ λοιπὸν πλῆθος ὑποτεμνόμενος εἴργει τῆς
61 ἀνόδου. καὶ οἱ μὲν τὸ Ἰταβύριον καταλιπόντες
ἐπὶ Ἱεροσολύμων ἔφευγον, οἱ δ᾽ ἐπιχώριοι πίστεις
λαβόντες, ἐπιλελοίπει δ᾽ αὐτοὺς ὕδωρ, τό τε ὄρος
καὶ σφᾶς αὐτοὺς Πλακίδῳ παρέδοσαν.
62 (9) Τῶν δ᾽ ἐπὶ τῆς Γαμάλας οἱ παραβολώτεροι
μὲν φεύγοντες διελάνθανον, οἱ δ᾽ ἀσθενεῖς διεφθεί-
63 ροντο λιμῷ· τὸ μάχιμον δ᾽ ἀντεῖχεν τῇ πολιορκίᾳ,
μέχρι δευτέρᾳ καὶ εἰκάδι μηνὸς Ὑπερβερεταίου
τρεῖς τῶν ἀπὸ τοῦ πέμπτου καὶ δεκάτου τάγματος
στρατιῶται περὶ τὴν ἑωθινὴν φυλακὴν ὑπο-
δύντες τὸν προύχοντα κατὰ τούτους πύργον ὑπ-
64 ορύσσουσιν ἡσυχῇ. τοῖς δ᾽ ὑπὲρ αὐτοῦ φύλαξιν
οὔτε προσιόντων αἴσθησις, νὺξ γὰρ ἦν, οὔτε προσ-
ελθόντων ἐγένετο. οἱ δὲ στρατιῶται φειδόμενοι

---

[1] L: παρακλήσεως the rest.
[2] Destinon: προσεκαλεῖτο MSS.

[a] The tribune who had seen service in Galilee before
Vespasian's arrival (*Vita* 213) and after (*ib.* 411, *B.* iii. 59,

176

Placidus [a] with six hundred horse. That officer, finding the ascent of the mountain impracticable, made peaceable overtures to the crowd, holding out hopes of terms and exhorting them to avail themselves of the offer. They descended accordingly, but with counter-designs of their own ; for while the object of Placidus with his mild address was to capture them in the plain, they came down ostensibly in compliance with his proposal, but with the real intention of attacking him while off his guard. The craft of Placidus, however, won the day ; for when the Jews opened hostilities he feigned flight and, having drawn his pursuers far into the plain, suddenly wheeled his cavalry round and routed them. Masses of them were slain; the remainder he intercepted and prevented from reascending the mountain. These fugitives abandoning Mount Tabor made off to Jerusalem ; the natives, under promise of protection, and pressed by the failure of their water-supply, surrendered the mountain and themselves to Placidus.

(9) At Gamala, while the more adventurous were stealthily escaping and the feebler folk dying of famine,[b] the effective combatants continued to sustain the siege until the twenty-second of the month Hyperberetaeus, when three soldiers of the fifteenth legion, about the time of the morning watch, crept up to the base of a projecting tower opposite to them and began secretly undermining it ; the sentries on guard above failing, in the darkness, to detect them either when approaching or after they had reached it. These soldiers, with as little noise as

Overthrow of a tower at Gamala

c. 9 November A.D. 67

110, etc.), and who subsequently subdued Peraea (*B.* iv. 419 ff.).

[b] Resuming and partly repeating the narrative in §§ 52 f.

τοῦ ψόφου [καὶ] πέντε τοὺς κραταιοτάτους ἐκ-
65 κυλίσαντες λίθους ὑποπηδῶσι. κατερείπεται[1] δ'
ὁ πύργος ἐξαίφνης μετὰ μεγίστου ψόφου, καὶ
συγκατακρημνίζονται μὲν οἱ φύλακες αὐτῷ, θορυ-
βηθέντες δὲ οἱ κατὰ τὰς ἄλλας φυλακὰς ἔφευγον·
66 καὶ πολλοὺς διεκπαίειν τολμῶντας οἱ Ῥωμαῖοι
διέφθειραν, ἐν οἷς καὶ Ἰώσηπόν[2] τις ὑπὲρ τὸ
παρερρηγμένον τοῦ τείχους ἐκδιδράσκοντα βαλὼν
67 ἀναιρεῖ. τῶν δ' ἀνὰ τὴν πόλιν διασεισθέντων
ὑπὸ τοῦ ψόφου διαδρομή τε ἦν καὶ πτόα πολλή,
καθάπερ εἰσπεπαικότων πάντων τῶν πολεμίων.
68 ἔνθα καὶ Χάρης κατακείμενος καὶ νοσηλευόμενος
ἐκλείπει, πολλὰ τοῦ[3] δέους συνεργήσαντος εἰς
69 θάνατον τῇ νόσῳ. Ῥωμαῖοί γε μὴν μεμνημένοι
τοῦ προτέρου πταίσματος οὐκ εἰσέβαλλον ἕως
70 τρίτῃ καὶ εἰκάδι τοῦ προειρημένου μηνὸς (10)
Τίτος,[4] ἤδη γὰρ παρῆν, ὀργῇ τῆς πληγῆς ἦν
παρ' αὐτὸν ἐπλήγησαν ἀπόντα Ῥωμαῖοι, τῶν
ἱππέων ἐπιλέξας διακοσίους, πρὸς οἷς πεζούς,[5] εἰσ-
71 έρχεται τὴν πόλιν ἡσυχῇ. καὶ παρελθόντος οἱ
μὲν φύλακες αἰσθόμενοι μετὰ βοῆς ἐχώρουν ἐπὶ
τὰ ὅπλα, δήλης δὲ τῆς εἰσβολῆς ταχέως καὶ τοῖς
εἴσω γενομένης, οἱ μὲν ἁρπάζοντες τὰ τέκνα καὶ
γυναῖκας ἐπισυρόμενοι πρὸς τὴν ἄκραν ἀνέφευγον
μετὰ κωκυτοῦ καὶ βοῆς, οἱ δὲ τὸν Τίτον ὑπ-
72 αντιάζοντες ἀδιαλείπτως ἔπιπτον· ὅσοι δὲ ἀπ-
εκωλύθησαν ἐπὶ τὴν κορυφὴν ἀναδραμεῖν ὑπ'
ἀμηχανίας εἰς τὰς τῶν Ῥωμαίων φρουρὰς ἐξ-
έπιπτον. ἄπειρος δ' ἦν πανταχοῦ φονευομένων ὁ

---

[1] Niese: κατηρείπετο or καταρρίπτεται mss.
[2] Ἰώσην L[1] Lat.; cf. § 18.
[3] πολλὰ τοῦ Niese: πολλοῦ mss.

possible, succeeded in rolling away the five chief
stones and then leapt back; whereupon the tower
suddenly collapsed with a tremendous crash, carrying
the sentries headlong with it. The guards at the
other posts fled in alarm; many who essayed to cut
their way out were killed by the Romans, and among
them Joseph, who was struck dead while making his
escape across the breach. The people throughout
the town, confounded by the crash, ran hither and
thither in great trepidation, believing that the whole
of the enemy had burst in. At that same moment
Chares, who was bedridden and in the hands of
physicians, expired, terror largely contributing to the
fatal termination of his illness. The Romans, however, with the memory of their former disaster,
deferred their entry until the twenty-third of the
month.

(10) On that day Titus, who had now returned,[a] leads to the
indignant at the reverse which the Romans had sus- capture of
tained in his absence, selected two hundred cavalry the town.
and a body of infantry, and quietly entered the
town. The guards, apprised of his entry, flew with
shouts to arms. News of the incursion rapidly
spreading to the interior of the town, some, snatching
up their children and dragging their wives after
them, fled with their wailing and weeping families
up to the citadel; those who faced Titus were incessantly dropping; while any who were debarred
from escape to the heights fell in their bewilderment
into the hands of the Roman sentries. On all sides
was heard the never ending moan of the dying, and

---

[a] From his visit to Mucianus in Syria, § 32.

[4] + δὲ MSS.: omit Destinon and Niese (ed. min.).
[5] A numeral has perhaps dropped out.

στόνος, καὶ τὸ αἷμα πᾶσαν ἐπέκλυζε τὴν πόλιν
73 κατὰ πρανοῦς χεόμενον. πρὸς δὲ τοὺς ἀναφεύγοντας εἰς τὴν ἄκραν ἐπεβοήθει Οὐεσπασιανὸς
74 πᾶσαν εἰσαγαγὼν τὴν δύναμιν. ἦν δ᾽ ἥ τε κορυφὴ
πάντοθεν πετρώδης καὶ δύσβατος, εἰς ἄπειρον
ὕψος ἐπηρμένη, καὶ πανταχόθεν τοῦ † βάθους¹
κατέγεμεν περιειλημμένη κρημνοῖς [κατέτεμνόν
75 τε]. ἐνταῦθα τοὺς προσβαίνοντας οἱ Ἰουδαῖοι
τοῖς τε ἄλλοις βέλεσι καὶ πέτρας κατακυλινδοῦντες
ἐκάκουν· αὐτοὶ δὲ δι᾽ ὕψος ἦσαν δυσέφικτοι βέλει.
76 γίνεται δὲ πρὸς ἀπώλειαν αὐτῶν ἄντικρυς θύελλα
δαιμόνιος, ᾗ τὰ μὲν Ῥωμαίων ἔφερεν εἰς αὐτοὺς
βέλη, τὰ δ᾽ αὐτῶν ἀνέστρεφεν καὶ πλάγια παρ-
77 έσυρεν. οὔτε δὲ τοῖς ὑποκρήμνοις ἐφίστασθαι διὰ
τὴν βίαν ἐδύναντο τοῦ πνεύματος, μηδὲν ἑδραῖον
78 ἔχοντες, οὔτε τοὺς προσβαίνοντας καθορᾶν. ἐπανα-
βαίνουσι δὲ Ῥωμαῖοι, καὶ περισχόντες οὓς μὲν
ἀμυνομένους ἔφθανον, οὓς δὲ χεῖρας προΐσχοντας·
ἐτόνου δὲ τὸν θυμὸν αὐτοῖς ἐπὶ πάντας ἡ μνήμη
τῶν ἐπὶ τῆς πρώτης εἰσβολῆς ἀπολωλότων.
79 ἀπογινώσκοντες δὲ τὴν σωτηρίαν πανταχόθεν οἱ
πολλοὶ περισχόμενοι τέκνα καὶ γυναῖκας αὐτούς
τε κατεκρήμνιζον εἰς τὴν φάραγγα· βαθυτάτη δ᾽
80 αὕτη κατὰ τὴν ἄκραν ὑπώρυκτο. συνέβη δὲ τὴν
Ῥωμαίων ὀργὴν τῆς. εἰς ἑαυτοὺς ἀπονοίας τῶν
ἁλόντων πραοτέραν φανῆναι· τετρακισχίλιοι μέν γε
ὑπὸ τούτων ἐσφάγησαν, οἱ δὲ ῥίψαντες ἑαυτοὺς
81 ὑπὲρ πεντακισχιλίους εὑρέθησαν. διεσώθη δὲ πλὴν
δύο γυναικῶν οὐδείς· τῆς Φιλίππου δ᾽ ἦσαν

---

¹ πλήθους LP²M², "crowded with people": text doubtful:
? read πάθους, "fraught with tragedy." The words in
brackets appear to be a doublet of κατέγεμεν.

the whole city was deluged with blood pouring down
the slopes. To aid the attack on the fugitives in
the citadel Vespasian now brought up his entire
force. The summit, all rock-strewn, difficult of access,
towering to an immense height, and surrounded with
precipices, everywhere yawned to depths below.[a]
Here the Jews worked havoc among the advancing
enemy with missiles of all kinds and rocks which
they rolled down upon them, being themselves from
their elevated position no easy mark for an arrow.
However, to seal their ruin, a storm miraculously
arose which, blowing full in their faces, carried
against them the arrows of the Romans and checked
and deflected their own. Owing to the force of the
gale they could neither stand on the edge of the
precipices, having no firm foothold, nor see the
approaching enemy. The Romans mounted the crest
and quickly surrounded and slew them, some offering
resistance, others holding out their hands for quarter ;
but the recollection of those who fell in the first
assault whetted their fury against all. Despairing
of their lives and hemmed in on every side, multitudes plunged headlong with their wives and children
into the ravine which had been excavated [b] to a vast
depth beneath the citadel. Indeed, the rage of the
Romans was thus made to appear milder than the
frantic self-immolation of the vanquished, four thousand only being slain by the former, while those who
flung themselves over the cliff were found to exceed
five thousand. Not a soul escaped save two women ;

[a] Literally " was full of depth " : see critical note.
[b] See § 9.

ἀδελφῆς θυγατέρες αὗται, αὐτὸς δ' ὁ Φίλιππος
Ἰακίμου τινὸς ἀνδρὸς ἐπισήμου, στραταρχήσαντος[1]
82 Ἀγρίππᾳ τῷ βασιλεῖ. διεσώθησαν δὲ τὰς παρὰ
τὴν ἅλωσιν ὀργὰς Ῥωμαίων λαθοῦσαι· τότε γὰρ
οὐδὲ νηπίων ἐφείδοντο, πολλὰ δ' ἑκάστοτε ἁρπά-
83 ζοντες ἐσφενδόνων ἀπὸ τῆς ἄκρας. Γάμαλα μὲν
[οὖν][2] οὕτως ἑάλω τρίτῃ καὶ εἰκάδι μηνὸς Ὑπερβερεταίου, τῆς ἀποστάσεως ἀρξαμένης Γορπιαίου
μηνὸς τετάρτῃ καὶ εἰκάδι.
84 (ii. 1) Μόνη δὲ Γίσχαλα πολίχνη τῆς Γαλιλαίας
ἀχείρωτος κατελείπετο, τοῦ μὲν πλήθους εἰρηνικὰ
φρονοῦντος, καὶ γὰρ ἦσαν τὸ πλέον γεωργοὶ καὶ
ταῖς ἀπὸ τῶν καρπῶν ἐλπίσιν ἀεὶ προσανέχοντες,
παρεισεφθαρμένου δ' αὐτοῖς οὐκ ὀλίγου λῃστρικοῦ
τάγματος, ᾧ τινες καὶ τοῦ πολιτικοῦ συνενόσουν.
85 ἐνῆγε δὲ τούτους εἰς τὴν ἀπόστασιν καὶ συν-
εκρότει Ληΐου τινὸς υἱὸς Ἰωάννης, γόης ἀνὴρ καὶ
ποικιλώτατος τὸ ἦθος, πρόχειρος μὲν ἐλπίσαι
μεγάλα, δεινὸς δὲ τῶν ἐλπισθέντων περιγενέσθαι,
παντί τε ὢν δῆλος ἀγαπᾶν τὸν πόλεμον εἰς
86 δυναστείας ἐπίθεσιν. ὑπὸ τούτῳ τὸ στασιῶδες
ἐν τοῖς Γισχάλοις ἐτέτακτο, δι' οὓς τάχ' ἂν[3] καὶ
πρεσβευσάμενον περὶ παραδόσεως τὸ δημοτικὸν
ἐν πολεμίου[4] μοίρᾳ τὴν Ῥωμαίων ἔφοδον ἐξεδέχετο.
87 Οὐεσπασιανὸς δὲ ἐπὶ μὲν τούτους Τίτον ἐκπέμπει

---

[1] τετραρχήσαντος PAL Lat.
[2] om. PA Lat.
[3] τάχα ἂν L: τυχὸν the rest.
[4] conj.: πολέμου mss. For the phrase ἐν πολεμίου μοίρᾳ
cf. Demosthenes 639.

---

[a] Vita 46, etc., B. ii. 421, 556, with note a on § 2 above.
[b] El-Jish, in the north of Galilee.

these were nieces, on the mother's side, of Philip, son of Jacimus, a distinguished man who had been commander-in-chief to King Agrippa.[a] They owed their escape to their having concealed themselves at the time of the capture of the town ; for at that moment the rage of the Romans was such that they spared not even infants, but time after time snatched up numbers of them and slung them from the citadel. Thus on the twenty-third of the month Hyperbere- _{c. 10 Nov.} taeus was Gamala taken, after a revolt which began on the twenty-fourth of Gorpiaeus. _{c. 12 Oct.}

(ii. 1) Only Gischala,[b] a small town in Galilee, ^{GISCHALA} now remained unsubdued. The inhabitants were ^{incited to revolt by} inclined to peace, being mainly agricultural labourers, ^{John.} whose whole attention was devoted to the prospects of the crops ; but they had been afflicted by the invasion of a numerous gang of brigands, from whom some members of the community had caught the contagion. These had been incited to rebel and organized for the purpose by John, son of Levi, a charlatan of an extremely subtle character, always ready to indulge great expectations and an adept in realizing them ; all knew that he had set his heart on war in order to attain supreme power.[c] Under him the malcontents of Gischala had ranged themselves and it was through their influence that the townsfolk, who would otherwise probably have sent deputies offering to surrender, now awaited the Roman onset in an attitude of defiance. To meet ^{Titus, sent} these rebels Vespasian dispatched Titus with a ^{against Gischala,}

^c *Cf.* the character sketch of John in ii. 585 ff., with the parallel there quoted from Sallust's description of Catiline ; here ποικιλώτατος recalls "varius" of Sallust, and with the last clause *cf.* "hunc . . . lubido maxuma invaserat rei publicae capiundae " (*De Cat. conj.* 5).

σὺν χιλίοις ἱππεῦσιν, τὸ δέκατον δὲ τάγμα ἀπαίρει
88 εἰς Σκυθόπολιν. αὐτὸς δὲ σὺν δυσὶ τοῖς λοιποῖς
ἐπανῆλθεν εἰς Καισάρειαν, τοῦ τε συνεχοῦς καμάτου
διδοὺς ἀνάπαυσιν αὐτοῖς καὶ δι' εὐθηνίαν τῶν
πόλεων τά τε σώματα καὶ τὸ πρόθυμον ὑποθρέψειν
89 οἰόμενος ἐπὶ τοὺς μέλλοντας ἀγῶνας· οὐ γὰρ ὀλίγον αὐτῷ πόνον ἑώρα περὶ τοῖς Ἱεροσολύμοις
λειπόμενον, ἅτε δὴ βασιλείου μὲν οὔσης τῆς
πόλεως καὶ προανεχούσης ὅλου τοῦ ἔθνους, συρ-
ρεόντων δὲ εἰς αὐτὴν τῶν ἐκ τοῦ πολέμου δια-
90 διδρασκόντων. τό γε μὴν φύσει <τε>[1] ὀχυρὸν
αὐτῆς καὶ διὰ κατασκευὴν τειχῶν ἀγωνίαν οὐ
τὴν τυχοῦσαν ἐνεποίει· τὰ δὲ φρονήματα τῶν
ἀνδρῶν καὶ τὰς τόλμας δυσμεταχειρίστους καὶ
91 δίχα τειχῶν ὑπελάμβανεν. διὸ δὴ τοὺς στρατιώτας καθάπερ ἀθλητὰς προήσκει τῶν ἀγώνων.
92 (2) Τίτῳ δὲ προσιππασαμένῳ τοῖς Γισχάλοις
εὐπετὲς μὲν ἦν ἐξ ἐφόδου τὴν πόλιν ἑλεῖν, εἰδὼς
δέ, εἰ βίᾳ ληφθείη, διαφθαρησόμενον ὑπὸ τῶν
στρατιωτῶν ἀνέδην τὸ πλῆθος, ἦν δ' αὐτῷ κόρος
ἤδη φόνων καὶ δι' οἴκτου τὸ πλέον ἀκρίτως
συναπολλύμενον τοῖς αἰτίοις,[2] ἐβούλετο μᾶλλον
93 ὁμολογίαις παραστήσασθαι τὴν πόλιν. καὶ δὴ τοῦ
τείχους ἀνδρῶν καταγέμοντος, οἳ τὸ πλέον ἦσαν
ἐκ τοῦ διεφθαρμένου τάγματος, θαυμάζειν ἔφη
πρὸς αὐτούς, τίνι πεποιθότες πάσης ἑαλωκυίας
πόλεως μόνοι τὰ Ῥωμαίων ὅπλα μένουσιν,
94 ἑωρακότες μὲν ὀχυρωτέρας πολλῷ πόλεις ὑπὸ
μίαν προσβολὴν κατεστραμμένας, ἐν ἀσφαλείᾳ δὲ
τῶν ἰδίων κτημάτων ἀπολαύοντας ὅσοι ταῖς
Ῥωμαίων δεξιαῖς ἐπίστευσαν, ἃς καὶ νῦν προ-

_____
[1] ins. Bekker. [2] +τὸ μὴ αἴτιον M.

184

thousand horse; the tenth legion he dismissed to Scythopolis. He himself with the two remaining legions returned to Caesarea, to recruit them after their incessant toil, and with the idea that the abundance of city life would invigorate their bodies and impart fresh alacrity for coming struggles. For he foresaw that no light toil was in store for him under the walls of Jerusalem, seeing that it was not only the royal city and the capital of the whole nation, but the rendezvous to which all fugitives had flocked from the seat of war. The strength of its defences, both natural and artificial, caused him serious solicitude; and he conjectured that the spirit and daring of its defenders would, even without walls, render their reduction a difficult task. He accordingly trained his soldiers, like athletes, for the fray.

(2) Titus, on riding up to Gischala, saw that the town might easily be carried by assault. But he knew that were it taken by storm a general massacre of the population by his troops would ensue; he was already satiated with slaughter and pitied the masses doomed along with the guilty to indiscriminate destruction; he therefore preferred to induce the town to capitulate. Finding the ramparts crowded with men, mainly of the corrupted gang, he told them that he wondered on what they were relying that, when every other city had fallen, they alone stood out to face the Roman arms. They had seen cities far stronger than their own overthrown at the first assault, but beheld in the secure enjoyment of their possessions all who had trusted the pledges proffered by Roman hands—hands which he now

urges the inhabitants to surrender.

185

τείνειν αὐτοῖς μηδὲν μνησικακῶν τῆς αὐθαδείας.
95 εἶναι γὰρ συγγνωστὸν ἐλευθερίας ἐλπίδα, μηκέτι
96 μέντοι τὴν ἐν τοῖς ἀδυνάτοις ἐπιμονήν· εἰ γὰρ οὐ
πεισθήσονται λόγοις φιλανθρώποις καὶ δεξιαῖς
πίστεως, πειράσειν αὐτοὺς ἀφειδῆ τὰ ὅπλα, καὶ
ὅσον οὐδέπω γνώσεσθαι[1] παιζόμενον[2] τοῖς Ῥωμαίων μηχανήμασιν τὸ τεῖχος, ᾧ πεποιθότες
ἐπιδείκνυνται μόνοι Γαλιλαίων, ὅτι εἰσὶν αὐθάδεις
αἰχμάλωτοι.
97 (3) Πρὸς ταῦτα τῶν μὲν δημοτικῶν οὐ μόνον
οὐκ ἀποκρίνεσθαί τινι μετῆν, ἀλλ' οὐδ' ἐπὶ τὸ
τεῖχος ἀναβῆναι· προδιείληπτο γὰρ ἅπαν τοῖς
λῃστρικοῖς, καὶ φύλακες τῶν πυλῶν ἦσαν, ὡς μή
τινες ἢ προέλθοιεν ἐπὶ τὰς σπονδὰς ἢ δέξαιντό
98 τινας τῶν ἱππέων εἰς τὴν πόλιν. ὁ δ' Ἰωάννης
αὐτός τε ἀγαπᾶν ἔφη τὰς προκλήσεις καὶ τοὺς
99 ἀπιστοῦντας[3] ἢ πείσειν ἢ συναναγκάσειν· δεῖν
μέντοι τὴν ἡμέραν αὐτὸν ἐκείνην, ἑβδομὰς γὰρ
ἦν, χαρίσασθαι τῷ[4] Ἰουδαίων νόμῳ, καθ' ἣν
ὥσπερ ὅπλα κινεῖν αὐτοῖς, οὕτω καὶ τὸ συν-
100 τίθεσθαι περὶ εἰρήνης ἀθέμιτον. οὐκ ἀγνοεῖν δὲ
οὐδὲ Ῥωμαίους, ὡς ἀργὴ πάντων αὐτοῖς ἐστιν
ἡ τῆς ἑβδομάδος περίοδος, ἔν τε τῷ παραβαίνειν
αὐτὴν οὐχ ἧττον ἀσεβεῖν τῶν βιασθέντων τὸν
101 βιασάμενον. φέρειν δ' ἐκείνῳ μὲν οὐδεμίαν βλάβην
τὰ τῆς ὑπερθέσεως, τί γὰρ ἄν τις ἐν νυκτὶ βου-
λεύσαιτο δρασμοῦ πλέον, ἐξὸν περιστρατοπεδεύ-
102 σαντα παραφυλάξαι; μέγα δὲ κέρδος αὐτοῖς τὸ

---

[1] AM : γνωσθήσεσθαι the rest.
[2] L[1], cf. Lat. ludum fore : πιεζόμενον the rest.
[3] ἀπειθοῦντας P.
[4] + τῶν L.

extended to them without a thought of vindictiveness for their obstinacy. If hopes of liberty were pardonable, there was no excuse for holding out under impossible conditions. For, should they decline his humane proposals and pledges of good faith, they would experience the relentlessness of his arms and learn all too soon that their walls were a mere plaything for the Roman engines—those walls on the strength of which they alone of the Galilaeans were displaying the obstinacy of prisoners.

(3) To this speech not one of the townsfolk had an opportunity of replying, not being allowed even to mount the wall; for it had all been already occupied by the brigands, while sentries had been posted at the gates to prevent either the exit of any anxious to make terms or the admission of any of the cavalry into the town. It was John who replied, saying that for his part he acquiesced in the proposals and would either persuade or coerce refractory opponents. Titus must, however (he said), in deference to the Jewish law, allow them that day, being the seventh, on which they were forbidden alike to have resort to arms and to conclude a treaty of peace. Even the Romans must be aware that the recurrence of the seventh day brought them repose from all labour; and one who compelled them to transgress that law was no less impious than those who so acted under compulsion. To Titus the delay could cause no injury; for what plot could be laid in a single night, except for flight, and that he could guard against by camping round the city? To

John of Gischala imposes upon Titus.

187

μηδὲν παραβῆναι τῶν πατρίων ἐθῶν. πρέπει[1]
δὲ τῷ παρὰ προσδοκίαν εἰρήνην χαριζομένῳ τοῖς
103 σωζομένοις τηρεῖν καὶ τοὺς νόμους. τοιούτοις
ἐσοφίζετο τὸν Τίτον, οὐ τοσοῦτον τῆς ἑβδομάδος
στοχαζόμενος, ὅσον τῆς ἑαυτοῦ σωτηρίας· ἐδε-
δοίκει δὲ ἐγκαταληφθῆναι[2] παραχρῆμα τῆς πόλεως
ἁλούσης, ἐν νυκτὶ καὶ φυγῇ τὰς ἐλπίδας ἔχων τοῦ
104 βίου. θεοῦ δ᾽ ἦν ἔργον ἄρα τοῦ σώζοντος τὸν
Ἰωάννην ἐπὶ τὸν τῶν Ἱεροσολυμιτῶν[3] ὄλεθροι
τὸ μὴ μόνον πεισθῆναι Τίτον τῇ σκήψει τῆς
ὑπερθέσεως, ἀλλὰ καὶ τῆς πόλεως πορρωτέρω
105 στρατοπεδεύσασθαι πρὸς Κυδασοῖς· μεσόγειος δ᾽
ἐστὶ Τυρίων κώμη καρτερά, διὰ μίσους ἀεὶ καὶ
πολέμου Γαλιλαίοις, ἔχουσα πλῆθός τε οἰκητόρων
καὶ τὴν ὀχυρότητα τῆς πρὸς τὸ ἔθνος διαφορᾶς
ἐφόδια.
106   (4) Νυκτὸς δ᾽ ὁ Ἰωάννης ὡς οὐδεμίαν περὶ τῇ
πόλει Ῥωμαίων ἑώρα φυλακήν, τὸν καιρὸν ἁρ-
πασάμενος, οὐ μόνον τοὺς περὶ αὐτὸν ὁπλίτας
ἀλλὰ καὶ τῶν ἀργοτέρων συχνοὺς ἅμα ταῖς
107 γενεαῖς ἀναλαβὼν ἐπὶ Ἱεροσολύμων ἔφευγε. μέχρι
μὲν οὖν εἴκοσι σταδίων οἷόν τε ἦν συνεξαγαγεῖν
γυναικῶν καὶ παιδίων ὄχλον ἀνθρώπῳ κατα-
σπερχομένῳ τοῖς ὑπὲρ αἰχμαλωσίας καὶ τοῦ ζῆν
φόβοις, περαιτέρω δὲ προκόπτοντος ἀπελείποντο,
108 καὶ δειναὶ τῶν ἐωμένων ἦσαν ὀλοφύρσεις· ὅσον
γὰρ ἕκαστος τῶν οἰκείων ἐγίνετο πορρωτέρω,
τοσοῦτον ἐγγὺς ὑπελάμβανεν εἶναι τῶν πολεμίων,
παρεῖναί τε ἤδη τοὺς αἰχμαλωτισομένους δοκοῦντες

---

[1] πρέπειν Dindorf with Lat. decere; but speeches tend
to drift into *oratio recta* at the close.
[2] ἐγκαταλειφθῆναι, "deserted," PA[1]LV[2] Lat.

them there would be great gain in being spared any
transgression of their national customs.   Moreover,
it would be becoming in the gracious bestower of an
unexpected peace to preserve the laws as well as the
lives of his beneficiaries.   By such language John
imposed on Titus ; for he was concerned not so much
for the seventh day as for his own safety, and, fearing
that he would be caught the instant the city was
taken, rested his hopes of life on darkness and
flight.   But after all it was by the act of God, who
was preserving John to bring ruin upon Jerusalem,
that Titus was not only influenced by this pretext
for delay, but even pitched his camp farther from
the city, at Cydasa.[a]   This is a strong inland village
of the Tyrians, always at feud and strife with the
Galilaeans, having its large population and stout
defences as resources behind it in its quarrel with
the nation.

(4) At nightfall John, seeing no Roman guard
about the town, seized his opportunity and, accompanied not only by his armed followers but by a
multitude of non-combatants with their families,
fled for Jerusalem.   For the first twenty furlongs
he succeeded in dragging with him this mob of women
and children, goaded though he was by terror of
captivity and of his life ; but after that point as he
pushed on they were left behind, and dreadful were
their lamentations when thus deserted.   For, the
farther each was removed from his friends, the nearer
did he fancy himself to his foes ; and believing that
their captors were already upon them they were

John's flight to Jerusalem.

[a] Probably Kedesh-Naphtali = Kedasa (Kad-) in ii. 459.

---

[3] P²AM : Ἱεροσολύμων the rest.

ἐπτόηντο, καὶ πρὸς τὸν ἀλλήλων ἐκ τοῦ δρόμου
ψόφον ἐπεστρέφοντο καθάπερ ἤδη παρόντων οὓς
109 ἔφευγον· ἀνοδίαις τ᾽ ἐνέπιπτον οἱ πολλοί, καὶ περὶ
τὴν λεωφόρον ἡ τῶν φθανόντων ἔρις συνέτριβεν
110 τοὺς πολλούς. οἰκτρὸς δὲ γυναικῶν καὶ παιδίων
ὄλεθρος ἦν, καί ᾽τινες πρὸς ἀνακλήσεις ἀνδρῶν
τε καὶ συγγενῶν ἐθάρσησαν μετὰ κωκυτῶν ἱκε-
111 τεύουσαι περιμένειν. ἀλλ᾽ ἑνίκα τὸ Ἰωάννου
παρακέλευσμα σῴζειν ἑαυτοὺς ἐμβοῶντος καὶ
καταφεύγειν ἔνθα καὶ περὶ τῶν ἀπολειπομένων
ἀμυνοῦνται Ῥωμαίους ἂν ἁρπαγῶσι. τὸ μὲν
οὖν τῶν διαδιδρασκόντων πλῆθος ὡς ἕκαστος
ἰσχύος εἶχεν ἢ τάχους ἐσκέδαστο.
112   (5) Τίτος δὲ μεθ᾽ ἡμέραν ἐπὶ τὰς συνθήκας πρὸς
113 τὸ τεῖχος παρῆν. ἀνοίγει δ᾽ αὐτῷ τὰς πύλας ὁ
δῆμος, καὶ μετὰ τῶν γενεῶν προελθόντες[1] ἀνευ-
φήμουν ὡς εὐεργέτην καὶ φρουρᾶς ἐλευθερώσαντα
114 τὴν πόλιν· ἐδήλουν γὰρ ἅμα τὴν τοῦ Ἰωάννου
φυγὴν καὶ παρεκάλουν φείσασθαί τε αὐτῶν καὶ
παρελθόντα τοὺς ὑπολειπομένους τῶν νεωτερι-
115 ζόντων κολάσαι. ὁ δὲ τὰς τοῦ δήμου δεήσεις
ἐν δευτέρῳ θέμενος μοῖραν ἔπεμπε τῶν ἱππέων
Ἰωάννην διώξουσαν, οἳ τὸν μὲν οὐ καταλαμ-
βάνουσιν, ἔφθη γὰρ εἰς Ἱεροσόλυμα διαφυγών,
τῶν δὲ συναπαράντων ἀποκτείνουσι μὲν εἰς
ἑξακισχιλίους, γύναια δὲ καὶ παιδία τρισχιλίων
116 ὀλίγον ἀποδέοντα περιελάσαντες ἀνήγαγον. ὁ δὲ
Τίτος ἤχθετο μὲν ἐπὶ τῷ μὴ παραχρῆμα τιμωρήσασθαι τὸν Ἰωάννην τῆς ἀπάτης, ἱκανὸν δὲ
ἀστοχήσαντι τῷ θυμῷ παραμύθιον ἔχων τὸ
πλῆθος τῶν αἰχμαλώτων καὶ τοὺς διεφθαρμένους,
117 εἰσῄει τε ἀνευφημούμενος εἰς τὴν πόλιν, καὶ τοῖς

panic-stricken and turned at every sound made by their comrades in flight, under the impression that their pursuers had overtaken them. Many strayed off the track, and on the highway many were crushed in the struggle to keep ahead. Piteous was the fate of the women and children, some making bold to call back their husbands or relatives and imploring them with shrieks to wait for them. But John's orders prevailed : " Save yourselves," he cried, " and flee where you can have your revenge on the Romans for any left behind, if they are caught." So this crowd of fugitives straggled away, each putting out the best strength and speed he had.

(5) Early next day Titus appeared before the walls to conclude the treaty. The gates were opened to him by the people, who came out with their wives and children and hailed him as benefactor and the liberator of their town from bondage ; for they proceeded to tell him of John's flight and besought him to spare them, and to enter the town and punish the insurgents who remained. Titus, regarding the citizens' petition as of secondary importance, at once dispatched a squadron of cavalry in pursuit of John. These failed to overtake him, the fugitive making good his escape to Jerusalem, but of his companions in flight they killed some six thousand and rounded up and brought back nearly three thousand women and children. Titus was mortified at failing to visit John's trickery with instant chastisement, but, with this host of prisoners and the slain as a sufficient solace to his disappointed resentment, he now entered the city amidst general

Titus enters Gischala.

---

[1] Niese: προσελθόντες MSS.

στρατιώταις ὀλίγον τοῦ τείχους παρασπάσαι κελεύσας νόμῳ καταλήψεως, ἀπειλαῖς μᾶλλον ἢ
κολάσει τοὺς ταράσσοντας τὴν πόλιν ἀνέστελλε·
118 πολλοὺς γὰρ ἂν καὶ διὰ τὰ οἰκεῖα μίση καὶ δια-
φορὰς ἰδίας ἐνδείξασθαι τοὺς ἀναιτίους, εἰ δια-
κρίνοι τοὺς τιμωρίας ἀξίους· ἄμεινον δ' εἶναι
μετέωρον ἐν φόβῳ τὸν αἴτιον καταλιπεῖν ἢ τινα
119 τῶν οὐκ ἀξίων αὐτῷ συναπολεῖν· τὸν μὲν γὰρ ἴσως
κἂν[1] σωφρονῆσαι δέει κολάσεως, τὴν ἐπὶ τοῖς
παρῳχηκόσι συγγνώμην αἰδούμενον, ἀδιόρθωτον
δὲ τὴν ἐπὶ τοῖς παραναλωθεῖσι τιμωρίαν εἶναι.
120 φρουρᾷ μέντοι τὴν πόλιν ἠσφαλίσατο, δι' ἧς τούς
τε νεωτερίζοντας ἐφέξειν καὶ τοὺς εἰρηνικὰ
φρονοῦντας θαρραλεωτέρους καταλείψειν ἔμελλεν.
Γαλιλαία μὲν [οὖν][2] οὕτως ἑάλω πᾶσα, πολλοῖς
ἱδρῶσι προγυμνάσασα Ῥωμαίους ἐπὶ τὰ Ἱεροσόλυμα.

121 (iii. 1) Πρὸς δὲ τὴν εἴσοδον τοῦ Ἰωάννου ὁ πᾶς
δῆμος ἐξεκέχυτο, καὶ περὶ ἕκαστον τῶν συμ-
πεφευγότων μυρίος ὅμιλος συνηθροισμένοι τὰς
122 ἔξωθεν συμφορὰς ἀνεπυνθάνοντο. τῶν δὲ τὸ μὲν
ἄσθμα θερμὸν ἔτι κοπτόμενον ἐδήλου τὴν ἀνάγκην,
ἠλαζονεύοντο δὲ κἂν κακοῖς, οὐ πεφευγέναι
Ῥωμαίους φάσκοντες, ἀλλ' ἥκειν πολεμήσοντες
123 αὐτοὺς ἐξ ἀσφαλοῦς· ἀλογίστων γὰρ εἶναι καὶ
ἀχρήστων παραβόλως προκινδυνεύειν περὶ Γίσχαλα
καὶ πολίχνας ἀσθενεῖς, δέον τὰ ὅπλα καὶ τὰς
ἀκμὰς ταμιεύεσθαι τῇ μητροπόλει καὶ συμφυλάσ-
124 σειν. ἔνθα δὴ παρεδήλουν τὴν ἅλωσιν τῶν
Γισχάλων, καὶ τὴν λεγομένην εὐσχημόνως ὑπο-

_____
[1] Bekker: καὶ mss.   [2] P: om. the rest.

acclamations ; and, after directing his troops to pull down a small portion of the wall in token of capture, he proceeded to repress the disturbers of the city's peace rather by threats than by punishment. For he feared that, should he attempt to pick out the offenders who deserved chastisement, many from private animosity and personal quarrels would accuse the guiltless, and he thought it better to leave the guilty in suspense and alarm than to involve any innocent persons in their destruction ; since the sinner might perhaps learn wisdom through fear of punishment and respect for the pardon granted him for past offences, whereas the death penalty unjustly inflicted was irremediable. He secured the town, however, by a garrison, calculated to check the rebels and to give confidence to the peaceable citizens on his departure. Galilee was thus now wholly subdued, All Galilee after affording the Romans a strenuous training for subdued. the impending Jerusalem campaign.

(iii. 1) When John entered the capital, the whole JERUSALEM : population poured forth and each of the fugitives reception of was surrounded by a vast crowd, eagerly asking John of Gischala. what had befallen outside. The newcomers, though their breath, still hot and gasping, betrayed their recent stress, nevertheless blustered under their misfortunes, declaring that they had not fled from the Romans, but had come to fight them on safe ground. " It would have been stupid and useless," they said, " recklessly to risk our lives for Gischala and such defenceless little towns, when we ought to husband our arms and energies for the metropolis and combine to defend it." Then they casually mentioned the fall of Gischala and their own

125 χώρησιν αὐτῶν οἱ πολλοὶ δρασμὸν ἐνενόουν. ὡς
μέντοι τὰ περὶ τοὺς αἰχμαλωτισθέντας ἠκούσθη,
σύγχυσις οὐ μετρία κατέσχε τὸν δῆμον, καὶ
μεγάλα τῆς ἑαυτῶν ἁλώσεως συνελογίζοντο τὰ
126 τεκμήρια. Ἰωάννης δ' ἐπὶ μὲν τοῖς καταλει-
φθεῖσιν[1] ἧττον ἠρυθρία, περιιὼν δ' ἑκάστους ἐπὶ τὸν
πόλεμον ἐνῆγεν ταῖς ἐλπίσιν, τὰ μὲν Ῥωμαίων
ἀσθενῆ κατασκευάζων, τὴν δ' οἰκείαν δύναμιν
127 ἐξαίρων, καὶ κατειρωνευόμενος τῆς τῶν ἀπείρων
ἀγνοίας, ὡς οὐδ' ἂν πτερὰ λαβόντες ὑπερβαῖέν
ποτε Ῥωμαῖοι τὸ Ἱεροσολύμων τεῖχος οἱ περὶ
ταῖς Γαλιλαίων κώμαις κακοπαθοῦντες καὶ πρὸς
τοῖς ἐκεῖ τείχεσι κατατρίψαντες τὰς μηχανάς.
128 (2) Τούτοις τὸ πολὺ μὲν τῶν νέων προσδι-
εφθείρετο καὶ πρὸς[2] τὸν πόλεμον ἦρτο, τῶν δὲ
σωφρονούντων καὶ γηραιῶν οὐκ ἦν ὅστις οὐ τὰ
μέλλοντα προορώμενος ὡς ἤδη τῆς πόλεως
129 οἰχομένης ἐπένθει. ὁ μὲν οὖν δῆμος ἦν ἐν τοιαύτῃ
συγχύσει, προδιέστη δὲ τὸ κατὰ τὴν χώραν
130 πλῆθος τῆς ἐν Ἱεροσολύμοις στάσεως. ὁ μὲν γὰρ
Τίτος ἀπὸ Γισχάλων εἰς Καισάρειαν, Οὐεσπασιανὸς δὲ ἀπὸ Καισαρείας εἰς Ἰάμνειαν καὶ
Ἄζωτον ἀφικόμενος παρίσταταί τε αὐτὰς[3] καὶ
φρουροὺς ἐγκαταστήσας ὑπέστρεψε, πολὺ πλῆθος
ἐπαγόμενος τῶν ἐπὶ δεξιᾷ προσκεχωρηκότων.
131 ἐκινεῖτο δ' ἐν ἑκάστῃ πόλει ταραχὴ καὶ πόλεμος
ἐμφύλιος, ὅσον τε ἀπὸ Ῥωμαίων ἀνέπνεον εἰς

---

[1] A¹L¹ Lat.: καταληφθεῖσιν the rest.

[2] + μὲν mss.   [3] C: αὐταῖς the rest.

ᵃ § 130, describing the movements of Titus and Vespasian,
comes in rather awkwardly, breaking the close connexion
between §§ 129 and 131.

" retreat," as they decently called it, though most
of their hearers understood them to mean flight.
When, however, the story of the prisoners came out,
profound consternation took possession of the people,
who drew therefrom plain indications of their own
impending capture. But John, little abashed at
the desertion of his friends, went round the several
groups, instigating them to war by the hopes he
raised, making out the Romans to be weak, extolling
their own power, and ridiculing the ignorance of the
inexperienced; even had they wings, he remarked,
the Romans would never surmount the walls of
Jerusalem, after having found such difficulty with
the villages of Galilee and worn out their engines
against their walls.

John as
leader of
war-party in
Jerusalem.

(2) By these harangues most of the youth were
seduced into his service and incited to war ; but of
the sober and elder men there was not one who did
not foresee the future and mourn for the city as if
it had already met its doom. Such was the confusion
prevailing among the citizens, but even before
sedition appeared in Jerusalem, party strife had
broken out in the country. For when Titus moved
from Gischala to Caesarea, Vespasian proceeded
from Caesarea to Jamnia and Azotus, and, having
reduced those towns and garrisoned them, returned
with a large multitude who had surrendered under
treaty.[a] Every city [b] was now agitated by tumult
and civil war, and the moment they had a respite
from the Romans they turned their hands against

Sedition
and party
strife in
Judaea.

[b] In this picture of the effects of sedition the historian
probably has in mind, as elsewhere, the famous reflections
of Thucydides (iii. 81-84) on revolution.

ἀλλήλους τὰς χεῖρας ἐπέστρεφον. ἦν δὲ τῶν
ἐρώντων τοῦ πολέμου πρὸς τοὺς ἐπιθυμοῦντας
132 εἰρήνης ἔρις χαλεπή. καὶ πρῶτον μὲν ἐν οἰκίαις
ἥπτετο τῶν ὁμονοούντων πάλαι τὸ φιλόνεικον,
ἔπειτα ἀφηνιάζοντες ἀλλήλων οἱ φίλτατοι¹ καὶ
συνιὼν ἕκαστος πρὸς τοὺς τὰ αὐτὰ προαιρου-
133 μένους ἤδη κατὰ πλῆθος ἀντετάσσοντο. καὶ
στάσις μὲν ἦν πανταχοῦ, τὸ νεωτερίζον δὲ καὶ τῶν
ὅπλων ἐπιθυμοῦν ἐπεκράτει νεότητι καὶ τόλμῃ
134 γηραιῶν καὶ σωφρόνων. ἐτράποντο δὲ πρῶτον
μὲν εἰς ἁρπαγὰς ἕκαστοι τῶν ἐπιχωρίων, ἔπειτα
συντασσόμενοι κατὰ λόχους ἐπὶ λῃστείαν τῶν
κατὰ τὴν χώραν, ὡς ὠμότητος καὶ παρανομίας
ἕνεκεν αὐτοῖς μηδὲν Ῥωμαίων τοὺς ὁμοφύλους
διαφέρειν καὶ πολὺ τοῖς πορθουμένοις κουφο-
τέραν δοκεῖν τὴν ὑπὸ Ῥωμαίοις ἅλωσιν.
135 (3) Οἱ φρουροὶ δὲ τῶν πόλεων τὰ μὲν ὄκνῳ τοῦ
κακοπαθεῖν, τὰ δὲ μίσει τοῦ ἔθνους, οὐδὲν ἢ μικρὰ
προσήμυνον τοῖς κακουμένοις, μέχρι κόρῳ τῶν
κατὰ τὴν χώραν ἁρπαγῶν ἀθροισθέντες οἱ τῶν
πανταχοῦ συνταγμάτων ἀρχιλῃσταὶ καὶ γενόμενοι
πονηρίας στῖφος εἰς τὰ Ἱεροσόλυμα παρεισ-
136 φθείρονται, πόλιν ἀστρατήγητον καὶ πατρίῳ μὲν
ἔθει πᾶν ἀπαρατηρήτως δεχομένην τὸ ὁμόφυλον,
τότε δ' οἰομένων ἁπάντων τοὺς ἐπιχεομένους²
137 πάντας ἀπ' εὐνοίας ἥκειν συμμάχους. ὃ δὴ καὶ
δίχα τῆς στάσεως ὕστερον ἐβάπτισεν τὴν πόλιν·
πλήθει γὰρ ἀχρήστῳ καὶ ἀργῷ προεξαναλώθη
τὰ τοῖς μαχίμοις διαρκεῖν δυνάμενα, καὶ πρὸς

¹ + λαοί mss.: expunged in A.
² ἐπεισχεομένους MC (similar variant in § 307).

each other. Between the enthusiasts for war and
the friends of peace contention raged fiercely.
Beginning in the home this party rivalry first attacked
those who had long been bosom friends ; then the
nearest relations severed their connexions and joining those who shared their respective views ranged
themselves henceforth in opposite camps. Faction
reigned everywhere ; and the revolutionary and
militant party overpowered by their youth and recklessness the old and prudent. The various cliques
began by pillaging their neighbours, then banding
together in companies they carried their depreda-
tions throughout the country ; insomuch that in
cruelty and lawlessness the sufferers found no differ-
ence between compatriots and Romans, indeed to
be captured by the latter seemed to the unfortunate
victims far the lighter fate.

(3) The garrisons of the towns, partly from Irruption
of the
brigands
(Zealots)
into
Jerusalem.
reluctance to take risks, partly from their hatred
of the nation, afforded little or no protection to
the distressed. In the end, satiated with their
pillage of the country, the brigand chiefs of all
these scattered bands joined forces and, now merged
into one pack of villainy, stole into poor Jerusalem—
a city under no commanding officer and one which,
according to hereditary custom, unguardedly
admitted all of Jewish blood, and the more readily
at that moment when it was universally believed
that all who were pouring into it came out of goodwill as its allies. Yet it was just this circumstance
which, irrespectively of the sedition, eventually
wrecked the city ; for supplies which might have
sufficed for the combatants were squandered upon
a useless and idle mob, who brought upon themselves,

197

JOSEPHUS

τῷ πολέμῳ στάσιν τε ἑαυτοῖς καὶ λιμὸν ἐπικατ-
εσκεύασαν.
138 (4) Ἄλλοι τε ἀπὸ τῆς χώρας λῃσταὶ παρελ-
θόντες εἰς τὴν πόλιν καὶ τοὺς ἔνδον προσλαβόντες
χαλεπωτέρους οὐδὲν ἔτι τῶν δεινῶν παρίεσαν·
139 οἵ γε οὐ μόνον¹ ἁρπαγαῖς καὶ λωποδυσίαις τὴν
τόλμαν ἐμέτρουν, ἀλλὰ καὶ μέχρι φόνων ἐχώρουν,
οὐ νυκτὸς ἢ λαθραίως ἢ ἐπὶ τοὺς τυχόντας, ἀλλὰ
φανερῶς καὶ μεθ' ἡμέραν καὶ τῶν ἐπισημοτάτων
140 καταρχόμενοι. πρῶτον μὲν γὰρ Ἀντίπαν, ἄνδρα
τοῦ βασιλικοῦ γένους καὶ τῶν κατὰ τὴν πόλιν
δυνατωτάτων, ὡς καὶ τοὺς δημοσίους θησαυροὺς
141 πεπιστεῦσθαι, συλλαβόντες εἶρξαν· ἐπὶ τούτῳ
Ληουΐαν τινὰ τῶν ἐπισήμων καὶ Συφὰν υἱὸν
Ἀρεγέτου,² βασιλικὸν δ' ἦν καὶ τούτων τὸ γένος,
πρὸς δὲ τοὺς κατὰ τὴν χώραν προύχειν δοκοῦντας.
142 δεινὴ δὲ κατάπληξις εἶχε τὸν δῆμον, καὶ καθάπερ
κατειλημμένης τῆς πόλεως πολέμῳ τὴν καθ'
αὑτὸν ἕκαστος σωτηρίαν ἠγάπα.
143 (5) Τοῖς δ' οὐκ ἀπέχρη τὰ δεσμὰ τῶν συνειλημ-
μένων, οὐδὲ ἀσφαλὲς ᾤοντο τὸ μέχρι πολλοῦ
144 δυνατοὺς ἄνδρας οὕτω φυλάσσειν· ἱκανοὺς μὲν γὰρ
εἶναι καὶ τοὺς οἴκους αὐτῶν πρὸς ἄμυναν οὐκ
ὀλιγάνδρους ὄντας, οὐ μὴν ἀλλὰ καὶ τὸν δῆμον
ἐπαναστήσεσθαι τάχα κινηθέντα πρὸς τὴν παρα-
145 νομίαν. δόξαν οὖν ἀναιρεῖν αὐτούς, Ἰωάννην τινὰ
πέμπουσιν τὸν ἐξ αὐτῶν εἰς φόνους προχειρότατον·

¹ ? read μόναις.
² PA, cf. Ῥεγέτου L, Rageti Lat.: Ραγ(Ρεγ-)ώλου, Ραγουήλου
the rest.

ᵃ He, with two other relatives of Agrippa II, Saul and
Costobar, had sought through the king's influence to nip
198

in addition to the war, the miseries of sedition and famine.

(4) Fresh brigands from the country entering the city and joining the yet more formidable gang within, abstained henceforth from no enormities. For, not restricting their audacity to raids and highway robberies, they now proceeded to murders, committed not under cover of night or clandestinely or on ordinary folk, but openly, in broad daylight, and with the most eminent citizens for their earliest victims. The first was Antipas,[a] one of the royal family and he carried such weight in the city that he was entrusted with the charge of the public treasury. Him they arrested and imprisoned, and after him Levias, one of the nobles, and Syphas, son of Aregetes—both also of royal blood—besides other persons of high reputation throughout the country. Dire panic now seized the people, and as if the city had been captured by the enemy none cherished any thought but that of his personal security. They arrest and murder eminent citizens.

(5) The brigands, however, were not satisfied with having put their captives in irons, and considered it unsafe thus to keep for long in custody influential persons, with numerous families quite capable of avenging them; they feared, moreover, that the people might be moved by their outrageous action to rise against them. They accordingly decided to kill their victims and commissioned for this purpose the most handy assassin among them, one John,

the Jewish revolt in the bud (ii. 418); later, he remained in Jerusalem when the others fled (ii. 557).

Δορκάδος οὗτος ἐκαλεῖτο παῖς κατὰ τὴν ἐπιχώριον
γλῶσσαν· ᾧ δέκα συνελθόντες εἰς τὴν εἰρκτὴν
ξιφήρεις ἀποσφάττουσιν τοὺς συνειλημμένους.[1]

146 παρανομήματι δ᾽ ἐν[2] τηλικούτῳ μεγάλως ἐπεψεύ-
δοντο[3] καὶ πρόφασιν[4]· διαλεχθῆναι γὰρ αὐτοὺς
Ῥωμαίοις περὶ παραδόσεως τῶν Ἱεροσολύμων,
καὶ προδότας ἀνῃρηκέναι τῆς κοινῆς ἐλευθερίας
ἔφασκον, καθόλου τ᾽ ἐπηλαζονεύοντο τοῖς τολμήμασιν ὡς εὐεργέται καὶ σωτῆρες τῆς πόλεως
γεγενημένοι.

147 (6) Συνέβη δὲ εἰς τοσοῦτον τὸν μὲν δῆμον
ταπεινότητος καὶ δέους, ἐκείνους δ᾽ ἀπονοίας
προελθεῖν, ὡς ἐπ᾽ αὐτοῖς εἶναι καὶ τὰς χειροτονίας

148 τῶν ἀρχιερέων. ἄκυρα γοῦν τὰ γένη ποιήσαντες,
ἐξ ὧν κατὰ διαδοχὰς οἱ ἀρχιερεῖς ἀπεδείκνυντο,
καθίστασαν ἀσήμους καὶ ἀγενεῖς, ἵν᾽ ἔχοιεν

149 συνεργοὺς τῶν ἀσεβημάτων· τοῖς γὰρ παρ᾽ ἀξίαν
ἐπιτυχοῦσι τῆς ἀνωτάτω τιμῆς ὑπακούειν ἦν

150 ἀνάγκη τοῖς παρασχοῦσι. συνέκρουον δὲ καὶ
τοὺς ἐν τέλει ποικίλαις ἐπινοίαις καὶ λογοποιίαις,
καιρὸν ἑαυτοῖς ἐν ταῖς πρὸς ἀλλήλους τῶν κωλυόν-
των φιλονεικίαις ποιούμενοι, μέχρι τῶν εἰς ἀνθρώπους ὑπερεμπλησθέντες ἀδικημάτων ἐπὶ τὸ θεῖον
μετήνεγκαν τὴν ὕβριν καὶ μεμιασμένοις τοῖς ποσὶ
παρῄεσαν εἰς τὸ ἅγιον.

151 (7) Ἐπανισταμένου τε αὐτοῖς ἤδη τοῦ πλήθους,

---

[1] εἰργμένους LC Exc. and margin of PAM.
[2] ἐπὶ CA[marg.]: Niese (ed. min.) omits.
[3] Dindorf: ἀπεψεύδοντο mss.
[4] προφάσεις ἀνέπλαττον PAM.

---

[a] i.e. " Gazelle," in Aramaic Bar Tabitha (cf. Acts ix. 36) ;
Dorcas was used also by Greeks as a woman's name (Wetstein).

known in their native tongue as son of Dorcas [a] ;
he with ten others entered the gaol with drawn
swords and butchered the prisoners. For such a
monstrous crime they invented as monstrous an
excuse, declaring that their victims had conferred
with the Romans concerning the surrender of Jerusalem and had been slain as traitors to the liberty
of the state. In short, they boasted of their audacious
acts as though they had been the benefactors and
saviours of the city.

(6) In the end, to such abject prostration and
terror were the people reduced and to such heights
of madness rose these brigands, that they actually
took upon themselves the election to the high priesthood. Abrogating the claims of those families from
which in turn the high priests had always been
drawn,[b] they appointed to that office ignoble and
low born individuals, in order to gain accomplices in
their impious crimes ; for persons who had unde-
servedly attained to the highest dignity were bound
to obey those who had conferred it. Moreover, by
various devices and libellous statements, they brought
the official authorities into collision with each other,
finding their own opportunity in the bickerings of
those who should have kept them in check ; until,
glutted with the wrongs which they had done to
men, they transferred their insolence to the Deity
and with polluted feet invaded the sanctuary.

(7) An insurrection of the populace was at length

[b] For this limitation of the high priesthood to a few
privileged families see Schürer, *G.J.V.* (ed. 3) ii. 222. The
contents of this section are partly repeated in that which
follows ; a duplication perhaps indicating imperfect editorial
revision.

ἐνῆγε γὰρ ὁ γεραίτατος[1] τῶν ἀρχιερέων Ἄνανος,
ἀνὴρ σωφρονέστατος καὶ τάχα ἂν διασώσας τὴν
πόλιν, εἰ τὰς τῶν ἐπιβούλων χεῖρας ἐξέφυγεν, οἱ
δὲ τὸν νεὼν τοῦ θεοῦ φρούριον αὑτοῖς καὶ τῶν
ἀπὸ τοῦ δήμου ταραχῶν ποιοῦνται καταφυγήν,
152 καὶ τυραννεῖον ἦν αὐτοῖς τὸ ἅγιον. παρεκίρνατο
δὲ τοῖς δεινοῖς εἰρωνεία, τὸ τῶν ἐνεργουμένων
153 ἀλγεινότερον· ἀποπειρώμενοι γὰρ τῆς τοῦ δήμου
καταπλήξεως καὶ τὴν αὑτῶν δοκιμάζοντες ἰσχὺν
κληρωτοὺς ἐπεχείρησαν ποιεῖν τοὺς ἀρχιερεῖς
οὔσης, ὡς ἔφαμεν, κατὰ γένος αὐτῶν τῆς διαδοχῆς.
154 ἦν δὲ πρόσχημα μὲν τῆς ἐπιβολῆς[2] ἔθος ἀρχαῖον,
ἐπειδὴ καὶ πάλαι κληρωτὴν ἔφασαν εἶναι τὴν
ἀρχιερωσύνην, τὸ δ᾽ ἀληθὲς τοῦ βεβαιοτέρου[3]
κατάλυσις καὶ τέχνη πρὸς δυναστείαν τὰς ἀρχὰς
δι᾽ αὑτῶν καθισταμένοις.
155 (8) Καὶ δὴ μεταπεμψάμενοι μίαν τῶν ἀρχ-
ιερατικῶν φυλήν, Ἐνιάχιν καλεῖται, διεκλήρουν
ἀρχιερέα, λαγχάνει δ᾽ ἀπὸ τύχης ὁ μάλιστα
διαδείξας αὐτῶν τὴν παρανομίαν, Φαννί τις ὄνομα,
υἱὸς Σαμουήλου κώμης Ἀφθίας, ἀνὴρ οὐ μόνον
οὐκ ἐξ ἀρχιερέων, ἀλλ᾽ οὐδ᾽ ἐπιστάμενος σαφῶς
156 τί ποτ᾽ ἦν ἀρχιερωσύνη δι᾽ ἀγροικίαν. ἀπὸ γοῦν
τῆς χώρας αὐτὸν ἄκοντα σύραντες ὥσπερ ἐπὶ
σκηνῆς ἀλλοτρίῳ κατεκόσμουν προσωπείῳ, τήν

---

[1] γεραίτερος PAM.
[2] Niese: ἐπιβουλῆς mss.
[3] L[1]: + νόμου the rest.

---

[a] For his murder and an encomium on his character see
§§ 316-325.   [b] Or " by families "; see § 148.
[c] The φυλή (" clan ") is a subdivision of the πατρία or
ἐφημερίς (" course ").   Josephus himself belonged to the
202

pending, instigated by Ananus, the senior of the Insurrection against
chief priests, a man of profound sanity, who might Zealots
possibly have saved the city, had he escaped the headed by Ananus.
conspirators' hands.[a]   At this threat these wretches
converted the temple of God into their fortress and The Zealots
refuge from any outbreak of popular violence, and occupy the temple
made the Holy Place the headquarters of their
tyranny.   To these horrors was added a spice of and select
mockery more galling than their actions.   For, to a high-priest by lot.
test the abject submission of the populace and make
trial of their own strength, they essayed to appoint
the high priests by lot, although, as we have stated,
the succession was hereditary.[b]   As pretext for this
scheme they adduced ancient custom, asserting that
in old days the high priesthood had been determined
by lot; but in reality their action was the abrogation
of established practice and a trick to make themselves supreme by getting these appointments into
their own hands.

(8) They accordingly summoned one of the high-
priestly clans,[c] called Eniachin, and cast lots for a
high priest.   By chance the lot fell to one who proved
a signal illustration of their depravity; he was an
individual named Phanni, son of Samuel, of the
village of Aphthia,[d] a man who not only was not
descended from high priests, but was such a clown
that he scarcely knew what the high priesthood
meant.   At any rate they dragged their reluctant
victim out of the country and, dressing him up for
his assumed part, as on the stage, put the sacred

first of the twenty-four priestly courses, and to the most
eminent of its constituent clans, *Vita* 2.   The clan Eniachin
is mentioned here only; the suggestion of Lowth to read
ἡ Ἰακὶμ for Ἐνιάχιν (Ἐνιακείμ), comparing 1 Chron. xxiv. 12
(the *course* Jakim), is uncalled for.   [d] Site unknown.

τ' ἐσθῆτα περιτιθέντες τὴν ἱερὰν καὶ τὸ τί δεῖ
157 ποιεῖν ἐπὶ καιροῦ διδάσκοντες. χλεύη δ' ἦν
ἐκείνοις καὶ παιδιὰ τὸ τηλικοῦτον ἀσέβημα, τοῖς
δ' ἄλλοις ἱερεῦσιν ἐπιθεωμένοις πόρρωθεν παιζόμενον τὸν νόμον δακρύειν ἐπήει καὶ κατέστενον
τὴν τῶν ἱερῶν τιμῶν κατάλυσιν.

158 (9) Ταύτην τὴν τόλμαν αὐτῶν οὐκ ἤνεγκεν ὁ
δῆμος, ἀλλ' ὥσπερ ἐπὶ τυραννίδος κατάλυσιν
159 ὥρμηντο πάντες· καὶ γὰρ οἱ προύχειν αὐτῶν
δοκοῦντες, Γωρίων τε υἱὸς Ἰωσήπου καὶ ὁ
Γαμαλιήλου Συμεών, παρεκρότουν ἔν τε ταῖς
ἐκκλησίαις ἀθρόους καὶ κατ' ἰδίαν περιιόντες
ἕκαστον ἤδη ποτὲ τίσασθαι τοὺς λυμεῶνας τῆς
ἐλευθερίας καὶ καθᾶραι τῶν μιαιφόνων τὸ ἅγιον,
160 οἵ τε δοκιμώτατοι τῶν ἀρχιερέων, Γαμάλα μὲν
υἱὸς Ἰησοῦς Ἀνάνου δὲ Ἄνανος, πολλὰ τὸν
δῆμον εἰς νωθείαν κατονειδίζοντες ἐν ταῖς συνόδοις
161 ἐπήγειρον τοῖς ζηλωταῖς· τοῦτο γὰρ αὐτοὺς
ἐκάλεσαν ὡς ἐπ' ἀγαθοῖς ἐπιτηδεύμασιν, ἀλλ'
οὐχὶ[1] ζηλώσαντες τὰ κάκιστα τῶν ἔργων [καὶ][2]
ὑπερβαλλόμενοι.

162 (10) Καὶ δὴ συνελθόντος τοῦ πλήθους εἰς
ἐκκλησίαν καὶ πάντων ἀγανακτούντων μὲν ἐπὶ
τῇ καταλήψει τῶν ἁγίων ταῖς τε ἁρπαγαῖς καὶ
τοῖς πεφονευμένοις, οὔπω δὲ πρὸς τὴν ἄμυναν
ὡρμημένων τῷ δυσεπιχειρήτους, ὅπερ ἦν, τοὺς
ζηλωτὰς ὑπολαμβάνειν, καταστὰς ἐν μέσοις ὁ

---

[1] ἀλλ' οὐχί L Lat.: ἄλλους the rest.   [2] om. PA Lat.

---

[a] Probably the Joseph, son of Gorion, who, along with
Ananus, was given supreme control in Jerusalem at the outbreak of war, ii. 563 ; the younger Gorion here mentioned
bears his grandfather's name.

vestments upon him and instructed him how to act in keeping with the occasion. To them this monstrous impiety was a subject for jesting and sport, but the other priests, beholding from a distance this mockery of their law, could not restrain their tears and bemoaned the degradation of the sacred honours.

(9) This latest outrage was more than the people could stand, and as if for the overthrow of a despotism one and all were now roused. For their leaders of outstanding reputation, such as Gorion, son of Joseph,[a] and Symeon,[b] son of Gamaliel, by public addresses to the whole assembly and by private visits to individuals, urged them to delay no longer to punish these wreckers of liberty and purge the sanctuary of its bloodstained polluters. Their efforts were supported by the most eminent of the high priests, Jesus,[c] son of Gamalas, and Ananus, son of Ananus, who at their meetings vehemently upbraided the people for their apathy and incited them against the Zealots ; for so these miscreants called themselves, as though they were zealous in the cause of virtue and not for vice in its basest and most extravagant form.

(10) And now, the populace being convened to a general assembly, when indignation was universally expressed at the occupation of the sanctuary, at the raids and murders, but no attempt at resistance had yet been made, owing to a belief, not unfounded, that the Zealots would prove difficult to dislodge,

Popular indignation roused.

General Assembly and speech of Ananus.

---

[b] Probably identical with Simon, son of Gamaliel, of whom, notwithstanding his opposition to Josephus, the historian, writes in the highest terms in *Vita* 190 ff.

[c] Befriended Josephus, *Vita* 193, 204 ; for his death and the historian's encomium upon him see §§ 316 ff.

Ἄνανος καὶ πολλάκις εἰς τὸν ναὸν ἀπιδὼν ἐμ-
163 πλήσας τε τοὺς ὀφθαλμοὺς δακρύων " ἦ καλόν
γ'," εἶπεν, " ἦν ἐμοὶ τεθνάναι πρὶν ἐπιδεῖν τὸν
οἶκον τοῦ θεοῦ τοσούτοις ἄγεσι καταγέμοντα καὶ
τὰς ἀβάτους καὶ ἁγίας χώρας ποσὶ μιαιφόνων
164 στενοχωρουμένας. ἀλλὰ περικείμενος τὴν ἀρχιερα-
τικὴν ἐσθῆτα καὶ τὸ τιμιώτατον καλούμενος τῶν
σεβασμίων ὀνομάτων, ζῶ καὶ φιλοψυχῶ, μηδ'[1]
ὑπὲρ τοὐμοῦ γήρως ὑπομένων εὐκλεῆ θάνατον·
†εἰ δὲ δεῖ[2] μόνος εἰμι[3] καὶ καθάπερ ἐν ἐρημίᾳ τὴν
ἐμαυτοῦ ψυχὴν ἐπιδώσω μόνην ὑπὲρ τοῦ θεοῦ.
165 τί γὰρ καὶ δεῖ ζῆν ἐν δήμῳ συμφορῶν ἀναισ-
θητοῦντι καὶ παρ' οἷς ἀπόλωλεν ἡ τῶν ἐν χερσὶ
παθῶν ἀντίληψις; ἁρπαζόμενοι γοῦν ἀνέχεσθε
καὶ τυπτόμενοι σιωπᾶτε, καὶ τοῖς φονευομένοις
166 οὐδ' ἐπιστένει τις ἀναφανδόν. ὢ τῆς πικρᾶς
τυραννίδος. τί [δὲ] μέμφομαι τοὺς τυράννους;
μὴ γὰρ οὐκ ἐτράφησαν ὑφ' ὑμῶν καὶ τῆς ὑμετέρας
167 ἀνεξικακίας; μὴ γὰρ οὐχ ὑμεῖς περιιδόντες τοὺς
πρώτους συνισταμένους, ἔτι δ' ἦσαν ὀλίγοι,
πλείους ἐποιήσατε τῇ σιωπῇ καὶ καθοπλιζομένων
ἠρεμοῦντες καθ' ἑαυτῶν ἐπεστρέψατε τὰ ὅπλα,
168 δέον τὰς πρώτας αὐτῶν ἐπικόπτειν ὁρμάς, ὅτε
λοιδορίαις καθήπτοντο τῶν εὐγενῶν,[4] ·ὑμεῖς δ'
ἀμελήσαντες ἐφ' ἁρπαγὰς παρωξύνατε τοὺς ἀλιτηρίους, καὶ πορθουμένων οἴκων λόγος ἦν οὐδείς·
τοιγαροῦν αὐτοὺς ἥρπαζον τοὺς δεσπότας, καὶ
συρομένοις διὰ μέσης τῆς πόλεως οὐδεὶς ἐπήμυνεν.

---

[1] Destinon (Lat. nec . . quidem): μήθ' PAML: μηκέτι
the rest.
[2] εἰ δὲ δεῖ conj.: εἰ δεῖ μὴ PA: εἰ δὴ μὴ L: εἰ δὲ δὴ
the rest.

Ananus arose in the midst and, often gazing on the
Temple with eyes filled with tears, spoke as follows :
    " Truly well had it been for me to have died ere
I had seen the house of God laden with such abom-
inations and its unapproachable and hallowed places
crowded with the feet of murderers ! And yet I
who wear the high priest's vestments, who bear that
most honoured of venerated names, am alive and
clinging to life, instead of braving a death which
would shed lustre on my old age. If it must be
then, alone will I go and, as in utter desolation,
devote this single life of mine in the cause of
God. Why, indeed, should I live amongst a people
insensible to calamities, who have lost the will to
grapple with the troubles on their hands ? When
plundered you submit, when beaten you are silent,
nay over the murdered none dares audibly to groan !
What bitter tyranny ! Yes, but why blame I the
tyrants ? For have they not been fostered by you
and your forbearance ? Was it not you who by
allowing those first recruits to combine, when they
were yet but few, swelled their numbers by your
silence, and by your inaction when they were arming
drew those arms upon yourselves ? You should have
cut short their opening attacks when they were
assailing the nobles with abuse ; instead, by your
negligence you incited the miscreants to rapine.
Then, when houses were pillaged, not a word was
said—consequently they laid hands on their owners
as well ; and when these were dragged through the
midst of the city, none rose in their defence. They

---

³ Destinon with Lat.: εἰμὶ MSS.
⁴ Destinon: συγγενῶν MSS.

169 οἱ δὲ καὶ δεσμοῖς ἠκίσαντο τοὺς ὑφ' ὑμῶν προ-
δοθέντας, ἐῶ λέγειν πόσους καὶ ποδαπούς· ἀλλ'
ἀκαταιτιάτοις ἀκρίτοις οὐδεὶς ἐβοήθησε τοῖς δεδε-
170 μένοις. ἀκόλουθον ἦν ἐπιδεῖν τοὺς αὐτοὺς φο-
νευομένους. ἐπείδομεν καὶ τοῦτο, καθάπερ ἐξ
ἀγέλης ζῴων ἀλόγων ἑλκομένου τοῦ κρατι-
στεύοντος ἀεὶ θύματος, οὐδὲ φωνήν τις ἀφῆκεν,
171 οὐχ ὅπως ἐκίνησε τὴν δεξιάν. φέρετε δὴ τοίνυν,
φέρετε πατούμενα βλέποντες [καὶ]¹ τὰ ἅγια καὶ
πάντας ὑποθέντες αὐτοὶ τοῖς ἀνοσίοις τοὺς τῶν
τολμημάτων βαθμοὺς μὴ βαρύνεσθε τὴν ὑπεροχήν·
καὶ γὰρ νῦν πάντως ἂν ἐπὶ μεῖζον προύκοψαν,
172 εἴ τι τῶν ἁγίων καταλῦσαι μεῖζον εἶχον. κεκράτη-
ται μὲν οὖν τὸ ὀχυρώτατον τῆς πόλεως· λεγέσθω
γὰρ νῦν τὸ ἱερὸν ὡς ἄκρα τις ἢ φρούριον· ἔχοντες
δ' ἐπιτετειχισμένην τυραννίδα τοσαύτην καὶ τοὺς
ἐχθροὺς ὑπὲρ κορυφὴν βλέποντες, τί βουλεύεσθε
173 καὶ τίσι τὰς γνώμας προσθάλπετε; Ῥωμαίους
ἄρα περιμενεῖτε, ἵν' ἡμῶν βοηθήσωσι τοῖς ἁγίοις;
ἔχει μὲν οὕτως τὰ πράγματα τῇ πόλει, καὶ πρὸς
τοσοῦτον ἥκομεν συμφορῶν, ἵν' ἡμᾶς ἐλεήσωσι
174 καὶ πολέμιοι;² οὐκ ἐξαναστήσεσθε, ὦ τλημονέ-
στατοι, καὶ πρὸς τὰς πληγὰς ἐπιστραφέντες, ὃ
κἀπὶ τῶν θηρίων ἔστιν ἰδεῖν, τοὺς τύπτοντας
ἀμυνεῖσθε; οὐκ ἀναμνήσεσθε τῶν ἰδίων ἕκαστος
συμφορῶν, οὐδ' ἃ πεπόνθατε πρὸ ὀφθαλμῶν
θέμενοι τὰς ψυχὰς ἐπ' αὐτοὺς θήξετε πρὸς τὴν

---

¹ ins. L¹ Lat.: om. the rest.
² Mark of interrogation substituted for full stop in mss.

ᵃ ἐπιτετειχισμένην τυραννίδα; the phrase comes from
τυραννίδα . . . ἐπετείχισεν ὑμῖν in the fourth Philippic attributed to Demosthenes (133).

next proceeded to inflict the indignity of bonds upon
those whom you had betrayed.   The number and
nature of these I forbear to state, but though they were
unimpeached, uncondemned, not a man assisted them
in their bondage.   The natural sequel was to watch
these same men massacred ; that spectacle also we
have witnessed, when as from a herd of dumb cattle
one prize victim after another was dragged to the
slaughter ; yet not a voice, much less a hand, was
raised.   Bear then, yes bear, I say, this further sight
of the trampling of your sanctuary ; and, after yourselves laying each step of the ladder for the audacity
of these profane wretches to mount, do not grudge
them the attainment of the climax ! Indeed by
now they would assuredly have proceeded to greater
heights, had aught greater than the sanctuary remained for them to overthrow.

" Well, they have mastered the strongest point in
the city—for henceforth the Temple must be spoken
of as a mere citadel or fortress— ; but with such a
tyrants' stronghold entrenched in your midst,[a] with
the spectacle of your foes above your heads, what
plans have you, what further cherished hopes console
your minds ? Will you wait for the Romans to
succour our holy places ?   Has the city come to such
a pass, are we reduced to such misery, that even
enemies must pity us ? Will you never rise, most
long-suffering of men, and turning to meet the lash,
as even the beast may be seen to turn, retaliate on
them that smite you ? Will you not call to mind
each one of you his personal calamities and, holding
before your eyes all that you have undergone, whet

JOSEPHUS

175 ἄμυναν; ἀπόλωλεν ἄρα παρ' ὑμῖν τὸ τιμιώτατον
τῶν παθῶν καὶ φυσικώτατον, ἐλευθερίας ἐπιθυμία,
φιλόδουλοι δὲ καὶ φιλοδέσποτοι γεγόναμεν, ὥσπερ
ἐκ προγόνων τὸ ὑποτάσσεσθαι παραλαβόντες.
176 ἀλλ' ἐκεῖνοί γε πολλοὺς καὶ μεγάλους ὑπὲρ τῆς
αὐτονομίας πολέμους διήνεγκαν καὶ οὔτε τῆς
Αἰγυπτίων οὔτε τῆς Μήδων δυναστείας ἡττήθησαν
177 ὑπὲρ τοῦ μὴ ποιεῖν τὸ κελευόμενον. καὶ τί δεῖ
τὰ τῶν προγόνων λέγειν; ἀλλ' ὁ νῦν πρὸς Ῥωμαίους πόλεμος, ἐῶ διελέγχειν πότερον λυσιτελὴς
ὢν καὶ σύμφορος ἢ τοὐναντίον, τίνα δ' οὖν ἔχει
178 πρόφασιν; οὐ τὴν ἐλευθερίαν; εἶτα τοὺς τῆς
οἰκουμένης δεσπότας μὴ φέροντες τῶν ὁμοφύλων
179 τυράννων ἀνεξόμεθα; καίτοι τὸ μὲν τοῖς ἔξωθεν
ὑπακούειν ἀνενέγκαι τις ἂν εἰς τὴν ἅπαξ ἡττή-
σασαν τύχην, τὸ δὲ τοῖς οἰκείοις εἴκειν πονηροῖς
180 ἀγεννῶν ἐστι καὶ προαιρουμένων. ἐπειδὴ δὲ
ἅπαξ ἐμνήσθην Ῥωμαίων, οὐκ ἀποκρύψομαι
πρὸς ὑμᾶς εἰπεῖν ὃ μεταξὺ τῶν λόγων ἐμπεσὸν
ἐπέστρεψε τὴν διάνοιαν, ὅτι κἂν ἁλῶμεν ὑπ'
ἐκείνοις, ἀπείη δὲ ἡ πεῖρα τοῦ λόγου, χαλεπώτερον
οὐδὲν παθεῖν ἔχομεν ὧν ἡμᾶς διατεθείκασιν οὗτοι.
181 πῶς δ' οὐ δακρύων ἄξιον ἐκείνων μὲν ἐν τῷ ἱερῷ
καὶ ἀναθήματα βλέπειν, τῶν δὲ ὁμοφύλων τὰ
σκῦλα σεσυληκότων καὶ ἀνελόντων τὴν τῆς
μητροπόλεως εὐγένειαν, καὶ πεφονευμένους ἄνδρας
182 ὧν ἀπέσχοντο ἂν κἀκεῖνοι κρατήσαντες; καὶ
Ῥωμαίους μὲν μηδέποτε ὑπερβῆναι τὸν ὅρον τῶν

your souls for revenge upon them ? Have you then
lost that most honourable, that most instinctive, of
passions—the desire for liberty ? Have we fallen in
love with slavery, in love with our masters, as though
submission were a heritage from our forefathers ?
Nay, they sustained many a mighty struggle for
independence and yielded neither to Egyptian nor
to Median domination, in their determination to
refuse obedience to a conqueror's behests. But why
need I speak of the deeds of our forefathers ? We
are now at war with Rome ; I forbear to inquire
whether such war is profitable and expedient or
the reverse, but what is its pretext ? Is it not
liberty ? If, then, we refuse to bow to the lords of
the inhabited world, are we to tolerate domestic
tyrants ? Yet subservience to the foreigner might
be attributed to fortune having once for all proved
too strong for us ; whereas to surrender to villains
of one's own country argues a base and deliberate
servility.

" Now that I have mentioned the Romans, I will
not conceal from you the thought which struck me
while I was speaking and turned my mind to them :
I mean that even should we fall beneath their arms
—God forbid that those words should ever be our
lot !—we can suffer no greater cruelty than what
these men have already inflicted upon us. Is it not
enough to bring tears to the eyes to see on the one
hand in our Temple courts the very votive offerings
of the Romans, on the other the spoils of our fellow-
countrymen who have plundered and slain the
nobility of the metropolis, massacring men whom
even the Romans, if victorious, would have spared ?
Is it not lamentable, that, while the Romans never

211

βεβήλων μηδὲ παραβῆναί τι τῶν ἱερῶν ἐθῶν,
πεφρικέναι δὲ πόρρωθεν ὁρῶντας τοὺς τῶν ἁγίων
183 περιβόλους, γεννηθέντας[1] δέ τινας ἐν τῇδε τῇ
χώρᾳ καὶ τραφέντας ὑπὸ τοῖς ἡμετέροις ἔθεσι
καὶ Ἰουδαίους καλουμένους ἐμπεριπατεῖν μέσοις
τοῖς ἁγίοις, θερμὰς ἔτι τὰς χεῖρας ἐξ ὁμοφύλων
184 ἔχοντας φόνων; εἶτά τις δέδοικεν τὸν ἔξωθεν
πόλεμον καὶ τοὺς ἐν συγκρίσει πολλῷ τῶν οἰκείων
ἡμῖν μετριωτέρους; καὶ γὰρ ἄν,[2] εἰ ἐτύμους δεῖ
τοῖς πράγμασι τὰς κλήσεις ἐφαρμόζειν, τάχα ἂν
εὕροι τις Ῥωμαίους μὲν ἡμῖν βεβαιωτὰς τῶν
185 νόμων, πολεμίους δὲ τοὺς ἔνδον. ἀλλ' ὅτι μὲν
ἐξώλεις οἱ ἐπίβουλοι τῆς ἐλευθερίας, καὶ πρὸς
ἃ δεδράκασιν οὐκ ἄν τις ἐπινοήσειεν δίκην ἀξίαν
κατ' αὐτῶν, οἶμαι πάντας ἥκειν πεπεισμένους
οἴκοθεν καὶ πρὸ τῶν ἐμῶν λόγων παρωξύνθαι
186 τοῖς ἔργοις ἐπ' αὐτούς, ἃ πεπόνθατε. καταπλήσ-
σονται δ' ἴσως οἱ πολλοὶ τό τε πλῆθος αὐτῶν καὶ
τὴν τόλμαν, ἔτι δὲ καὶ τὴν ἐκ τοῦ τόπου πλεονεξίαν.
187 ταῦτα δ' ὥσπερ συνέστη διὰ τὴν ὑμετέραν ἀμέ-
λειαν, καὶ νῦν αὐξηθήσεται πλέον ὑπερθεμένων·
καὶ γὰρ τὸ πλῆθος αὐτοῖς ἐπιτρέφεται καθ'
ἡμέραν, παντὸς πονηροῦ πρὸς τοὺς ὁμοίους αὐτο-
188 μολοῦντος, καὶ τὴν τόλμαν ἐξάπτει μέχρι νῦν
μηδὲν ἐμπόδιον, τῷ τε τόπῳ καθύπερθεν ὄντες
χρήσαιντ' ἄν[3] καὶ μετὰ παρασκευῆς, ἂν ἡμεῖς

---

[1] natos Lat.: γεννηθέντας Niese.
[2] om. ἄν L.
[3] Niese: χρήσαιντο mss.

---

[a] Or, if τῶν βεβήλων is neuter, " the limit of the unhallowed
(permitted) ground." The reference is to the stone balustrade
(δρύφακτος) separating the inner temple from the outer
court, with its warning inscriptions in Greek and Latin,

overstepped the limit fixed for the profane,[a] never violated one of our sacred usages, but beheld with awe from afar the walls that enclose our sanctuary, persons born in this very country, nurtured under our institutions and calling themselves Jews should freely perambulate our holy places, with hands yet hot with the blood of their countrymen ? After that, can any still dread the war with the foreigner and foes who by comparison are far more lenient to us than our own people ? Indeed, if one must nicely fit the phrase to the fact, it is the Romans who may well be found to have been the upholders of our laws, while their enemies were within the walls.

" However, of the abandoned character of these conspirators against liberty and that it would be impossible to conceive any adequate punishment for what they have done, I feel sure that you were all convinced when you left your homes, and that before this address of mine you were already driven to exasperation against them by those misdeeds from which you have suffered. Perhaps, however, most of you are overawed by their numbers, their audacity, and the further advantage which they derive from their position. But, as these arose through your supineness, so will they now be increased, the longer you delay. Indeed, their numbers are growing daily, as every villain deserts to his like ; their audacity is fired by meeting so far with no obstruction ; and they will doubtless avail themselves of their superior position, with the added benefit of

forbidding foreigners to pass under pain of death, v. 193 f. While the ordinary Roman scrupulously observed the rule, (ii. 341 Neapolitanus pays his devotions " from the permitted area "), conquerors such as Pompey, and even Titus himself, penetrated to the Holy Place (*Ap.* ii. 82, *B.* i. 152, vi. 260).

189 χρόνον δῶμεν. πιστεύσατε δ' ὡς, ἐὰν προσ-
βαίνωμεν ἐπ' αὐτούς, ἔσονται τῇ συνειδήσει
ταπεινότεροι, καὶ τὸ πλεονέκτημα τοῦ ὕψους ὁ
190 λογισμὸς ἀπολεῖ. τάχα τὸ θεῖον ὑβρισμένον ἀνα-
στρέψει κατ' αὐτῶν τὰ βαλλόμενα, καὶ τοῖς σφετέ-
ροις διαφθαρήσονται βέλεσιν οἱ δυσσεβεῖς. μόνον
191 ὀφθῶμεν αὐτοῖς, καὶ καταλέλυνται. καλὸν δέ,
κἂν προσῇ τις κίνδυνος, ἀποθνήσκειν πρὸς τοῖς
ἱεροῖς πυλῶσι κἂν τὴν ψυχήν, εἰ καὶ μὴ πρὸ
παίδων ἢ γυναικῶν, ἀλλ' ὑπὲρ τοῦ θεοῦ καὶ τῶν
192 ἁγίων προέσθαι. προστήσομαι δ' ἐγὼ γνώμῃ
τε καὶ χειρί, καὶ οὔτ' ἐπίνοιά τις ὑμῖν λείψει πρὸς
ἀσφάλειαν ἐξ ἡμῶν οὔτε τοῦ σώματος ὄψεσθε
φειδόμενον."
193 (11) Τούτοις ὁ Ἄνανος παρακροτεῖ τὸ πλῆθος
ἐπὶ τοὺς ζηλωτάς, οὐκ ἀγνοῶν μὲν ὡς εἶεν ἤδη
δυσκατάλυτοι πλήθει τε καὶ νεότητι καὶ παρα-
στήματι ψυχῆς, τὸ πλέον δὲ συνειδήσει τῶν εἰρ-
γασμένων· οὐ γὰρ ἐνδώσειν αὐτοὺς εἰς ἔσχατον[1]
194 συγγνώμην ἐφ' οἷς ἔδρασαν ἀπελπίσαντας[2]· ὅμως
δὲ πᾶν ὁτιοῦν παθεῖν προῃρεῖτο μᾶλλον ἢ περιιδεῖν
195 ἐν τοιαύτῃ τὰ πράγματα συγχύσει. τὸ δὲ πλῆθος
ἄγειν αὐτοὺς ἐβόα καθ' ὧν παρεκάλει, καὶ προκινδυνεύειν ἕκαστος ἦν ἑτοιμότατος.
196 (12) Ἐν ὅσῳ δὲ ὁ Ἄνανος κατέλεγέ τε καὶ
συνέτασσε τοὺς ἐπιτηδείους πρὸς μάχην, οἱ
ζηλωταὶ πυνθανόμενοι τὴν ἐπιχείρησιν, παρῆσαν
γὰρ οἱ ἀγγέλλοντες αὐτοῖς πάντα τὰ παρὰ τοῦ
δήμου, παροξύνονται κἀκ τοῦ ἱεροῦ προπηδῶντες
ἀθρόοι τε καὶ κατὰ λόχους οὐδενὸς ἐφείδοντο τῶν

---

[1] Hudson with one ms.: ἐσχάτην the rest.

214

preparation, if we give them time. But, believe me, if we mount to the attack, conscience will humble them and the advantage of superior height will be neutralized by reflection. Maybe, the Deity, whom they have outraged, will turn their missiles back upon them,[a] and their own weapons will bring destruction upon the impious wretches. Only let us face them and their doom is sealed. And, if the venture has its attendant risks, it were a noble end to die at the sacred portals and to sacrifice our lives if not for wives and children, yet for God and for the sanctuary. But I will support you both with head and hand : there shall be no lack on my part of thought to ensure your safety, nor shall you see me spare my person."

(11) Thus did Ananus incite the populace against the Zealots. He knew full well how difficult their extermination had already become through their numbers, vigour, and intrepidity, but above all through their consciousness of their deeds ; since, in despair of obtaining pardon for all they had done, they would never give in to the end. Nevertheless, he preferred to undergo any suffering rather than allow affairs to remain in such confusion. The people too now clamoured for him to lead them against the foe whom he urged them to attack, each man fully ready to brave the first danger.

Ananus and the citizens prepare to attack the Zealots.

(12) But while Ananus was enlisting and marshalling efficient recruits, the Zealots hearing of the projected attack—for word was brought to them of all the people's proceedings—were furious, and dashed out of the Temple, in regiments and smaller units,

Fierce fighting.

---

[a] As at Gamala, § 76.

[a] Destinon (*cf.* v. 354): ἐλπίσαντας (or -ες) MSS.

197 προστυγχανόντων. ἀθροίζεται δ' ὑπ' Ἀνάνου ταχέως τὸ δημοτικόν, πλήθει μὲν ὑπερέχον, ὅπλοις
δὲ καὶ τῷ μὴ συγκεκροτῆσθαι λειπόμενον τῶν
198 ζηλωτῶν. τὸ πρόθυμον δὲ παρ' ἑκατέροις ἀνεπλήρου τὰ λείποντα, τῶν μὲν ἀπὸ τῆς πόλεως
ἀνειληφότων ὀργὴν ἰσχυροτέραν τῶν ὅπλων, τῶν
δ' ἀπὸ τοῦ ἱεροῦ τόλμαν παντὸς πλήθους ὑπερ-
199 έχουσαν· καὶ οἱ μὲν ἀοίκητον ὑπολαμβάνοντες
αὐτοῖς τὴν πόλιν εἰ μὴ τοὺς λῃστὰς ἐκκόψειαν
αὐτῆς, οἱ ζηλωταὶ δ' εἰ μὴ κρατοῖεν οὐκ ἔστιν
ἧστινος ὑστερήσειν τιμωρίας, συνερρήγνυντο[1] στρα-
200 τηγούμενοι τοῖς πάθεσι, τὸ μὲν πρῶτον κατὰ τὴν
πόλιν καὶ πρὸ τοῦ ἱεροῦ λίθοις βάλλοντες ἀλλήλους
καὶ πόρρωθεν διακοντιζόμενοι, κατὰ δὲ τὰς
τροπὰς οἱ κρατοῦντες ἐχρῶντο τοῖς ξίφεσι· καὶ
πολὺς ἦν ἑκατέρων φόνος, τραυματίαι τε ἐγίνοντο
201 συχνοί. καὶ τοὺς μὲν ἀπὸ τοῦ δήμου διεκόμιζον
εἰς τὰς οἰκίας οἱ προσήκοντες, ὁ δὲ βληθεὶς τῶν
ζηλωτῶν εἰς τὸ ἱερὸν ἀνῄει καθαιμάσσων τὸ θεῖον
ἔδαφος· καὶ μόνον ἄν τις εἴποι τὸ ἐκείνων αἷμα
202 μιᾶναι τὰ ἅγια. κατὰ μὲν οὖν τὰς συμβολὰς
ἐκτρέχοντες ἀεὶ περιῆσαν οἱ λῃστρικοί, τεθυμω-
μένοι δ' οἱ δημοτικοὶ καὶ πλείους ἀεὶ γινόμενοι,
κακίζοντες τοὺς ἐνδιδόντας καὶ μὴ διδόντες τοῖς
τρεπομένοις ἀναχώρησιν οἱ κατόπιν βιαζόμενοι,
πᾶν μὲν ἐπιστρέφουσι τὸ σφέτερον εἰς τοὺς
203 ὑπεναντίους· κἀκείνων μηκέτ' ἀντεχόντων τῇ βίᾳ,
κατὰ μικρὸν δ' ἀναχωρούντων εἰς τὸ ἱερὸν συν-
204 εισπίπτουσιν οἱ περὶ τὸν Ἄνανον. τοῖς δὲ κατάπληξις ἐμπίπτει στερομένοις τοῦ πρώτου περιβόλου, καὶ καταφυγόντες εἰς τὸ ἐνδοτέρω ταχέως

[1] A² : + δὲ the rest.

and spared none who fell in their way. Ananus
promptly collected his citizen force, which, though
superior in numbers, in arms and through lack of
training was no match for the Zealots. Ardour,
however, supplied either party's deficiencies, those
from the city being armed with a fury more powerful
than weapons, those from the Temple with a recklessness outweighing all numerical superiority ; the
former persuaded that the city would be uninhabit-
able by them unless the brigands were eradicated,
the Zealots that unless they were victorious no form
of punishment would be spared them. Thus, swayed
by their passions, they met in conflict. This opened
with a mutual discharge of stones from all parts of
the city and from the front of the Temple and a
long range javelin combat ; but, when either party
gave way, the victors employed their swords, and
there was great slaughter on both sides and multitudes were wounded. The injured civilians were
carried into the houses by their relatives, while any
Zealot who was struck climbed up into the Temple,
staining with his blood the sacred pavement ; and
it might be said that no blood but theirs defiled the
sanctuary. In these engagements the sallies of the
brigands proved invariably successful ; but the
populace, roused to fury and continually growing
in numbers, upbraiding those who gave way, while
those pressing forward in rear refused passage to
the fugitives, finally turned their whole force upon
their opponents. The latter no longer able to withstand this pressure gradually withdrew into the
Temple, Ananus and his men rushing in along with Ananus
them. Dismayed by the loss of the outer court, the masters the
Zealots fled into the inner and instantly barred the outer court

217

JOSEPHUS

205 ἀποκλείουσι τὰς πύλας. τῷ δ' Ἀνάνῳ προσ-
βαλεῖν μὲν οὐκ ἐδόκει τοῖς ἱεροῖς πυλῶσιν,
ἄλλως τε κἀκείνων βαλλόντων ἄνωθεν, ἀθέμιτον
δ' ἡγεῖτο, κἂν κρατήσῃ, μὴ προηγνευκὸς εἰσ-
206 αγαγεῖν τὸ πλῆθος· διακληρώσας δ' ἐκ πάντων εἰς
ἑξακισχιλίους ὁπλίτας καθίστησιν ἐπὶ ταῖς στοαῖς
207 φρουρούς· διεδέχοντο δ' ἄλλοι τούτους, καὶ παντὶ
μὲν ἀνάγκη παρεῖναι πρὸς τὴν φυλακὴν ἐκ περιόδου,
πολλοὶ δὲ τῶν ἐν ἀξιώμασιν ἐφεθέντες ὑπὸ τῶν
ἄρχειν δοκούντων μισθούμενοι πενιχροτέρους ἀνθ'
ἑαυτῶν ἐπὶ τὴν φρουρὰν ἔπεμπον.
208 (13) Γίνεται δὲ τούτοις πᾶσιν ὀλέθρου παραίτιος
Ἰωάννης, ὃν ἔφαμεν ἀπὸ Γισχάλων διαδρᾶναι,
δολιώτατος ἀνὴρ καὶ δεινὸν ἔρωτα τυραννίδος ἐν
τῇ ψυχῇ περιφέρων, ὃς πόρρωθεν ἐπεβούλευε τοῖς
209 πράγμασιν. καὶ δὴ τότε τὰ τοῦ δήμου φρονεῖν
ὑποκρινόμενος συμπεριῄει μὲν τῷ Ἀνάνῳ βου-
λευομένῳ¹ σὺν τοῖς δυνατοῖς μεθ' ἡμέραν καὶ
νύκτωρ ἐπιόντι τὰς φυλακάς, διήγγελλε δὲ τὰ
ἀπόρρητα τοῖς ζηλωταῖς, καὶ πᾶν σκέμμα τοῦ
δήμου πρὶν καλῶς βουλευθῆναι παρὰ τοῖς ἐχθροῖς
210 ἐγινώσκετο δι' αὐτοῦ. μηχανώμενος δὲ τὸ μὴ
δι' ὑποψίας ἐλθεῖν ἀμέτροις ἐχρῆτο ταῖς θερα-
πείαις εἰς τόν τε Ἄνανον καὶ τοὺς τοῦ δήμου
211 προεστῶτας. ἐχώρει δ' εἰς τοὐναντίον αὐτῷ τὸ
φιλότιμον· διὰ γὰρ τὰς ἀλόγους κολακείας μᾶλλον
ὑπωπτεύετο, καὶ τὸ πανταχοῦ παρεῖναι μὴ καλούμενον ἔμφασιν προδοσίας τῶν ἀπορρήτων παρεῖχε.

¹ + μὲν PAVR : + τε Destinon.

ᵃ §§ 106 ff.
ᵇ Cf. § 85 with note. This passage again recalls Sallust's
218

gates. Ananus did not think fit to assail the sacred portals, especially under the enemy's hail of missiles from above, but considered it unlawful, even were he victorious, to introduce these crowds without previous purification ; instead, he selected by lot from the whole number six thousand armed men, whom he posted to guard the porticoes. These were to be relieved by others, and every man was bound to fall in for sentry duty in rotation ; but many persons of rank, with the permission of their superior officers, hired some of the lower classes and sent them to mount guard in their stead.

and blockades the Zealots in the temple.

(13) The subsequent destruction of this entire party was largely due to John, whose escape from Gischala we have related.[a] He was a man of extreme cunning who carried in his breast a dire passion for despotic power and had long been plotting against the state.[b] At this juncture, feigning to side with the people, he would accompany Ananus on his rounds, whether holding consultations with the leaders by day or visiting the sentries by night, and then divulge his secrets to the Zealots ; so that every idea proposed by the people, even before it had been thoroughly considered, was through his agency known to their opponents. Seeking to escape suspicion, he displayed unbounded servility to Ananus and the heads of the popular party, but this obsequiousness had the reverse effect ; for his extravagant flatteries only brought more suspicion upon him, and his ubiquitous and uninvited presence produced the impression that he was betraying

John of Gischala, the traitor to Ananus,

portrait of Catiline : "animus audax, subdolus (parallel to δολιώτατος here) . . hunc . . lubido maxuma invaserat rei publicae capiundae."

212 συνεώρων μὲν γὰρ αἰσθανομένους ἅπαντα τοὺς
ἐχθροὺς τῶν παρ' αὐτοῖς βουλευμάτων, πιθανώ-
τερος δ' οὐδεὶς ἦν Ἰωάννου πρὸς ὑποψίας τοῦ
213 διαγγέλλειν. ἀποσκευάσασθαι μὲν οὖν αὐτὸν οὐκ
ἦν ῥᾴδιον, ὄντα ⟨τε⟩[1] δυνατὸν ἐκ πονηρίας καὶ
ἄλλως οὐ τῶν ἀσήμων, ὑπεζωσμένον τε πολλοὺς
τῶν συνεδρευόντων τοῖς ὅλοις,[2] ἐδόκει δ' αὐτὸν
214 ὅρκοις πιστώσασθαι πρὸς εὔνοιαν. ὤμνυε δ' ὁ
Ἰωάννης ἑτοίμως εὐνοήσειν τε τῷ δήμῳ καὶ μήτε
βουλήν τινα μήτε πρᾶξιν προδώσειν τοῖς ἐχθροῖς,
συγκαταλύσειν δὲ τοὺς ἐπιτιθεμένους καὶ χειρὶ
215 καὶ γνώμῃ. οἱ δὲ περὶ τὸν Ἄνανον πιστεύσαντες
τοῖς ὅρκοις ἤδη χωρὶς ὑπονοίας εἰς τὰς συμ-
βουλίας αὐτὸν παρελάμβανον, καὶ δὴ καὶ πρε-
σβευτὴν εἰσπέμπουσι πρὸς τοὺς ζηλωτὰς περὶ
διαλύσεων· ἦν γὰρ αὐτοῖς σπουδὴ τὸ παρ' αὐτοῖς
μὴ μιᾶναι τὸ ἱερὸν μηδέ τινα τῶν ὁμοφύλων ἐν
αὐτῷ πεσεῖν.

216 (14) Ὁ δ' ὥσπερ τοῖς ζηλωταῖς ὑπὲρ εὐνοίας
ὀμόσας καὶ οὐ κατ' αὐτῶν, παρελθὼν εἴσω καὶ
καταστὰς εἰς μέσους πολλάκις μὲν ἔφη κινδυνεῦσαι
δι' αὐτούς, ἵνα μηδὲν ἀγνοήσωσι τῶν ἀπορρήτων,
ὅσα κατ' αὐτῶν οἱ περὶ τὸν Ἄνανον ἐβουλεύσαντο·
217 νῦν δὲ τὸν μέγιστον ἀναρριπτεῖν κίνδυνον σὺν
πᾶσιν αὐτοῖς, εἰ μή τις προσγένοιτο βοήθεια
218 δαιμόνιος. οὐ γὰρ ἔτι μέλλειν Ἄνανον, ἀλλὰ
πείσαντα μὲν τὸν δῆμον πεπομφέναι πρέσβεις
πρὸς Οὐεσπασιανόν, ἵν' ἐλθὼν κατὰ τάχος παρα-

---

[1] ὄντα τε Dindorf: ὄντα most mss. : οὔτε VR.
[2] ὅπλοις PAL[2].

---

[a] Literally "girt about (or 'under') him many," cf. ii.
275 ἴδιον στῖφος ὑπεζωσμένος " with his own band of followers

secrets. For it was observed that their enemies were aware of all their plans, and there was no one more open to the suspicion of disclosing them than John. It was, however, no easy matter to shake off one who had gained such influence through his villainy, who was in any case a man of mark, and who had won many followers[a] among those who met in council on the general weal; it was therefore decided to bind him over to loyalty by oath. John promptly swore that he would be true to the people, that he would betray neither counsel nor act to their foes, and would assist both with his arm and his advice in putting down their assailants. Relying on these oaths, Ananus and his party now admitted him without suspicion to their deliberations, and even went so far as to send him as their delegate to the Zealots to arrange a treaty; for they were anxious on their side to preserve the Temple from pollution and that none of their countrymen should fall within its walls.

(14) But John, as though he had given his oath of allegiance to the Zealots instead of against them, went in and, standing in their midst, addressed them as follows. " Often have I risked my life on your behalf, to keep you fully informed of all the secret schemes devised against you by Ananus and his followers; but now I am exposing myself to the greatest of perils, in which you will all be involved, unless some providential aid intervene to avert it. For Ananus, impatient of delay, has prevailed on the people to send an embassy to Vespasian, inviting

is bound over to loyalty

and sent as delegate to the Zealots.

John incites the Zealots to seek aid from outside against Ananus.

grouped around him "; a metaphorical use of the verb unattested elsewhere.

JOSEPHUS

λάβῃ τὴν πόλιν, ἀγνείαν δὲ παρηγγελκέναι κατ'
αὐτῶν εἰς τὴν ἑξῆς ἡμέραν, ἵν' ἢ κατὰ θρησκείαν
εἰσελθόντες ἢ καὶ βιασάμενοι συμμίξωσιν αὐτοῖς.
219 οὐχ ὁρᾶν δὲ μέχρι τίνος ἢ τὴν φρουρὰν οἴσουσιν
ἢ παρατάξονται πρὸς τοσούτους. προσετίθει δ'
ὡς αὐτὸς εἰσπεμφθείη κατὰ θεοῦ πρόνοιαν ὡς
πρεσβευτὴς ὑπὲρ¹ διαλύσεων· τὸν γὰρ Ἄνανον
ταύτας αὐτοῖς προτείνειν, ὅπως ἀνυποπτοτέροις²
220 ἐπέλθῃ. δεῖν οὖν ἢ τῷ λόγῳ τοῦ ζῆν τοὺς φρου-
ροῦντας ἱκετεύειν ἢ πορίζεσθαί τινα παρὰ τῶν
221 ἔξωθεν ἐπικουρίαν· τοὺς δὲ θαλπομένους ἐλπίδι
συγγνώμης εἰ κρατηθεῖεν, ἐπιλελῆσθαι τῶν ἰδίων
τολμημάτων ἢ νομίζειν ἅμα τῷ μετανοεῖν τοὺς
δεδρακότας εὐθέως ὀφείλειν διηλλάχθαι καὶ τοὺς
222 παθόντας. ἀλλὰ τῶν μὲν ἀδικησάντων διὰ μίσους
πολλάκις γίνεσθαι καὶ τὴν μεταμέλειαν, τοῖς
ἀδικηθεῖσι δὲ τὰς ὀργὰς ἐπ' ἐξουσίας χαλεπωτέρας·
223 ἐφεδρεύειν δέ γε ἐκείνοις φίλους καὶ συγγενεῖς
τῶν ἀπολωλότων καὶ δῆμον τοσοῦτον ὑπὲρ καταλύσεως νόμων καὶ δικαστηρίων τεθυμωμένον,
ὅπου κἂν ᾖ τι μέρος τὸ ἐλεοῦν, ὑπὸ πλείονος ἂν
αὐτὸ τοῦ διαγανακτοῦντος ἀφανισθῆναι.
224 (iv. 1) Τοιαῦτα μὲν ἐποίκιλλεν ἀθρόως δεδισσόμενος, καὶ τὴν ἔξωθεν βοήθειαν ἀναφανδὸν μὲν
οὐκ ἐθάρρει λέγειν, ἠνίσσετο δὲ τοὺς Ἰδουμαίους·
ἵνα δὲ καὶ τοὺς ἡγεμόνας τῶν ζηλωτῶν ἰδίᾳ

¹ περὶ P.
² L¹ (Lat. nihil suspicantes): ἀνοπλοτέροις PAL²: ἀ(ν)όπλοις
the rest.

ᵃ A specious statement, in view of his known reluctance to
allow his followers to enter the Temple without previous
purification (§ 205).
ᵇ In the collocation of " laws and law-courts " we seem

him to come at once and take possession of the city. To your further injury, he has announced a purification service [a] for to-morrow, in order that his followers may obtain admission here, either on the plea of worship or by force of arms, and attack you hand to hand. Nor do I see how you can long sustain either the present siege or a contest with such a host of opponents." He added that it was by the providence of God that he had himself been deputed to negotiate a treaty, as Ananus was offering them terms, only to fall upon them when off their guard. " It behoves you, therefore," he continued, " if you care for your lives, either to sue for mercy from your besiegers, or to procure some external aid. But any who cherish hopes of being pardoned in the event of defeat must either have forgotten their own daring deeds, or suppose that the penitence of the perpetrators should be followed by the instant reconciliation of the victims. On the contrary, the very repentance of wrongdoers is often detested and the resentment of the wronged is embittered by power. Watching their opportunity to retaliate are the friends and relatives of the slain and a whole host of people infuriated at the dissolution of their laws and law-courts.[b] In such a crowd, even if some few were moved to compassion, they would be crushed by an indignant majority."

(iv. 1) Such was the embroidered tale he told to create a general scare ; what " external aid " was intended he did not venture to say outright, but he was hinting ·at the Idumaeans. But in order to incense the personal feelings of the Zealots' leaders

The Zealots invoke the aid of the Idumaeans.

to hear the historian's Greek assistant speaking ; *cf.* § 258 and Vol. II. Introd. p. xiii.

παροξύνη, τὸν Ἄνανον εἴς τε ὠμότητα διέβαλλε
225 καὶ ἀπειλεῖν ἐκείνοις ἐξαιρέτως ἔλεγεν. ἦσαν δὲ
Ἐλεάζαρος μὲν υἱὸς Γίωνος,[1] ὃς δὴ καὶ πιθανώ-
τατος ἐδόκει τῶν ἐν αὐτοῖς νοῆσαί τε τὰ δέοντα
καὶ τὰ νοηθέντα πρᾶξαι, Ζαχαρίας δέ τις υἱὸς
226 Ἀμφικάλλει,[2] γένος ἐκ τῶν ἱερέων ἑκάτερος. οὗτοι
πρὸς ταῖς κοιναῖς τὰς ἰδίας καθ᾽ ἑαυτῶν ἀπειλὰς
ἀκούσαντες, ἔτι δ᾽ ὡς οἱ περὶ τὸν Ἄνανον δυναστείαν αὐτοῖς περιποιούμενοι Ῥωμαίους ἐπι-
καλοῖντο, καὶ γὰρ τοῦτο Ἰωάννης προσεψεύσατο,
μέχρι πολλοῦ μὲν ἠποροῦντο, τί χρὴ πράττειν εἰς
227 ὀξὺν οὕτως καιρὸν συνεωσμένους· παρεσκευάσθαι
μὲν γὰρ τὸν δῆμον ἐπιχειρεῖν αὐτοῖς οὐκ εἰς
μακράν, αὐτῶν δὲ τὸ σύντομον[3] τῆς ἐπιβολῆς[4]
ὑποτετμῆσθαι τὰς ἔξωθεν ἐπικουρίας· πάντα γὰρ
ἂν φθῆναι παθεῖν πρὶν καὶ πυθέσθαι τινὰ τῶν συμ-
228 μάχων. ἔδοξε δ᾽ ὅμως ἐπικαλεῖσθαι τοὺς Ἰδουμαίους, καὶ γράψαντες ἐπιστολὴν σύντομον, ὡς
Ἄνανος μὲν προδιδοίη Ῥωμαίοις τὴν μητρόπολιν
ἐξαπατήσας τὸν δῆμον, αὐτοὶ δ᾽ ὑπὲρ τῆς ἐλευ-
229 θερίας ἀποστάντες ἐν τῷ ἱερῷ φρουροῖντο, ὀλίγος
δ᾽ ἔτι χρόνος αὐτοῖς βραβεύοι τὴν σωτηρίαν, εἰ
δὲ μὴ βοηθήσουσιν ἐκεῖνοι κατὰ τάχος, αὐτοὶ μὲν
ὑπ᾽ Ἀνάνῳ τε καὶ τοῖς ἐχθροῖς, ἡ πόλις δ᾽ ὑπὸ
Ῥωμαίοις[5] φθάσει γενομένη. τὰ δὲ πολλὰ τοῖς
ἀγγέλοις ἐνετέλλοντο πρὸς τοὺς ἄρχοντας τῶν
230 Ἰδουμαίων διαλέγεσθαι. προεβλήθησαν δ᾽ ἐπὶ τὴν
ἀγγελίαν δύο τῶν δραστηρίων ἀνδρῶν, εἰπεῖν τε

---

[1] PAL Lat.: Σίμωνος the rest.
[2] Φαλέκου CM²V².
[3] PAL Lat.: σύντονον the rest.
[4] Niese: ἐπιβουλῆς mss.　　　[5] Ῥωμαίους PL¹.

as well, he accused Ananus of brutality, asserting that his special threats were directed at them. These leaders were Eleazar, son of Gion,[a] the most influential man of the party, from his ability both in conceiving appropriate measures and in carrying them into effect, and a certain Zacharias,[b] son of Amphicalleus, both being of priestly descent. They, on hearing first the menaces against the whole party and then those specially levelled at themselves, and, moreover, how Ananus and his friends were summoning the Romans in order to secure supreme power for themselves—this was another of John's libels—were long in doubt what action they should take, being so hard pressed for time; since the people were prepared to attack them ere long, and the suddenness of the scheme cut short their chances of aid from without, as all would be over before any of their allies even heard of their situation. They decided, nevertheless, to summon the Idumaeans, and drafted a letter concisely stating that Ananus had imposed on the people and was proposing to betray the capital to the Romans; that they themselves having revolted in the cause of freedom were imprisoned in the Temple; that a few hours would now decide their fate, and that unless the Idumaeans sent prompt relief, they would soon have succumbed to Ananus and their foes, and the city be in possession of the Romans. The messengers were instructed to communicate further details to the Idumaean chiefs by word of mouth. Those selected for this errand were two active individuals, eloquent and

[a] Or, with the other reading, E. son of Simon, who plays an important part elsewhere, ii. 564 f., v. 5 ff.

[b] Not mentioned again.

ἱκανοὶ καὶ πεῖσαι περὶ πραγμάτων, τὸ δὲ τούτων
231 χρησιμώτερον, ὠκύτητι ποδῶν διαφέροντες· τοὺς
μὲν γὰρ Ἰδουμαίους αὐτόθεν ᾔδεισαν πεισθησο-
μένους, ἅτε θορυβῶδες καὶ ἄτακτον ἔθνος αἰεί τε
μετέωρον πρὸς τὰ κινήματα καὶ μεταβολαῖς χαῖρον,
πρὸς ὀλίγην τε κολακείαν τῶν δεομένων τὰ ὅπλα
κινοῦν καὶ καθάπερ εἰς ἑορτὴν εἰς τὰς παρατάξεις
232 ἐπειγόμενον. ἔδει δὲ τάχους εἰς τὴν ἀγγελίαν·
εἰς ὃ μηδὲν ἐλλείποντες προθυμίας οἱ πεμφθέντες,
ἐκαλεῖτο δ' αὐτῶν Ἀνανίας ἑκάτερος, καὶ δὴ πρὸς
τοὺς ἄρχοντας τῶν Ἰδουμαίων παρῆσαν.

233   (2) Οἱ δὲ πρὸς τὴν ἐπιστολὴν καὶ τὰ ῥηθέντα
παρὰ τῶν ἀφιγμένων ἐκπλαγέντες, ὥσπερ ἐμμανεῖς
περιέθεόν τε τὸ ἔθνος καὶ διεκήρυσσον τὴν στρα-
234 τείαν. ἤθροιστο δ' ἡ πληθὺς τάχιον τοῦ παρ-
αγγέλματος, καὶ πάντες ὡς ἐπ' ἐλευθερίᾳ τῆς
235 μητροπόλεως ἥρπαζον τὰ ὅπλα. συνταχθέντες δ'
εἰς δύο μυριάδας παραγίνονται πρὸς τὰ Ἱεροσόλυμα, χρώμενοι τέσσαρσιν ἡγεμόσιν, Ἰωάννῃ
τε καὶ Ἰακώβῳ παιδὶ[1] Σωσᾶ, πρὸς δὲ τούτοις·ἦν
Σίμων υἱὸς Θακήου[2] καὶ Φινέας Κλουσώθ.

236   (3) Τὸν δὲ Ἄνανον ἡ μὲν ἔξοδος τῶν ἀγγέλων
ὥσπερ καὶ τοὺς φρουροὺς ἔλαθεν, ἡ δ' ἔφοδος
τῶν Ἰδουμαίων οὐκέτι· προγνοὺς γὰρ ἀποκλείει
τε[3] τὰς πύλας αὐτοῖς καὶ διὰ φυλακῆς εἶχε τὰ
237 τείχη. καθάπαν γε μὴν αὐτοὺς ἐκπολεμεῖν οὐκ
ἔδοξεν, ἀλλὰ λόγοις πείθειν πρὸ τῶν ὅπλων.
238 στὰς οὖν ἐπὶ τὸν ἀντικρὺς αὐτῶν πύργον ὁ μετὰ

---

[1] Perhaps παισὶ should be read (Niese).
[2] Κλαθᾶ or Καθλᾶ the inferior mss.; cf. 271, v. 249, vi. 148.
[3] ἀποκλείει τε Destinon : ἀποκλείεται or ἀποκλείει mss.

---

[a] Or perhaps "John and James, sons of S." John was

persuasive speakers on public affairs, and, what was
still more useful, remarkably fleet of foot. For the
Zealots knew that the Idumaeans would comply
forthwith, as they were a turbulent and disorderly
people, ever on the alert for commotion and delight-
ing in revolutionary changes, and only needed a
little flattery from their suitors to seize their arms
and rush into battle as to a feast. Speed was
essential to the errand; in this no want of alacrity
was shown by the delegates, each named Ananias,
and they were soon in the presence of the Idumaean
chiefs.

(2) The leaders, astounded by the letter and the
statements of their visitors, raced round the nation
like madmen, making proclamation of the campaign.
The mustering of the clan outstripped the orders,
and all snatched up their arms to defend the freedom
of the capital. No less than twenty thousand joined
the ranks and marched to Jerusalem, under the
command of four generals: John, James son of
Sosas,[a] Simon son of Thaceas, and Phineas son of
Clusoth. *The
Idumaeans
march to
Jerusalem.*

(3) Though the departure of the messengers had
eluded the vigilance alike of Ananus and of the
sentries, not so the approach of the Idumaeans.
Forewarned of this, he shut the gates against them
and posted guards upon the walls. Unwilling, however, to make complete enemies of them, he determined to try persuasion before having recourse to
arms. Accordingly Jesus, the chief priest next in

[a] subsequently slain by an Arab archer in the Roman army,
v. 290; James appears often in the sequel, iv. 521, v. 249,
vi. 92, 148, 380. Simon is the orator of the party, iv. 271,
and wins special distinction in the field, v. 249, vi. 148.
Phineas is not heard of again.

Ἄνανον γεραίτατος τῶν ἀρχιερέων Ἰησοῦς, πολλῶν ἔφη καὶ ποικίλων τὴν πόλιν κατεσχηκότων
θορύβων ἐν οὐδενὶ θαυμάσαι τὴν τύχην· οὕτως,
ὡς τῷ συμπράττειν τοῖς πονηροῖς καὶ τὰ παρά-
239 δοξα· παρεῖναι γοῦν ὑμᾶς ἀνθρώποις ἐξωλε-
στάτοις μετὰ τοσαύτης προθυμίας ἐπαμυνοῦντας
καθ' ἡμῶν, μεθ' ὅσης εἰκὸς ἦν ἐλθεῖν οὐδὲ τῆς
240 μητροπόλεως καλούσης ἐπὶ βαρβάρους. "καὶ εἰ
μὲν ἑώρων τὴν σύνταξιν ὑμῶν ἐξ ὁμοίων τοῖς
καλέσασιν ἀνδρῶν, οὐκ ἂν ἄλογον τὴν ὁρμὴν
ὑπελάμβανον· οὐδὲν γὰρ οὕτως συνίστησι τὰς
εὐνοίας ὡς τρόπων συγγένεια· νῦν δ', εἰ μέν τις
αὐτοὺς ἐξετάζοι καθ' ἕνα, μυρίων ἕκαστος εὑρε-
241 θήσεται θανάτων ἄξιος. τὰ γὰρ λύματα[1] καὶ
καθάρματα τῆς χώρας[2] ὅλης, κατασωτευσάμενα
τὰς ἰδίας οὐσίας καὶ προγυμνάσαντα τὴν ἀπόνοιαν
ἐν ταῖς πέριξ κώμαις τε καὶ πόλεσι, τελευταῖα
λεληθότως παρεισέρρευσαν εἰς τὴν ἱερὰν πόλιν,
242 λῃσταὶ δι' ὑπερβολὴν ἀσεβημάτων μιαίνοντες καὶ
τὸ ἀβέβηλον ἔδαφος, οὓς ὁρᾶν ἔστι νῦν ἀδεεῖς
ἐμμεθυσκομένους τοῖς ἁγίοις καὶ τὰ σκῦλα τῶν
πεφονευμένων καταναλίσκοντας εἰς τὰς ἀπλήστους
243 γαστέρας. τὸ δ' ὑμέτερον πλῆθος καὶ τὸν κόσμον
τῶν ὅπλων ὁρᾶν ἔστιν οἷος ἔπρεπεν καλούσης μὲν
τῆς μητροπόλεως κοινῷ βουλευτηρίῳ, συμμάχους
δὲ κατ' ἀλλοφύλων. τί ἂν οὖν εἴποι τοῦτό τις ἢ
τύχης ἐπήρειαν, ὅταν λογάσι πονηροῖς αὔτανδρον
244 ἔθνος ὁρᾷ συνασπίζον[3]; μέχρι πολλοῦ μὲν ἀπορῶ,

---

[1] Lowth: θύματα mss.: ludibria Lat., whence ἀθύρματα
Hudson.
[2] πόλεως PAL.
[3] +αὐτοῖς mss.: συνασπίζοντας (Destinon) or, with altered

seniority to Ananus, mounted the tower opposite to the Idumaeans and addressed them as follows :

"Among the many and manifold disorders which this city has witnessed, nothing has astonished me more than the decree of fortune by which even the most unexpected things co-operate to aid the wicked. Here, for instance, are you, come to assist these most abandoned of men against us, with such alacrity as was hardly to be looked for even had the mother city summoned you to meet a barbarian invasion. Had I seen your ranks composed of men like those who invited you, I should not have thought such ardour unreasonable ; for nothing so unites men's affections as congeniality of character. But as it is, were one to review these friends of yours one by one, each would be found deserving of a myriad deaths. The scum and offscourings of the whole country, after squandering their own means and exercising their madness first upon the surrounding villages and towns, these pests have ended by stealthily streaming into the holy city : brigands of such rank impiety as to pollute even that hallowed ground, they may be seen now recklessly intoxicating themselves in the sanctuary and expending the spoils of their slaughtered victims upon their insatiable bellies. You, on the other hand, in your numbers and shining armour present an appearance such as would become you had the capital in public council summoned you to its aid against the foreigner. What, then, can this be called but a spiteful freak of fortune, when one sees a nation armed to a man on behalf of notorious scoundrels ?

Jesus the chief priest addresses the Idumaeans from the walls. The paradox of a nation in arms on behalf of scoundrels.

punctuation, συνάσπιζον : αὐτὸς (Bekker) should perhaps be read.

τί δή ποτε καὶ τὸ κινῆσαν ὑμᾶς οὕτω ταχέως
ἐγένετο· μὴ γὰρ ἂν δίχα μεγάλης αἰτίας ἀναλαβεῖν
τὰς πανοπλίας ὑπὲρ λῃστῶν καὶ κατὰ δήμου
245 συγγενοῦς. ἐπεὶ δὲ ἠκούσαμεν Ῥωμαίους καὶ
προδοσίαν, ταῦτα γὰρ ὑμῶν ἐθορύβουν τινὲς ἀρτίως,
καὶ τῆς μητροπόλεως ἐπ' ἐλευθερώσει παρεῖναι,
πλέον τῶν ἄλλων τολμημάτων ἐθαυμάσαμεν τοὺς
246 ἀλιτηρίους τῆς περὶ τοῦτο ψευδοῦς ἐπινοίας· ἄνδρας
γὰρ φύσει φιλελευθέρους καὶ διὰ τοῦτο μάλιστα
τοῖς ἔξωθεν πολεμίοις μάχεσθαι παρεσκευασμέ-
νους οὐκ ἐνῆν ἄλλως ἐξαγριῶσαι καθ' ἡμῶν ἢ
λογοποιήσαντας προδοσίαν τῆς ποθουμένης[1] ἐλευ-
247 θερίας. ἀλλ' ὑμᾶς γε χρὴ σκέπτεσθαι τούς τε
διαβάλλοντας καὶ καθ' ὧν, συνάγειν τε τὴν
ἀλήθειαν οὐκ ἐκ τῶν ἐπιπλάστων λόγων ἀλλ' ἐκ τῶν
248 κοινῶν πραγμάτων. τί γὰρ δὴ καὶ παθόντες ἂν
ἡμεῖς Ῥωμαίοις προσπωλοῖμεν[2] ἑαυτοὺς νῦν. παρὸν
ἢ μηδὲ ἀποστῆναι τὸ πρῶτον ἢ προσχωρῆσαι
ταχέως ἀποστάντας, ὄντων ἔτι τῶν πέριξ ἀπορ-
249 θήτων; νῦν μὲν γὰρ οὐδὲ βουλομένοις διαλύσα-
σθαι ῥάδιον, ὅτε Ῥωμαίους μὲν ὑπερόπτας πε-
ποίηκεν ὑποχείριος ἡ Γαλιλαία, φέρει δ' αἰσχύνην
ἡμῖν θανάτου χαλεπωτέραν τὸ θεραπεύειν αὐτοὺς
250 ὄντας ἤδη πλησίον. κἀγὼ καθ' ἑαυτὸν μὲν ἂν
εἰρήνην προτιμήσαιμι θανάτου, πολεμούμενος δ'
ἅπαξ καὶ συμβαλὼν θάνατον εὐκλεᾶ τοῦ ζῆν
251 αἰχμάλωτος. πότερον δέ φασιν ἡμᾶς τοὺς τοῦ
δήμου προεστῶτας πέμψαι κρύφα πρὸς Ῥωμαίους
252 ἢ καὶ τὸν δῆμον κοινῇ ψηφισάμενον; εἰ μὲν

---

[1] πορθουμένης PMV¹R Lat.
[2] Havercamp with one ms.: προσπωλοῦμεν the majority.

[a] *i.e.* like yourselves.

" I have long been wondering what motive could The charge have brought you so promptly; for never, without of treachery grave cause, would you have armed yourselves from ridiculous. head to foot for the sake of brigands, and against a kindred people. But now that we have heard the words ' Romans ' and ' treason '—for that was what some of you were clamouring just now, and how they were here to protect the freedom of the metropolis—no other audacity of these wretches has amazed us more than this ingenious lie. For indeed men with an inborn passion for liberty,[a] and for it above all ready to fight a foreign foe, could by no other means be infuriated against us than by the fabrication of a charge that we were betraying their darling liberty. You, however, ought to reflect who are the authors of this calumny and at whom it is aimed, and to form your opinion of the truth not from fictitious tales but from public events. For what could induce us to sell ourselves to the Romans *now*? It was open to us either to refrain from revolt in the first instance or, having revolted, promptly to return to our allegiance, while the surrounding country was still undevastated. But now, even if we desired it, a reconciliation would be no easy matter, when their conquest of Galilee has made the Romans contemptuous, and to court them, now that they are at our doors, would bring upon us a disgrace even worse than death. For my own part, though I should prefer peace to death, yet having once declared war and entered the lists, I would rather die nobly than live a captive.

" Do they say, however, that we, the leaders of the people, communicated secretly with the Romans, or that the people themselves so decided by public

JOSEPHUS

ἡμᾶς, εἰπάτωσαν τοὺς πεμφθέντας φίλους, τοὺς
διακονήσαντας τὴν προδοσίαν οἰκέτας. ἐφωράθη
τις ἀπιών; ἀνακομιζόμενος ἑάλω; γραμμάτων
253 γεγόνασιν ἐγκρατεῖς; πῶς δὲ τοὺς μὲν τοσούτους
πολίτας ἐλάθομεν, οἷς κατὰ πᾶσαν ὥραν συνανα-
στρεφόμεθα, τοῖς δὲ ὀλίγοις καὶ φρουρουμένοις καὶ
μηδ' εἰς τὴν πόλιν ἐκ τοῦ ἱεροῦ προελθεῖν δυναμένοις ἐγνώσθη τὰ κατὰ τὴν χώραν λαθραίως
254 ἐνεργούμενα; νῦν δ' ἔγνωσαν, ὅτε[1] δεῖ δοῦναι
δίκας τῶν τετολμημένων, ἕως δ' ἦσαν ἀδεεῖς
255 αὐτοί, προδότης ἡμῶν οὐδεὶς ὑπωπτεύετο; εἰ δ'
ἐπὶ τὸν δῆμον ἀναφέρουσι τὴν αἰτίαν, ἐν φανερῷ
δήπουθεν ἐβουλεύσαντο, οὐδεὶς ἀπεστάτει τῆς
ἐκκλησίας, ὥστε τάχιον ἂν τῆς μηνύσεως ἔσπευσεν
256 ἡ φήμη πρὸς ὑμᾶς φανερωτέρα. τί δέ; οὐχὶ καὶ
πρέσβεις ἔδει πέμπειν ψηφισαμένους[2] τὰς δια-
λύσεις; καὶ τίς ὁ χειροτονηθείς; εἰπάτωσαν.
257 ἀλλὰ τοῦτο μὲν δυσθανατούντων καὶ πλησίον
οὔσας τὰς τιμωρίας διακρουομένων σκῆψίς ἐστιν·
εἰ γὰρ δὴ καὶ προδοθῆναι τὴν πόλιν εἵμαρτο,
μόνους ἂν τολμῆσαι καὶ τοῦτο τοὺς διαβάλλοντας,
ὧν τοῖς τολμήμασιν ἓν μόνον [κακὸν] λείπει, προ-
258 δοσία. χρὴ δὲ ὑμᾶς, ἐπειδήπερ ἅπαξ πάρεστε
μετὰ τῶν ὅπλων, τὸ μὲν δικαιότατον, ἀμύνειν τῇ
μητροπόλει καὶ συνεξαιρεῖν τοὺς τὰ δικαστήρια
καταλύσαντας τυράννους, οἳ πατήσαντες τοὺς
νόμους ἐπὶ τοῖς αὐτῶν ξίφεσι πεποίηνται τὰς
259 κρίσεις. ἄνδρας γοῦν ἀκαταιτιάτους τῶν ἐπι-

---

[1] Bekker with Lat.: ὅτι mss.
[2] L: ψηφισομένους the rest.

decree ? If they accuse us, let them name the
friends whom we sent, the underlings who negotiated
the betrayal. Was anyone detected leaving on his
errand, or caught on his return ? Have any letters
fallen into their hands ? How could we have concealed our action from all our numerous fellow-
citizens, with whom we are hourly associating, while
their small and beleaguered party, unable to advance
one step into the city from the Temple, were, it
seems, acquainted with these underhand proceedings
in the country ? Have they heard of them only
now, when they must pay the penalty for their
crimes, and, so long as they felt themselves secure,
was none of us suspected of treason ? If, on the
other hand, it is the people whom they incriminate,
the matter presumably was openly discussed and
none was absent from the assembly ; in which case
rumour would have brought you speedier and more
open intelligence than your private informer. Again,
must they not have followed up their vote for capitulation by sending ambassadors ? Who was elected
to that office ? Let them tell us. No, this is a mere
pretext of die-hards who are struggling to avert
impending punishment. For had this city been
indeed fated to be betrayed, none would have
ventured on the deed save our present accusers, to
complete whose tale of crimes one only is lacking—
that of treason.

" But now that you are actually here in arms, the *Three*
duty which has the highest claims upon you is to *courses are*
now open
defend the metropolis and to join us in extirpating *to you.*
these tyrants, who have annulled our tribunals,
trampled on our laws, and passed sentence with the
sword. Have they not haled men of eminence and

233

φανῶν ἐκ μέσης τῆς ἀγορᾶς ἁρπάσαντες δεσμοῖς
τε προηκίσαντο καὶ μηδὲ φωνῆς μηδ᾽ ἱκεσίας
260 ἀνασχόμενοι διέφθειραν. ἔξεστιν δ᾽ ὑμῖν παρελθοῦσιν εἴσω μὴ πολέμου νόμῳ θεάσασθαι τὰ
τεκμήρια τῶν λεγομένων, οἴκους ἠρημωμένους
ταῖς ἐκείνων ἁρπαγαῖς καὶ γύναια καὶ γενεὰς
τῶν ἀπεσφαγμένων μελανειμονούσας, κωκυτὸν δὲ
καὶ θρῆνον ἀνὰ τὴν πόλιν ὅλην· οὐδεὶς γάρ ἐστιν,
261 ὃς οὐ γέγευται τῆς τῶν ἀνοσίων καταδρομῆς· οἵ
γε ἐπὶ τοσοῦτον ἐξώκειλαν ἀπονοίας, ὥστε μὴ
μόνον ἐκ τῆς χώρας καὶ τῶν ἔξωθεν πόλεων ἐπὶ
τὸ πρόσωπον καὶ τὴν κεφαλὴν ὅλου τοῦ ἔθνους
μετενεγκεῖν τὴν λῃστρικὴν τόλμαν, ἀλλὰ καὶ ἀπὸ
262 τῆς πόλεως ἐπὶ τὸ ἱερόν. ὁρμητήριον γοῦν αὐτοῖς
τοῦτο καὶ καταφυγὴ ταμιεῖόν τε τῶν ἐφ᾽ ἡμᾶς
παρασκευῶν γέγονεν, ὁ δ᾽ ὑπὸ τῆς οἰκουμένης
προσκυνούμενος χῶρος καὶ τοῖς ἀπὸ περάτων γῆς
ἀλλοφύλοις ἀκοῇ τετιμημένος παρὰ τῶν γεννη-
263 θέντων ἐνθάδε θηρίων καταπατεῖται· νεανιεύονταί
τε ἐν ταῖς ἀπογνώσεσιν ἤδη δήμους τε δήμοις καὶ
πόλεσι πόλεις συγκρούειν καὶ κατὰ τῶν σπλάγχνων
264 τῶν ἰδίων τὸ ἔθνος στρατολογεῖν. ἀνθ᾽ ὧν τὸ μὲν
κάλλιστον καὶ πρέπον, ὡς ἔφην, ὑμῖν συνεξαιρεῖν
τοὺς ἀλιτηρίους καὶ ὑπὲρ αὐτῆς τῆς ἀπάτης
ἀμυνομένους, ὅτι συμμάχους ἐτόλμησαν καλεῖν
265 οὓς ἔδει τιμωροὺς δεδιέναι· εἰ δ᾽ αἰδεῖσθε τὰς
τῶν τοιούτων ἐπικλήσεις, ἀλλά τοι πάρεστι
θεμένοις τὰ ὅπλα καὶ παρελθοῦσιν εἰς τὴν πόλιν
σχήματι συγγενῶν ἀναλαβεῖν τὸ μέσον συμμάχων
τε καὶ πολεμίων ὄνομα, δικαστὰς γενομένους.

unimpeached from the open market-place, ignomin-
ously placed them in irons and then, refusing to
listen to expostulation or entreaty, put them to
death ? You are at liberty to enter, though not by
right of war, and behold the proofs of these statements : houses desolated by their rapine, poor widows
and orphans of the murdered in black attire, wailing
and lamentation throughout the city ; for there is not
one who has not felt the raids of these impious
wretches. To such extremes of insanity have they
run as not only to transfer their brigands' exploits
from the country and outlying towns to this front
and head of the whole nation, but actually from the
city to the Temple. That has now become their
base and refuge, the magazine for their armament
against us ; and the spot which is revered by the
world and honoured by aliens from the ends of the
earth who have heard its fame, is trampled on by
these monsters engendered in this very place. And
now in desperation they wantonly proceed to set at
variance township against township, city against city,
and to enlist the nation to prey upon its own vitals.
Wherefore,[a] as I said before, the most honourable
and becoming course for you is to assist in extirpating
these reprobates, and to chastise them for this deceit
which they have practised on yourselves in daring
to summon as allies those whom they should have
dreaded as avengers.

" If, however, you still respect the appeals made
to you by men such as these, it is surely open to
you to lay down your arms and, entering the city in
the guise of kinsmen, to assume a neutral rôle by

---

[a] Or perhaps " On the contrary " or " Instead of aiding
such a cause " (Traill).

266 καίτοι λογίσασθε, πόσον κερδήσουσιν ἐφ' ὁμο-
λογουμένοις καὶ τηλικούτοις κρινόμενοι παρ' ὑμῖν
οἱ τοῖς ἀκαταιτιάτοις μηδὲ λόγου μεταδόντες·
λαμβανέτωσαν δ' οὖν ταύτην ἐκ τῆς ὑμετέρας
267 ἀφίξεως τὴν χάριν. εἰ δ' οὔτε συναγανακτεῖν
ἡμῖν οὔτε κρίνεσθαι δεῖ,[1] τρίτον ἐστὶ καταλιπεῖν
ἑκατέρους καὶ μήτε ταῖς ἡμετέραις ἐπεμβαίνειν[2]
συμφοραῖς μήτε τοῖς ἐπιβούλοις τῆς μητροπόλεως
268 συνέρχεσθαι. εἰ γὰρ καὶ τὰ μάλιστα Ῥωμαίοις
ὑποπτεύετε διειλέχθαι τινάς, παρατηρεῖν ἔξεστι
τὰς ἐφόδους, κἄν τι τῶν διαβεβλημένων ἔργῳ
διακαλύπτηται, τότε φρουρεῖν τὴν μητρόπολιν
ἐλθόντας, κολάζειν τε τοὺς αἰτίους πεφωραμένους·
οὐ γὰρ ἂν ὑμᾶς φθάσειαν οἱ πολέμιοι τῇ πόλει
269 προσῳκημένους.[3] εἰ δ' οὐδὲν ὑμῖν τούτων εὔ-
γνωμον ἢ μέτριον δοκεῖ, μὴ θαυμάζετε τὰ κλεῖθρα
τῶν πυλῶν, ἕως ἂν φέρητε τὰ ὅπλα."

270 (4) Τοιαῦτα μὲν ὁ Ἰησοῦς ἔλεγε· τῶν δὲ
Ἰδουμαίων οὐδὲν[4] τὸ πλῆθος προσεῖχεν, ἀλλὰ
τεθύμωτο μὴ τυχὸν ἑτοίμης τῆς εἰσόδου, καὶ
διηγανάκτουν οἱ στρατηγοὶ πρὸς ἀπόθεσιν τῶν
ὅπλων, αἰχμαλωσίαν ἡγούμενοι τὸ κελεύοντος
271 τινῶν αὐτὰ ῥῖψαι. Σίμων δὲ υἱὸς Κααθᾶ[5] τῶν
ἡγεμόνων εἷς, μόλις τῶν οἰκείων καταστείλας τὸν
θόρυβον καὶ στὰς εἰς ἐπήκοον τοῖς ἀρχιερεῦσιν,
272 οὐκέτι θαυμάζειν ἔφη φρουρουμένων ἐν τῷ ἱερῷ
τῶν προμάχων τῆς ἐλευθερίας, εἴ γε καὶ τῷ
273 ἔθνει κλείουσί τινες ἤδη τὴν κοινὴν πόλιν, καὶ

---

[1] δοκεῖ Hudson with one ms.
[2] MVC: ἐπιβαίνειν the rest.
[3] L: προσῳκισμένους the rest.
[4] PAML (Lat.?): οὔτε the rest.
[5] Κλαθᾶ M: Καθλᾶ VRC Lat.; cf. § 235.

becoming arbitrators. Consider, too, what they will gain by being tried by you for such undeniable and flagrant offences, whereas they would not suffer unimpeached persons to speak a word in their defence ; however, let them derive this benefit from your coming. But if you will neither share our indignation nor act as umpires, a third course remains, namely to leave both parties to themselves and neither to insult us in our calamities nor join with these conspirators against the mother city. For, however strongly you suspect some of us of having communicated with the Romans, you are in a position to watch the approaches, and if any of these calumnies is actually discovered to be true, you can then come to the protection of the metropolis and punish the detected culprits ; for the enemy could never take you by surprise while you are quartered here hard by the city. If, however, none of these proposals appears to you reasonable or fair, do not wonder that these gates are barred, so long as you remain in arms."

(4) Such was the speech of Jesus. But the Idumaean troops paid no heed to it, infuriated at not obtaining instant admission ; while their generals were indignant at the thought of laying down their arms, accounting it captivity to fling them away at any man's bidding. Thereupon Simon, son of Caathas, one of the officers, having with difficulty quelled the uproar among his men and taken his stand within hearing of the chief priests, thus replied :

"I am no longer surprised that the champions of liberty are imprisoned in the Temple, now that I find that there are men who close against this nation the city common to us all ; men who, while

Abusive reply of Simon, the Idumaean chief.

Ῥωμαίους μὲν εἰσδέχεσθαι παρασκευάζονται, τάχα
καὶ στεφανώσαντες τὰς πύλας, Ἰδουμαίοις δὲ ἀπὸ
τῶν πύργων διαλέγονται καὶ τὰ ὑπὲρ τῆς ἐλευ-
274 θερίας ὅπλα κελεύουσι ῥῖψαι, μὴ πιστεύοντες δὲ
τοῖς συγγενέσι τὴν τῆς μητροπόλεως φυλακὴν τοὺς
αὐτοὺς δικαστὰς ποιοῦνται τῶν διαφόρων, καὶ κατ-
ηγοροῦντές τινων ὡς ἀποκτείνειαν ἀκρίτους,
αὐτοὶ καταδικάζοιεν ὅλου τοῦ ἔθνους ἀτιμίαν·
275 τὴν γοῦν ἅπασι τοῖς ἀλλοφύλοις ἀναπεπταμένην
εἰς θρησκείαν πόλιν τοῖς οἰκείοις νῦν ἀπο-
276 τετειχίσθαι.[1] "πάνυ γὰρ ἐπὶ σφαγὰς ἐσπεύ-
δομεν καὶ τὸν κατὰ τῶν ὁμοφύλων πόλεμον
οἱ διὰ τοῦτο ταχύναντες, ἵν' ὑμᾶς τηρήσωμεν
277 ἐλευθέρους. τοιαῦτα μέντοι καὶ πρὸς τῶν φρουρουμένων ἠδίκησθε, καὶ πιθανὰς οὕτως ὑποψίας οἶμαι
278 κατ' ἐκείνων συνελέξατε. ἔπειτα τῶν ἔνδον φρουρᾷ
κρατοῦντες ὅσοι κήδονται τῶν κοινῶν πραγμάτων, καὶ τοῖς συγγενεστάτοις ἔθνεσιν ἀθρόοις
ἀποκλείσαντες μὲν τὴν πόλιν ὑβριστικὰ δ' οὕτως
προστάγματα κελεύοντες, τυραννεῖσθαι λέγετε καὶ
τὸ τῆς δυναστείας ὄνομα τοῖς ὑφ' ὑμῶν τυραννου-
279 μένοις περιάπτετε. τίς ἂν ἐνέγκαι τὴν εἰρωνείαν
τῶν λόγων ἀφορῶν εἰς τὴν ἐναντιότητα τῶν
πραγμάτων; εἰ μὴ καὶ νῦν ὑμᾶς[2] ἀποκλείουσιν
Ἰδουμαῖοι[3] τῆς μητροπόλεως, οὓς αὐτοὶ τῶν
280 πατρίων ἱερῶν εἴργετε. μέμψαιτ' ἂν εἰκότως τις
τοὺς ἐν τῷ ἱερῷ πολιορκουμένους, ὅτι θαρσήσαντες
τοὺς προδότας κολάζειν, οὓς ὑμεῖς ἄνδρας ἐπισή-
μους καὶ ἀκαταιτιάτους λέγετε διὰ τὴν κοινωνίαν,

---

[1] ἀποτετείχισθε A, making the drift into *oratio recta* begin
earlier.
[2] ἡμᾶς PAL. [3] Ἰδουμαίους PAL Lat.

preparing to admit the Romans, maybe crowning the gates with garlands, parley with Idumaeans from their towers and bid them fling down the arms which they took up in defence of liberty ; men who, refusing to entrust to their kinsmen the protection of the mother city, would make them arbitrators in their disputes, and, while accusing certain individuals of putting others to death without trial, would themselves condemn the whole nation to dishonour. At any rate, this city, which flung wide its gates to every foreigner for worship, is now barricaded by you against your own people. And why ? Because forsooth, we were hurrying hither to slaughter and make war on our fellow-countrymen—we whose sole reason for haste was to keep you free ! Such doubtless was the nature of your grievance against your prisoners,[a] and equally credible, I imagine, is your list of insinuations against them. And then, while detaining in custody all within the walls who care for the public welfare, after closing your gates against a whole body of people who are your nearest kinsmen and issuing to them such insulting orders, you profess to be tyrant-ridden and attach the stigma of despotism to the victims of your own tyranny ! Who can tolerate such ironical language, which he sees to be flatly contrary to the facts, unless indeed it is the Idumaeans who are now excluding you from the metropolis, and not you who are debarring them from the national sacred rites ? One complaint might fairly be made against the men blockaded in the Temple, that, while they had the courage to punish those traitors whom you, as their partners in guilt, describe as distinguished persons and un-

---

[a] Viz. that they wished to keep you free.

οὐκ ἀφ' ὑμῶν ἤρξαντο καὶ τὰ καιριώτατα τῆς
281 προδοσίας μέρη προαπέκοψαν. ἀλλ' εἰ κἀκεῖνοι
τῆς χρείας ἐγένοντο μαλακώτεροι, τηρήσομεν[1]
Ἰδουμαῖοι τὸν οἶκον τοῦ θεοῦ καὶ τῆς κοινῆς
πατρίδος προπολεμήσομεν,[1] ἅμα τούς τε ἔξωθεν
ἐπιόντας καὶ τοὺς ἔνδον προδιδόντας ἀμυνόμενοι
282 πολεμίους. ἐνθάδε πρὸ τῶν τειχῶν μενοῦμεν ἐν
τοῖς ὅπλοις, ἕως ἂν Ῥωμαῖοι κάμωσι προσέχοντες
ὑμῖν[2] ἢ ὑμεῖς ἐλεύθερα φρονήσαντες μεταβάλησθε.''
283 (5) Τούτοις τὸ μὲν τῶν Ἰδουμαίων ἐπεβόα
πλῆθος, ὁ δὲ Ἰησοῦς ἀθυμῶν ἀνεχώρει τοὺς μὲν
Ἰδουμαίους μηδὲν φρονοῦντας ὁρῶν μέτριον,
284 διχόθεν δὲ τὴν πόλιν πολεμουμένην. ἦν δ' οὐδὲ
τοῖς Ἰδουμαίοις ἐν ἠρεμίᾳ τὰ φρονήματα· καὶ
γὰρ τεθύμωντο πρὸς τὴν ὕβριν εἰρχθέντες τῆς
πόλεως καὶ τὰ τῶν ζηλωτῶν ἰσχυρὰ δοκοῦντες,
ὡς οὐδὲν ἐπαμύνοντας ἑώρων, ἠποροῦντο καὶ
285 μετενόουν πολλοὶ τὴν ἄφιξιν. ἡ δὲ αἰδὼς τοῦ
τέλεον ἀπράκτους ὑποστρέφειν ἐνίκα τὴν μεταμέλειαν, ὥστε μένειν[3] αὐτόθι πρὸ τοῦ τείχους
286 κακῶς αὐλιζομένους· διὰ γὰρ τῆς νυκτὸς ἀμήχανος
ἐκρήγνυται χειμὼν ἄνεμοί τε βίαιοι σὺν ὄμβροις
λαβροτάτοις καὶ συνεχεῖς ἀστραπαὶ βρονταί τε
φρικώδεις καὶ μυκήματα σειομένης τῆς γῆς
287 ἐξαίσια. πρόδηλον δ' ἦν ἐπ' ἀνθρώπων ὀλέθρῳ
τὸ κατάστημα τῶν ὅλων συγκεχυμένον, καὶ οὐχὶ
μικροῦ τις ἂν εἰκάσαι συμπτώματος τὰ τέρατα.
288 (6) Μία δὲ τοῖς Ἰδουμαίοις καὶ τοῖς ἐν τῇ
πόλει παρέστη δόξα, τοῖς μὲν ὀργίζεσθαι τὸν
θεὸν ἐπὶ τῇ στρατείᾳ καὶ οὐκ ἂν διαφυγεῖν ἐπενεγ-

---

[1] Many mss. have τηρήσωμεν . . . προπολεμήσωμεν.
[2] Hudson: ἡμῖν mss.   [3] ἐμμένειν PAM.

impeached, they did not begin with you and cut off
at the outset the most vital members of this treasonable conspiracy. But if they were more lenient
than they should have been, we Idumaeans will
preserve God's house and fight to defend our common
country from both her foes, the invaders from without and the traitors within. Here before these walls
will we remain in arms, until the Romans are tired
of listening to you or you become converts to the
cause of liberty."

(5) This speech being loudly applauded by the
Idumaeans, Jesus withdrew despondent, finding them
opposed to all moderate counsels and the city
exposed to war from two quarters. Nor indeed were
the minds of the Idumaeans at ease : infuriated at
the insult offered them in being excluded from the
city and seeing no aid forthcoming from the Zealots
whom they believed to be in considerable strength,
they were sorely perplexed, and many repented of
having come. But the shame of returning, having
accomplished absolutely nothing, so far overcame
their regrets that they kept their ground, bivouacking
before the walls under miserable conditions. For
in the course of the night a terrific storm broke out :
the winds blew a hurricane, rain fell in torrents,
lightning was continuous, accompanied by fearful
thunder-claps and extraordinary rumblings of earth-
quake. Such a convulsion of the very fabric of the
universe clearly foretokened destruction for mankind,
and the conjecture was natural that these were
portents of no trifling calamity.

(6) In this the Idumaeans and the city folk were
of one mind : the former being persuaded that God
was wroth at their expedition and that they were

The
Idumaeans
encamp
before the
walls in a
thunder-
storm.

κόντας ὅπλα τῇ μητροπόλει, τοῖς δὲ περὶ τὸν
Ἄνανον νενικηκέναι χωρὶς παρατάξεως καὶ τὸν
289 θεὸν ὑπὲρ αὐτῶν στρατηγεῖν. κακοὶ δ' ἦσαν ἄρα
τῶν μελλόντων στοχασταὶ καὶ κατεμαντεύοντο
290 τῶν ἐχθρῶν ἃ τοῖς ἰδίοις αὐτῶν ἐπῄει παθεῖν· οἱ
μὲν γὰρ Ἰδουμαῖοι συσπειραθέντες τοῖς σώμασιν
ἀλλήλους ἀντέθαλπον καὶ τοὺς θυρεοὺς ὑπὲρ
κεφαλῆς συμφράξαντες ἧττον ἐκακοῦντο τοῖς
291 ὑετοῖς, οἱ δὲ ζηλωταὶ μᾶλλον τοῦ καθ' αὑτοὺς
κινδύνου ὑπὲρ ἐκείνων ἐβασανίζοντο καὶ συνελθόντες ἐσκόπουν, εἴ τινα μηχανὴν αὑτοῖς ἀμύνης
292 ἐπινοήσειαν. τοῖς μὲν οὖν θερμοτέροις ἐδόκει
μετὰ τῶν ὅπλων βιάζεσθαι τοὺς παραφυλάσσοντας,
ἔπειτα δ' εἰσπεσόντας εἰς μέσον τῆς πόλεως
ἀναφανδὸν ἀνοίγειν τοῖς συμμάχοις τὰς πύλας·
293 τούς τε γὰρ φύλακας εἴξειν πρὸς τὸ ἀδόκητον
αὐτῶν τεταραγμένους, ἄλλως τε καὶ τοὺς πλείονας[1]
ὄντας ἀνόπλους καὶ πολέμων ἀπείρους, καὶ τῶν
κατὰ τὴν πόλιν δυσσύνακτον ἔσεσθαι τὸ πλῆθος
κατειλημμένον[2] ὑπὸ τοῦ χειμῶνος εἰς τὰς οἰκίας.
294 εἰ δὲ καί τις γένοιτο κίνδυνος, πρέπειν αὐτοῖς πᾶν
ὁτιοῦν παθεῖν ἢ περιιδεῖν τοσοῦτον πλῆθος δι'
295 αὐτοὺς αἰσχρῶς ἀπολλύμενον. οἱ δὲ συνετώτεροι
βιάζεσθαι μὲν ἀπεγίνωσκον, ὁρῶντες οὐ μόνον τὴν
αὐτῶν φρουρὰν πληθύουσαν ἀλλὰ καὶ τὸ τῆς
πόλεως τεῖχος διὰ τοὺς Ἰδουμαίους ἐπιμελῶς
296 φυλασσόμενον, ᾤοντό τε πανταχοῦ τὸν Ἄνανον
παρεῖναι καὶ κατὰ πᾶσαν ὥραν ἐπισκέπτεσθαι
297 τὰς φυλακάς· ὃ δὴ ταῖς μὲν ἄλλαις νυξὶν οὕτως
εἶχεν, ἀνείθη δὲ κατ' ἐκείνην, οὔτι κατὰ τὴν

---

[1] L: + αὐτῶν the rest.   [2] Bekker: κατειλημμένον MSS.

not to escape retribution for bearing arms against
the metropolis, Ananus and his party believing that
they had won the day without a contest and that
God was directing the battle on their behalf. But
they proved mistaken in their divination of the future,
and the fate which they predicted for their foes was
destined to befall their friends. For the Idumaeans,
huddling together, kept each other warm, and by
making a penthouse of bucklers above their heads
were not seriously affected by the torrents of rain ;
while the Zealots, more concerned for their allies
than for their own danger, met to consider whether
any means could be devised for their relief. The
more ardent advocated forcing a way through the
sentries at the point of the sword, and then plunging
boldly into the heart of the city and opening the
gates to their allies : the guards, disconcerted by
their unexpected assault, would give way, especially
as the majority were unarmed and had never been
in action, while the citizens could not easily be
collected in force, being confined to their houses by
the storm ; even if this involved hazard, it was only
right that they should suffer anything rather than
leave such a vast host disgracefully to perish on
their account. The more prudent, however, disapproved of these violent measures, seeing that not
only was the guard surrounding them in full strength,
but the city wall carefully watched on account of
the Idumaeans ; they imagined, moreover, that
Ananus would be everywhere, inspecting the sentries
at all hours. Such, indeed, had been his practice on
other nights, but on this one it was omitted ; not

JOSEPHUS

Ἀνάνου ῥαθυμίαν, ἀλλ' ὡς αὐτός ⟨τε⟩[1] ἐκεῖνος
ἀπόλοιτο καὶ τὸ πλῆθος τῶν φυλάκων στρατη-
298 γούσης τῆς εἱμαρμένης. ἢ δὴ καὶ τότε τῆς νυκτὸς
προκοπτούσης καὶ τοῦ χειμῶνος ἐπακμάζοντος
κοιμίζει μὲν τοὺς ἐπὶ τῇ στοᾷ φρουρούς, τοῖς δὲ
ζηλωταῖς ἐπίνοιαν ἐμβάλλει τῶν ἱερῶν αἴροντας
πριόνων ἐκτεμεῖν τοὺς μοχλοὺς τῶν πυλῶν.
299 συνήργησε δ' αὐτοῖς πρὸς τὸ μὴ κατακουσθῆναι
τὸν ψόφον ὅ τε τῶν ἀνέμων ἦχος καὶ τὸ τῶν
βροντῶν ἐπάλληλον.
300 (7) Διαλαθόντες δ' ἐκ τοῦ ἱεροῦ παραγίνονται
πρὸς τὸ τεῖχος καὶ τοῖς αὐτοῖς πρίοσι χρώμενοι
τὴν κατὰ τοὺς Ἰδουμαίους ἀνοίγουσι πύλην.
301 τοῖς δὲ τὸ μὲν πρῶτον ἐμπίπτει ταραχὴ τοὺς
περὶ τὸν Ἄνανον ἐπιχειρεῖν οἰηθεῖσι, καὶ πᾶς ἐπὶ
τοῦ ξίφους ἔσχε τὴν δεξιὰν ὡς ἀμυνόμενος[2]·
ταχέως δὲ γνωρίζοντες τοὺς ἥκοντας εἰσῄεσαν.
302 εἰ μὲν οὖν ἐτράποντο περὶ τὴν πόλιν, οὐδὲν
ἐκώλυσεν ἂν ἀπολωλέναι τὸν δῆμον αὔτανδρον,
οὕτως εἶχον ὀργῆς· νῦν δὲ πρώτους τοὺς ζηλωτὰς
ἔσπευδον[3] τῆς φρουρᾶς ἐξελέσθαι, δεομένων πολλὰ
καὶ τῶν εἰσδεξαμένων μὴ περιιδεῖν δι' οὓς ἦλθον
ἐν μέσοις τοῖς δεινοῖς μηδ' αὐτοῖς χαλεπώτερον
303 ἐπισεῖσαι τὸν κίνδυνον· τῶν μὲν γὰρ φρουρῶν
ἁλόντων ῥάδιον αὐτοῖς εἶναι χωρεῖν ἐπὶ τὴν πόλιν,
εἰ δ' ἅπαξ ταύτην προκινήσειαν, οὐκ ἂν ἔτ'
304 ἐκείνων κρατῆσαι· πρὸς γὰρ τὴν αἴσθησιν συν-
τάξεσθαι[4] αὐτοὺς καὶ τὰς ἀνόδους ἀποφράξειν.

---

[1] ins. Herwerden: the τε appears to have been misplaced
in most mss., which read ὥστε for ὡς.
[2] ἀμυνόμενος R.   [3] C : σπεύδοντες the rest.
[4] Bekker: συντάξασθαι mss.
244

through any remissness on his part, but by the over-ruling decree of Destiny that he and all his guards should perish. She it was who as that night advanced and the storm approached its climax lulled to sleep the sentinels posted at the colonnade, and suggested to the Zealots the thought of taking some of the temple saws and severing the bars of the gates. They were aided by the blustering wind and the successive peals of thunder, which prevented the noise from being heard.[a]

A party of Zealots sally from the temple

(7) Escaping unperceived from the Temple, they[b] reached the walls and, employing their saws once more, opened the gate nearest to the Idumaeans. They, supposing themselves attacked by the troops of Ananus, were at first seized with alarm, and every man's hand was on his sword to defend himself, but, quickly recognizing their visitors, they entered the city. Had they then turned upon it in all directions, such was their fury that nothing could have saved the inhabitants from wholesale destruction ; but, as it was, they first hastened to liberate the Zealots from custody, at the earnest entreaty of the men who had let them in. " Do not," these urged, " leave those for whose sake you have come in the thick of peril, nor expose us to graver risks. Over-power the guards and you can then easily march upon the city, but once begin by rousing the city, and you will never master the guards ; for at the first intimation the citizens will fall into line and block every ascent."

and open the city gates to the Idumaeans.

---

[a] Reminiscent of Thucydides' account of the escape from Plataea : ψόφῳ δὲ . . . ἀντιπαταγοῦντος τοῦ ἀνέμου οὐ κατακουσάντων (iii. 22).

[b] i.e. a small party of the Zealots, as the sequel shows.

JOSEPHUS

305 (v. 1) Συνεδόκει ταῦτα τοῖς Ἰδουμαίοις, καὶ διὰ τῆς πόλεως ἀνέβαινον πρὸς τὸ ἱερόν, μετέωροί τε οἱ ζηλωταὶ τὴν ἄφιξιν αὐτῶν ἐκαραδόκουν καὶ παριόντων εἴσω καὶ αὐτοὶ θαρροῦντες προῄεσαν ἐκ
306 τοῦ ἐνδοτέρου ἱεροῦ. μιγέντες δὲ τοῖς Ἰδουμαίοις προσέβαλλον ταῖς φυλακαῖς, καὶ τινὰς μὲν τῶν προκοιτούντων ἀπέσφαξαν κοιμωμένους, πρὸς δὲ τὴν τῶν ἐγρηγορότων βοὴν διανέστη πᾶν τὸ πλῆθος καὶ μετ᾽ ἐκπλήξεως ἁρπάζοντες τὰ ὅπλα
307 πρὸς τὴν ἄμυναν ἐχώρουν. ἕως μὲν οὖν μόνους τοὺς ζηλωτὰς ἐπιχειρεῖν ὑπελάμβανον, ἐθάρρουν ὡς τῷ πλήθει περιεσόμενοι, κατιδόντες δ᾽ ἔξωθεν ἐπεισχεομένους[1] ἄλλους ᾔσθοντο τὴν εἰσβολὴν τῶν
308 Ἰδουμαίων, καὶ τὸ μὲν πλέον αὐτῶν ἅμα ταῖς ψυχαῖς κατέβαλλε τὰ ὅπλα καὶ πρὸς οἰμωγαῖς ἦν, φραξάμενοι δὲ ὀλίγοι τῶν νέων γενναίως ἐδέχοντο τοὺς Ἰδουμαίους καὶ μέχρι πολλοῦ τὴν
309 ἀργοτέραν πληθὺν ἔσκεπον. οἱ δὲ κραυγῇ διεσήμαινον τοῖς κατὰ τὴν πόλιν τὰς συμφοράς, κἀκείνων ἀμῦναι μὲν οὐδεὶς ἐτόλμησεν, ὡς ἔμαθον εἰσπεπαικότας τοὺς Ἰδουμαίους, ἀργὰ δ᾽ ἀντεβόων καὶ ἀντωλοφύροντο, καὶ πολὺς κωκυτὸς γυναικῶν ἠγείρετο κινδυνεύοντος ἑκάστῃ τινὸς
310 τῶν φυλάκων. οἱ δὲ ζηλωταὶ τοῖς Ἰδουμαίοις συνεπηλάλαζον καὶ τὴν ἐκ πάντων βοὴν ὁ χειμὼν ἐποίει φοβερωτέραν. ἐφείδοντό τε οὐδενὸς Ἰδουμαῖοι, φύσει τε ὠμότατοι φονεύειν ὄντες καὶ τῷ χειμῶνι κεκακωμένοι κατὰ τῶν ἀποκλεισάντων

[1] ἐπιχεομένους PA.

246

(v. 1) Yielding to these representations, the Idu- Wholesale slaughter of the guards of Ananus.
maeans marched up through the city to the
Temple. The Zealots, who were anxiously awaiting
their arrival, on their entering the building boldly
advanced from the inner court, joined the Idumaeans
and fell upon the guards. Some of the outlying
sentries they slew in their sleep, till, roused by the
cries of those who were awake, the whole force in
consternation snatched up their arms and advanced
to the defence. So long as they believed the Zealots
to be their only assailants, they did not lose heart,
hoping to overpower them by numbers ; but the
sight of others pouring in from outside brought home
to them the irruption of the Idumaeans. Thereupon, the greater number of them flung courage
and armour away together and abandoned themselves to lamentation ; a few of the younger men,
however, fencing themselves in, gallantly received
the Idumaeans and for a good while protected the
feebler crowd. The cries of the latter signified their
distress to their friends in the city, but not one of
these ventured to their assistance, when they learnt
that the Idumaeans had broken in ; instead they
responded with futile shouts and lamentations on
their side, while a great wail went up from the
women, each having some relative in the guards
whose life was at stake. The Zealots joined in the
war-whoop of the Idumaeans, and the din from all
quarters was rendered more terrific by the howling
of the storm.[a] The Idumaeans spared none. Naturally of a most savage and murderous disposition, they
had been buffeted by the storm and wreaked their

---

[a] *Cf.* iii. 247 ff. (Jotapata : the din of battle heightened by
the echo from the mountains), vi. 272 ff. (Jerusalem : similar).

311 ἐχρῶντο τοῖς θυμοῖς[1]· ἦσαν δ' ὅμοιοι τοῖς ἱκε-
τεύουσι καὶ τοῖς ἀμυνομένοις καὶ πολλοὺς τήν
τε συγγένειαν ἀναμιμνήσκοντας καὶ δεομένους
τοῦ κοινοῦ ἱεροῦ λαβεῖν αἰδῶ διήλαυνον τοῖς
312 ξίφεσιν. ἦν δὲ φυγῆς μὲν οὐδεὶς τόπος οὐδὲ
σωτηρίας ἐλπίς, συνωθούμενοι δὲ περὶ ἀλλήλους
κατεκόπτοντο, καὶ τὸ πλέον ἐκβιαζόμενοι, ὡς
οὐκέτ' ἦν ὑποχωρήσεως τόπος ἐπῄεσαν δ' οἱ
φονεύοντες, ὑπ' ἀμηχανίας κατεκρήμνιζον ἑαυτοὺς
εἰς τὴν πόλιν, οἰκτρότερον ἔμοιγε δοκεῖν[2] οὗ
διέφευγον ὀλέθρου τὸν αὐθαίρετον ὑπομένοντες.
313 ἐπεκλύσθη δὲ τὸ ἔξωθεν ἱερὸν πᾶν αἵματι, καὶ
νεκροὺς ὀκτακισχιλίους πεντακοσίους ἡ ἡμέρα
κατελάμβανεν.

314 (2) Οὐκ ἐκορέσθησαν δὲ τούτοις οἱ θυμοὶ τῶν
Ἰδουμαίων, ἀλλ' ἐπὶ τὴν πόλιν τραπόμενοι πᾶσαν
μὲν οἰκίαν διήρπαζον, ἔκτεινον δὲ τὸν περιτυχόντα.
315 καὶ τὸ μὲν ἄλλο πλῆθος αὐτοῖς ἐδόκει παρανάλωμα,
τοὺς δ' ἀρχιερεῖς ἀνεζήτουν, καὶ κατ' ἐκείνων ἦν
316 τοῖς πλείστοις ἡ φορά. ταχέως δ' ἁλόντες διεφθείροντο, καὶ τοῖς νεκροῖς αὐτῶν ἐπιστάντες τὸν
μὲν Ἄνανον τῆς πρὸς τὸν δῆμον εὐνοίας, τὸν δὲ
Ἰησοῦν τῶν ἀπὸ τοῦ τείχους λόγων ἐπέσκωπτον.
317 προῆλθον δὲ εἰς τοσοῦτον ἀσεβείας, ὥστε καὶ
ἀτάφους ῥῖψαι, καίτοι τοσαύτην Ἰουδαίων περὶ
τὰς ταφὰς πρόνοιαν ποιουμένων, ὥστε καὶ τοὺς
ἐκ καταδίκης ἀνεσταυρωμένους πρὸ δύντος ἡλίου
318 καθελεῖν τε καὶ θάπτειν. οὐκ ἂν ἁμάρτοιμι δ'

---

[1] VM[2]: ὅπλοις or ἐχθροῖς the rest.
[2] Dindorf: δοκεῖ mss.

---

a At the outset of the blockade the guards on duty at
248

rage on those who had shut them out; suppliants
and combatants were treated alike, and many while
reminding them of their kinship and imploring them
to respect their common Temple were transfixed by
their swords. No room for flight, no hope of escape
remained; crushed together upon each other they
were cut down, and the greater part, finding themselves forced back until further retreat was impossible,
with their murderers closing upon them, in their
helplessness flung themselves headlong into the
city, devoting themselves to a fate more piteous in
my opinion than that from which they fled. The
whole outer court of the Temple was deluged with
blood, and day dawned upon eight thousand five
hundred [a] dead.

(2) The fury of the Idumaeans being still un-
satiated, they now turned to the city, looting every
house and killing all who fell in their way. But,
thinking their energies wasted on the common people,
they went in search of the chief priests; it was for
them that the main rush was made, and they were
soon captured and slain. Then, standing over their
dead bodies, they scoffed at Ananus for his patronage
of the people and at Jesus for the address which he
had delivered from the wall.[b] They actually went
so far in their impiety as to cast out the corpses
without burial, although the Jews are so careful
about funeral rites that even malefactors who have
been sentenced to crucifixion are taken down and
buried before sunset.[c] I should not be wrong in

The Idumaeans murder Ananus and Jesus.

one time numbered not more than 6000 (εἰς ἑξακισχιλίους
§ 206). That number was apparently afterwards increased.
We are told that on this night they were " in full strength "
or " above strength " (πληθύουσαν § 295).

  [b] §§ 238 ff.   [c] Cf. Deut. xxi. 22 f.; John xix. 31.

εἰπὼν ἁλώσεως ἄρξαι τῇ πόλει τὸν Ἀνάνου
θάνατον, καὶ ἀπ' ἐκείνης τῆς ἡμέρας ἀνατραπῆναι
τὸ τεῖχος καὶ διαφθαρῆναι τὰ πράγματα Ἰουδαίοις, ἐν ᾗ τὸν ἀρχιερέα καὶ ἡγεμόνα τῆς ἰδίας
σωτηρίας αὐτῶν ἐπὶ μέσης τῆς πόλεως εἶδον
319 ἀπεσφαγμένον. ἦν γὰρ δὴ τά τε ἄλλα σεμνὸς
ἀνὴρ καὶ δικαιότατος, καὶ παρὰ τὸν ὄγκον τῆς
τε εὐγενείας καὶ τῆς ἀξίας καὶ ἧς εἶχε τιμῆς
ἠγαπηκὼς τὸ ἰσότιμον καὶ πρὸς τοὺς ταπεινοτά-
320 τους, φιλελεύθερός τε ἐκτόπως καὶ δημοκρατίας
ἐραστής, πρό τε τῶν ἰδίων λυσιτελῶν τὸ κοινῇ
συμφέρον ἀεὶ τιθέμενος καὶ περὶ παντὸς ποιού-
μενος τὴν εἰρήνην· ἄμαχα γὰρ ᾔδει τὰ Ῥωμαίων·
προσκοπούμενος δ' ὑπ' ἀνάγκης καὶ τὰ κατὰ τὸν
πόλεμον, ὅπως, εἰ μὴ διαλύσαιντο Ἰουδαῖοι,
321 δεξιῶς διαφέροιντο. καθόλου δ' εἰπεῖν, ζῶντος
Ἀνάνου πάντως ἂν ⟨ἢ⟩[1] διελύθησαν· δεινὸς γὰρ
ἦν εἰπεῖν τε καὶ πεῖσαι τὸν δῆμον, ἤδη δὲ ἐχειροῦτο
καὶ τοὺς ἐμποδίζοντας· ἢ πολεμοῦντες[2] πλείστην
ἂν τριβὴν Ῥωμαίοις παρέσχον ὑπὸ τοιούτῳ
322 στρατηγῷ. παρέζευκτο δ' αὐτῷ καὶ ὁ Ἰησοῦς,
αὐτοῦ μὲν λειπόμενος κατὰ σύγκρισιν, προύχων
323 δὲ τῶν ἄλλων. ἀλλ' οἶμαι κατακρίνας ὁ θεὸς ὡς
μεμιασμένης τῆς πόλεως ἀπώλειαν καὶ πυρὶ
βουλόμενος ἐκκαθαρθῆναι τὰ ἅγια τοὺς ἀντεχο-
μένους αὐτῶν καὶ φιλοστοργοῦντας περιέκοπτεν.
324 οἱ δὲ πρὸ ὀλίγου τὴν ἱερὰν ἐσθῆτα περικείμενοι

[1] ins. Niese.
[2] Destinon : πολεμοῦντας MSS.

[a] Ananus is here almost the counterpart of Pericles ; the
250

saying that the capture of the city began with the death of Ananus ; and that the overthrow of the walls and the downfall of the Jewish state dated from the day on which the Jews beheld their high priest, the captain of their salvation, butchered in the heart of Jerusalem. A man on every ground revered and of the highest integrity, Ananus,[a] with all the distinction of his birth, his rank and the honours to which he had attained, yet delighted to treat the very humblest as his equals. Unique in his love of liberty and an enthusiast for democracy, he on all occasions put the public welfare above his private interests. To maintain peace was his supreme object. He knew that the Roman power was irresistible, but, when driven to provide for a state of war, he endeavoured to secure that, if the Jews would not come to terms, the struggle should at least be skilfully conducted. In a word, had Ananus lived, they would undoubtedly either have arranged terms —for he was an effective speaker, whose words carried weight with the people, and was already gaining control even over those who thwarted him—or else, had hostilities continued, they would have greatly retarded the victory of the Romans under such a general. With him was linked Jesus, who, though not comparable with Ananus, stood far above the rest. But it was, I suppose, because God had, for its pollutions, condemned the city to destruction and desired to purge the sanctuary by fire, that He thus cut off those who clung to them with such tender affection. So they who but lately had worn the

Encomium on Ananus and Jesus.

encomium on the latter in Thuc. ii. 65 is doubtless in our historian's mind.

καὶ τῆς κοσμικῆς θρησκείας κατάρχοντες προσ-
κυνούμενοί τε τοῖς ἐκ τῆς οἰκουμένης παρα-
βάλλουσιν εἰς τὴν πόλιν, ἐρριμμένοι γυμνοὶ βορὰ
325 κυνῶν καὶ θηρίων ἐβλέποντο. αὐτὴν ἐπ᾽ ἐκείνοις
στενάξαι τοῖς ἀνδράσι δοκῶ τὴν ἀρετήν, ὀλο-
φυρομένην ὅτι τοσοῦτον ἥττητο τῆς κακίας. ἀλλὰ
γὰρ τὸ μὲν Ἀνάνου καὶ Ἰησοῦ τέλος τοιοῦτον
ἀπέβη.
326 (3) Μετὰ δ᾽ ἐκείνους οἵ τε ζηλωταὶ καὶ τῶν
Ἰδουμαίων τὸ πλῆθος τὸν λαὸν ὥσπερ ἀνοσίων
327 ζώων ἀγέλην ἐπιόντες ἔσφαζον. καὶ τὸ μὲν
εἰκαῖον ἐφ᾽ οὗ καταληφθείη τόπου διεφθείρετο,
τοὺς δὲ εὐγενεῖς καὶ νέους συλλαμβάνοντες εἰς
εἱρκτὴν κατέκλειον δεδεμένους, κατ᾽ ἐλπίδα τοῦ
προσθήσεσθαί τινας αὐτοῖς τὴν ἀναίρεσιν ὑπερ-
328 τιθέμενοι. προσέσχε δ᾽ οὐδείς, ἀλλὰ πάντες τοῦ
τάξασθαι μετὰ τῶν πονηρῶν κατὰ τῆς πατρίδος
329 προείλοντο τὸν θάνατον. δεινὰς δὲ τῆς ἀρνήσεως
αἰκίας ὑπέμενον μαστιγούμενοί τε καὶ στρε-
βλούμενοι, μετὰ δὲ τὸ μηκέτ᾽ ἀρκεῖν τὸ σῶμα
330 ταῖς βασάνοις μόλις ἠξιοῦντο τοῦ ξίφους. οἱ
συλληφθέντες δὲ μεθ᾽ ἡμέραν ἀνῃροῦντο[1] νύκτωρ,
καὶ τοὺς νεκροὺς ἐκφοροῦντες ἔρριπτον, ὡς ἑτέροις
331 εἴη δεσμώταις τόπος. ἦν δὲ τοσαύτη τοῦ δήμου
κατάπληξις, ὡς μηδένα τολμῆσαι μήτε κλαίειν
φανερῶς τὸν προσήκοντα νεκρὸν μήτε θάπτειν,
ἀλλὰ λαθραῖα μὲν ἦν αὐτῶν κατακεκλεισμένων τὰ
δάκρυα καὶ μετὰ περισκέψεως, μή τις ἐπακούσῃ
332 τῶν ἐχθρῶν, ἔστενον· ἴσα γὰρ τοῖς πενθουμένοις ὁ

---

[1] ἀνήγοντο L Lat.

[a] Literally " cosmical," meaning either " open to the
whole world " or perhaps " emblematic of the mundane

252

sacred vestments, led those ceremonies of world-wide[a]
significance and been reverenced by visitors to the
city from every quarter of the earth, were now seen
cast out naked, to be devoured by dogs and beasts
of prey. Virtue herself, I think, groaned for these
men's fate, bewailing such utter defeat at the hands
of vice. Such, however, was the end of Ananus and
Jesus.

(3) Having disposed of them, the Zealots and the
Idumaean hordes fell upon and butchered the people
as though they had been a herd of unclean animals.
Ordinary folk were slain on the spot where they
were caught ; but the young nobles[b] they arrested
and threw into prison in irons, postponing their
execution in the hope that some would come over
to their party. Not one, however, listened to their
overtures, all preferring to die rather than side with
these criminals against their country, notwithstanding the fearful agonies which they underwent for
their refusal : they were scourged and racked, and
only when their bodies could no longer sustain these
tortures were they grudgingly consigned to the
sword. Those arrested by day were dispatched at
night and their bodies cast forth to make room for
fresh prisoners. To such consternation were the
people reduced that none dared openly weep for or
bury a deceased relative ; but in secret and behind
closed doors were their tears shed and their groans
uttered with circumspection, for fear of being overheard by any of their foes. For the mourner in-

The Zealots and Idumaeans torture and kill the nobility.

system " (Traill) ; cf. Ant. iii. 123, 180 ff. (the Tabernacle a
symbol of the universe), with Westcott's note on Heb. ix. 1
(τὸ ἅγιον κοσμικόν).

[b] τοὺς εὐγενεῖς καὶ νέους parallel with τῶν εὐγενῶν νέων
below (§ 333).

πενθήσας εὐθὺς ἔπασχε· νύκτωρ δὲ κόνιν αἴροντες
χεροῖν ὀλίγην ἐπερρίπτουν τοῖς σώμασι, καὶ μεθ᾽
333 ἡμέραν εἴ τις παράβολος. μύριοι καὶ δισχίλιοι
τῶν εὐγενῶν νέων οὕτως διεφθάρησαν.

334 (4) Οἱ δὲ ἤδη διαμεμισηκότες τὸ φονεύειν ἀνέδην
335 εἰρωνεύοντο δικαστήρια καὶ κρίσεις. καὶ δή τινα
τῶν ἐπιφανεστάτων ἀποκτείνειν προθέμενοι Ζαχαρίαν υἱὸν Βάρεις[1]· παρώξυνε δ᾽ αὐτοὺς τὸ λίαν
τἀνδρὸς μισοπόνηρον καὶ φιλελεύθερον, ἦν δὲ καὶ
πλούσιος, ὥστε μὴ μόνον ἐλπίζειν τὴν ἁρπαγὴν
τῆς οὐσίας, ἀλλὰ καὶ προσαποσκευάσεσθαι[2] δυνα-
336 τὸν ἄνθρωπον εἰς τὴν ἑαυτῶν κατάλυσιν· συγ-
καλοῦσι μὲν ἐξ ἐπιτάγματος ἑβδομήκοντα τῶν ἐν
τέλει δημοτῶν εἰς τὸ ἱερόν, περιθέντες δ᾽ αὐτοῖς
ὥσπερ ἐπὶ σκηνῆς σχῆμα δικαστῶν ἔρημον
ἐξουσίας τοῦ Ζαχαρίου κατηγόρουν, ὡς ἐνδιδοίη
τὰ πράγματα Ῥωμαίοις καὶ περὶ προδοσίας δια-
337 πέμψαιτο πρὸς Οὐεσπασιανόν. ἦν δὲ οὔτ᾽ ἔλεγχός
τις τῶν κατηγορουμένων οὔτε τεκμήριον, ἀλλ᾽
αὐτοὶ πεπεῖσθαι καλῶς ἔφασαν καὶ τοῦτ᾽ εἶναι
338 πίστιν τῆς ἀληθείας ἠξίουν. ὅ γε μὴν Ζαχαρίας
συνιδὼν μηδεμίαν αὐτῷ καταλειπομένην σωτηρίας
ἐλπίδα, κεκλῆσθαι γὰρ κατ᾽ ἐνέδραν εἰς εἱρκτήν,
οὐκ ἐπὶ δικαστήριον, ἐποιήσατο τὴν τοῦ ζῆν ἀπόγνωσιν οὐκ ἀπαρρησίαστον, ἀλλὰ καταστὰς τὸ

[1] PAVR Lat.: Βαρούχου M[1]C: Βαρισκαίου LM[2].
[2] ed. pr. and Lat.: προσαποσκενάζεσθαι mss.

[a] This incident has gained an interest for N.T. students
from an old suggestion revived by Wellhausen (*Einleitung
in die drei ersten Evangelien*, ed. 2, 1911, pp. 118 ff.) to identify
this Zacharias son of Baris (or Bariscaeus: the reading
Baruch is negligible) with the "Zachariah, son of Barachiah,"
whose death in the temple is referred to by Christ in Matt.

stantly suffered the same fate as the mourned. Only
by night would they take a little dust in both hands
and strew it on the bodies, though some venturous
persons did this by day. Twelve thousand of the
youthful nobility thus perished.

(4) Having now come to loathe indiscriminate *Mock trial*
massacre, the Zealots instituted mock trials and *and*
courts of justice. They had determined to put to *Zacharias.*
death Zacharias, son of Baris,[a] one of the most
eminent of the citizens. The man exasperated them
by his pronounced hatred of wrong and love of liberty,
and, as he was also rich, they had the double prospect
of plundering his property and of getting rid of a
powerful and dangerous opponent. So they issued
a peremptory summons to seventy of the leading
citizens to appear in the Temple, assigning to them,
as in a play, the rôle, without the authority, of
judges; they then accused Zacharias of betraying
the state to the Romans and of holding treasonable
communications with Vespasian. They adduced no
evidence or proof in support of these charges, but
declared that they were fully convinced of his guilt
themselves and claimed this as sufficiently establish-
ing the fact. Zacharias, aware that no hope of
escape was left him, as he had been treacherously
summoned to a prison rather than a court of justice,
did not allow despair of life to rob him of liberty of
speech. He rose and ridiculed the probability of

xxiii. 35, as the last of a series of Jewish murders beginning
with that of Abel. The theory, which rests on a rather
remote resemblance of names, is on many grounds untenable.
The author of the first Gospel refers to the murder of Z.
ben Jehoiada (2 Chron. xxiv. 19 ff.) whom, like some Jewish
Rabbis, he confused with Z. ben Berechiah, the prophet of
the Restoration (Zech. i. 1).

μὲν πιθανὸν τῶν κατηγορημένων διεχλεύασε καὶ
διὰ βραχέων ἀπελύσατο τὰς ἐπιφερομένας αἰτίας.
339 ἔπειτα δὲ τὸν λόγον εἰς τοὺς κατηγόρους ἀπο-
στρέψας ἑξῆς πάσας αὐτῶν διεξῄει τὰς παρανομίας
καὶ πολλὰ περὶ τῆς συγχύσεως κατωλοφύρατο
340 τῶν πραγμάτων. οἱ ζηλωταὶ δ' ἐθορύβουν καὶ
μόλις τῶν ξιφῶν ἀπεκράτουν, τὸ σχῆμα καὶ τὴν
εἰρωνείαν τοῦ δικαστηρίου μέχρι τέλους παῖξαι
προαιρούμενοι, καὶ ἄλλως πειράσαι θέλοντες τοὺς
δικαστάς, εἰ παρὰ τὸν αὐτῶν κίνδυνον μνησθή-
341 σονται τοῦ δικαίου. φέρουσι δ' οἱ ἑβδομήκοντα
τῷ κρινομένῳ τὰς ψήφους ἅπαντες καὶ σὺν αὐτῷ
προείλοντο τεθνάναι μᾶλλον ἢ τῆς ἀναιρέσεως
342 αὐτοῦ λαβεῖν τὴν ἐπιγραφήν. ἤρθη δὲ βοὴ τῶν
ζηλωτῶν πρὸς τὴν ἀπόλυσιν, καὶ πάντων μὲν ἦν
ἀγανάκτησις ἐπὶ τοῖς δικασταῖς ὡς μὴ συνιεῖσι
343 τὴν εἰρωνείαν τῆς δοθείσης αὐτοῖς ἐξουσίας, δύο
δὲ τῶν τολμηροτάτων προσπεσόντες ἐν μέσῳ τῷ
ἱερῷ διαφθείρουσι τὸν Ζαχαρίαν καὶ πεσόντι
ἐπιχλευάσαντες ἔφασαν "καὶ παρ' ἡμῶν τὴν
ψῆφον ἔχεις καὶ βεβαιοτέραν ἀπόλυσιν," ῥίπτουσί
τε αὐτὸν εὐθέως ἀπὸ τοῦ ἱεροῦ κατὰ τῆς ὑπο-
344 κειμένης φάραγγος. τοὺς δὲ δικαστὰς πρὸς ὕβριν
ἀπεστραμμένοις τοῖς ξίφεσι τύπτοντες ἐξέωσαν τοῦ
περιβόλου, δι' ἓν τοῦτο φεισάμενοι τῆς σφαγῆς
αὐτῶν, ἵνα σκεδασθέντες ἀνὰ τὴν πόλιν ἄγγελοι
πᾶσι τῆς δουλείας γένωνται.
345 (5) Τοῖς δ' Ἰδουμαίοις ἤδη τῆς παρουσίας
346 μετέμελε καὶ προσίστατο τὰ πραττόμενα. συναγαγὼν δὲ αὐτούς τις ἀπὸ τῶν ζηλωτῶν κατ'
ἰδίαν ἐλθὼν ἐνεδείκνυτο τὰ συμπαρανομηθέντα
τοῖς καλέσασι καὶ τὸ κατὰ τῆς μητροπόλεως

the accusation, and in few words quashed the charges
laid against him. Then, rounding upon his accusers,
he went over all their enormities in order, and bitterly
lamented the confusion of public affairs. The Zealots
were in an uproar and could scarce refrain from
drawing their swords, although they were anxious to
play out their part and this farce of a trial to the
close, and desired, moreover, to test whether the
judges would put considerations of justice above their
own peril. The seventy, however, brought in a
unanimous verdict for the defendant, preferring to
die with him rather than be held answerable for his
destruction. The Zealots raised an outcry at his
acquittal, and were all indignant with the judges for
not understanding that the authority entrusted to
them was a mere pretence. Two of the most daring
of them then set upon Zacharias and slew him in the
midst of the Temple, and exclaiming in jest over his
prostrate body " Now you have our verdict also and
a more certain release,[a] " forthwith cast him out
of the Temple into the ravine below. Then they
insolently struck the judges with the backs of their
swords and drove them from the precincts ; sparing
their lives for the sole reason that they might disperse through the city and proclaim to all the
servitude to which they were reduced.

(5) The Idumaeans now began to regret that they
had come, taking offence at these proceedings. In
this mood they were called together by one of the
Zealots, who came to them privately and showed up
the crimes which they had committed in conjunction
with those who had summoned them, and gave a

A Zealot
secretly
denounces
the crimes
of his party
to the
Idumaeans
and urges
them to
depart.

---

[a] The Greek word ἀπόλυσις means both " acquittal " and
" decease."

347 διεξῄει· παρατάσσεσθαι μὲν γὰρ ὡς ὑπὸ τῶν
ἀρχιερέων προδιδομένης Ῥωμαίοις τῆς μητροπόλεως, εὑρηκέναι δὲ προδοσίας μὲν τεκμήριον
οὐδέν, τοὺς δ᾽ ἐκείνην ὑποκρινομένους φυλάτ-
τεσθαι καὶ πολέμου καὶ τυραννίδος ἔργα τολμῶν-
348 τας. προσήκειν μὲν οὖν αὐτοῖς διακωλύειν ἀπ᾽
ἀρχῆς· ἐπειδὴ δ᾽ ἅπαξ εἰς κοινωνίαν ἐμφυλίου
φόνου προέπεσον,[1] ὅρον γοῦν ἐπιθεῖναι τοῖς ἁμαρτή-
μασι καὶ μὴ παραμένειν χορηγοῦντας ἰσχὺν τοῖς
349 καταλύουσι τὰ πάτρια. καὶ γὰρ εἴ τινες χαλε-
παίνουσι τῷ[2] κλεισθῆναι τὰς πύλας καὶ μὴ δοθῆναι
μετὰ τῶν ὅπλων αὐτοῖς ἑτοίμην τὴν εἴσοδον,
ἀλλὰ τοὺς εἴρξαντας τετιμωρῆσθαι· καὶ τεθνάναι
μὲν Ἄνανον, διεφθάρθαι δ᾽ ἐπὶ μιᾶς νυκτὸς
350 ὀλίγου δεῖν πάντα τὸν δῆμον. ἐφ᾽ οἷς τῶν μὲν
οἰκείων πολλοὺς αἰσθάνεσθαι μετανοοῦντας, τῶν
ἐπικαλεσαμένων δὲ ὁρᾶν ἄμετρον τὴν ὠμότητα
351 μηδὲ δι᾽ οὓς ἐσώθησαν αἰδουμένων· ἐν ὄμμασι
γοῦν τῶν συμμάχων τὰ αἴσχιστα τολμᾶν, καὶ τὰς
ἐκείνων παρανομίας Ἰδουμαίοις προσάπτεσθαι,
μέχρις ἂν μήτε κωλύῃ τις μήτε χωρίζηται τῶν
352 δρωμένων. δεῖν οὖν, ἐπειδὴ διαβολὴ μὲν πέφηνε
τὰ τῆς προδοσίας, ἔφοδος δὲ Ῥωμαίων οὐδεμία
προσδοκᾶται, δυναστεία δ᾽ ἐπιτετείχισται τῇ
πόλει δυσκατάλυτος, αὐτοὺς ἀναχωρεῖν ἐπ᾽ οἴκου
καὶ τῷ μὴ κοινωνεῖν τοῖς φαύλοις ἁπάντων
ἀπολογήσασθαι πέρι, ὧν φενακισθέντες μετά-
σχοιεν.
353   (vi. 1) Τούτοις πεισθέντες οἱ Ἰδουμαῖοι πρῶ-

---

[1] R : προσέπεσον most MSS. : μετέπεσον L.
[2] Dindorf: τὸ MSS.

detailed account of the situation in the capital.
They had enlisted, he reminded them, in the belief
that the chief priests were betraying the metropolis
to the Romans ; but they had discovered no evidence
of treason, whereas its professed defenders were the
daring perpetrators of acts of war and despotism.
These proceedings, he said, the Idumaeans should
have checked at the outset ; but having once become
their partners and plunged into civil war, they ought
now at least to put a limit to their sins and no longer
continue to lend support to men who were subverting
the institutions of their forefathers.   Even were there
any still indignant at the closure of the gates and the
refusal of prompt admission to them while bearing
arms, well, those who had excluded them had now
been punished : Ananus was dead and in one night
almost the whole population had been destroyed.
Such actions, he could perceive, had produced repentance in many of their own party, but among
those who had invited them he saw nothing but
unmeasured brutality, without the slightest respect
for their deliverers : under the very eyes of their
allies they dared to commit the foulest atrocities,
and their iniquities would be ascribed to the Idumaeans, so long as no one vetoed or dissociated himself
from these proceedings.   Since, then, the charge of
treason had been shown to be a calumny and no
invasion of the Romans was expected, while the city
had had planted upon it a despotism not easily to be
overthrown, their duty (he said) was to return home
and by severing their connexion with these scoundrels
to make some amends for all the crimes in which
they had been duped into taking a part.

(vi. 1) Acting on this advice, the Idumaeans first

τον μὲν λύουσι τοὺς ἐν τοῖς δεσμωτηρίοις περὶ
δισχιλίους δημότας, οἳ παραχρῆμα φυγόντες ἐκ
τῆς πόλεως ἀφικνοῦνται πρὸς Σίμωνα, περὶ οὗ
μικρὸν ὕστερον ἐροῦμεν· ἔπειτα ἐκ τῶν Ἱερο-
354 σολύμων ἀνεχώρησαν ἐπ' οἴκου. καὶ συνέβη τὸν
χωρισμὸν αὐτῶν γενέσθαι παράδοξον ἀμφοτέροις·
ὅ τε γὰρ δῆμος ἀγνοῶν τὴν μετάνοιαν ἀνεθάρσησε
355 πρὸς ὀλίγον ὡς ἐχθρῶν κεκουφισμένος, οἵ τε
ζηλωταὶ μᾶλλον ἐπανέστησαν, οὐχ ὡς ὑπὸ συμμάχων καταλειφθέντες, ἀλλ' ἀπηλλαγμένοι τῶν
δυσωπούντων καὶ διατρεπόντων παρανομεῖν.
356 οὐκέτι γοῦν μέλλησις ἢ σκέψις ἦν τῶν ἀδικημάτων,
ἀλλ' ὀξυτάταις μὲν ἐχρῶντο ταῖς ἐπινοίαις εἰς
ἕκαστα, τὰ δοχθέντα δὲ τάχιον καὶ τῆς ἐπινοίας
357 ἐνήργουν. μάλιστα δ' ἐπ' ἀνδρείαν τε καὶ εὐγένειαν ἐφόνων, τὴν μὲν φθόνῳ λυμαινόμενοι, τὸ
δὲ γενναῖον δέει· μόνην γὰρ αὐτῶν[1] ἀσφάλειαν
ὑπελάμβανον τὸ μηδένα τῶν δυνατῶν καταλιπεῖν.
358 ἀνηρέθη γοῦν σὺν πολλοῖς ἑτέροις καὶ Γουρίων,
ἀξιώματι μὲν καὶ γένει προύχων, δημοκρατικὸς
δὲ καὶ φρονήματος ἐλευθερίου μεστός, εἰ καί τις
ἕτερος Ἰουδαίων· ἀπώλεσε δ' αὐτὸν ἡ παρρησία
359 μάλιστα πρὸς τοῖς ἄλλοις πλεονεκτήμασιν. οὐδ'
ὁ Περαΐτης Νίγερ αὐτῶν τὰς χεῖρας διέφυγεν,
ἀνὴρ ἄριστος ἐν τοῖς πρὸς Ῥωμαίους πολέμοις
γενόμενος· ὃς καὶ βοῶν πολλάκις τάς τε ὠτειλὰς
360 ἐπιδεικνὺς διὰ μέσης ἐσύρετο τῆς πόλεως. ἐπεὶ

[1] αὐτῶν mss. (as often).

[a] §§ 503 ff.
[b] Probably identical with Gorion ben Joseph, § 159.
[c] "Teeming"; cf. Plato, Rep. 563 D μεστὰ ἐλευθερίας,
"ready to burst with liberty" (Jowett).

liberated the citizens confined in the prisons, numbering about two thousand (these immediately fled from
the city and joined Simon, of whom we shall speak
presently [a]); they then left Jerusalem and returned
home. Their departure produced an unlooked-for
effect on both parties : the citizens, unaware of their
repentance, recovered momentary confidence, as if
relieved of an enemy ; the Zealots, on the other
hand, grew yet more insolent, not as though they
had been abandoned by allies, but as quit of critics
who discountenanced and sought to deter them from
their lawlessness. No longer now was there any
delay or deliberation about their crimes ; they devised their plans with lightning rapidity, and in each
case put their decisions into effect even more swiftly
than they devised them. They thirsted above all for
the blood of the brave and the nobility, massacring
the latter out of envy, the former from fear ; for
they imagined that their own safety depended solely
on their leaving no person of authority alive. Thus,
to take one instance among many, they murdered
Gurion,[b] a person of exalted rank and birth, and
yet a democrat and filled [c] with liberal principles,
if ever Jew was ; his outspokenness, added to the
privileges of his position, was the main cause of his
ruin. Nor did even Niger the Peraean [d] escape
their hands, a man who had shown exceptional
gallantry in his battles with the Romans : vehemently
protesting and pointing to his scars, this veteran
was dragged through the midst of the city. When

The departure of the Idumaeans in disgust leads the Zealots to greater atrocities. Further victims : Gurion and Niger.

[d] He distinguished himself in the opening battle with
Cestius, *B.* ii. 520 ; was at one time governor of Idumaea, ii.
566 ; and led two unsuccessful attacks on the Roman
garrison at Ascalon, when he again won distinction and had a
miraculous escape, iii. 11-28.

δ' ἔξω τῶν πυλῶν ἦκτο, τὴν σωτηρίαν ἀπογνοὺς
περὶ ταφῆς ἱκέτευεν· οἱ δὲ προαπειλήσαντες ἧς
ἐπεθύμει μάλιστα γῆς μὴ μεταδώσειν αὐτῷ, τὸν
361 φόνον ἐνήργουν. ἀναιρούμενος δὲ ὁ Νίγερ τιμωροὺς Ῥωμαίους αὐτοῖς ἐπηράσατο, λιμόν τε καὶ
λοιμὸν ἐπὶ τῷ πολέμῳ καὶ πρὸς ἅπασι τὰς ἀλλήλων
362 χεῖρας· ἃ δὴ πάντα · κατὰ τῶν ἀσεβῶν ἐκύρωσεν
ὁ θεός, καὶ τὸ δικαιότατον, ὅτι γεύσασθαι τῆς
ἀλλήλων ἀπονοίας ἔμελλον οὐκ εἰς μακρὰν στασιά-
363 σαντες. Νίγερ μὲν οὖν ἀνῃρημένος τοὺς περὶ
τῆς καταλύσεως αὐτῶν φόβους ἐπεκούφισε, τοῦ
λαοῦ δὲ μέρος οὐδὲν ἦν, ᾧ μὴ πρὸς ἀπώλειαν
364 ἐπενοεῖτο πρόφασις. τὸ μὲν γὰρ αὐτῶν διενεχθέν
τινι πάλαι διέφθαρτο, τὸ δὲ μὴ προσκροῦσαν κατ'
εἰρήνην ἐπικαίρους ἐλάμβανε τὰς αἰτίας· καὶ ὁ
μὲν μηδ' ὅλως αὐτοῖς προσιὼν ὡς ὑπερήφανος,
ὁ προσιὼν δὲ μετὰ παρρησίας ὡς καταφρονῶν, ὁ
365 θεραπεύων δ' ὡς ἐπίβουλος ὑπωπτεύετο. μία
δὲ ἦν τῶν τε μεγίστων καὶ μετριωτάτων ἐγ-
κλημάτων τιμωρία θάνατος, καὶ διέφυγεν οὐδείς,
εἰ μὴ σφόδρα τις ἦν ταπεινὸς [ἢ]¹ δι' ἀγένειαν ἢ
διὰ τύχην.
366   (2) Ῥωμαίων δὲ οἱ μὲν ἄλλοι πάντες ἡγεμόνες
ἕρμαιον ἡγούμενοι τὴν στάσιν τῶν πολεμίων
ὥρμηντο πρὸς τὴν πόλιν καὶ τὸν Οὐεσπασιανὸν
ἤπειγον ὡς ἂν ὄντα κύριον τῶν ὅλων, φάμενοι
πρόνοιαν θεοῦ σύμμαχον σφίσι τῷ τετράφθαι

¹ om. ἢ L.

ᵃ Or " . . . had quarrels having long since been ":
πάλαι in the central position may be intended as adverb to
both verbs.

ᵇ In the manner of Thucydides in his reflections on civil
dissensions (στάσεις), iii. 82.

brought without the gates, he, despairing of his life, besought them to give him burial; but they fiercely declared that they would not grant him the one desire of his heart—a grave—and then proceeded to murder him. In his dying moments Niger imprecated upon their heads the vengeance of the Romans, famine and pestilence to add to the horrors of war, and, to crown all, internecine strife; all which curses upon the wretches were ratified by God, including that most righteous fate, by which they were doomed ere long to taste in party conflict the effects of their comrades' frenzy. Niger's removal anyhow relieved their fear of being deposed from power; but there was no section of the people for whose destruction some pretext was not devised. Those with whom any had ancient quarrels having been[a] put to death, against those who had given them no umbrage in peace-time accusations suitable to the occasion were invented: the man who never approached them was suspected of pride; he who approached them with freedom, of treating them with contempt; he who courted them, of conspiracy.[b] The one penalty for charges of the gravest or the most trifling nature was death; and none escaped save those whose humble birth put them utterly beneath notice, unless by accident.[c]

(2) The Roman generals, regarding the dissension in the enemy's ranks as a godsend, were all eager to march against the capital, and urged Vespasian, as commander-in-chief, to take this course. " Divine providence," they said, " has come to our aid by

Vespasian deliberates with his generals about attacking Jerusalem.

---

[c] I omit the first ἤ with L. The natural rendering " those whose humble birth or fortune " etc. gives τύχη a sense which appears unwarranted.

367 τοὺς ἐχθροὺς κατ᾽ ἀλλήλων· εἶναι μέντοι τὴν
ῥοπὴν ὀξεῖαν, καὶ ταχέως Ἰουδαίους ὁμονοήσειν[1]
ἢ κοπιάσαντας ἐν τοῖς ἐμφυλίοις κακοῖς ἢ μετα-
368 νοήσαντας. Οὐεσπασιανὸς δὲ πλεῖστον αὐτοὺς ἔφη
τοῦ δέοντος ἁμαρτάνειν, ὥσπερ ἐν θεάτρῳ χειρῶν
τε καὶ ὅπλων ἐπίδειξιν ποιήσασθαι γλιχομένους
οὐκ ἀκίνδυνον, ἀλλὰ μὴ τὸ συμφέρον καὶ τὰσφαλὲς
369 σκοποῦντας. εἰ μὲν γὰρ εὐθέως ὁρμήσειεν ἐπὶ
τὴν πόλιν, αἴτιος ὁμονοίας ἔσεσθαι τοῖς πολεμίοις
καὶ τὴν ἰσχὺν αὐτῶν ἀκμάζουσαν ἐφ᾽ ἑαυτὸν
ἐπιστρέψειν[2]· εἰ δὲ περιμείνειεν, ὀλιγωτέροις χρή-
370 σεσθαι δαπανηθεῖσιν ἐν τῇ στάσει. στρατηγεῖν
μὲν γὰρ ἄμεινον αὐτοῦ τὸν θεόν, ἀπονητὶ[3] Ῥωμαίοις παραδιδόντα Ἰουδαίους καὶ τὴν νίκην ἀκιν
371 δύνως τῇ στρατηγίᾳ[4] χαριζόμενον· ὥστε χρῆναι,
διαφθειρομένων χερσὶν οἰκείαις τῶν ἐχθρῶν καὶ
τῷ μεγίστῳ κακῷ στάσει χρωμένων, θεατὰς
μᾶλλον αὐτοὺς ἀποκαθῆσθαι τῶν κινδύνων ἢ
θανατῶσιν ἀνθρώποις καὶ λελυσσηκόσιν κατ᾽
372 ἀλλήλων χεῖρα μίσγειν. "εἰ δέ τις οἴεται τὴν
δόξαν τῆς νίκης ἑωλοτέραν ἔσεσθαι δίχα μάχης,
γνώτω τοῦ διὰ τῶν ὅπλων σφαλεροῦ τὸ μεθ᾽
373 ἡσυχίας κατόρθωμα λυσιτελέστερον ⟨ὄν⟩[5]· καὶ γὰρ
οὐχ ἧττον εὐκλεεῖς οἴεσθαι χρὴ τῶν κατὰ χεῖρα
λαμπρῶν τοὺς ἐγκρατείᾳ καὶ συνέσει τὰ ἴσα
πράξαντας." ἅμα μέντοι μειουμένων τῶν πολεμίων καὶ τὴν αὐτοῦ στρατιάν, ἀναληφθεῖσαν ἐκ
374 τῶν συνεχῶν πόνων, ἐρρωμενεστέραν ἕξειν. ἄλλως

---

[1] ed. pr. with Lat.: + ἡμῖν MSS.
[2] Bekker with Lat.: ἐπιστρέφειν MSS.
[3] ἀκονιτὶ VRC (ἀκοντὶ L).   [4] στρατιᾷ LVC.
[5] ins. Herwerden with Cobet.

turning our adversaries against each other; but
changes come rapidly and the Jews will quickly
return to unanimity through weariness or repentance
of civil strife." To this Vespasian replied that they
were gravely mistaken as to the right policy, and
were anxious to make a theatrical, though hazardous,
display of their gallantry and arms, without regard
to expediency and safety. For, were he immediately
to attack the city, the effect would be merely to
reunite their opponents and to turn their forces in
fullest strength against himself; whereas by waiting
he would find fewer enemies, when they had wasted
their numbers in sedition. God was a better general
than he, and was delivering the Jews to the Romans
without any exertion on their part and bestowing
victory upon them without risk to Roman generalship. Consequently, while their adversaries were
perishing by their own hands and suffering from that
worst of calamities, civil strife, their part was rather
to sit as distant spectators [a] of their perils, than to
contend with men who courted death and were
raving against each other. " But," he continued,
" if anyone thinks that the glory of victory will lose
its zest without a fight, let him learn that success
obtained by sitting still is more fruitful than when
won by the uncertainty of arms; indeed those who
attain the same ends by self-restraint and sagacity
should be deemed no less famous than those who
distinguish themselves in action." Moreover, while
the enemy's numbers were diminishing, his own
army would have recruited their strength after their
continuous labours and be at his service reinvigorated.

"Our strength is to sit still.

[a] As at gladiatorial shows.

τε καὶ τῶν στοχαζομένων τῆς περὶ τὴν νίκην
375 λαμπρότητος οὐ τοῦτον εἶναι τὸν καιρόν· οὐ γὰρ
περὶ κατασκευὴν ὅπλων ἢ τειχῶν οὐδὲ περὶ
συλλογὴν ἐπικούρων Ἰουδαίους ἀσχολεῖσθαι καὶ[1]
τὴν ὑπέρθεσιν ἔσεσθαι κατὰ τῶν διδόντων, ἀλλ'
ἐμφυλίῳ πολέμῳ καὶ διχονοίᾳ τραχηλιζομένους
καθ' ἡμέραν οἰκτρότερα πάσχειν ὧν ἂν ἐπελθόντες
376 αὐτοὶ διαθεῖεν αὐτοὺς ἁλόντας. εἴτ' οὖν τἀσφαλές
τις σκοποίη, χρῆναι τοὺς ὑφ' ἑαυτῶν ἀναλισκο-
μένους ἐᾶν, εἴτε τὸ εὐκλεέστερον τοῦ κατορθώ-
ματος, οὐ δεῖν τοῖς οἴκοι νοσοῦσιν ἐπιχειρεῖν·
ῥηθήσεσθαι γὰρ εὐλόγως οὐκ αὐτῶν τὴν νίκην
ἀλλὰ τῆς στάσεως.

377 (3) Ταῦτα Οὐεσπασιανῷ λέγοντι συνῄνουν οἱ
ἡγεμόνες, καὶ παραχρῆμα τὸ στρατηγικὸν τῆς
γνώμης ἀνεφαίνετο· πολλοὶ γοῦν[2] καθ' ἡμέραν
378 ηὐτομόλουν τοὺς ζηλωτὰς διαδιδράσκοντες. χα-
λεπὴ δ' ἦν ἡ φυγὴ φρουραῖς διειληφότων τὰς
διεξόδους πάσας καὶ τὸν ὁπωσοῦν ἐν αὐταῖς
ἁλισκόμενον ὡς πρὸς Ῥωμαίους ἀπιόντα δια-
379 χρωμένων. ὅ γε μὴν χρήματα δοὺς ἐξηφίετο
καὶ μόνος ἦν ὁ μὴ διδοὺς προδότης, ὥστε κατελείπετο τῶν εὐπόρων τὴν φυγὴν ὠνουμένων μόνους
380 ἐναποσφάττεσθαι τοὺς πένητας. νεκροὶ δὲ κατὰ
τὰς λεωφόρους πάσας ἐσωρεύοντο παμπληθεῖς,
καὶ πολλοὶ τῶν ὡρμημένων αὐτομολεῖν πάλιν τὴν
ἔνδον ἀπώλειαν ᾑροῦντο· τὸν γὰρ ἐπὶ τῆς πατρίδος
θάνατον ἐλπὶς ταφῆς ἐποίει δοκεῖν μετριώτερον.
381 οἱ δ' εἰς τοσοῦτον ὠμότητος ἐξώκειλαν, ὡς μήτε

---

[1] ὡς Destinon : atque ideo Lat.   Text doubtful.
[2] L : δὲ the rest.

Above all, this was not the occasion for aspiring to
the honours of a brilliant victory; for the Jews were
not busily engaged in forging arms, erecting fortifications or levying auxiliaries, in which case delay would
be prejudicial to those who granted it, but were
risking their necks in civil war and dissension and
daily enduring greater miseries than they themselves
would inflict on them after defeat, if they advanced
to the assault. Whether, therefore, they looked to
the path of safety, these Jews should be left to
continue their own destruction; or whether they
considered the success which would bring the greater
renown, they ought not to attack patients suffering
from their own domestic disorders; for it would be
said, with reason, that they owed their victory not
to themselves but to sedition.

(3) In these observations of Vespasian the officers
concurred, and the soundness of the general's judgement was soon made evident by the numbers who
daily deserted, eluding the Zealots. But flight was
difficult, because guards were posted at all the outlets and anyone caught there, on whatever business,
was slain, on the assumption that he was going off
to the Romans. If, however, he paid the price, he
was allowed to go, and only he who offered nothing
was a traitor; the result being that the wealthy
purchased their escape and the poor alone were
slaughtered. Along all the highways the dead were
piled in heaps; and many starting [a] to desert changed
their minds and chose to die within the walls, since
the hope of burial made death in their native city
appear more tolerable. The Zealots, however, carried
barbarity so far as to grant interment to none,

Many Jews desert to the Romans.

---

[a] Or " who had been eager."

τοῖς ἔνδον ἀναιρουμένοις μήτε τοῖς ἀνὰ τὰς
382 ὁδοὺς μεταδοῦναι γῆς, ἀλλὰ καθάπερ συνθήκας
πεποιημένοι τοῖς τῆς πατρίδος συγκαταλῦσαι καὶ
τοὺς τῆς φύσεως νόμους ἅμα τε τοῖς εἰς ἀνθρώ-
383 πους ἀδικήμασιν συμμιᾶναι καὶ τὸ θεῖον, ὑφ' ἡλίῳ
τοὺς νεκροὺς μυδῶντας ἀπέλειπον. τοῖς δὲ θάπ-
τουσί τινα τῶν προσηκόντων, ὃ καὶ τοῖς αὐτο-
μολοῦσιν, ἐπιτίμιον θάνατος ἦν, καὶ δεῖσθαι
παραχρῆμα ταφῆς ἔδει τὸν ἑτέρῳ χαριζόμενον.
384 καθόλου τε εἰπεῖν, οὐδὲν οὕτως ἀπολώλει χρηστὸν
πάθος ἐν ταῖς τότε συμφοραῖς ὡς ἔλεος· ἃ γὰρ
ἐχρῆν οἰκτείρειν, ταῦτα παρώξυνε τοὺς ἀλιτηρίους,
καὶ ἀπὸ μὲν τῶν ζώντων ἐπὶ τοὺς ἀνῃρημένους,
ἀπὸ δὲ τῶν νεκρῶν ἐπὶ τοὺς ζῶντας τὰς ὀργὰς
385 μετέφερον· καὶ δι' ὑπερβολὴν δέους ὁ περιὼν
τοὺς προληφθέντας ὡς ἀναπαυσαμένους ἐμακά-
ριζεν, οἵ τε ἐν τοῖς δεσμωτηρίοις αἰκιζόμενοι
κατὰ σύγκρισιν καὶ τοὺς ἀτάφους ἀπέφαινον
386 εὐδαίμονας. κατεπατεῖτο μὲν οὖν πᾶς αὐτοῖς
θεσμὸς ἀνθρώπων, ἐγελᾶτο δὲ τὰ θεῖα, καὶ τοὺς
τῶν προφητῶν χρησμοὺς[1] ὥσπερ ἀγυρτικὰς λογο-
387 ποιίας ἐχλεύαζον. πολλὰ δ' οὗτοι περὶ ἀρετῆς
καὶ κακίας προεθέσπισαν, ἃ παραβάντες οἱ
ζηλωταὶ καὶ τὴν κατὰ τῆς πατρίδος προφητείαν
388 τέλους ἠξίωσαν. ἦν γὰρ δή τις παλαιὸς λόγος
ἀνδρῶν ἐνθέων[2] τότε τὴν πόλιν ἁλώσεσθαι καὶ
καταφλέξεσθαι τὸ ἁγιώτατον νόμῳ πολέμου,
στάσις ἐὰν κατασκήψῃ καὶ χεῖρες οἰκεῖαι προ-

[1] L Exc. : θεσμοὺς the rest (from previous line).

whether slain within the city or on the roads ; but, as though they had covenanted to annul the laws of nature along with those of their country, and to their outrages upon humanity to add pollution of Heaven [a] itself, they left the dead putrefying in the sun. For burying a relative, as for desertion, the penalty was death, and one who granted this boon to another instantly stood in need of it himself. In short, none of the nobler emotions was so utterly lost amid the miseries of those days, as pity : what should have roused their compassion, only exasperated these miscreants, whose fury shifted alternately from the living to the slain and from the dead to the living. Such terror prevailed that the survivors deemed blessed the lot of the earlier victims, now at rest, while the tortured wretches in the prisons pronounced even the unburied happy in comparison with themselves. Every human ordinance was trampled under foot, every dictate of religion ridiculed by these men, who scoffed at the oracles of the prophets as impostors' fables. Yet those predictions of theirs contained much concerning virtue and vice, by the transgression of which the Zealots brought upon their country the fulfilment of the prophecies directed against it. For there was an ancient saying of inspired men that the city would be taken and the sanctuary burnt to the ground by right of war, whensoever it should be visited by sedition and native hands should be the first

Barbarity of Zealots to dead and living.

They fulfil the predictions of ancient prophecy.

---

[a] Literally "the deity" ; *cf.* ii. 148 of the scrupulous care of the Essenes "not to offend the rays of the deity," *i.e.* the sun.

---

[2] Holwerda : ἔνθεον ms. quoted by Havercamp : ἔνθα the rest.

μιάνωσι τὸ τοῦ θεοῦ τέμενος· οἷς οὐκ ἀπιστήσαντες
οἱ ζηλωταὶ διακόνους αὐτοὺς ἐπέδοσαν.

389 (vii. 1). Ἤδη δὲ Ἰωάννῃ τυραννιῶντι τὸ πρὸς
τοὺς ὁμοίους ἰσότιμον ἠδοξεῖτο, καὶ κατ' ὀλίγους
προσποιούμενος τῶν πονηροτέρων ἀφηνίαζε[1] τοῦ
390 συντάγματος. ἀεὶ δὲ τοῖς μὲν τῶν ἄλλων δόγ-
μασιν ἀπειθῶν, τὰ δὲ αὐτοῦ προστάσσων δεσπο-
τικώτερον, δῆλος ἦν μοναρχίας ἀντιποιούμενος.
391 εἶκον δ' αὐτῷ τινὲς μὲν δέει, τινὲς δὲ κατ' εὔνοιαν,
δεινὸς γὰρ ἦν ἀπάτῃ καὶ λόγῳ προσαγαγέσθαι,
πολλοὶ δὲ πρὸς ἀσφαλείας ἡγούμενοι τῆς αὐτῶν
τὰς αἰτίας ἤδη τῶν τολμωμένων ἐφ' ἕνα καὶ
392 μὴ πολλοὺς ἀναφέρεσθαι. τό γε μὴν δραστήριον
αὐτοῦ κατά τε χεῖρα καὶ κατὰ γνώμην δορυφόρους
393 εἶχεν οὐκ ὀλίγους. πολλὴ δὲ μοῖρα τῶν ἀντι-
καθισταμένων[2] ἀπελείπετο, παρ' οἷς ἴσχυε μὲν
καὶ φθόνος, δεινὸν ἡγουμένων ὑποτετάχθαι τὸ[3]
πρὶν ἰσοτίμῳ, τὸ πλέον δ' εὐλάβεια τῆς μοναρχίας
394 ἀπέτρεπεν· οὔτε γὰρ καταλύσειν ῥᾳδίως ἤλπιζον
αὐτὸν ἅπαξ κρατήσαντα, καὶ καθ' αὑτῶν πρόφασιν
ἕξειν τὸ τὴν ἀρχὴν ἀντιπρᾶξαι· προῃρεῖτο δ' οὖν
πολεμῶν ἕκαστος ὁτιοῦν παθεῖν ἢ δουλεύσας
ἑκουσίως ἐν ἀνδραπόδου μοίρᾳ παραπολέσθαι.

---

[1] ἀφηνιάζετο L Exc.
[2] PC : ἀντικαθημένων the rest.
[3] PAC : τῷ the rest.

---

[a] I can quote no " ancient " authority for the saying.
The following *vaticinium post eventum* occurs in a work
written c. A.D. 80 : ἡνίκα δ' ἀφροσύνῃσι πεποιθότες εὐσεβίην
τε | ῥίψουσιν στυγερούς τε τελοῦσι φόνους περὶ νηόν, | καὶ τότ'
. . [reference follows to flight of Nero and the Roman civil

to defile God's sacred precincts.[a] This saying the
Zealots did not disbelieve ; yet they lent themselves
as instruments of its accomplishment.

(vii. 1) But now John, aspiring to despotic power, *Split in the*
began to disdain the position of mere equality in *Zealot party:*
honours with his peers, and, gradually gathering *John*
round him a group of the more depraved, broke *assumes despotic*
away from the coalition. Invariably disregarding *power.*
the decisions of the rest, and issuing imperious orders
of his own, he was evidently laying claim to absolute
sovereignty. Some yielded to him through fear,
others from devotion (for he was an expert in gaining
supporters by fraud and rhetoric) ; a large number
thought that it would conduce to their own safety
that the blame for their daring crimes should henceforth rest upon one individual rather than upon
many ; while his energy both of body and mind pro-
cured him not a few retainers. On the other hand,
he was abandoned by a large section of antagonists,
partly influenced by envy—they scorned subjection
to a former equal—but mainly deterred by dread
of monarchical rule ; for they could not expect easily
to depose him when once in power, and thought
that they would have an excuse for themselves if
they opposed him at the outset.[b] Anyhow, each man
preferred war, whatever sufferings it might entail,
to voluntary servitude and being killed off like slaves.

---

war] ἐκ Συρίης δ' ἥξει Ῥώμης πρόμος ὃς πυρὶ νηὸν | συμφλέξας
Σολύμων κτλ., *Orac. Sibyll.* iv. 117 ff.

[b] Meaning doubtful. τὴν ἀρχὴν (which is certainly
adverbial, not a noun as in Whiston's rendering, " that they
had opposed *his having power* ") usually has a negative ;
possibly we should read τὸ ⟨μὴ⟩ τὴν ἀρχὴν ἀντιπρᾶξαι, *i.e.*
" that he would have a pretext against them if they did not
oppose him at the outset."

395 διαιρεῖται μὲν οὖν ἡ στάσις ἐκ τούτων, καὶ τοῖς
396 ἐναντιωθεῖσιν Ἰωάννης ἀντεβασίλευσεν. ἀλλὰ τὰ
μὲν πρὸς ἀλλήλους αὐτοῖς διὰ φυλακῆς ἦν, καὶ
οὐδὲν ἢ μικρὸν εἴ ποτε διηκροβολίζοντο τοῖς
ὅπλοις, ἤριζον δὲ κατὰ τοῦ δήμου καὶ πότεροι
397 πλείονα λείαν ἄξουσιν¹ ἀντεφιλονείκουν. ἐπεὶ δὲ
ἡ πόλις τρισὶ τοῖς μεγίστοις κακοῖς ἐχειμάζετο,
πολέμῳ καὶ τυραννίδι καὶ στάσει, κατὰ σύγκρισιν
μετριώτερον ἦν τοῖς δημοτικοῖς ὁ πόλεμος·
ἀμέλει διαδιδράσκοντες ἐκ τῶν οἰκείων ἔφευγον
πρὸς τοὺς ἀλλοφύλους καὶ παρὰ Ῥωμαίοις ἧς
ἀπήλπισαν ἐν τοῖς ἰδίοις σωτηρίας ἠξιοῦντο.

398 (2) Τέταρτον δὲ ἄλλο κακὸν ἐκινεῖτο πρὸς τὴν
399 τοῦ ἔθνους κατάλυσιν. φρούριον ἦν οὐ πόρρω
Ἱεροσολύμων καρτερώτατον, ὑπὸ τῶν ἀρχαίων
βασιλέων εἴς τε ὑπέκθεσιν κτήσεως ἐν πολέμου
ῥοπαῖς καὶ σωμάτων ἀσφάλειαν κατεσκευασμέ-
400 νον, ὃ ἐκαλεῖτο Μασάδα. τοῦτο κατειληφότες
οἱ προσαγορευόμενοι σικάριοι τέως μὲν τὰς
πλησίον χώρας κατέτρεχον οὐδὲν πλέον τῶν ἐπιτηδείων ποριζόμενοι· δέει γὰρ ἀνεστέλλοντο
401 τῆς πλείονος ἁρπαγῆς· ὡς δὲ² τὴν Ῥωμαίων μὲν
στρατιὰν ἠρεμοῦσαν, στάσει δὲ καὶ τυραννίδι
ἰδίᾳ τοὺς ἐν Ἱεροσολύμοις Ἰουδαίους ἐπύθοντο
διῃρημένους, ἁδροτέρων ἥπτοντο τολμημάτων.
402 καὶ κατὰ τὴν ἑορτὴν τῶν ἀζύμων, ἣν ἄγουσιν
Ἰουδαῖοι³ σωτήρια ἐξ οὗ τῆς ὑπ᾽ Αἰγυπτίοις

¹ PA : ἀνάξουσιν the rest.
² ὡς δὲ] ὡς PA¹ Lat.: εἶθ᾽ ὡς Niese with A².
³ Ἑβραῖοι L Lat.

ᵃ *Sebbeh*, above the W. coast of the Dead Sea, near its

Such, then, was the origin of the split in the party, and John confronted his adversaries as a rival sovereign. However, their attitude to each other was purely defensive, and there were seldom if ever any skirmishes in arms between them; but they were rival oppressors of the people and vied with each other in carrying off the larger spoils. While the ship of state was thus labouring under the three greatest of calamities—war, tyranny, and faction—to the populace the war was comparatively the mildest; in fact they fled from their countrymen to take refuge with aliens and obtained at Roman hands the security which they despaired of finding among their own people.

(2) But yet a fourth misfortune was on foot to consummate the nation's ruin. Not far from Jerusalem was a fortress of redoubtable strength, built by the kings of old as a repository for their property and a refuge for their persons during the vicissitudes of war; it was called Masada.[a] Of this the so-called Sicarii had taken possession. So far they had confined themselves to raids upon the neighbouring districts, merely with the object of procuring supplies, fear restraining them from further ravages; but now when they learnt that the Roman army was inactive and that in Jerusalem the Jews were distracted by sedition and domestic tyranny, they embarked on more ambitious enterprises. Thus, during the feast of unleavened bread—a feast which has been kept by the Jews in thanksgiving for deliverance ever since their return to their native land on their

The Sicarii occupy Masada and make raids on the country.

lower end. Its capture by the insurgents is mentioned in *B.* ii. 408; a detailed description of the fortress and of its final capture by the Romans is given in vii. 280 ff.

δουλείας ἀνεθέντες εἰς τὴν πάτριον γῆν κατῆλθον,
νύκτωρ τοὺς ἐμποδὼν ὄντας διαλαθόντες πολίχνην τινὰ κατατρέχουσιν καλουμένην Ἐνγαδδί,
403 ἐν ᾗ τὸ μὲν ἀμύνεσθαι δυνάμενον, πρὶν ὅπλων
ἅψασθαι καὶ συνελθεῖν, φθάσαντες ἐσκέδασαν[1] καὶ
τῆς πόλεως ἐξέβαλον, τὸ δὲ φυγεῖν ἧττον ὄν,
γύναιά τε καὶ παῖδας, ὑπὲρ ἑπτακοσίους ἀναι-
404 ροῦσιν. ἔπειτα τούς τε οἴκους ἐξεσκευασμένοι
καὶ τῶν καρπῶν τοὺς ἀκμαιοτάτους[2] ἁρπάσαντες
405 ἀνήνεγκαν εἰς τὴν Μασάδαν. καὶ οἱ μὲν ἐλή-
ζοντο πάσας τὰς περὶ τὸ φρούριον κώμας καὶ
τὴν χώραν ἐπόρθουν ἅπασαν, προσδιαφθειρομένων
αὐτοῖς καθ᾽ ἡμέραν ἑκασταχόθεν οὐκ ὀλίγων·
406 ἐκινεῖτο δὲ καὶ κατὰ τἆλλα τῆς Ἰουδαίας κλίματα
τὸ τέως ἠρεμοῦν τὸ ληστρικόν, καθάπερ δὲ ἐν
σώματι τοῦ κυριωτάτου φλεγμαίνοντος πάντα τὰ
407 μέλη συνενόσει· διὰ γοῦν τὴν ἐν τῇ μητροπόλει
στάσιν καὶ ταραχὴν ἄδειαν ἔσχον οἱ κατὰ τὴν
χώραν πονηροὶ τῶν ἁρπαγῶν καὶ τὰς οἰκείας
ἕκαστοι[3] κώμας ἁρπάζοντες ἔπειτα εἰς τὴν ἐρη-
408 μίαν ἀφίσταντο. συναθροιζόμενοί τε καὶ συν-
ομνύμενοι κατὰ λόχους, στρατιᾶς μὲν ὀλιγώτεροι
πλείους δὲ ληστηρίου, προσέπιπτον ἱεροῖς καὶ
409 πόλεσιν, καὶ κακοῦσθαι μὲν συνέβαινεν ἐφ᾽ οὓς
ὁρμήσειαν ὡς ἐν πολέμῳ καταληφθέντας, φθάνε-
σθαι δὲ τὰς ἀμύνας ὡς λῃστῶν ἅμα ταῖς ἁρπαγαῖς

---

[1] ἐκόλασαν P[1]A[1]VR.
[2] PAM: ἀκμαίους the rest.   [3] L: ἕκαστος the rest.

---

[a] And when, consequently, the bulk of the population
would be absent at Jerusalem.

[b] Engedi, ʿAin Jidy, on the W. coast of the Dead Sea,
some 10 miles N. of Masada.

release from bondage in Egypt [a]—these assassins,
eluding under cover of night those who might have
obstructed them, made a raiding descent upon a
small town called Engaddi.[b] Those of the inhabitants who were capable of resistance were, before
they could seize their arms and assemble, dispersed
and driven out of the town ; those unable to fly,
women and children numbering upwards of seven
hundred, were massacred. They then rifled the
houses, seized the ripest of the crops, and carried off
their spoil to Masada. They made similar raids on
all the villages around the fortress, and laid waste
the whole district, being joined daily by numerous
dissolute recruits from every quarter. Throughout Similar
the other parts of Judaea, moreover, the predatory brigandage throughout
bands, hitherto quiescent, now began to bestir them- Judaea.
selves. And as in the body when inflammation
attacks the principal member all the members catch
the infection,[c] so the sedition and disorder in the
capital gave the scoundrels in the country free
licence to plunder ; and each gang after pillaging
their own village made off into the wilderness. Then
joining forces and swearing mutual allegiance, they
would proceed by companies—smaller than an army
but larger than a mere band of robbers—to fall upon
temples [d] and cities. The unfortunate victims of
their attacks suffered the miseries of captives of war,
but were deprived of the chance of retaliation, because their foes in robber fashion at once decamped

[c] Cf. 1 Cor. xii. 26 εἴτε πάσχει ἓν μέλος, συνπάσχει πάντα τὰ
μέλη, and for the same simile B. i. 507.

[d] Apparently synagogues or " prayer-houses " are meant ;
these were often built outside the towns near rivers or sea
coast for purification purposes. Judaea had but the one
" temple " at Jerusalem.

JOSEPHUS

ἀποδιδρασκόντων. οὐδὲν δὲ μέρος ἦν τῆς Ἰουδαίας, ὃ μὴ τῇ προανεχούσῃ πόλει συναπώλλυτο.
410 (3) Ταῦτα. Οὐεσπασιανῷ παρὰ τῶν αὐτομόλων
διηγγέλλετο· καίπερ γὰρ φρουρούντων τὰς ἐξόδους τῶν στασιαστῶν ἁπάσας καὶ διαφθειρόντων
τοὺς ὁπωσοῦν προσιόντας, ὅμως ἦσαν οἱ διελάνθανον καὶ καταφεύγοντες εἰς τοὺς Ῥωμαίους
τὸν στρατηγὸν ἐνῆγον ἀμῦναι τῇ πόλει καὶ τὰ
411 τοῦ δήμου περισῶσαι λείψανα· διὰ γὰρ τὴν πρὸς
Ῥωμαίους εὔνοιαν ἀνῃρῆσθαί τε τοὺς πολλοὺς
412 καὶ κινδυνεύειν τοὺς περιόντας. ὁ δὲ οἰκτείρων
ἤδη τὰς συμφορὰς αὐτῶν τὸ¹ μὲν δοκεῖν ἐκ-
πολιορκήσων ἀφίσταται² τὰ Ἱεροσόλυμα, τὸ δ᾽
413 ἀληθὲς ἀπαλλάξων πολιορκίας. ἔδει μέντοι³ προ-
καταστρέψασθαι τὰ λειπόμενα καὶ μηδὲν ἔξωθεν
ἐμπόδιον τῇ πολιορκίᾳ καταλιπεῖν· ἐλθὼν οὖν ἐπὶ
τὰ Γάδαρα μητρόπολιν τῆς Περαίας καρτερὰν
τετράδι Δύστρου μηνὸς εἴσεισιν εἰς τὴν πόλιν.
414 καὶ γὰρ ἔτυχον οἱ δυνατοὶ λάθρα τῶν στασιωδῶν
πρεσβευσάμενοι πρὸς αὐτὸν περὶ παραδόσεως
πόθῳ τε εἰρήνης καὶ διὰ τὰς οὐσίας· πολλοὶ δὲ
415 τὰ Γάδαρα κατῴκουν πλούσιοι. τούτων τὴν

¹ PC : τῷ the rest.
² Niese (ed. min.): ἐφίσταται PAML (which should perhaps
stand = propius accedit Lat.): ἀνίσταται the rest.
³ Destinon: μὲν τοῦ L : μὲν PA : δὲ the rest.

ᵃ § 378.
ᵇ Gadara is here identified by all commentators with the
important place of that name S.E. of the Sea of Galilee,
modern *Umm Keis* or *Mukes*, a principal city of Decapolis,
and a seat of Greek culture, being the home, among other
writers, of Meleager the epigrammatist and Philodemus the
Epicurean. This identification, though favoured by the
reference to its " many wealthy residents," is open to serious
276

with their prey. There was, in fact, no portion of
Judaea which did not share in the ruin of the capital.

(3) Of these proceedings Vespasian was informed
by deserters. For, although the insurgents guarded
all the exits and slew any who for whatever reason
approached them,[a] there were notwithstanding some
who evaded them and, fleeing to the Romans, urged
the general to protect the city and rescue the remnant
of its inhabitants, assuring him that it was owing to
their loyalty to the Romans that so many had been
slain and the survivors were in peril. Vespasian,
who already pitied their misfortunes, broke up his
camp, with the apparent purpose of taking Jerusalem
by siege, but in reality to deliver it from siege. It
was, however, first necessary to reduce any places
still outstanding, so as to leave no external impedi-
ment to hinder his operations. He accordingly
marched on Gádara,[b] the capital of Peraea and a
city of some strength, and entered it on the fourth
of the month Dystrus. For the leading men had,
unbeknown to the rebels, sent an embassy to him
offering to capitulate, alike from a desire for peace
and from concern for their property, for Gadara had
many wealthy residents. Of the leaders' deputation

Vespasian, instigated by deserters, prepares to advance on Jerusalem

and occupies GADARA (in Peraea) c. 21 March A.D. 68.

objections. (1) *Mukes* was in Decapolis, whereas the
Gadara here mentioned is called the capital or metropolis of
Peraea, of which district Pella, some 15 miles S. of *Mukes*,
was the northern boundary (*B.* iii. 46 f.); (2) Gadora
(Gadara ?) *es Salt*, is actually in Peraea and satisfies the other
data, for (3) it is not far from the village to which the
Gadarene fugitives fled (§ 420 note); (4) that village was on
the direct line to Jericho, for which they were making
(§ 431), an unnatural refuge for fugitives from the northern
Gadara; (5) Vespasian was marching southwards from
Caesarea upon Jerusalem (§ 412), not northwards towards
Galilee, which was already subdued.

πρεσβείαν ἠγνοήκεσαν οἱ διάφοροι, πλησίον δὲ
ἤδη ὄντος Οὐεσπασιανοῦ διεπύθοντο, καὶ κατα-
σχεῖν μὲν αὐτοὶ τὴν πόλιν ἀπέγνωσαν δύνασθαι,
τῶν τε ἔνδον ἐχθρῶν πλήθει λειπόμενοι καὶ
Ῥωμαίους ὁρῶντες οὐ μακρὰν τῆς πόλεως,
φεύγειν δὲ κρίνοντες[1] ἠδόξουν ἀναιμωτὶ καὶ
μηδεμίαν παρὰ τῶν αἰτίων εἰσπραξάμενοι τι-
416 μωρίαν. συλλαβόντες δὴ τὸν Δόλεσον, οὗτος γὰρ
ἦν οὐ μόνον ἀξιώματι καὶ γένει τῆς πόλεως
πρῶτος, ἀλλ᾽ ἐδόκει καὶ τῆς πρεσβείας αἴτιος,
κτείνουσί τε αὐτὸν καὶ δι᾽ ὑπερβολὴν ὀργῆς
νεκρὸν αἰκισάμενοι διέδρασαν ἐκ τῆς πόλεως.
417 ἐπιούσης δὲ ἤδη τῆς Ῥωμαϊκῆς δυνάμεως ὅ τε
δῆμος τῶν Γαδαρέων μετ᾽ εὐφημίας τὸν Οὐεσπασιανὸν εἰσδεξάμενοι δεξιὰς παρ᾽ αὐτοῦ πίστεως
ἔλαβον καὶ φρουρὰν ἱππέων τε καὶ πεζῶν πρὸς
418 τὰς τῶν φυγάδων καταδρομάς· τὸ γὰρ τεῖχος
αὐτοὶ πρὶν ἀξιῶσαι Ῥωμαίους καθεῖλον, ὅπως
εἴη πίστις αὐτοῖς τοῦ τὴν εἰρήνην ἀγαπᾶν τὸ μηδὲ
βουληθέντας δύνασθαι[2] πολεμεῖν.
419 (4) Οὐεσπασιανὸς δ᾽ ἐπὶ μὲν τοὺς διαδράντας ἐκ
τῶν Γαδάρων Πλάκιδον σὺν ἱππεῦσιν πεντακοσίοις
καὶ πεζοῖς τρισχιλίοις πέμπει, αὐτὸς δὲ μετὰ τῆς
420 ἄλλης στρατιᾶς ὑπέστρεψεν εἰς Καισάρειαν. οἱ
δὲ φυγάδες ὡς αἰφνίδιον τοὺς διώκοντας ἱππεῖς
ἐθεάσαντο, πρὶν εἰς χεῖρας ἐλθεῖν εἴς τινα κώμην
421 συνειλοῦνται Βηθεννάβριν προσαγορευομένην· ἐν
ᾗ νέων[3] πλῆθος οὐκ ὀλίγον εὑρόντες καὶ τοὺς μὲν
ἑκόντας τοὺς δὲ βίᾳ καθοπλίσαντες εἰκαίως,

---

[1] κρίναντες MVRC.
[2] δύνασθαι A[2] Lat.: om. the rest.
[3] VRC Lat. Heg.: Ἰουδαίων the rest.

their adversaries were ignorant and only discovered it on the approach of Vespasian. Despairing of their ability to hold the city themselves, in view of their inferiority in numbers to their opponents within the walls and the proximity of the Romans, visible not far without, they determined to flee, but scorned to do so without shedding blood and exacting punishment from those responsible for their situation. So they seized Dolesus, who was not only by rank and family the first man in the town, but was also regarded as the originator of the embassy; having slain him and in their furious rage mangled his body, they fled from the city. The Roman army now appearing, the Gadarenes admitted Vespasian with acclamation and received from him pledges of security together with a garrison of horse and foot to protect them against invasions of the fugitives; for they had pulled down their walls of their own accord without requisition from the Romans, in order that their powerlessness to make war, even if they wished, might testify to their love of peace.

(4) Vespasian sent Placidus [a] with 500 horse and 3000 foot to pursue those who had fled from Gadara, while he himself with the remainder of his army returned to Caesarea. The fugitives, on suddenly catching sight of the pursuing cavalry, before any engagement took place swarmed into a village called Bethennabris [b]; finding here a considerable number of young men, they armed these with any available weapons, some consenting, others by force, and

Placidus defeats the Gadarene fugitives.

[a] § 57 n.
[b] Doubtless Beth-Nimrah, *Tell Nimrin*, some 12 miles S.W. of the Peraean Gadara, and on the direct line for Jericho, which lay nearly opposite it on the other side of the Jordan.

422 προπηδῶσιν ἐπὶ τοὺς περὶ τὸν Πλάκιδον. οἱ δὲ
πρὸς μὲν τὴν πρώτην ἐμβολὴν ὀλίγον εἶξαν, ἅμα
καὶ προκαλέσασθαι τεχνιτεύοντες αὐτοὺς ἀπὸ
423 τοῦ τείχους πορρωτέρω, λαβόντες δ᾽ εἰς ἐπιτήδειον περιήλαυνόν τε καὶ κατηκόντιζον, καὶ
τὰς μὲν φυγὰς¹ αὐτῶν οἱ ἱππεῖς ὑπετέμνοντο, τὰς
424 συμπλοκὰς δὲ τὸ πεζὸν εὐτόνως διέφθειρον.² οὐ
μέντοι πλέον τι τόλμης ἐπιδεικνύμενοι οἱ Ἰουδαῖοι
διεφθείροντο· πεπυκνωμένοις γὰρ τοῖς Ῥωμαίοις
προσπίπτοντες καὶ ταῖς πανοπλίαις ὥσπερ τε-
τειχισμένοις, αὐτοὶ μὲν οὐχ εὕρισκον βέλους
παράδυσιν οὐδ᾽ ηὐτόνουν ῥῆξαι τὴν φάλαγγα,
425 περιεπείροντο δὲ τοῖς ἐκείνων βέλεσι· καὶ τοῖς
ἀγριωτάτοις παραπλήσιοι θηρίοις ὥρμων ἐπὶ
τὸν σίδηρον, διεφθείροντο δ᾽ οἱ μὲν κατὰ στόμα
παιόμενοι τοῖς ξίφεσιν, οἱ δὲ ὑπὸ τῶν ἱππέων
σκεδαννύμενοι.
426   (5) Σπουδὴ γὰρ ἦν τῷ Πλακίδῳ τὰς ἐπὶ τὴν
427 κώμην ὁρμὰς αὐτῶν διακλείειν, καὶ συνεχῶς
παρελαύνων κατ᾽ ἐκεῖνο τὸ μέρος, ἔπειτα ἐπι-
στρέφων ἅμα καὶ τοῖς βέλεσι χρώμενος εὐστόχως
ἀνήρει τοὺς πλησιάζοντας καὶ δέει τοὺς πόρρωθεν
ἀνέστρεφεν, μέχρι βίᾳ διεκπεσόντες οἱ γενναιό-
428 τατοι πρὸς τὸ τεῖχος διέφευγον. ἀπορία δ᾽ εἶχε
τοὺς φύλακας· οὔτε γὰρ ἀποκλεῖσαι τοὺς ἀπὸ
τῶν Γαδάρων ὑπέμενον διὰ τοὺς σφετέρους καὶ
429 δεξάμενοι συναπολεῖσθαι προσεδόκων. ὃ δὴ καὶ
συνέβη· συνωσθέντων γὰρ αὐτῶν εἰς τὸ τεῖχος
παρ᾽ ὀλίγον μὲν οἱ τῶν Ῥωμαίων ἱππεῖς συνεισ-
έπεσον, οὐ μὴν ἀλλὰ καὶ φθασάντων ἀποκλεῖσαι
τὰς πύλας προσβαλὼν ὁ Πλάκιδος καὶ μέχρι

¹ τὰς μὲν φυγὰς Destinon : τοὺς μὲν φυγάδας MSS.

dashed out upon the troops of Placidus. The Romans
at their first onset fell back a little, manœuvring to
entice them further from the walls, and then, having
drawn them to a suitable spot, rode round them and
with their javelins shot them down; the cavalry
intercepting their flight, while the infantry vigorously
broke up their entangled masses. The Jews, in fact,
were cut to pieces after a display of mere audacity;
for, flinging themselves upon the serried Roman
ranks, walled in, as it were, by their armour, they
found no loophole for their missiles and were powerless to break the line, whilst their own men were
transfixed by their enemy's javelins and rushed, like
the most savage of beasts, upon the blade. So they
perished, some struck down by the sword facing the
foe, others in disorderly flight before the cavalry.

(5) For Placidus, anxious to intercept their rushes
for the village, kept riding his cavalry past them in
that direction, and then, wheeling round, with one
and the same well-aimed volley of missiles killed
those who were nearing it and intimidated and beat
back those further off; but in the end the most
courageous cut their way through and fled for the
ramparts. Here the sentries were in doubt what
they should do: they could not bring themselves to
exclude the Gadarenes because of their own men,[a]
whereas if they admitted them they expected to
perish with them. That was in fact what happened;
for in the crush of fugitives at the wall, the Roman
cavalry very nearly burst in with them, and, although
the guards succeeded in shutting the gates, Placidus

---

[a] The recruits obtained from the village, § 421.

[2] διέφερον of Destinon is needless; cf. διαφθείρειν τὴν
συνουσίαν, "break up the party," Plato, *Prot.* 338 D.

δείλης γενναίως ἀγωνισάμενος τοῦ τείχους καὶ
430 τῶν ἐν τῇ κώμῃ κρατεῖ.¹ τὰ μὲν οὖν ἀργὰ πλήθη
διεφθείρετο, φυγὴ δ᾽ ἦν τῶν δυνατωτέρων, τὰς δ᾽
οἰκίας οἱ στρατιῶται διήρπασαν καὶ τὴν κώμην
431 ἐνέπρησαν. οἱ δὲ διαδράντες ἐξ αὐτῆς τοὺς
κατὰ τὴν χώραν συνανέστησαν, καὶ τὰς μὲν
αὐτῶν συμφορὰς ἐξαίροντες ἐπὶ μεῖζον, τῶν δὲ
Ῥωμαίων τὴν στρατιὰν πᾶσαν ἐπιέναι λέγοντες
πάντας πανταχόθεν ἐξέσεισαν τῷ δέει, γενόμενοί
432 τε παμπληθεῖς ἔφευγον ἐπὶ Ἱεριχοῦντος· αὕτη
γὰρ ἔτι μόνη τὰς ἐλπίδας αὐτῶν ἔθαλπε τῆς σω-
433 τηρίας καρτερὰ πλήθει γε οἰκητόρων. Πλάκιδος
δὲ τοῖς ἱππεῦσι καὶ ταῖς προαγούσαις εὐπραγίαις
τεθαρρηκὼς εἵπετο, καὶ μέχρι μὲν Ἰορδάνου τοὺς
ἀεὶ καταλαμβανομένους ἀνῄρει, συνελάσας δὲ
πρὸς τὸν ποταμὸν πᾶν τὸ πλῆθος εἰργομένους²
ὑπὸ τοῦ ῥεύματος, τραφὲν γὰρ ὑπ᾽ ὄμβρων ἄβατον
434 ἦν, ἀντικρὺ παρετάσσετο. παρώξυνε δ᾽ ἡ ἀνάγκη
πρὸς μάχην τοὺς φυγῆς τόπον οὐκ ἔχοντας, καὶ
ταῖς ὄχθαις ἐπὶ μήκιστον παρεκτείναντες σφᾶς
αὐτοὺς ἐδέχοντο τὰ βέλη καὶ τὰς τῶν ἱππέων
ἐμβολάς, οἳ πολλοὺς αὐτῶν παίοντες εἰς τὸ ῥεῦμα
435 κατέβαλον. καὶ τὸ μὲν ἐν χερσὶν αὐτῶν δια-
φθαρὲν μύριοι πεντακισχίλιοι, τὸ δὲ βιασθὲν
ἐμπηδῆσαι εἰς τὸν Ἰορδάνην πλῆθος ἑκουσίως³
436 ἄπειρον ἦν. ἑάλωσαν δὲ περὶ δισχιλίους καὶ διακοσίους, λεία τε παμπληθὴς ὄνων τε καὶ προ-
βάτων καὶ καμήλων καὶ βοῶν.
437 (6) Ἰουδαίοις μὲν οὖν οὐδενὸς⁴ ἐλάττων ἥδε ἡ
πληγὴ προσπεσοῦσα καὶ μείζων ἔδοξεν ἑαυτῆς

---

¹ Niese: δὲ κρατεῖ L: ἐκράτει the rest.
² εἰργομένους PM.   ³ ἀκουσίως L.   ⁴ οὐδὲν MSS.

led an assault and by a gallant struggle prolonged until evening became master of the wall and of the occupants of the village. The helpless were slaughtered wholesale, the more able-bodied fled, and the soldiers rifled the houses and then set the village alight. The fugitives, meanwhile, roused the country-side, and by exaggerating their own calamities and stating that the entire Roman army was upon them drove all from their homes in universal panic, and with the whole population fled for Jericho ; that being the one remaining city strong enough, at least in virtue of its numerous inhabitants, to encourage hopes of salvation. Placidus, relying on his cavalry and emboldened by his previous success, pursued them, killing all whom he overtook, as far as the Jordan. Having driven the whole multitude up to the river, where they were blocked by the stream, which being swollen by the rain was unfordable, he drew up his troops in line opposite them. Necessity goaded them to battle, flight being impossible, and deploying their forces as far as possible along the bank[a] they met the missiles and the charges of the cavalry, who wounded and drove many down into the stream. Fifteen thousand perished by the enemy's hands, while the number of those who were driven to fling themselves of their own accord into the Jordan was incalculable ; about two thousand two hundred were captured, together with vast spoils of asses, sheep, camels, and oxen.

(6) This blow was the greatest that had befallen the Jews, and appeared even greater than it was ;

General flight of Peraeans for Jericho.

They are defeated with great slaughter at the Jordan.

---

[a] The plural can only refer to the one (left) bank, or rather perhaps to the terraces, one above the other, on that bank of the stream.

διὰ τὸ μὴ μόνον τὴν χώραν ἅπασαν δι' ἧς ἔφευγον
πληρωθῆναι φόνου, μηδὲ νεκροῖς διαβατὸν γενέσθαι τὸν Ἰορδάνην, ἐμπλησθῆναι δὲ τῶν σωμάτων
καὶ τὴν Ἀσφαλτῖτιν¹ λίμνην, εἰς ἣν παμπληθεῖς
438 ὑπὸ τοῦ ποταμοῦ κατεσύρησαν. Πλάκιδος δὲ
δεξιᾷ τύχῃ χρώμενος ὥρμησεν ἐπὶ τὰς πέριξ
πολίχνας τε καὶ κώμας, καταλαμβανόμενός² τε
Ἄβιλα καὶ Ἰουλιάδα καὶ Βησιμώθ³ τάς τε μέχρι
τῆς Ἀσφαλτίτιδος πάσας ἐγκαθίστησιν ἑκάστῃ
439 τοὺς ἐπιτηδείους τῶν αὐτομόλων. ἔπειτα σκάφεσιν ἐπιβήσας τοὺς στρατιώτας αἱρεῖ τοὺς εἰς
τὴν λίμνην καταφεύγοντας. καὶ τὰ μὲν κατὰ τὴν
Περαίαν προσεχώρησεν ἢ ἑάλω πάντα μέχρι
Μαχαιροῦντος.
440 (viii. 1) Ἐν δὲ τούτῳ τὸ περὶ τὴν Γαλατίαν⁴
ἀγγέλλεται κίνημα καὶ Οὐίνδιξ ἅμα τοῖς δυνατοῖς
τῶν ἐπιχωρίων ἀφεστὼς Νέρωνος, περὶ ὧν ἐν
441 ἀκριβεστέροις ἀναγέγραπται. Οὐεσπασιανὸν δ' ἐπήγειρεν εἰς τὴν ὁρμὴν τοῦ πολέμου τὰ ἠγγελ-
μένα, προορώμενον ἤδη τοὺς μέλλοντας ἐμφυλίους
πολέμους καὶ τὸν ὅλης κίνδυνον τῆς ἡγεμονίας,
ἐν ᾧ προειρηνεύσας τὰ κατὰ τὴν ἀνατολὴν ἐπι-
κουφίσειν ᾤετο τοὺς κατὰ τὴν Ἰταλίαν φόβους.

¹ Ἀσφαλτικὴν PA.
² καταλαβόμενός ML.   ³ Βησιμὼ PA.
⁴ C: τῆς Γαλατίας the rest.

ᵃ The Bituminous Lake=the Dead Sea.
ᵇ Probably Abel-Shittim (*Khurbet el-Keffrein*),some 5 miles
due S. of Beth-Nimrah : mentioned in conjunction with
Julias, *B.* ii. 252.
ᶜ Julias or Livias, formerly Beth-Haram (Betharamatha),

for not only was the whole countryside through which their flight had lain one scene of carnage, and the Jordan choked with dead, but even the Lake Asphaltitis [a] was filled with bodies, masses of which were carried down into it by the river. Placidus, following up his good fortune, hastened to attack the small towns and villages in the neighbourhood, and taking Abila,[b] Julias,[c] Besimoth,[d] and all as far as the Lake Asphaltitis, posted in each a garrison of such deserters as he thought fit ; then embarking his soldiers on shipboard he captured those who had taken refuge on the lake. Thus the whole of Peraea as far as Machaerus [e] either surrendered or was subdued.

All Peraea subdued.

(viii. 1) Meanwhile tidings arrived of the rising in Gaul and that Vindex [f] with the chiefs of that country had revolted from Nero, of which events fuller accounts have been given elsewhere. Vespasian was stimulated by the news to prosecute the war more vigorously, for he already foresaw the impending civil dissensions and the peril to the empire at large, and thought that, in the circumstances, by an early pacification of the east he would allay the anxiety of Italy. Accordingly, while the

Vespasian learns of Gallic revolt from Nero: winter of A.D. 67-68.

modern *Tell Rameh*, 2 miles S. of Abel-Shittim, opposite Jericho : *B.* ii. 59 n., 168 n.

[d] Beth-Jeshimoth, *Sueimeh*, S. of Julias.

[e] E. of the upper region of the Dead Sea.

[f] C. Julius Vindex, prefect of Gallia Celtica, headed a Gallic revolt against Nero ; and Virginius Rufus was sent with the legions of Lower Germany to oppose him. At Vesontio, where the armies met, Vindex and Virginius secretly agreed to conspire together, but the armies coming to no similar understanding, the troops of Vindex were cut to pieces and Vindex committed suicide. Dio Cass. lxiii. 22 ff., Plut. *Galba*, 4 ff., etc.

442 ἔως μὲν οὖν ἐπεῖχεν ὁ χειμὼν τὰς ὑπηγμένας
διησφαλίζετο κώμας τε καὶ πολίχνας φρουραῖς,
δεκαδάρχας μὲν κώμαις ἐγκαθιστάς, ἑκατοντάρχας
δὲ πόλεσι· πολλὰ δὲ ἀνῴκιζε καὶ τῶν πεπορ-
443 θημένων. ὑπὸ δὲ τὴν ἀρχὴν τοῦ ἔαρος ἀναλαβὼν
τὸ πλέον τῆς δυνάμεως ἤγαγεν ἀπὸ τῆς Καισαρείας ἐπὶ Ἀντιπατρίδος, ἔνθα δυσὶν ἡμέραις
καταστησάμενος¹ τὴν πόλιν τῇ τρίτῃ προῄει
444 πορθῶν καὶ καίων τὰς πέριξ πάσας. καταστρεψάμενος δὲ τὰ περὶ τὴν Θαμνᾶ τοπαρχίαν² ἐπὶ
Λύδδων καὶ Ἰαμνείας ἐχώρει καὶ προκεχειρω-
μέναις³ ἑκατέραις ἐγκαταστήσας οἰκήτορας τῶν
προσκεχωρηκότων ἱκανοὺς εἰς Ἀμμαοῦντα ἀφ-
445 ικνεῖται. καταλαβόμενος δὲ τὰς ἐπὶ τὴν μητρόπολιν αὐτῶν εἰσβολὰς στρατόπεδόν τε τειχίζει
καὶ τὸ πέμπτον ἐν αὐτῇ τάγμα καταλιπὼν πρόεισι⁴
μετὰ τῆς ἄλλης δυνάμεως ἐπὶ τὴν Βεθλεπτηνφῶν
446 τοπαρχίαν. πυρὶ δὲ αὐτήν τε καὶ τὴν γειτνιῶσαν
ἀνελὼν καὶ τὰ πέριξ τῆς Ἰδουμαίας, φρούρια μὲν
447 τοῖς ἐπικαίροις τόποις ἐπετείχισε, καταλαβόμενος
δὲ δύο κώμας τὰς μεσαιτάτας τῆς Ἰδουμαίας,
Βήταβριν καὶ Καφάρτοβαν,⁵ κτείνει μὲν ὑπὲρ
448 μυρίους, αἰχμαλωτίζεται δὲ ὑπὲρ χιλίους, καὶ
τὸ λοιπὸν πλῆθος ἐξελάσας ἐγκαθίστησιν τῆς
οἰκείας δυνάμεως οὐκ ὀλίγην, οἳ κατατρέχοντες

---

¹ L Lat. (composita): ἐγκαταστησάμενος the rest.
² τὰς π. τ. Θ. τοπαρχίας L Lat.
³ προσκεχωρημέναις L Lat.   ⁴ L: πρόσεισι the rest.
⁵ ed. pr.: Καταφάρτοβαν most mss.

ᵃ Ras el-'Ain, in the S. of the plain of Sharon, N.E. of
Joppa.   ᵇ "toparchy."
ᶜ S.E. of Antipatris. Here he turns S.W. towards the
coast to Ludd and Yebnah.

winter lasted, he employed himself in securing with
garrisons the villages and smaller towns which had
been reduced, posting decurions in the villages and
centurions in the towns ; he also rebuilt many places
that had been devastated. Then, at the first approach of spring, he marched the main body of his
army from Caesarea to Antipatris.[a] After two days
spent in restoring order in that town, on the third he
advanced, laying waste and burning all the surrounding places. Having reduced the neighbourhood of
the province [b] of Thamna,[c] he moved to Lydda and
Jamnia ; both these districts being already subdued,[d]
he quartered upon them an adequate number of
residents from those who had surrendered, and
passed to Ammaus.[e] Having occupied the approaches to the capital of this province, he fortified
a camp and, leaving the fifth legion there, advanced
with the rest of his forces to the province of Beth-
leptenpha.[f] After devastating with fire this and
the neighbouring district and the outskirts of
Idumaea, he built fortresses in suitable situations ;
finally having taken two villages right in the heart
of Idumaea, Betabris [g] and Caphartoba,[g] he put
upwards of ten thousand of the inhabitants to death,
made prisoners of over a thousand, expelled the
remainder and stationed in the district a large
division of his own troops, who overran and devastated

*spring
A.D. 68.
He moves
southward
from
Caesarea,
subduing
Judaea*

*and
Idumaea.*

---

[d] § 130 (for Jamnia).

[e] The toparchy (iii. 55) which took its name from Ammaus
(or Emmaus), *Amwas*, N.W. of Jerusalem.

[f] The correct form is probably Bethleptepha (or Bethle-
tepha), Schürer, *G.J.V.* ii. 184 n. ; it is the modern *Beit
Nettif*, S.W. of Jerusalem, and gave its name to one of the
provinces of Judaea, *B.* iii. 54 n.

[g] Unidentified.

449 ἐπόρθουν ἅπασαν τὴν ὀρεινήν. αὐτὸς δὲ μετὰ τῆς
λοιπῆς δυνάμεως ὑπέστρεψεν εἰς Ἀμμαοῦν, ὅθεν
διὰ τῆς Σαμαρείτιδος καὶ παρὰ τὴν Νέαν πόλιν[1]
καλουμένην, Μαβαρθὰ δ' ὑπὸ τῶν ἐπιχωρίων,
καταβὰς εἰς Κορέαν δευτέρᾳ Δαισίου μηνὸς
450 στρατοπεδεύεται. τῇ δ' ἑξῆς εἰς Ἱεριχοῦντα
ἀφικνεῖται, καθ' ἣν αὐτῷ συμμίσγει Τραϊανὸς εἷς
τῶν ἡγεμόνων τὴν ἐκ τῆς Περαίας ἄγων δύναμιν,
ἤδη τῶν ὑπὲρ τὸν Ἰορδάνην κεχειρωμένων.

451 (2) Τὸ μὲν οὖν πολὺ πλῆθος ἐκ τῆς Ἱεριχοῦς
φθάσαν τὴν ἔφοδον αὐτῶν εἰς τὴν ἄντικρυς Ἱεροσολύμων ὀρεινὴν διαπεφεύγει, καταλειφθὲν δ' οὐκ
452 ὀλίγον διαφθείρεται. τὴν δὲ πόλιν ἔρημον κατ-
ειλήφεσαν, ἥτις ἵδρυται μὲν ἐν πεδίῳ, ψιλὸν δὲ
ὑπέρκειται αὐτῇ καὶ ἄκαρπον ὄρος μήκιστον·
453 κατὰ γὰρ τὸ βόρειον κλίμα μέχρι τῆς Σκυθο-
πολιτῶν γῆς ἐκτείνεται, κατὰ δὲ τὸ μεσημβρινὸν
μέχρι τῆς Σοδομιτῶν χώρας καὶ τῶν περάτων τῆς
Ἀσφαλτίτιδος. ἔστιν δὲ ἀνώμαλόν τε πᾶν καὶ
454 ἀοίκητον διὰ τὴν ἀγονίαν. ἀντίκειται δὲ τούτῳ
τὸ περὶ[2] τὸν Ἰορδάνην ὄρος ἀρχόμενον ἀπὸ

---

[1] L: Νεάπολιν the rest.
[2] ὑπὲρ Destinon with Heg. (supra).

---

[a] Flavia Neapolis, mod. Nablus, the new town founded by
Vespasian c. A.D. 72 on the site of the older Mabartha
(Mamortha according to Pliny, H.N. v. 13. 69) in the immediate vicinity of Shechem. The most probable meaning
of Mabartha is " pass " or " passage " (ma 'abartā), the
name, like that of Shechem (" shoulder "), being taken from
the watershed on which both places stood, forming an easy

the whole of the hill country. He then returned
with the rest of his forces to Ammaus, and thence by
way of Samaria, passing Neapolis [a] or, as the natives
call it, Mabartha, he descended to Corea,[b] where he
encamped on the second of the month Daesius. On the following day he reached Jericho, where he was joined by Trajan,[c] one of his generals, with the force which he had led from Peraea, all the country beyond Jordan being now subjugated.

c. 20 June
A.D. 68.
Vespasian at
Jericho.

(2) The mass of the population, anticipating their arrival, had fled from Jericho [d] to the hill country over against Jerusalem, but a considerable number remained behind and were put to death ; the city itself the Romans found deserted. Jericho lies in a plain, but above it hangs a bare and barren mountain range of immense length, extending northwards as far as the territory of Scythopolis [e] and southwards to the region of Sodom and the extremities of the Lake Asphaltitis ; this hill district is all rugged and owing to its sterility uninhabited. Opposite to it and flanking the Jordan lies a second range,

Description
of neigh-
bourhood
of Jericho

pass between the Mediterranean and Jordan basins. Schürer, *G.J.V.* i. 650, *Encycl. Bibl.*, and Hastings, *D.B.*

[b] From the pass of Shechem a Roman road followed the course of a tributary of the Jordan in a S.E. direction down to Corea or Coreae, *Tell el-Mazar*, on the N. frontier of Judaea, *B.* i. 134, *A.* xiv. 49.

[c] Commander of the 10th legion and father of the future emperor of that name, *B.* iii. 289 ff.

[d] Apparently the larger area of the toparchy (*B.* iii. 55) is meant, as opposed to "the city itself" mentioned below.

[e] Bethshan, *Beisan*, the one city of Decapolis which lay W. of the Jordan. The name Scythopolis may owe its origin to the great Scythian invasion of Palestine in the 7th cent. B.C., mentioned by Herodotus i. 105 ; Syncellus (quoted by Schürer) writes Σκύθαι τὴν Παλαιστίνην κατέδραμον καὶ τὴν Βασὰν κατέσχον τὴν ἐξ αὐτῶν κληθεῖσαν Σκυθόπολιν.

'Ιουλιάδος καὶ τῶν βορείων κλιμάτων, παρατεῖνον
δὲ εἰς μεσημβρίαν ἕως Σομόρων, ἥπερ ὁρίζει τὴν
Πέτραν τῆς 'Αραβίας. ἐν τούτῳ δ' ἐστὶ καὶ τὸ
Σιδηροῦν καλούμενον ὄρος μηκυνόμενον μέχρι τῆς
455 Μωαβίτιδος. ἡ μέση δὲ τῶν δύο ὀρέων χώρα τὸ
μέγα πεδίον καλεῖται, ἀπὸ κώμης Γινναβρὶν[1]
456 διῆκον μέχρι τῆς 'Ασφαλτίτιδος.[2] ἔστι δ' αὐτοῦ
μῆκος μὲν σταδίων χιλίων διακοσίων,[3] εὖρος δ'
εἴκοσι καὶ ἑκατόν, καὶ μέσον ὑπὸ τοῦ 'Ιορδάνου
τέμνεται, λίμνας τε ἔχει τήν τε 'Ασφαλτῖτιν καὶ
τὴν Τιβεριέων φύσιν ἐναντίας· ἡ μὲν γὰρ ἁλ-
μυρώδης καὶ ἄγονος, ἡ Τιβεριέων δὲ γλυκεῖα καὶ
457 γόνιμος. ἐκπυροῦται δὲ ὥρᾳ θέρους τὸ πεδίον
καὶ δι' ὑπερβολὴν αὐχμοῦ περιέχει νοσώδη τὸν
458 ἀέρα· πᾶν γὰρ ἄνυδρον πλὴν τοῦ 'Ιορδάνου, παρὸ
καὶ τοὺς μὲν ἐπὶ ταῖς ὄχθαις φοινικῶνας εὐθαλε-
στέρους καὶ πολυφορωτέρους εἶναι συμβέβηκεν,
ἧττον δὲ τοὺς πόρρω κεχωρισμένους.

459 (3) Παρὰ μέντοι τὴν 'Ιεριχοῦν ἐστι πηγὴ δαψιλής
τε καὶ πρὸς ἀρδείας λιπαρωτάτη, παρὰ τὴν
παλαιὰν ἀναβλύζουσα πόλιν, ἣν 'Ιησοῦς ὁ Ναυῆ

---

[1] Δενναβρὶ L; cf. iii. 447 Σενναβρίς, whence Σενναβρῖ Niese
(ed. min.) here.
[2] P: +χώρας A: +λίμνης the rest.
[3] χιλ. διακοσ.] τριάκοντα καὶ διακοσίων L Lat. Heg., through
misreading of ᾽AC′ as ΛC′.

---

[a] Bethsaida Julias, et-Tell, at the head of the sea of
Galilee, founded by Philip the Tetrarch, B. ii. 168.
[b] Literally " and the northern regions," perhaps=" or
regions farther north."
[c] Perhaps Khirbat al Samra shown in map (facing p. 1)
in Kennedy's Petra (1925).

which, beginning at Julias *a* in the north,*b* stretches parallel to the former chain southwards as far as Somora,*c* which borders on Petra in Arabia ; this range includes also the so-called Iron mountain *d* stretching into Moab. The region enclosed between these two mountain ranges is called the Great Plain.*e* This extends from the village of Ginnabris *f* to the Lake Asphaltitis, and is twelve hundred furlongs in length, and a hundred and twenty in breadth ; *g* it is intersected by the Jordan and contains two lakes, Asphaltitis and that of Tiberias, contrary in their nature, the former being salt and barren, the latter sweet and prolific. In summer the plain is burnt up, and the excessive drought renders the surrounding atmosphere pestilential ; for it is wholly without water, apart from the Jordan, which, moreover, explains why the palm-groves on the banks of that river are more luxuriant and productive than those further off.

(3) Hard by Jericho, however, is a copious spring *h* of excellent value for irrigation ; it gushes up near the old town, which was the first in the land of the

and of the Great Plain (Jordan valley).

Elisha's spring near Jericho.

---

d Unidentified ; " stretching " (μηκυνόμενον) probably means running out laterally from W. to E. (as in *B*. iii. 40).

e The *Ghôr* (=" Rift ") or Jordan valley. " The Great Plain " (similarly used in *A*. iv. 100) elsewhere is the name for the plain of Esdraelon.

f Called Sennabris (iii. 447), between Tiberias and Tarichaeae.

g *i.e.* (the " stade " being *c.* 606 feet) about 137 miles by 13. The actual length of the Jordan valley from the Sea of Galilee to the Dead Sea is 65 miles ; the breadth varies from 3 to 14 miles (G. A. Smith, *Hist. Geography of Holy Land*, 482). Josephus apparently includes the two lakes ; this would increase the length to *c.* 124 miles.

h Commonly identified with the Sultan's Spring, 1½ miles N. of the road from Jerusalem.

παῖς στρατηγὸς Ἑβραίων πρώτην εἷλε γῆς
460 Χαναναίων δορίκτητον. ταύτην τὴν πηγὴν λόγος
ἔχει κατ' ἀρχὰς οὐ μόνον γῆς καὶ δένδρων καρποὺς
ἀπαμβλύνειν, ἀλλὰ καὶ γυναικῶν γονάς, καθόλου
τε πᾶσιν εἶναι νοσώδη τε καὶ φθαρτικήν, ἐξ-
ημερωθῆναι δὲ καὶ γενέσθαι τοὐναντίον ὑγιεινο-
τάτην τε καὶ γονιμωτάτην ὑπὸ Ἐλισσαίου τινὸς[1]
προφήτου· γνώριμος δ' ἦν οὗτος Ἠλίᾳ καὶ
461 διάδοχος· ὃς ἐπιξενωθεὶς τοῖς κατὰ τὴν Ἱεριχοῦν,
περισσὸν δή τι φιλοφρονησαμένων αὐτὸν τῶν
ἀνθρώπων, αὐτούς τε ἀμείβεται καὶ τὴν χώραν
462 αἰωνίῳ χάριτι. προελθὼν γὰρ ἐπὶ τὴν πηγὴν
καὶ καταβαλὼν εἰς τὸ ῥεῦμα πλῆρες ἁλῶν ἀγγεῖον
κεραμοῦν,[2] ἔπειτα εἰς οὐρανὸν δεξιὰν ἀνατείνας
δικαίαν κἀπὶ γῆς[3] σπονδὰς μειλικτηρίους χεόμενος,
τὴν μὲν ᾐτεῖτο μαλάξαι τὸ ῥεῦμα καὶ γλυκυτέρας
463 φλέβας ἀνοῖξαι, τὸν δ' ἐγκεράσασθαι τῷ ῥεύματι
γονιμωτέρους ἀέρας δοῦναί τε ἅμα καὶ καρπῶν
εὐθηνίαν τοῖς ἐπιχωρίοις καὶ τέκνων διαδοχήν, μηδ'
ἐπιλιπεῖν αὐτοῖς τὸ τούτων γεννητικὸν ὕδωρ,
464 ἕως μενοῦσι δίκαιοι. ταύταις ταῖς εὐχαῖς πολλὰ
προσχειρουργήσας[4] ἐξ ἐπιστήμης ἔτρεψε τὴν
πηγήν, καὶ τὸ πρὶν ὀρφανίας αὐτοῖς καὶ λιμοῦ
παραίτιον ὕδωρ ἔκτοτε εὐτεκνίας καὶ κόρου
465 χορηγὸν κατέστη. τοσαύτην γοῦν ἐν ταῖς ἀρδείαις
ἔχει δύναμιν ὥς, εἰ καὶ μόνον ἐφάψαιτο τῆς
χώρας, νοστιμώτερον εἶναι τῶν μέχρι κόρου
466 χρονιζόντων. παρὸ καὶ τῶν μέν, δαψιλεστέρως
χρωμένων, ἡ ὄνησίς ἐστιν ὀλίγη, τούτου δὲ τοῦ

---

[1] L Lat.: τοῦ the rest.   [2] Naber: κεράμου MSS.
[3] καὶ ἐπὶ γῆς A[2]: καὶ πηγῆς or καὶ (τῇ) πηγῇ the rest.
[4] Destinon with Lat.: προ(περι- R)χειρουργήσας MSS.

Canaanites to fall before the arms of Jesus the son
of Naue,[a] general of the Hebrews. Tradition avers
that this spring originally not only blighted the fruits
of the earth and of trees but also caused women to
miscarry, and that to everything alike it brought
disease and destruction, until it was reclaimed and
converted into a most salubrious and fertilizing source
by a certain prophet Elisha, the disciple and successor
of Elijah.[b] Having been the guest of the people of
Jericho and been treated by them with extreme
hospitality, he requited their kindness by conferring
a boon for all time upon them and their country.
For he went out to this spring and cast into the
stream an earthenware vessel full of salt, and then
raising his righteous right hand to heaven and
pouring propitiatory libations upon the ground, he
besought the earth to mollify the stream and to
open sweeter channels, and heaven to temper its
waters with more genial airs and to grant to the
inhabitants alike an abundance of fruits, a succession
of children, and an unfailing supply of water con-
ducive to their production, so long as they remained
a righteous people. By these prayers, supplemented
by various ritual ceremonies,[c] he changed the nature
of the spring, and the water which had before
been to them a cause of childlessness and famine
thenceforth became a source of fecundity and plenty.
Such, in fact, are its powers of irrigation, that if it
but skim the soil, it is more salubrious than waters
which stand and saturate it. Hence, too, while the
benefit derived from other streams is slight, though

[a] The Septuagint name for Joshua, son of Nun.
[b] *Cf.* 2 Kings. ii. 19-22.
[c] Literally "working many things besides with his hands
from (professional) skill."

467 ὀλίγου [χορηγία]¹ δαψιλής. ἄρδει γοῦν πλέονα
τῶν ἄλλων ἁπάντων, καὶ πεδίον μὲν ἔπεισιν
ἑβδομήκοντα σταδίων μῆκος εὖρος δ᾽ εἴκοσιν,
ἐκτρέφει δ᾽ ἐν αὐτῷ παραδείσους καλλίστους τε
468 καὶ πυκνοτάτους. τῶν δὲ φοινίκων ἐπαρδομένων
γένη πολλὰ ταῖς γεύσεσι καὶ ταῖς παρηγορίαις²
διάφορα· τούτων οἱ πιότεροι πατούμενοι καὶ μέλι
469 δαψιλὲς ἀνιᾶσιν οὐ πολλῷ τοῦ λοιποῦ χεῖρον. καὶ
μελιττοτρόφος δ᾽ ἡ χώρα· φέρει δὲ καὶ ὀπο-
βάλσαμον, ὃ δὴ τιμιώτατον τῶν τῇδε καρπῶν,
κύπρον τε καὶ μυροβάλανον, ὡς οὐκ ἂν ἁμαρτεῖν
τινα εἰπόντα θεῖον εἶναι τὸ χωρίον, ἐν ᾧ δαψιλῆ τὰ
470 σπανιώτατα καὶ κάλλιστα γεννᾶται. τῶν μὲν
γὰρ ἄλλων αὐτῷ καρπῶν ἕνεκεν οὐκ ἂν ῥᾳδίως τι
παραβληθείη κλίμα τῆς οἰκουμένης· οὕτως τὸ
471 καταβληθὲν πολύχουν ἀναδίδωσιν. αἴτιόν μοι
δοκεῖ τὸ θερμὸν τῶν ἀέρων καὶ τὸ τῶν ὑδάτων
εὔτονον,³ τῶν μὲν προκαλουμένων⁴ τὰ φυόμενα
καὶ διαχεόντων, τῆς δ᾽ ἰκμάδος ῥιζούσης ἕκαστον
ἰσχυρῶς καὶ χορηγούσης τὴν ἐν θέρει δύναμιν·
περικαὲς δέ ἐστιν οὕτως τὸ χωρίον, ὡς μηδένα
472 ῥᾳδίως προϊέναι. τὸ δὲ ὕδωρ πρὸ ἀνατολῆς

¹ PMA²: ἡ χορηγία L: om. the rest.
² προσηγορίαις Niese with Lat. nominibus.
³ Margin of PAM: εὔγονον the rest.
⁴ ed. pr. with Lat.: προσκαλουμένων mss.

^a The article τῶν (sc. ἄλλων ὑδάτων) must be dissociated from the following genitive absolute δαψιλεστέρως χρωμένων (cf. A. vii. 159).
^b Jericho was " the city of palm-trees," Deut. xxxiv. 3, Judges i. 16.
^c Legend said that the first roots of the balsam were imported into Palestine from Arabia by the Queen of Sheba, A. viii. 174; the method of collecting the juice is described

they use them more lavishly,[a] this little rill yields an ample return. Indeed, this spring irrigates a larger tract than all others, permeating a plain seventy furlongs in length and twenty in breadth, and fostering within that area the most charming and luxuriant parks. Of the date-palms[b] watered by it there are numerous varieties differing in flavour and in medicinal properties; the richer species of this fruit when pressed under foot emit copious honey, not much inferior to that of bees, which are also abundant in this region. Here, too, grow the juicy balsam,[c] the most precious of all the local products, the cypress and the myrobalanus[d]; so that it would be no misnomer to describe as "divine" this spot in which the rarest and choicest plants are produced in abundance.[e] For, with regard to its other fruits, it would be difficult to find another region in the habitable world comparable to this; so manifold are the returns from whatever is sown. I attribute these results to the warmth of the air and the bracing[f] effects of the water, the one calling forth and diffusing the young plants, while the moisture enables them all to take firm root and supplies them with vitality in summer, when the surrounding region is so parched up, that one can scarcely venture out of doors. The water if drawn

The rich products of the region watered by it.

in *B.* i. 138, *A.* xiv. 54; Cleopatra appropriated from Herod's realm "the palm grove of Jericho where the balsam grows," *B.* i. 361, *A.* xv. 96; in the last passage Josephus speaks of the balsam as peculiar to Jericho, but in *A.* ix. 7 he mentions another habitat, Engedi on the Dead Sea. Strabo (xvi. 763) and other writers mention the balsam of Jericho.

[d] "Perhaps the ben-nut" (Liddell and Scott).

[e] *Cf.* the description of the fertile plain of Gennesareth, iii. 516 ff.

[f] Or, with the reading εὔγονον, "fertilizing."

ἀντλούμενον. ἔπειτα ἐξαιθριασθὲν γίνεται ψυχρό-
τατον καὶ τὴν ἐναντίαν πρὸς τὸ περιέχον φύσιν
λαμβάνει, χειμῶνος δὲ ἀνάπαλιν χλιαίνεται καὶ
473 τοῖς ἐμβαίνουσι γίνεται προσηνέστατον. ἔστι δὲ
καὶ τὸ περιέχον οὕτως εὔκρατον, ὡς λινοῦν
ἀμφιέννυσθαι τοὺς ἐπιχωρίους νιφομένης τῆς
474 ἄλλης Ἰουδαίας. ἀπέχει δ᾽ ἀπὸ Ἱεροσολύμων
μὲν σταδίους ἑκατὸν πεντήκοντα, τοῦ δὲ Ἰορδάνου
ἑξήκοντα, καὶ τὸ μὲν μέχρι Ἱεροσολύμων αὐτῆς
ἔρημον καὶ πετρῶδες, τὸ δὲ μέχρι τοῦ Ἰορδάνου
καὶ τῆς Ἀσφαλτίτιδος χθαμαλώτερον μέν, ἔρημον
475 δὲ ὁμοίως καὶ ἄκαρπον. ἀλλὰ γὰρ τὰ μὲν περὶ
Ἱεριχοῦν εὐδαιμονεστάτην οὖσαν ἀποχρώντως
δεδήλωται.

476   (4) Ἄξιον δ᾽ ἀφηγήσασθαι καὶ τὴν φύσιν τῆς
Ἀσφαλτίτιδος λίμνης, ἥτις ἐστὶ μέν, ὡς ἔφην,
πικρὰ καὶ ἄγονος, ὑπὸ δὲ κουφότητος καὶ τὰ
βαρύτατα τῶν εἰς αὐτὴν ῥιφέντων ἀναφέρει, κατα-
δῦναι δ᾽ εἰς τὸν βυθὸν οὐδὲ ἐπιτηδεύσαντα ῥάδιον.
477 ἀφικόμενος γοῦν καθ᾽ ἱστορίαν ἐπ᾽ αὐτὴν Οὐεσπασιανὸς ἐκέλευσέ τινας τῶν νεῖν οὐκ ἐπιστα-
μένων, δεθέντας ὀπίσω τὰς χεῖρας, ῥιφῆναι κατὰ
τοῦ βυθοῦ, καὶ συνέβη πάντας ἐπινήξασθαι
478 καθάπερ ὑπὸ πνεύματος ἄνω βιαζομένους. ἔστι
δ᾽ ἐπὶ τούτῳ καὶ ἡ τῆς χρόας μεταβολὴ θαυμάσιος·
τρὶς γὰρ ἑκάστης ἡμέρας τὴν ἐπιφάνειαν ἀλλάσ-
σεται καὶ πρὸς τὰς ἡλιακὰς ἀκτῖνας ἀνταυγεῖ ποι-
479 κίλως. τῆς μέντοι ἀσφάλτου κατὰ πολλὰ μέρη

before sunrise and then exposed to the air becomes intensely cold,[a] assuming a character the reverse of the surrounding atmosphere ; in winter, on the contrary, it is warm and quite pleasant to bathe in. Moreover, the climate is so mild that the inhabitants wear linen when snow is falling throughout the rest of Judaea. The distance from Jerusalem is a hundred and fifty furlongs and from the Jordan sixty.[b] The country from Jericho to Jerusalem is desert and rocky ; to the Jordan and the Lake Asphaltitis the ground is lower, though equally wild and barren. But of Jericho, that most favoured spot, enough has been said.

(4) The natural properties of the Lake Asphaltitis also merit remark. Its waters are, as I said,[c] bitter and unproductive, but owing to their buoyancy send up to the surface the very heaviest of objects cast into them, and it is difficult, even of set purpose, to sink to the bottom.[d] Thus, when Vespasian came to explore the lake, he ordered certain persons who were unable to swim to be flung into the deep water with their hands tied behind them ; with the result that all rose to the surface and floated, as if impelled upward by a current of air. Another remarkable feature is its change of colour : three times a day it alters its appearance and throws off a different reflection of the solar rays. Again, in many parts it

Description of the Lake Asphaltitis (Dead Sea).

Vespasian visits it.

---

[a] Cf. a similar statement on the water of the Sea of Galilee, iii. 508.

[b] i.e. 11½ and nearly 7 miles respectively. The actual distances appear to be about 16 and 5 miles.

[c] § 456.

[d] Cf. with this description Tac. Hist. v. 6 and Strabo, 763 f. (who confuses it with the Lake Sirbonis in Egypt; context and details show that he refers to the Dead Sea).

βώλους μελαίνας ἀναδίδωσιν· αἱ δ' ἐπινήχονται
τό τε σχῆμα καὶ τὸ μέγεθος ταύροις ἀκεφάλοις
480 παραπλήσιαι. προσελαύνοντες δὲ οἱ τῆς λίμνης
ἐργάται καὶ δρασσόμενοι τοῦ συνεστῶτος ἕλκουσιν
εἰς τὰ σκάφη, πληρώσασι δὲ ἀποκόπτειν οὐ
ῥᾴδιον, ἀλλὰ δι' εὐτονίαν προσήρτηται τῷ μηρύ-
ματι τὸ σκάφος, ἕως ἂν ἐμμηνίῳ γυναικῶν αἵματι
καὶ οὔρῳ διαλύσωσιν αὐτήν, οἷς μόνοις εἴκει.
481 καὶ χρήσιμος δὲ οὐ μόνον εἰς ἁρμονίας νεῶν ἀλλὰ
καὶ πρὸς· ἄκεσιν σωμάτων· εἰς πολλὰ γοῦν τῶν
482 φαρμάκων παραμίσγεται. ταύτης τῆς λίμνης μῆκος μὲν ὀγδοήκοντα καὶ πεντακόσιοι στάδιοι,
καθὸ δὴ μέχρι Ζοάρων τῆς Ἀραβίας ἐκτείνεται,
483 εὖρος δὲ πεντήκοντα καὶ ἑκατόν. γειτνιᾷ δ' ἡ
Σοδομῖτις αὐτῇ, πάλαι μὲν εὐδαίμων γῆ καρπῶν
τε ἕνεκεν καὶ τῆς κατὰ πόλιν περιουσίας, νῦν δὲ
484 κεκαυμένη πᾶσα. φασὶ δ' ὡς δι' ἀσέβειαν οἰκητόρων κεραυνοῖς καταφλεγῆναι[1]· ἔστι γοῦν ἔτι
λείψανα τοῦ θείου πυρός, καὶ πέντε μὲν πόλεων
ἰδεῖν σκιάς, ἔτι δὲ κἂν τοῖς καρποῖς σποδιὰν
ἀναγεννωμένην, οἳ χροιὰν μὲν ἔχουσι τῶν ἐδωδί-
μων ὁμοίαν, δρεψαμένων δὲ χερσὶν εἰς καπνὸν

----

[1] κατεφλέγη L.

----

[a] So Tac. *loc. cit.* " fugit cruorem vestemque infectam
sanguine, quo feminae per menses exsolvuntur. Sic veteres
auctores." From Strabo 764 we learn that one of these
" ancient authors " was Poseidonius (2nd-1st cent. B.C.). *Cf.*

casts up black masses of bitumen, which float on the Its bitumen. surface, in their shape and size resembling decapitated bulls. The labourers on the lake row up to these and catching hold of the lumps haul them into their boats ; but when they have filled them it is no easy task to detach their cargo, which owing to its tenacious and glutinous character clings to the boat until it is loosened by the monthly secretions of women,[a] to which alone it yields. It is useful not only for caulking ships, but also for the healing of the body, forming an ingredient in many medicines. The length of this lake is five hundred and eighty furlongs,[b] measured in a line reaching to Zoara[c] in Arabia, and its breadth one hundred and fifty.[d] Adjacent to it is the land of Sodom,[e] in days of old The blasted land of Sodom. a country blest in its produce and in the wealth of its various cities, but now all burnt up. It is said that, owing to the impiety of its inhabitants, it was consumed by thunderbolts ; and in fact vestiges of the divine fire and faint traces of five cities are still visible. Still, too, may one see ashes reproduced in the fruits, which from their outward appearance would be thought edible, but on being plucked with

also *B.* vii. 181, where the same secretions are named as aids to the extraction of a certain root with medicinal properties.

[b] This figure (=about 66½ miles) is greatly exaggerated ; the actual length is about 47 miles.

[c] The Biblical Zoar, familiar as Lot's city of refuge, Gen. xix. 22 ; perhaps (Smith and Bartholomew, *Atlas*) *el-Ḳeryeh*, a few miles S. of the Lake.

[d] *i.e.* about 11½ miles ; the actual breadth at the broadest part is about 10 miles.

[e] Perhaps the modern *Jebel Usdum* at the S.W. corner of the lake. Many older authorities located the cities of the plain to the *north* of the Dead Sea.

485 διαλύονται¹ καὶ τέφραν. τὰ μὲν δὴ περὶ τὴν Σοδομῖτιν μυθευόμενα τοιαύτην ἔχει πίστιν ἀπὸ τῆς ὄψεως.

486 (ix. 1) Ὁ δὲ Οὐεσπασιανὸς πανταχόσε² περιτειχίζων³ τοὺς ἐν τοῖς Ἱεροσολύμοις ἔν τε τῇ Ἱεριχοῖ καὶ ἐν Ἀδίδοις ἐγείρει στρατόπεδα καὶ φρουροὺς ἀμφοτέραις ἐγκαθίστησιν ἔκ τε τοῦ

487 Ῥωμαϊκοῦ καὶ συμμαχικοῦ τάγματος.⁴ πέμπει δὲ καὶ εἰς Γέρασα Λούκιον Ἄννιον παραδοὺς

488 μοῖραν ἱππέων καὶ συχνοὺς πεζούς. ὁ μὲν οὖν ἐξ ἐφόδου τὴν πόλιν ἑλὼν ἀποκτείνει μὲν χιλίους τῶν νέων, ὅσοι μὴ διαφυγεῖν ἔφθασαν, γενεὰς δὲ ἠχμαλωτίσατο καὶ τὰς κτήσεις διαρπάσαι τοῖς στρατιώταις ἐπέτρεψεν· ἔπειτα τὰς οἰκίας ἐμ-

489 πρήσας ἐπὶ τὰς πέριξ κώμας ἐχώρει. φυγαὶ δ' ἦσαν τῶν δυνατῶν καὶ φθοραὶ τῶν ἀσθενεστέρων,

490 τὸ καταλειφθὲν δὲ πᾶν ἐνεπίμπρατο. καὶ διειληφότος τοῦ πολέμου τήν τε ὀρεινὴν ὅλην καὶ τὴν πεδιάδα πάσας⁵ οἱ ἐν τοῖς Ἱεροσολύμοις τὰς ἐξόδους ἀφήρηντο· τοὺς μὲν γὰρ⁶ αὐτομολεῖν προαιρουμένους οἱ ζηλωταὶ παρεφυλάσσοντο, τοὺς δὲ οὔπω τὰ Ῥωμαίων φρονοῦντας εἶργεν ἡ στρατιὰ πανταχόθεν τὴν πόλιν περιέχουσα.

---

¹ ἀναλύονται L. ² πανταχόθεν LC.
³ ἐπιτειχίζων L. ⁴ συντάγματος A.
⁵ Destinon : πᾶσαν MSS.
⁶ μέντοι γε PA : μέν γε Destinon.

ᵃ Cf. Tac. Hist. v. 7 " et manere vestigia, terramque ipsam, specie torridam, vim frugiferam perdidisse. Nam cuncta . . . atra et inania velut in cinerem vanescunt " ; and from a writer of a thousand years later, Fulcher of Chartres, historian of the first crusade, Hist. Hierosol. ii. 4 (Migne) " illic inter arbores caeteras vidi quasdam poma ferentes, de quibus the hand dissolve into smoke and ashes.[a] So far are the legends about the land of Sodom borne out by ocular evidence.

(ix. 1) Vespasian, with a view to investing Jerusalem on all sides, now established camps at Jericho and at Adida,[b] placing in each a garrison composed jointly of Romans and auxiliaries. He also sent Lucius Annius to Gerasa[c] with a squadron of cavalry and a considerable body of infantry. Annius, having carried the city by assault, put to the sword a thousand of the youth who had not already escaped, made prisoners of women and children, gave his soldiers licence to plunder the property, and then set fire to the houses and advanced against the surrounding villages. The able-bodied fled, the feeble perished, and everything left was consigned to the flames. The war having now embraced the whole region, both hill and plain, all egress from Jerusalem was cut off; for those who desired to desert were closely watched by the Zealots, while those who were not yet pro-Romans were confined by the army which hemmed in the city on every side.

Vespasian establishes camps at Jericho and Adida.

L. Annius takes Gerasa.

Jerusalem isolated.

cum collegissem, scire volens cujus naturae essent, inveni rupto cortice interius quasi pulverem atrum, et inde inanem prodire fumum." Dr. C. Geikie, *The Holy Land and the Bible*, ii. 117, writes that "the 'osher' of the Arab is the true apple of Sodom. . . . Its fruit is like a large smooth apple or orange. . . . When ripe it is yellow and looks fair and attractive, and is soft to the touch, but if pressed, it bursts with a crack, and only the broken shell and a row of small seeds in a half-open pod, with a few dry filaments, remain in the hand."

[b] *Haditheh*, 3 miles E. of Lydda, and some 20 miles N.W. of Jerusalem.

[c] *Jerash*, in Gilead, on the N.E. frontier of Peraea, *B.* iii. 47.

491 (2) Οὐεσπασιανῷ δ' εἰς Καισάρειαν ἐπιστρέ-
ψαντι καὶ παρασκευαζομένῳ μετὰ πάσης τῆς
δυνάμεως ἐπ' αὐτῶν τῶν Ἱεροσολύμων ἐξ-
ελαύνειν ἀγγέλλεται Νέρων ἀνῃρημένος, τρία καὶ
δέκα βασιλεύσας ἔτη ⟨καὶ μῆνας ὀκτὼ⟩[1] καὶ
492 ἡμέρας ὀκτώ. περὶ οὗ λέγειν, ὃν τρόπον εἰς τὴν
ἀρχὴν ἐξύβρισεν πιστεύσας τὰ πράγματα τοῖς
493 πονηροτάτοις, Νυμφιδίῳ καὶ Τιγελλίνῳ, τοῖς γε[2]
ἀναξίοις τῶν ἐξελευθέρων, καὶ ὡς ὑπὸ τούτων
ἐπιβουλευθεὶς κατελείφθη μὲν ὑπὸ τῶν φυλάκων
ἁπάντων, διαδρὰς δὲ σὺν τέτρασι τῶν πιστῶν
ἀπελευθέρων ἐν τοῖς προαστείοις ἑαυτὸν ἀνεῖλεν,
καὶ ὡς οἱ καταλύσαντες αὐτὸν μετ' οὐ[3] πολὺν
494 χρόνον δίκας ἔδοσαν· τόν τε κατὰ τὴν Γαλατίαν
πόλεμον ὡς ἐτελεύτησε, καὶ πῶς Γάλβας ἀπο-
δειχθεὶς αὐτοκράτωρ εἰς Ῥώμην ἐπανῆλθεν ἐκ
τῆς Ἱσπανίας, καὶ ὡς ὑπὸ τῶν στρατιωτῶν
αἰτιαθεὶς ἐπὶ ταπεινοφροσύνῃ κατὰ μέσην ἐδολο-
φονήθη[4] τὴν Ῥωμαίων ἀγοράν, ἀπεδείχθη τε
495 αὐτοκράτωρ Ὄθων· τήν τε τούτου στρατείαν[5]

---

[1] ins. Niese.　　　[2] MRC: τε PAL: om. V.
[3] μετ' οὐ Cardwell: μετὰ MSS.
[4] κατὰ μέσ. ἐδ. Niese (avoiding hiatus): ἐδ. κατὰ μέσην MSS.
[5] Dindorf: στρατιὰν MSS.

---

[a] The actual length of his reign was 13 years 7 months 28
days (from 13th October 54 to 9th June 68). Dio Cassius
(lxiii. 29) reckons this in round numbers as 13 years 8 months.
With this figure the statement in Josephus may be brought
into conformity by altering ἡμέρας to μῆνας; more probably,
as suggested by Niese, καὶ μῆνας ὀκτὼ has dropped out
through homoioteleuton. With the insertion of those words,
Josephus makes the reign ten days too long; cf. similar
slight discrepancies in B. ii. 168, 180, 204.
[b] Nymphidius Sabinus, son of a freedwoman, was, along

302

(2) Vespasian had returned to Caesarea and was preparing to march in full strength upon Jerusalem itself, when the news reached him that Nero was slain, after a reign of thirteen years (eight months) and eight days.[a] To tell how that emperor wantonly abused his authority by entrusting the administration to the vilest wretches, Nymphidius[b] and Tigellinus,[c] the most worthless of freedmen[d]; how, when they conspired against him, he was abandoned by all his guards, and, escaping with four faithful freedmen,[e] put an end to himself[f] in the suburbs; and how punishment ere long overtook those who had caused his overthrow—falls outside my purpose. Nor do I propose to tell of the war in Gaul and its issue, of Galba's call to the imperial dignity and his return to Rome from Spain, of the charge of meanness[g] brought against him by the soldiers and how he was treacherously slain in the midst of the Roman forum[h] and Otho was made emperor; of Otho's

with Tigellinus, prefect of the praetorian guards towards the end of Nero's reign. On Nero's death he attempted to seize the empire for himself, but was slain by the friends of Galba.

[c] Sophonius Tigellinus. a man of obscure birth, appointed praetorian prefect A.D. 63, was the main instrument of the tyranny and profligacy which marked the end of Nero's reign; he committed suicide on the accession of Otho. Juv. *Sat.* i. 155 "pone Tigellinum" etc., "dare to portray T. and you will be burnt alive."

[d] Or, perhaps, "and to worthless freedmen."

[e] Phaon, who offered him refuge at his villa 4 miles out of Rome, Epaphroditus, Sporus, and another. The dramatic story is told by Suetonius, *Nero* 47 f. and Dio Cass. lxiii. 27.

[f] Epaphroditus assisting.

[g] He alienated the praetorians by refusing the donative which Nymphidius had promised in his name.

[h] Near the pool of Curtius.

JOSEPHUS

ἐπὶ τοὺς Οὐιτελλίου στρατηγοὺς καὶ κατάλυσιν,
ἔπειτα τοὺς κατὰ Οὐιτέλλιον ταράχους καὶ τὴν
περὶ τὸ Καπετώλιον συμβολήν, ὅπως τε Ἀντώνιος
Πρῖμος καὶ Μουκιανός, διαφθείραντες Οὐιτέλλιον
καὶ τὰ Γερμανικὰ τάγματα, κατέστειλαν τὸν ἐμ-
496 φύλιον πόλεμον· πάντα ταῦτα διεξιέναι μὲν ἐπ᾽
ἀκριβὲς παρῃτησάμην, ἐπειδὴ δι᾽ ὄχλου πᾶσίν
ἐστιν καὶ πολλοῖς Ἑλλήνων τε καὶ Ῥωμαίων
ἀναγέγραπται, συναφείας δὲ ἕνεκεν τῶν πραγμάτων καὶ τοῦ μὴ διηρτῆσθαι τὴν ἱστορίαν
κεφαλαιωδῶς ἕκαστον ἐπισημαίνομαι.
497   Οὐεσπασιανὸς τοίνυν τὸ μὲν πρῶτον ἀνεβάλλετο
τὴν τῶν Ἱεροσολύμων στρατείαν, καραδοκῶν
498 πρὸς τίνα ῥέψει τὸ κρατεῖν μετὰ Νέρωνα· αὖθις
δὲ Γάλβαν ἀκούσας αὐτοκράτορα, πρὶν ἐπιστεῖλαί
τι περὶ τοῦ πολέμου κἀκεῖνον, οὐκ ἐπεχείρει,
πέμπει δὲ πρὸς αὐτὸν [καὶ]¹ τὸν υἱὸν Τίτον
ἀσπασόμενόν τε καὶ ληψόμενον τὰς περὶ Ἰουδαίων
ἐντολάς. διὰ δὲ τὰς αὐτὰς αἰτίας ἅμα Τίτῳ καὶ
499 Ἀγρίππας ὁ βασιλεὺς πρὸς Γάλβαν ἔπλει. καὶ
διὰ τῆς Ἀχαΐας,² χειμῶνος γὰρ ἦν ὥρα, μακραῖς
ναυσὶ περιπλεόντων³ φθάνει Γάλβας ἀναιρεθεὶς
μετὰ μῆνας ἑπτὰ καὶ ἴσας ἡμέρας· ἐξ οὗ καὶ τὴν
ἡγεμονίαν παρέλαβεν Ὄθων ἀντιποιούμενος τῶν
500 πραγμάτων. ὁ μὲν οὖν Ἀγρίππας εἰς τὴν Ῥώμην

¹ om. Havercamp with one ms.   ² + αὐτῶν L.
³ παραπλεόντων Hudson with Lat. (praetervehuntur).

ᵃ These last incidents *are* narrated below, §§ 545-8, 585 ff.
ᵇ The meaning " *through* Achaea " is obscure. We might
expect, as has been suggested, " while [they were going by
land] through Achaea (for it was winter) [and the rest] were
sailing round " the Peloponnese ; possibly there is a lacuna
304

campaign against the generals of Vitellius and his overthrow ; of the subsequent commotions under Vitellius and the fighting around the Capitol, and how Antonius Primus and Mucianus, by the destruction of Vitellius and his German legions, finally suppressed the civil war.[a] All these matters I may be excused from narrating in detail, because they are commonly known and have been described by numerous Greek and Roman historians ; but to preserve the connexion of events and to avoid any break in the narrative, I have summarily touched upon each.

Vespasian, therefore, when the news first came, deferred his expedition against Jerusalem, anxiously waiting to see upon whom the empire would devolve after Nero's death ; nor when he subsequently heard that Galba was emperor would he undertake anything, until he had received further instructions from him concerning the war. But he sent his son Titus to the new emperor to salute him and to receive his orders with reference to the Jews ; king Agrippa also embarked with Titus on the same errand to Galba. However, before they reached their destination and while they were sailing round through Achaea [b] (for it was the winter season) in vessels of war, Galba was assassinated after a reign of seven months and as many days,[c] and was succeeded as emperor by Otho, the rival claimant to the sovereignty. Agrippa decided, notwithstanding, to proceed to Rome, in

and defers his march to Jerusalem.

Titus sent to salute Galba,

in the text. As the text stands, the parenthesis will account for the time taken over the voyage. The canal through the isthmus of Corinth begun by Nero (iii. 540) was never completed.

[c] From the death of Nero, 9th June 68, to that of Galba 15th January 69. The calculation is correct.

ἀφικέσθαι διέγνω μηδὲν ὀρρωδήσας πρὸς τὴν
501 μεταβολήν· Τίτος δὲ κατὰ δαιμόνιον ὁρμὴν ἀπὸ
τῆς Ἑλλάδος εἰς τὴν Συρίαν ἀνέπλει καὶ κατὰ
τάχος εἰς Καισάρειαν ἀφικνεῖται πρὸς τὸν πατέρα.
502 καὶ οἱ μὲν μετέωροι περὶ τῶν ὅλων ὄντες ὡς ἂν
σαλευομένης τῆς Ῥωμαίων ἡγεμονίας ὑπερεώρων
τὴν ἐπὶ Ἰουδαίους στρατείαν,[1] καὶ διὰ τὸν περὶ
τῆς πατρίδος φόβον τὴν ἐπὶ τοὺς ἀλλοφύλους
ὁρμὴν ἄωρον ἐνόμιζον.
503 (3) Ἐπανίσταται δ' ἄλλος τοῖς Ἱεροσολύμοις
πόλεμος. υἱὸς ἦν Γιώρα Σίμων τις Γερασηνὸς τὸ
γένος, νεανίας πανουργίᾳ μὲν ἡττώμενος Ἰωάννου
504 τοῦ προκατέχοντος ἤδη τὴν πόλιν, ἀλκῇ δὲ
σώματος καὶ τόλμῃ διαφέρων, δι' ἣν καὶ ὑπὸ
Ἀνάνου τοῦ ἀρχιερέως φυγαδευθεὶς ἐξ ἧς εἶχε[2]
τοπαρχίας Ἀκραβετηνῆς πρὸς τοὺς κατειληφότας
505 τὴν Μασάδαν λῃστὰς παραγίνεται. τὸ μὲν οὖν
πρῶτον ἦν αὐτοῖς δι' ὑποψίας· εἰς τὸ κατωτέρω
γοῦν φρούριον ἐπέτρεψαν αὐτῷ παρελθεῖν ἅμα
ταῖς γυναιξίν, ἃς ἄγων ἦκεν, αὐτοὶ τὸ ὑψηλότερον
506 οἰκοῦντες· αὖθις δὲ διὰ συγγένειαν ἠθῶν καὶ ὅτι
πιστὸς ἐδόκει, συμπροενόμενο γοῦν αὐτοῖς ἐξιὼν
507 καὶ συνεπόρθει τὰ περὶ τὴν Μασάδαν. οὐ μὴν
ἐπὶ τὰ μείζω παρακαλῶν ἔπεισεν· οἱ μὲν γὰρ
ἐν ἔθει ὄντες τῷ φρουρίῳ, καθάπερ φωλεοῦ χω-
508 ρίζεσθαι μακρὰν ἐδεδοίκεσαν, ὁ δὲ τυραννιῶν
καὶ μεγάλων ἐφιέμενος ἐπειδὴ καὶ τὴν Ἀνάνου
τελευτὴν ἤκουσεν, εἰς τὴν ὀρεινὴν ἀφίσταται,

---

[1] LC: στρατηγίαν PAM : στρατιάν VR.
[2] ἦρχε Dindorf with one ms.

---

[a] Active in the opening attack on Cestius, *B.* ii. 521, he
had afterwards become a marauder, ii. 652.

no way deterred by this change of affairs; but
Titus, under divine impulse, sailed back from Greece
to Syria and hastened to rejoin his father at Caesarea.
The two, being thus in suspense on these momentous
matters, when the Roman empire itself was reeling,
neglected the invasion of Judaea, regarding an
attack on a foreign country as unseasonable, while
in such anxiety concerning their own.

rejoins
Vespasian
on hearing
of accession
of Otho.
Hostilities
deferred.

(3) But another war was now impending over
Jerusalem. There was a certain Simon,[a] son of
Gioras and a native of Gerasa,[b] a youth less cunning
than John, who was already in possession of the city,
but his superior in physical strength and audacity;
the latter quality had led to his expulsion by the
high priest Ananus from the province of Acrabetene,[c]
once under his command, whereupon he had joined
the brigands who had seized Masada.[d] At first they
regarded him with suspicion, and permitted him and
his following of women access only to the lower part
of the fortress, occupying the upper quarters themselves; but afterwards, as a man of congenial disposition and apparently to be trusted, he was allowed
to accompany them on their marauding expeditions
and took part in their raids upon the surrounding
district. His efforts to tempt them to greater enterprises were, however, unsuccessful; for they had
grown accustomed to the fortress and were afraid
to venture far, so to speak, from their lair. He, on
the contrary, was aspiring to despotic power and
cherishing high ambitions; accordingly on hearing
of the death of Ananus,[e] he withdrew to the hills,

Simon, son
of Gioras,
joins the
brigands of
Masada,

---

[b] *Jerash*, § 487. [c] In the N. of Judaea.
[d] *Cf.* ii. 652 f., and for Masada, iv. 399. [e] § 316.

καὶ προκηρύξας δούλοις μὲν ἐλευθερίαν, γέρας
δὲ ἐλευθέροις, τοὺς πανταχόθεν πονηροὺς συν-
ήθροιζεν.

509 (4) Ὡς δ' ἦν αὐτῷ καρτερὸν ἤδη τὸ σύνταγμα,
τὰς ἀνὰ τὴν ὀρεινὴν κώμας κατέτρεχεν, ἀεὶ δὲ
προσγινομένων πλειόνων ἐθάρρει καταβαίνειν εἰς
510 τὰ χθαμαλώτερα. κἀπειδὴ πόλεσιν ἤδη φοβερὸς
ἦν, πολλοὶ πρὸς τὴν ἰσχὺν καὶ τὴν εὔροιαν τῶν
κατορθωμάτων ἐφθείροντο δυνατοί, καὶ οὐκέτι ἦν
δούλων μόνων οὐδὲ λῃστῶν στρατός, ἀλλὰ καὶ
δημοτικῶν οὐκ ὀλίγων ὡς πρὸς βασιλέα πειθαρχία.
511 κατέτρεχε δὲ τήν τε Ἀκραβετηνὴν τοπαρχίαν καὶ
τὰ μέχρι τῆς μεγάλης Ἰδουμαίας· κατὰ γὰρ
κώμην τινὰ καλουμένην Ναΐν¹ τεῖχος κατασκευάσας
512 ὥσπερ φρουρίῳ πρὸς ἀσφάλειαν ἐχρῆτο, κατὰ δὲ
τὴν φάραγγα προσαγορευομένην Φερεταΐ² πολλὰ
μὲν ἀνευρύνας σπήλαια, πολλὰ δ' εὑρὼν ἕτοιμα
ταμιείοις ἐχρῆτο θησαυρῶν καὶ τῆς λείας ἐκ-
513 δοχείοις. ἀνετίθει δὲ καὶ τοὺς ἁρπαζομένους εἰς
αὐτὰ καρπούς, οἵ τε πολλοὶ τῶν λόχων δίαιταν
εἶχον ἐν ἐκείνοις· δῆλος δ' ἦν τό τε σύνταγμα
προγυμνάζων καὶ τὰς παρασκευὰς κατὰ τῶν
Ἱεροσολύμων.

514 (5) Ὅθεν οἱ ζηλωταὶ δείσαντες αὐτοῦ τὴν ἐπι-
βολὴν³ καὶ προλαβεῖν βουλόμενοι τὸν κατ' αὐτῶν
τρεφόμενον ἐξίασι μετὰ τῶν ὅπλων οἱ πλείους·
ὑπαντιάζει δὲ Σίμων, καὶ παραταξάμενος συχνοὺς
μὲν αὐτῶν ἀναιρεῖ, συνελαύνει δὲ τοὺς λοιποὺς
515 εἰς τὴν πόλιν. οὔπω δὲ θαρρῶν τῇ δυνάμει τοῦ

¹ Ἀΐν PA : aiam Lat.
² φαρ. προσ. Φερεταΐ] Φαρὰ(ν) προσαγορευομένην φάραγγα
MVR(C).   ³ Destinon : ἐπιβουλὴν MSS.
308

where, by proclaiming liberty for slaves and rewards for the free, he gathered around him the villains from every quarter.

(4) Having now collected a strong force, he first overran the villages in the hills, and then through continual additions to his numbers was emboldened to descend into the lowlands. And now when he was becoming a terror to the towns, many men of standing were seduced by his strength and career of unbroken success into joining him ; and his was no longer an army of mere serfs or brigands, but one including numerous citizen recruits, subservient to his command as to a king. He now overran not only the province of Acrabetene but the whole district extending to greater Idumaea. For at a village called Nain [a] he had thrown up a wall and used the place as a fortress to secure his position ; while he turned to account numerous caves in the valley known as Pheretae,[b] widening some and finding others adapted to his purpose, as store chambers and repositories for plunder. Here, too, he laid up his spoils of corn, and here most of his troops were quartered. His object was evident : he was training his force and making all these preparations for an attack on Jerusalem.

and collects an army of marauders for an attack on the Zealots.

(5) The Zealots, in consequence, alarmed at his designs and anxious to forestall one whose growing strength was to their injury, went out with their main body under arms ; Simon met them and in the ensuing fight killed many of them and drove the remainder into the city. Misgivings about his

Simon repels attack of the Zealots

[a] Unidentified ; apparently not far N. of the Idumaean frontier, § 517 (not the Galilaean village so named).
[b] Perhaps *Khurbet Farah*, a gorge some 6 miles N.E. of Jerusalem.

μὲν τοῖς τείχεσιν προσβάλλειν ἀπετράπη, χειρώ-
σασθαι δὲ πρότερον τὴν Ἰδουμαίαν ἐπεβάλετο·
καὶ δὴ δισμυρίους ἔχων ὁπλίτας ἤλαυνεν ἐπὶ τοὺς
516 ὅρους αὐτῆς. οἱ δὲ ἄρχοντες τῆς Ἰδουμαίας κατὰ
τάχος ἀθροίσαντες ἐκ τῆς χώρας τὸ μαχιμώτατον
περὶ πεντακισχιλίους καὶ δισμυρίους, τοὺς δὲ
πολλοὺς ἐάσαντες φρουρεῖν τὰ σφέτερα διὰ τὰς
τῶν ἐν Μασάδῃ σικαρίων καταδρομάς, ἐδέχοντο
517 τὸν Σίμωνα πρὸς τοῖς ὅροις. ἔνθα συμβαλὼν
αὐτοῖς καὶ δι' ὅλης πολεμήσας ἡμέρας, οὔτε
νενικηκὼς οὔτε νενικημένος διεκρίθη, καὶ ὁ μὲν
εἰς τὴν Ναΐν,[1] οἱ δὲ Ἰδουμαῖοι διελύθησαν ἐπ'
518 οἴκου. καὶ μ⸍τ' οὐ πολὺ Σίμων μείζονι δυνάμει
πάλιν εἰς τὴν χώραν αὐτῶν ὥρμητο, στρατοπεδευ-
σάμενος δὲ κατά τινα κώμην, Θεκουὲ καλεῖται,
πρὸς τοὺς ἐν Ἡρωδείῳ φρουρούς, ὅπερ ἦν πλησίον, Ἐλεάζαρόν τινα τῶν ἑταίρων ἔπεμψε
519 πείσοντα παραδοῦναι τὸ ἔρυμα. τοῦτον οἱ φύλακες ἑτοίμως[2] ἐδέξαντο, τὴν αἰτίαν ἀγνοοῦντες
δι' ἣν ἥκοι, φθεγξάμενον δὲ περὶ παραδόσεως
ἐδίωκον σπασάμενοι τὰ ξίφη, μέχρι φυγῆς τόπον
οὐκ ἔχων ἔρριψεν ἀπὸ τοῦ τείχους ἑαυτὸν εἰς τὴν
520 ὑποκειμένην φάραγγα. καὶ ὁ μὲν αὐτίκα τελευτᾷ,
τοῖς δ' Ἰδουμαίοις ἤδη κατορρωδοῦσι τὴν ἰσχὺν
τοῦ Σίμωνος ἔδοξε πρὸ τοῦ συμβαλεῖν κατα-
σκέψασθαι τὴν στρατιὰν τῶν πολεμίων.
521 (6) Εἰς τοῦτο δὲ ὑπηρέτην αὐτὸν ἑτοίμως ἐπ-
εδίδου Ἰάκωβος, εἷς τῶν ἡγεμόνων, προδοσίαν
522 ἐνθυμούμενος. ὁρμήσας γοῦν ἀπὸ τῆς Ἀλούρου,

---

[1] aiam Lat. [2] προθύμως P.

[a] Tekoa, 5 miles S. of Bethlehem.

forces, however, still deterred him from an assault on the walls; instead he resolved first to subdue Idumaea, and now marched with an army of twenty thousand men towards the frontiers of that country. The chieftains of Idumaea hastily mustered from the country their most efficient troops, numbering about twenty-five thousand, and leaving the mass of the population to protect their property against incursions of the *sicarii* of Masada, met Simon at the frontier. There he fought them and, after a battle lasting all day, left the field neither victor nor vanquished; he then withdrew to Nain and the Idumaeans disbanded to their homes. Not long after, however, Simon with a yet larger force again invaded their territory, and, encamping at a village called Thekoue,[a] sent one of his comrades named Eleazar to the garrison at Herodion,[b] which was not far off, to persuade them to hand over that fortress. The guards, ignorant of the object of his visit, promptly admitted him, but at the first mention of the word " surrender " drew their swords and pursued him, until, finding escape impossible, he flung himself from the ramparts into the valley below and was killed on the spot. The Idumaeans, now gravely alarmed at Simon's strength, decided before risking an engagement to reconnoitre their enemy's army.

and invades Idumaea.

A drawn battle.

(6) For this service James, one of their officers, promptly volunteered, meditating treachery. He accordingly set out from Alurus,[c] the village where

James the Idumaean betrays his country to Simon.

[b] Some 3 miles N.E. of Tekoa; the fortress built by Herod the Great, i. 265, 419 ff., in which he was buried, i. 673.

[c] *Ḥulḥul*, some 4 miles N. of Hebron, and 7 miles S.W. of Simon's camp at Tekoa.

κατὰ γὰρ ταύτην συνήθροιστο τὴν κώμην τότε
τῶν Ἰδουμαίων τὸ στράτευμα, παραγίνεται πρὸς
523 Σίμωνα, καὶ πρώτην αὐτῷ παραδώσειν συντίθεται
τὴν αὐτοῦ πατρίδα, λαβὼν ὅρκους ὡς ἀεὶ τίμιος
ὢν διατελέσει,[1] συνεργήσειν δὲ ὑπέσχετο καὶ περὶ
524 τῆς ὅλης Ἰδουμαίας. ἐφ᾽ οἷς ἑστιαθεὶς φιλο-
φρόνως ὑπὸ τοῦ Σίμωνος καὶ λαμπραῖς ἐπαρθεὶς
ὑποσχέσεσιν, ἐπειδήπερ εἰς τοὺς σφετέρους ὑπέστρεψε, τὸ μὲν πρῶτον πολλαπλασίονα τὴν στρα-
525 τιὰν ἐψεύδετο τοῦ Σίμωνος, ἔπειτα δεξιούμενος[2]
τούς τε ἡγεμόνας καὶ κατ᾽ ὀλίγους πᾶν τὸ πλῆθος
ἐνῆγεν ὥστε δέξασθαι τὸν Σίμωνα καὶ παραδοῦναι
526 δίχα μάχης αὐτῷ τὴν τῶν ὅλων ἀρχήν. ἅμα δὲ
ταῦτα διαπραττόμενος καὶ Σίμωνα δι᾽ ἀγγέλων
ἐκάλει σκεδάσειν ὑπισχνούμενος τοὺς Ἰδουμαίους·
527 ὃ δὴ παρέσχεν. ὡς γὰρ ἦν ἤδη πλησίον ἡ στρατιά,
πρῶτος ἀναπηδήσας ἐπὶ τὸν ἵππον μετὰ τῶν
528 συνδιεφθαρμένων ἔφευγε. πτόα δ᾽ ἐμπίπτει παντὶ
τῷ πλήθει, καὶ πρὶν εἰς χεῖρας ἐλθεῖν λυθέντες
ἐκ τῆς τάξεως ἀνεχώρουν ἕκαστοι πρὸς τὰ ἴδια.
529   (7) Σίμων δὲ παρὰ δόξαν εἰς τὴν Ἰδουμαίαν
εἰσήλασεν ἀναιμωτὶ καὶ προσβαλὼν ἀδοκήτως
πρώτην αἱρεῖ τὴν πολίχνην Χεβρών, ἐν ᾗ πλείστης
ἐκράτησε λείας, πάμπολυν δὲ διήρπασε καρπόν.
530 ὡς δέ φασιν οἱ ἐπιχώριοι τὴν Χεβρὼν οὐ μόνον
τῶν τῇδε πόλεων ἀλλὰ καὶ τῆς ἐν Αἰγύπτῳ Μέμ-
φεως ἀρχαιοτέραν· δισχίλια γοῦν αὐτῇ καὶ τρια-

---

[1] διατελεῖ L.
[2] perterritis Lat. (reading ? δεδισσόμενος, Destinon).

---

[a] Cf. Numbers xiii. 22 (23) " Hebron was built seven years
before Zoan (= Tanis, LXX and Josephus, A. i. 170) in Egypt."
Tanis " was in any case built before 2000 B.C." (G. B.

the Idumaean army was then concentrated, and repaired to Simon. With him he made a compact, first to deliver up his own native place, after receiving an assurance on oath that he should always hold some post of honour ; he further undertook to assist in the subjugation of the whole of Idumaea. Being thereupon hospitably entertained by Simon and elated with dazzling promises, he, on his return to his own people, began by immensely exaggerating the strength of that general's army ; and then, by giving receptions to the officers and to the whole rank and file, in small parties, he instigated them to receive Simon and to surrender to him, without a struggle, the whole direction of affairs. While these negotiations were proceeding, he sent a message to Simon, summoning him to come and promising to disperse the Idumaeans—a promise which he duly fulfilled. For, on the approach of the army, he was the first to spring to the saddle and fly, followed by his corrupted accomplices. Panic-stricken the whole multitude, before a blow was struck, broke from the ranks and made off to their several homes.

(7) Simon having thus, beyond expectation, marched into Idumaea without bloodshed, first of all by a surprise attack captured the little town of Hebron, where he gained abundant booty and laid hands on vast supplies of corn. According to the statements of its inhabitants, Hebron is a town of greater antiquity not only than any other in the country, but even than Memphis in Egypt,[a] being reckoned to be

Simon takes Hebron.

Antiquities of Hebron.

Gray, *Internat. Crit. Comm. in loc.*) ; the foundation of Memphis goes back to the beginnings of Egyptian history. The antiquity of Hebron is undetermined, " but it certainly seems of pre-Israelitish origin " (*ibid.*).

531 κόσια ἔτη συναριθμεῖται. μυθεύουσι δὲ αὐτὴν
καὶ οἰκητήριον Ἀβράμου τοῦ Ἰουδαίων προγόνου
γεγονέναι μετὰ τὴν ἐκ τῆς Μεσοποταμίας ἀπανά-
στασιν, τούς τε παῖδας αὐτοῦ λέγουσι καταβῆναι
532 εἰς Αἴγυπτον ἔνθεν· ὧν καὶ τὰ μνημεῖα μέχρι νῦν
ἐν τῇδε τῇ πολίχνῃ δείκνυται, πάνυ καλῆς μαρ-
533 μάρου καὶ φιλοτίμως εἰργασμένα. δείκνυται δ'
ἀπὸ σταδίων ἓξ τοῦ ἄστεος τερέβινθος μεγίστη,
καὶ φασὶ τὸ δένδρον ἀπὸ τῆς κτίσεως μέχρι νῦν
534 διαμένειν. ἔνθεν ὁ Σίμων διὰ πάσης ἐχώρει τῆς
Ἰδουμαίας, οὐ μόνον κώμας καὶ πόλεις πορθῶν,
λυμαινόμενος δὲ καὶ τὴν χώραν, ὡς μηδὲ τῶν
ἐπιτηδείων ἐξαρκούντων πρὸς τὸ πλῆθος·[1] δίχα
γὰρ τῶν ὁπλιτῶν τέσσαρες αὐτῷ συνείποντο
535 μυριάδες. προσῆν δὲ ταῖς χρείαις ὠμότης τε
αὐτοῦ καὶ πρὸς τὸ γένος ὀργή, δι' ἃ μᾶλλον
536 ἐξερημοῦσθαι συνέβαινε τὴν Ἰδουμαίαν. καθάπερ δὲ [ὑπὸ] τῶν ἀκρίδων κατόπιν ὕλην ἔστιν
ἰδεῖν ἐψιλωμένην πᾶσαν, οὕτω τὸ κατὰ νώτου τῆς
537 Σίμωνος στρατιᾶς ἐρημία κατελείπετο· καὶ τὰ
μὲν ἐμπιπρῶντες τὰ δὲ κατασκάπτοντες, πᾶν δὲ
τὸ πεφυκὸς ἀνὰ τὴν χώραν ἢ συμπατοῦντες
ἠφάνιζον ἢ νεμόμενοι καὶ τὴν ἐνεργὸν ὑπὸ τῆς
πορείας σκληροτέραν ἐποίουν τῆς ἀκάρπου, καθ-

---

[1] ὡς μηδὲ . . πλῆθος in the mss. stand after μυριάδες: trans-
posed here by Bekker.

---

[a] Gen. xiii. 18.

[b] Jacob's residence in Hebron is mentioned in Gen. xxxv.
27, xxxvii. 14. The historian, however, is dependent on local
tradition, and ignores the Biblical narrative.

[c] The cave of Machpelah, the burial-place of Sarah

two thousand three hundred years old. They further
relate that it was there that Abraham, the progenitor
of the Jews, took up his abode after his migration
from Mesopotamia,[a] and from here that his posterity
went down into Egypt.[b] Their tombs are shown in
this little town to this day, of really fine marble and
of exquisite workmanship.[c] At a distance of six
furlongs from the town there is also shown a huge
terebinth-tree, which is said to have stood there ever
since the creation.[d] From Hebron Simon pursued
his march through the whole of Idumaea, not con-
fining his ravages to villages and towns, but making
havoc also of the country, since provisions proved
insufficient for such a multitude ; for, exclusive of
his troops, he had forty thousand followers. But,
besides his needs, his cruelty and animosity against
the nation contributed to complete the devastation
of Idumaea. Just as a forest in the wake of locusts
may be seen stripped quite bare, so in the rear of
Simon's army nothing remained but a desert. Some
places they burnt, others they razed to the ground ;
all vegetation throughout the country vanished,
either trodden under foot or consumed ; while the
tramp of their march rendered cultivated land
harder than the barren soil. In short, nothing

Simon
devastates
Idumaea.

(Gen. xxiii), Abraham (xxv. 9), Isaac (xxxv. 27 ff.), and
Jacob (l. 13) is believed to be below the present mosque ;
Jewish, Christian, and Moslem traditions are in agreement
as to the site. The wall surrounding the mosque has been
ascribed to the Herodian period (Conder, *Tent Work in
Palestine*, 239).

   [d] The " oak " of Abraham (so LXX; Heb. " oaks " or
" terebinths ") is mentioned in Gen. xiii. 18, xiv. 13, xviii. 1.
In the 5th cent. A.D. it was called Τερέβινθος, and was the
scene of an annual feast and fair, Sozomen, *H.E.* ii. 4
(Robertson Smith).

ὅλου τε εἰπεῖν, οὐδὲ σημεῖόν τι κατελείπετο τοῖς
πορθουμένοις[1] τοῦ γεγονέναι.

538 (8) Ταῦτα πάλιν τοὺς ζηλωτὰς ἐπήγειρεν, καὶ
φανερῶς μὲν ἀντιπαρατάξασθαι κατέδεισαν, προ-
λοχίσαντες δ' ἐν ταῖς παρόδοις ἁρπάζουσι τοῦ
Σίμωνος τὴν γυναῖκα καὶ τῆς περὶ αὐτὴν θεραπείας
539 συχνούς. ἔπειτα ὡς αὐτὸν αἰχμαλωτισάμενοι τὸν
Σίμωνα γεγηθότες εἰς τὴν πόλιν ὑπέστρεψαν καὶ
ὅσον οὐδέπω προσεδόκων καταθέμενον τὰ ὅπλα
540 περὶ τῆς γυναικὸς ἱκετεύσειν. τὸν δὲ οὐκ ἔλεος
εἰσῆλθεν ἀλλ' ὀργὴ περὶ τῆς ἡρπασμένης, καὶ
πρὸς τὸ τεῖχος τῶν Ἱεροσολύμων ἐλθὼν καθάπερ
τὰ τρωθέντα τῶν θηρίων, ἐπειδὴ τοὺς τρώσαντας
οὐ κατέλαβεν, ἐφ' οὓς εὗρε τὸν θυμὸν ἠφίει.
541 ὅσοι γοῦν λαχανείας ἕνεκεν ἢ φρυγανισμοῦ προ-
εληλύθεσαν ἔξω πυλῶν, ἀνόπλους καὶ γέροντας
συλλαμβάνων ᾐκίζετο καὶ διέφθειρεν, δι' ὑπερβολὴν ἀγανακτήσεως μονονουχὶ καὶ νεκρῶν γευό-
542 μενος τῶν σωμάτων. πολλοὺς δὲ καὶ χειρο-
κοπήσας εἰσέπεμπε καταπλήξασθαι τοὺς ἐχθροὺς
ἅμα καὶ διαστῆσαι[2] τὸν δῆμον ἐπιχειρῶν πρὸς
543 τοὺς αἰτίους. ἐντέταλτο δ' αὐτοῖς λέγειν ὅτι
Σίμων θεὸν ὄμνυσι τὸν πάντων ἔφορον, εἰ μὴ
θᾶττον ἀποδώσουσιν αὐτῷ τὴν γυναῖκα, ῥήξας τὸ
τεῖχος τοιαῦτα διαθήσειν πάντας τοὺς κατὰ τὴν
πόλιν, μηδεμιᾶς φεισάμενος ἡλικίας μηδ' ἀπὸ
544 τῶν ἀναιτίων διακρίνας τοὺς αἰτίους. τούτοις οὐ
μόνον ὁ δῆμος ἀλλὰ καὶ οἱ ζηλωταὶ καταπλαγέντες ἀποπέμπουσιν αὐτῷ τὴν γυναῖκα· καὶ τότε
μὲν ἐκμειλιχθεὶς ὀλίγον ἀνεπαύσατο τοῦ συνεχοῦς
φόνου.

---

[1] + τούτοις PA.   [2] διαστασιάσαι L.

touched by their ravages left any sign of its having
ever existed.

(8) These proceedings roused the Zealots anew ; The Zealots take Simon's wife prisoner
and, though afraid to meet Simon in open battle,
they laid ambushes in the passes and captured his
wife and a large number of her attendants. Then, as
if their prisoner had been Simon himself, they returned triumphant to the city, expecting that he
would instantly lay down his arms and come to sue
for his wife. It was, however, no tender feelings
but indignation which her capture aroused in his
breast, and advancing to the walls of Jerusalem like Simon by threats to Jerusalem recovers her.
some wounded beast, when it has failed to catch its
tormentors, he vented his wrath upon all whom he
met. Any who had ventured outside the gates to
gather herbs or fuel, unarmed and aged individuals,
he seized, tortured and killed, in the extravagance of
his rage almost gnawing their very corpses.[a] Many
others he sent back into the city with their hands
cut off, with the twofold object of intimidating his
foes and of causing the people to rise against the
responsible parties. These persons received injunctions to say that Simon had sworn by God, the over-
seer of all, that unless they restored his wife to him
forthwith, he would break down the wall and inflict
similar punishment on every soul in the city, sparing
neither young nor old, and making no distinction
between guilty and innocent. These threats so
terrified not only the people but even the Zealots,
that they sent him back his wife ; whereat, momentarily mollified, he paused for a while from his ceaseless
slaughter.

[a] A similar " hyperbole " (the historian supplies the word !)
occurs in vi. 373.

JOSEPHUS

545   (9) Οὐ μόνον δὲ κατὰ τὴν Ἰουδαίαν στάσις ἦν
καὶ πόλεμος ἐμφύλιος, ἀλλὰ κἀπὶ τῆς Ἰταλίας.
546 ἀνήρητο μὲν γὰρ κατὰ μέσην τὴν Ῥωμαίων
ἀγορὰν Γάλβας, ἀποδεδειγμένος δὲ αὐτοκράτωρ
Ὄθων ἐπολέμει Οὐιτελλίῳ βασιλειῶντι· τοῦτον
547 γὰρ ᾕρητο τὰ κατὰ Γερμανίαν τάγματα. καὶ
γενομένης συμβολῆς κατὰ Φρηγδίακον¹ τῆς Γαλατίας πρός τε Οὐάλεντα καὶ Καικίνναν² τοὺς
Οὐιτελλίου στρατηγούς, τῇ πρώτῃ μὲν ἡμέρᾳ
περιῆν Ὄθων, τῇ δὲ δευτέρᾳ τὸ Οὐιτελλίου
548 στρατιωτικόν· καὶ πολλοῦ φόνου γενομένου δι-
εχρήσατο μὲν Ὄθων αὐτὸν ἐν Βριξέλλῳ³ τὴν
ἧτταν πυθόμενος, ἡμέρας δύο καὶ τρεῖς μῆνας
549 κρατήσας τῶν πραγμάτων, προσεχώρησε δὲ τοῖς
Οὐιτελλίου στρατηγοῖς ἡ στρατιά, καὶ κατέβαινεν
αὐτὸς εἰς τὴν Ῥώμην μετὰ τῆς δυνάμεως.
550   Ἐν δὲ τούτῳ καὶ Οὐεσπασιανὸς ἀναστὰς ἐκ τῆς
Καισαρείας πέμπτῃ Δαισίου μηνὸς ὥρμησεν ἐπὶ
τὰ μηδέπω κατεστραμμένα τῶν τῆς Ἰουδαίας
551 χωρίων. ἀναβὰς δ᾽ εἰς τὴν ὀρεινὴν αἱρεῖ δύο
τοπαρχίας, τήν τε Γοφνιτικὴν καὶ τὴν Ἀκραβετηνὴν καλουμένην, μεθ᾽ ἃς Βήθηλά⁴ τε καὶ
Ἐφραὶμ πολίχνια, οἷς φρουροὺς ἐγκαταστήσας
μέχρι Ἱεροσολύμων ἱππάζετο· φθορὰ δ᾽ ἦν πολλῶν καταλαμβανομένων καὶ συχνοὺς ἠχμαλωτίζετο.

¹ Βηδριακὸν Hudson.   ² ed. pr.: Κίννα(ν) mss.
³ ed. pr.: Βριξέμῳ mss.
⁴ VRC: Βαίθηλά M: Βήθηγά the rest.

ᵃ §§ 494, 499.
ᵇ A small town in Cisalpine Gaul, between Verona and
318

(9) Sedition and civil war were not, however, confined to Judaea, but were rampant also in Italy.
For Galba had been murdered in the midst of the
Roman forum,[a] and Otho, being proclaimed emperor,
was at war with Vitellius, now aspiring to imperial
sovereignty, having been elected by the legions in
Germany. In the battle fought at Bedriacum[b] in
Gaul against Valens and Caecinna,[c] the generals of
Vitellius, on the first day Otho had the advantage,
but on the second the troops of Vitellius ; and such
was the slaughter that Otho put an end to himself
at Brixellum,[d] where he learnt of his defeat, having
held the reins of government for three months and
two days.[e] His army went over to the generals of
Vitellius, who now descended in person upon Rome
with his entire force.

Meanwhile, Vespasian had moved from Caesarea
on the fifth of the month Daesius and advanced
against those districts of Judaea which had not yet
been reduced. Ascending into the hill country he
subdued two provinces, those which take their names
from Gophna[f] and Acrabetta[g] ; next he captured
the small towns of Bethela[h] and Ephraim[i] ;
leaving garrisons in these, he then rode with his cavalry
up to the walls of Jerusalem, killing many of those
encountered on the route, and taking numerous

Marginal notes:

Civil war in Italy.

Galba slain. 15 January A.D. 69.

Otho's death. 17 April A.D. 69.

Vitellius.

Vespasian again invades Judaea (c. 23) June A.D. 68,

Cremona ; the Vitellians in their turn were defeated soon
after in the same neighbourhood, §§ 634 ff. Tacitus, *Hist.* ii.
41-49, describes the battle and the death of Otho.

    [c] Fabius Valens and A. Caecina Alienus.
    [d] *Brescello*, about 12 miles N.E. of Parma.
    [e] From January 15 to April 17, 69.
    [f] Some 12 miles due N. of Jerusalem.
    [g] In the N.E. corner of Judaea.
    [h] Bethel (*Beitin*) a few miles S.E. of Gophna.
    [i] *et-Taiyibeh* N.E. of Bethel.

552 Κερεάλιος δ' αὐτῷ τῶν ἡγεμόνων, μοῖραν ἱππέων
καὶ πεζῶν ἀναλαβών, τὴν ἄνω καλουμένην Ἰδουμαίαν ἐπόρθει, καὶ Κάφεθρα¹ μὲν ψευδοπολίχνιον
ἐξ ἐφόδου λαβὼν ἐμπίπρησιν, ἑτέραν δὲ καλου-
553 μένην Καφαραβὶν² προσβαλὼν ἐπολιόρκει. πάνυ
δ' ἦν ἰσχυρὸν τὸ τεῖχος, καὶ τρίψεσθαι προσ-
δοκῶντι πλείω χρόνον αἰφνιδίως ἀνοίγουσιν οἱ
ἔνδον τὰς πύλας καὶ μεθ' ἱκετηριῶν προελθόντες
554 ἑαυτοὺς παρέδοσαν. Κερεάλιος δὲ τούτους παρα-
στησάμενος ἐπὶ Χεβρὼν ἑτέρας πόλεως ἀρχαιο-
τάτης ἐχώρει· κεῖται δ', ὡς ἔφην, αὕτη κατὰ τὴν
ὀρεινὴν οὐ πόρρω Ἱεροσολύμων· βιασάμενος δὲ τὰς
εἰσόδους τὸ μὲν ἐγκαταληφθὲν πλῆθος ἡβηδὸν ἀναιρεῖ,
555 τὸ δ' ἄστυ καταπίμπρησι. καὶ πάντων ἤδη κεχειρωμένων πλὴν Ἡρωδείου καὶ Μασάδας καὶ Μαχαιροῦντος, ταῦτα δ' ὑπὸ τῶν λῃστῶν κατείληπτο, σκοπὸς
ἤδη τὰ Ἱεροσόλυμα προύκειτο Ῥωμαίοις.

556 (10) Ὁ δὲ Σίμων ὡς ἐρρύσατο παρὰ τῶν
ζηλωτῶν τὴν γυναῖκα, πάλιν ἐπὶ τὰ λείψανα τῆς
Ἰδουμαίας ὑπέστρεψεν, καὶ περιελαύνων πανταχόθεν τὸ ἔθνος εἰς Ἱεροσόλυμα τοὺς πολλοὺς
557 φεύγειν συνηνάγκασεν. εἵπετο δὲ καὶ αὐτὸς ἐπὶ
τὴν πόλιν καὶ κυκλωσάμενος αὖθις τὸ τεῖχος
ὅντινα λάβοι τῶν προϊόντων κατὰ τὴν χώραν
558 ἐργατῶν διέφθειρεν. ἦν δὲ τῷ δήμῳ Σίμων μὲν
ἔξωθεν Ῥωμαίων φοβερώτερος, οἱ ζηλωταὶ δ'
ἔνδον ἑκατέρων χαλεπώτεροι, κἂν τούτοις ἐπινοίᾳ
κακῶν καὶ τόλμῃ τὸ σύνταγμα τῶν Γαλιλαίων

¹ Hudson: Καφαίορα L: further corruption in other mss.
² Χαφαραβεὶν L: Χαραβὶν most mss.

ª Sextus Cerealius Vetilianus, legate of the 5th legion,
who had defeated the Samaritans, iii. 310 ff.

prisoners. Furthermore, Cerealius,[a] one of his officers, with a detachment of horse and foot, laid waste what is known as upper Idumaea; here he carried at the first assault the petty town (as it falsely calls itself) of Caphethra[b] and burnt it to the ground, and then attacked and proceeded to besiege another town called Capharabis.[b] The wall of this place was exceptionally strong and he was anticipating a prolonged delay, when the inhabitants suddenly opened their gates and, approaching him with olive-branches as suppliants, surrendered. Cerealius, after their capitulation, advanced on Hebron, another city and one of great antiquity, situated, as I have said,[c] in the hill country not far[d] from Jerusalem; having forced the approaches he slew all whom he found there, young or old, and burnt down the town. Every fortress being now subdued except Herodion, Masada, and Machaerus, which were held by the brigands, Jerusalem was henceforth the one objective before the Romans.

and Cerealius in Idumaea.

(10) Simon,[e] having now recovered his wife from the Zealots, returned once more to the relics of Idumaea and, harassing every quarter of the nation, drove multitudes to flee to Jerusalem. Thither he followed them himself, and again surrounding the wall killed any of the labouring class whom he caught going out into the country. The citizens thus found Simon without the walls a greater terror than the Romans, and the Zealots within more oppressive than either; while among the latter for mischievous ingenuity and audacity none surpassed the Galilaean contingent,

Jerusalem at the mercy of Simon without the walls

and the drunken horde of Zealots within.

---

[b] Unidentified.   [c] *Cf.* § 530.

[d] Some 18 miles as the crow flies.

[e] Resuming the narrative from § 544.

559 διέφερεν[1]· τόν τε γὰρ Ἰωάννην παρήγαγον εἰς
ἰσχὺν οὗτοι, κἀκεῖνος αὐτοὺς ἐξ ἧς περιεποίησαν[2]
δυναστείας ἡμείβετο, πάντα ἐπιτρέπων δρᾶν ὧν
560 ἕκαστος ἐπεθύμει. πόθοι δ' ἦσαν ἁρπαγῆς ἀ-
πλήρωτοι καὶ τῶν πλουσίων οἴκων ἔρευνα, φόνος
561 τε ἀνδρῶν καὶ γυναικῶν ὕβρεις ἐπαίζοντο, μεθ'
αἵματός τε τὰ συληθέντα κατέπινον καὶ μετ'
ἀδείας ἐνεθηλυπάθουν τῷ κόρῳ, κόμας συνθετι-
ζόμενοι καὶ γυναικείας ἐσθῆτας ἀναλαμβάνοντες,
κατ αντλούμενοι δὲ ·μύροις καὶ πρὸς εὐπρέπειαν
562 ὑπογράφοντες ὀφθαλμούς. οὐ μόνον δὲ κόσμον,
ἀλλὰ καὶ πάθη γυναικῶν ἐμιμοῦντο καὶ δι' ὑπερβολὴν[3] ἀσελγείας ἀθεμίτους ἐπενόησαν ἔρωτας·
ἐνηλινδοῦντο δ' ὡς πορνείῳ τῇ πόλει καὶ πᾶσαν
563 ἀκαθάρτοις ἐμίαναν ἔργοις. γυναικιζόμενοι δὲ
τὰς ὄψεις ἐφόνων ταῖς δεξιαῖς, θρυπτόμενοί τε
τοῖς βαδίσμασιν ἐπιόντες ἐξαπίνης ἐγίνοντο πολε-
μισταί, τά τε ξίφη προφέροντες ἀπὸ τῶν βε-
βαμμένων[4] χλανιδίων τὸν προστυχόντα διήλαυνον.
564 τοὺς ἀποδιδράσκοντας δὲ Ἰωάννην Σίμων φονικώ-
τερον ἐξεδέχετο, καὶ διαφυγών τις τὸν ἐντὸς
τείχους τύραννον ὑπὸ τοῦ πρὸ πυλῶν διεφθείρετο.
565 πᾶσα δὲ φυγῆς ὁδὸς τοῖς αὐτομολεῖν πρὸς Ῥωμαίους βουλομένοις ἀπεκέκοπτο.
566 (11) Διεστασιάζετο δὲ πρὸς τὸν Ἰωάννην ἡ
δύναμις, καὶ πᾶν ὅσον ἦν Ἰδουμαίων[5] ἐν αὐτῇ
χωρισθὲν ἐπεχείρει τῷ τυράννῳ φθόνῳ τε τῆς
567 ἰσχύος αὐτοῦ καὶ μίσει τῆς ὠμότητος. συμ-

---

[1] διέφθειρε(ν) mss.
[2] PAM : περιεποιήσαντο the rest : -ήσατο Lat.
[3] + ἀσωτίας P.
[4] L Exc. Lat. : περιβεβλημένων the rest.
[5] Ἰδουμαῖον ALR Exc.

322

for it was they who had promoted John to power, and he from the position of authority which they had won for him requited them by allowing every one to do whatever he desired. With an insatiable lust for loot, they ransacked the houses of the wealthy; the murder of men and the violation of women were their sport; they caroused on their spoils, with blood to wash them down,[a] and from mere satiety unscrupulously indulged in effeminate practices, plaiting their hair and attiring themselves in women's apparel, drenching themselves with perfumes and painting their eyelids to enhance their beauty. And not only did they imitate the dress, but also the passions[b] of women, devising in their excess of lasciviousness unlawful pleasures and wallowing as in a brothel in the city, which they polluted from end to end with their foul deeds. Yet, while they wore women's faces, their hands were murderous, and approaching with mincing steps they would suddenly become warriors and whipping out their swords from under their dyed mantles transfix whomsoever they met. Any who fled from John had a yet bloodier reception from Simon, and he who escaped the tyrant within the walls was slain by the other without the gates. Every avenue of escape was thus cut off from those desirous to desert to the Romans.

(11) But John's army now mutinied; and all the Idumaeans[c] within it broke away and made an attack on the tyrant, as much from envy of his power as from hatred of his cruelty. In the ensuing engage- *Sedition among the Zealots. John of Gischala is deserted by his Idumaean allies,*

---

[a] *Cf.* vi. 372 ἐσύλων καὶ . . . τροφὴν ἁρπάζοντες αἵματι πεφυρμένην κατέπινον.
[b] or "experiences."
[c] It appears from this that some of the Idumaeans still remained in Jerusalem when the main body withdrew (§ 353).

βαλόντες δὲ ἀναιροῦσί τε πολλοὺς τῶν ζηλωτῶν
καὶ συνελαύνουσι τοὺς λοιποὺς εἰς τὴν βασιλικὴν
αὐλὴν κατασκευασθεῖσαν ὑπὸ Γραπτῆς· συγγενὴς
δ' ἦν αὕτη τοῦ τῶν Ἀδιαβηνῶν βασιλέως Ἰζᾶ·
568 συνεισπίπτουσι δ' οἱ Ἰδουμαῖοι, κἀκεῖθεν εἰς τὸ
ἱερὸν ἐξώσαντες[1] τοὺς ζηλωτὰς ἐφ' ἁρπαγὴν ἐτρά-
569 ποντο τῶν Ἰωάννου χρημάτων· κατὰ γὰρ τὴν
προειρημένην αὐλὴν αὐτός τε ᾤκει[2] καὶ τὰ λάφυρα
570 τῆς τυραννίδος κατέθετο. ἐν δὲ τούτῳ τὸ κατὰ
τὴν πόλιν ἐσκεδασμένον πλῆθος τῶν ζηλωτῶν εἰς
τὸ ἱερὸν πρὸς τοὺς διαπεφευγότας ἠθροίσθη, καὶ
κατάγειν αὐτοὺς παρεσκευάσατο Ἰωάννης ἐπί τε
571 τὸν δῆμον καὶ τοὺς Ἰδουμαίους. τοῖς δὲ οὐχ
οὕτω τὴν ἔφοδον αὐτῶν καταδεῖσαι παρέστη
μαχιμωτέροις οὖσιν ὡς τὴν ἀπόνοιαν, μὴ νύκτωρ
ἐκ τοῦ ἱεροῦ παρεισδύντες αὐτούς τε διαφθείρωσι
572 καὶ τὸ ἄστυ καταπιμπρῶσι. συνελθόντες οὖν
μετὰ τῶν ἀρχιερέων ἐβουλεύοντο, τίνα χρὴ τρόπον
573 φυλάξασθαι τὴν ἐπίθεσιν. θεὸς δ' ἄρα τὰς γνώμας
αὐτῶν εἰς κακὸν ἔτρεψε, καὶ χαλεπώτερον ἀπωλείας ἐπενόησαν τὸ πρὸς σωτηρίαν φάρμακον·
ἵνα γοῦν καταλύσωσιν Ἰωάννην, ἔκριναν δέχεσθαι
Σίμωνα καὶ μεθ' ἱκετηριῶν δεύτερον εἰσαγαγεῖν
574 ἑαυτοῖς τύραννον. ἐπεραίνετο δ' ἡ βουλή, καὶ
τὸν ἀρχιερέα Ματθίαν πέμψαντες ἐδέοντο Σίμωνος

---

[1] περιώσαντες C: περιεξώσαντες L.
[2] Destinon from Lat.: ὧν (ἦν C) ἐκεῖ MSS.

---

[a] Elsewhere (B. v. 147, vi. 356; A. xx. 17, etc.) called
Izates, which should perhaps be read here. The story of the
conversion to Judaism of Helena, Queen of Adiabene (in the
upper Tigris region), and of her son Izates is told in full in
A. xx. 17 ff. This royal family adorned Jerusalem with

ment they killed many of the Zealots and drove the
remainder into the palace built by Grapte, a relative
of Izas,[a] king of Adiabene. Rushing in along with
them the Idumaeans chased them thence into the
Temple, and then proceeded to plunder John's
treasures ; he having made this palace his residence
and the repository for the spoils of his tyranny.
Meanwhile, the rank and file of the Zealots who
were scattered about the city mustered to the
fugitives in the Temple, and John prepared to lead
them down against the people and the Idumaeans.
The latter, as the better soldiers, had less fear of
their attack than of their frenzy, lest they should
steal out of the temple by night and murder them
and burn down the town. They accordingly held a
meeting with the chief priests and deliberated how
they should guard against the assault. But God,
as events proved, perverted their judgement, and
they devised for their salvation a remedy more
disastrous than destruction : in other words, in order
to overthrow John, they decided to admit Simon
and with suppliant appeals to introduce a second
tyrant over their heads. This resolution was carried
into effect, and the high priest Matthias[b] was
deputed to beg the Simon of whom they had such

*who invite
Simon into
Jerusalem·
to oppose
him.*

buildings. We hear of her palace within the city (v. 253),
and of the pyramidal tombs 3 furlongs outside, in which she
and Izates were interred (*A*. xx. 95 ; *B*. v. 55, 119, 147) ; also
of the palace of another son, Monobazus (*B*. v. 252). Of
Grapte we hear no more. Queen Helena, like Paul and
Barnabas, brought relief to Jerusalem during the famine
under Claudius (*A*. xx. 51 ff.).

   [b] Matthias, son of Boethus, belonging to one of the high-
priestly families (ἐκ τῶν ἀρχιερέων, *B*. v. 527 ; *cf.* iv. 148),
was afterwards, with his three sons, murdered by Simon
(v. 527 ff.).

εἰσελθεῖν ὃν πολλαὶ[1] ἔδεισαν· συμπαρεκάλουν δ'
οἱ ἐκ τῶν Ἱεροσολύμων τοὺς ζηλωτὰς φεύγοντες
575 πόθῳ τῶν οἴκων καὶ τῶν κτημάτων. ὁ δ' αὐτοῖς
ὑπερηφάνως κατανεύσας τὸ δεσπόζειν εἰσέρχεται
μὲν ὡς ἀπαλλάξων τῶν ζηλωτῶν τὴν πόλιν,
σωτὴρ ὑπὸ τοῦ δήμου καὶ κηδεμὼν εὐφημούμενος,
576 παρελθὼν δὲ μετὰ τῆς δυνάμεως ἐσκόπει τὰ περὶ
τῆς ἑαυτοῦ δυναστείας καὶ τοὺς καλέσαντας οὐχ
ἧττον ἐχθροὺς ἐνόμιζεν ἢ καθ' ὧν ἐκέκλητο.

577 (12) Σίμων μὲν οὕτως ἐνιαυτῷ τρίτῳ τοῦ πολέμου Ξανθικῷ μηνὶ Ἱεροσολύμων ἐγκρατὴς γίνεται·
Ἰωάννης δὲ καὶ τὸ τῶν ζηλωτῶν πλῆθος εἰργόμενοι τῶν ἐξόδων τοῦ ἱεροῦ καὶ τὰ[2] τῆς πόλεως
ἀπολωλεκότες, παραχρῆμα γὰρ τὰ ἐκείνων οἱ
περὶ τὸν Σίμωνα διήρπασαν, ἐν ἀπόρῳ τὴν
578 σωτηρίαν εἶχον. προσέβαλλε δὲ τῷ ἱερῷ Σίμων
τοῦ δήμου βοηθοῦντος, κἀκεῖνοι καταστάντες ἐπὶ
τῶν στοῶν καὶ τῶν ἐπάλξεων ἠμύνοντο τὰς
579 προσβολάς. συχνοὶ δ' ἔπιπτον τῶν περὶ Σίμωνα
καὶ πολλοὶ τραυματίαι κατεφέροντο· ῥᾳδίως γὰρ
ἐξ ὑπερδεξίου τὰς βολὰς οἱ ζηλωταὶ καὶ οὐκ
580 ἀστόχους ἐποιοῦντο. πλεονεκτοῦντες δὲ τῷ τόπῳ
καὶ πύργους ἔτι προσκατεσκεύασαν τέσσαρας
μεγίστους, ὡς ἀφ' ὑψηλοτέρων ποιοῖντο τὰς
581 ἀφέσεις, τὸν μὲν κατὰ τὴν ἀνατολικὴν καὶ βόρειον
γωνίαν, τὸν δὲ τοῦ ξυστοῦ καθύπερθεν, τὸν δὲ
τρίτον κατὰ γωνίαν ἄλλην ἀντικρὺ τῆς κάτω
582 πόλεως· ὁ δὲ λοιπὸς ὑπὲρ τὴν κορυφὴν κατ-
εσκεύαστο τῶν παστοφορίων, ἔνθα τῶν ἱερέων εἷς

---

[1] πολλάκις L Lat.   [2] τἀκ Bekker.

[a] On the W. side of the Temple ; the Xystus lay in or just
above the Tyropoeon valley (B. ii. 344 n.).

horror to enter the city; the request was backed
by natives of Jerusalem who sought refuge from the
Zealots and yearned for their homes and possessions.
Haughtily consenting to be their master, he entered
as one who was to rid the city of the Zealots, acclaimed by the people as their saviour and protector;
but, once admitted with his forces, his sole concern
was to secure his own authority, and he regarded
the men who had invited him as no less his enemies
than those whom he had been invited to oppose.

(12) Thus did Simon, in the third year of the war, Simon
in the month Xanthicus, become master of Jerusalem; master of
while John and the Zealots, being debarred from all April-May
egress from the Temple, and having lost their posses- A.D. 69.
sions in the city—for these had been instantly
plundered by Simon's party—began to despair of
deliverance. Simon now attacked the Temple, with Simon
the support of the citizens; their adversaries posting attacks the
themselves on the porticoes and battlements and Zealots
beating off their assaults. The casualties in Simon's the temple.
ranks were numerous, both in dead and wounded;
for the Zealots from their higher ground could maintain an easy and well-directed fire. They, moreover,
improved this advantage of position by erecting
four huge towers in order to increase the elevation
from which their missiles were discharged: one at
the north-east corner, the second above the Xystus,[a]
the third at another corner opposite the lower town.[b]
The last was erected above the roof of the priests'
chambers,[c] at the point where it was the custom for

[b] At the S.W. angle of the Temple.
[c] Small chambers, for the use of the priests and storage of
utensils, ranged in stories round three sides of the inner
court.

ἐξ ἔθους ἱστάμενος ἑκάστην ἑβδομάδα εἰσιοῦσαν
προεσήμαινε σάλπιγγι δείλης καὶ τελεσθεῖσαν
αὖθις περὶ ἑσπέραν, ὅτε μὲν ἀνέργειαν τῷ λαῷ
583 καταγγέλλων, ὅτε δ᾽ ἔργων ἔχεσθαι. διέστησαν
δ᾽ ἐπὶ τῶν πύργων ὀξυβελεῖς τε καὶ λιθοβόλους
584 μηχανὰς τούς τε τοξότας καὶ σφενδονήτας. ἔνθα
δὴ τὰς μὲν προσβολὰς ὀκνηροτέρας ἐποιεῖτο ὁ
Σίμων, μαλακιζομένων αὐτῷ τῶν πλειόνων, ἀντ-
εῖχε δ᾽ ὅμως περιουσίᾳ δυνάμεως· τὰ δ᾽ ἀπὸ
τῶν ὀργάνων βέλη πορρωτέρω φερόμενα πολλοὺς
τῶν μαχομένων ἀνῄρει.

585 (x. 1) Κατὰ δὲ τὸν αὐτὸν καιρὸν περιέσχε καὶ
586 τὴν Ῥώμην πάθη χαλεπά. παρῆν μὲν γὰρ ἀπὸ
Γερμανίας Οὐιτέλλιος ἅμα τῷ στρατιωτικῷ πολὺ
πλῆθος ἐπισυρόμενος ἕτερον, μὴ χωρούμενος δὲ
τοῖς ἀποδεδειγμένοις εἰς τοὺς στρατιώτας περι-
βόλοις ὅλην ἐποιήσατο τὴν Ῥώμην στρατόπεδον
587 καὶ πᾶσαν οἰκίαν ὁπλιτῶν ἐπλήρωσεν. οἱ δ᾽
ἀήθεσιν ὀφθαλμοῖς τὸν Ῥωμαίων πλοῦτον θεασά-
μενοι καὶ περιλαμφθέντες πάντοθεν ἀργύρῳ τε
καὶ χρυσῷ τὰς ἐπιθυμίας μόλις κατεῖχον, ὥστε
μὴ ἐφ᾽ ἁρπαγὰς τρέπεσθαί τε καὶ τοὺς ἐμποδὼν
γινομένους ἀναιρεῖν. καὶ τὰ μὲν κατὰ τὴν Ἰταλίαν
ἐν τούτοις ἦν.

588 (2) Οὐεσπασιανὸς δὲ ὡς τὰ πλησίον Ἱεροσολύμων καταστρεψάμενος ὑπέστρεψεν εἰς Καισά-

─────────────

a *Cf.* Talmud Bab. *Sukkah* v. 5 (trans. Greenup, S.P.C.K.,
1925) " On the eve of the Sabbath they sounded (the trumpets)
six times in addition [to the 21 daily blasts]—3 to cause the
people to cease from work, and 3 to mark the separation
between the sacred and the secular day " ; the custom is also

one of the priests to stand and to give notice, by sound of trumpet, in the afternoon of the approach, and on the following evening of the close, of every seventh day, announcing to the people the respective hours for ceasing work and for resuming their labours.[a] Along these towers they posted catapults and *ballistae*, together with archers and slingers. Thenceforth Simon's attacks grew less strenuous, as most of his men lost heart ; still by his superiority in numbers he was able to hold his ground, although the missiles from the engines with their longer range killed many of the combatants.

Custom of announcing the Sabbath by sound of trumpet.

(x. 1) About this very time[b] Rome also was beset by heavy calamities. Vitellius had arrived from Germany, dragging in the wake of his army a vast motley crowd besides ; and not finding room enough in the quarters assigned to the troops, he converted the whole of Rome into a camp and filled every house with armed men. These, beholding with unaccustomed eyes the wealth of the Romans and surrounded on every side by the glitter of silver and gold, could scarce restrain their avarice or refrain from plundering right and left and slaughtering any who obstructed them.[c] Such was the condition of affairs in Italy.

Vitellius converts Rome into a camp.

(2) Vespasian,[d] after reducing the whole of the environs of Jerusalem, returned to Caesarea, where

Vespasian is exasperated at the news of the accession of Vitellius.

mentioned in T.B. *Shabbath* 35 b, Talm. Jer. *Shabbath*, xvii. 16 a. [b] Resuming the narrative from § 549.
[c] The entry of Vitellius into Rome is described by Tacitus, *Hist.* ii. 89 (hardly prevented by his friends from marching in arms into Rome as into a captured city); Suetonius, *Vitell.* 11, represents him as entering in arms.
[d] Resuming the narrative from § 555.

ρειαν, ἀκούει τὰς κατὰ τὴν Ῥώμην ταραχὰς καὶ
589 Οὐιτέλλιον αὐτοκράτορα. τοῦτο αὐτόν, καίπερ
ἄρχεσθαι καθάπερ ἄρχειν καλῶς ἐπιστάμενον, εἰς
ἀγανάκτησιν προήγαγεν, καὶ τὸν μὲν ὡς ἐρήμου
καταμανέντα τῆς ἡγεμονίας ἠδόξει δεσπότην,
590 περιαλγήσας δὲ τῷ πάθει καρτερεῖν τὴν βάσανον
οὐχ οἷός τε ἦν καὶ τῆς πατρίδος πορθουμένης
591 ἑτέροις προσευσχολεῖν πολέμοις. ἀλλ' ὅσον ὁ θυμὸς
ἤπειγεν ἐπὶ τὴν ἄμυναν, τοσοῦτον εἶργεν ἔννοια τοῦ
διαστήματος· πολλὰ γὰρ ⟨ἂν⟩[1] φθάσαι πανουργή-
σασαν[2] τὴν τύχην πρὶν αὐτὸν εἰς τὴν Ἰταλίαν
περαιωθῆναι, καὶ ταῦτα χειμῶνος ὥρᾳ πλέοντα,
⟨καὶ⟩[3] σφαδάζουσαν ἤδη κατεῖχεν τὴν ὀργήν.

592 (3) Συνιόντες δὲ οἵ τε ἡγεμόνες καὶ στρατιῶται
καθ' ἑταιρίαν φανερῶς ἤδη μεταβολὴν ἐβουλεύοντο καὶ διαγανακτοῦντες ἐβόων, ὡς οἱ μὲν
ἐπὶ τῆς Ῥώμης στρατιῶται τρυφῶντες καὶ μηδ'
ἀκούειν πολέμου φήμην ὑπομένοντες διαχειρο-
τονοῦσιν οἷς βούλονται τὴν ἡγεμονίαν καὶ πρὸς
ἐλπίδα λημμάτων ἀποδεικνύουσιν αὐτοκράτορας,
593 αὐτοὶ δὲ διὰ τοσούτων κεχωρηκότες πόνων καὶ
γηρῶντες ὑπὸ τοῖς κράνεσιν ἑτέροις χαρίζονται
τὴν ἐξουσίαν, καὶ ταῦτα τὸν ἀξιώτερον ἄρχειν
594 παρ' αὐτοῖς ἔχοντες. ᾧ τίνα δικαιοτέραν ποτὲ
τῆς εἰς αὐτοὺς εὐνοίας ἀποδώσειν ἀμοιβήν, εἰ
τὴν νῦν καταπροοῖντο; τοσούτῳ δ' εἶναι Οὐεσπασιανὸν ἡγεμονεύειν Οὐιτελλίου δικαιότερον, ὅσῳ
595 καὶ αὐτοὺς τῶν ἐκείνον ἀποδειξάντων· οὐ γὰρ
δὴ μικροτέρους τῶν ἀπὸ Γερμανίας διενηνοχέναι

---

[1] ins. Herwerden.
[2] nova facere (=καινουργήσασαν) Lat.: καλλιουργήσασαν L.
[3] ins. Destinon.

he heard of the disturbances in Rome and that
Vitellius was emperor. Though he knew full as well
how to obey as how to command, this news roused
his indignation : he scorned to own as master one
who laid mad hands upon the empire as though it
were forlorn, and such was his agony at this calamity [a]
that he could not endure the torture or, while his
own country was being devastated, devote attention
to other wars. But, much as anger impelled him
to avenge her, the thought of the distance no less
deterred him : for fortune might forestall him
by many a knavish trick before he could cross to
Italy, especially as he must sail in the winter season.
This reflection checked what was now becoming a
paroxysm of wrath.

(3) However, his officers and men, in friendly
gatherings, were already frankly discussing a revolution. " Those soldiers in Rome," they indignantly
exclaimed, " now living in luxury, who cannot bear
to hear even a rumour of war, are electing whom
they choose to the sovereignty and in hope of lucre
creating emperors ; whilst we, who have undergone
such numerous toils and are growing grey beneath
our helmets, are giving up this privilege to others,
when all the time we have among us one more
worthy of the government. What juster return
can we ever render him for his kindness to us, if we
fling away the present opportunity ? Vespasian's
claim to the empire is as far superior to that of
Vitellius, as are we to the electors of that emperor ;
for, surely, we have waged wars no less arduous than

His
indignant
soldiers
take
matters into
their own
hands

---

[a] The phrase, περιαλγήσας τῷ πάθει comes from Thuc.
iv. 14.

πολέμους οὐδὲ τῶν ἐκεῖθεν καταγαγόντων τὸν
596 τύραννον ἡττῆσθαι τοῖς ὅπλοις. ἀγῶνος ἐνδεήσειν
δὲ οὐδέν· οὐ γὰρ τὴν σύγκλητον ἢ τὸν Ῥωμαίων
δῆμον ἀνέξεσθαι τῆς Οὐιτελλίου λαγνείας ἀντὶ τῆς
Οὐεσπασιανοῦ σωφροσύνης, οὐδ' ἀντὶ μὲν ἡγε-
μόνος ἀγαθοῦ τύραννον ὠμότατον, ἄπαιδα[1] δὲ
ἀντὶ πατρὸς αἱρήσεσθαι προστάτην· μέγιστον γὰρ
δὴ πρὸς ἀσφάλειαν εἰρήνης εἶναι τὰς γνησίους
597 τῶν βασιλέων διαδοχάς.[2] εἴτε οὖν ἐμπειρίᾳ γήρως
προσήκει τὸ ἄρχειν, Οὐεσπασιανὸν αὐτοὺς ἔχειν,
εἴτε νεότητος ἀλκῇ, Τίτον· κραθήσεσθαι γὰρ τῆς
598 παρ' ἀμφοῖν ἡλικίας τὸ ὠφέλιμον. χορηγήσειν δ'
οὐ μόνον αὐτοὶ[3] τὴν ἰσχὺν τοῖς ἀποδειχθεῖσι τρία
τάγματα καὶ τὰς παρὰ τῶν βασιλέων συμμαχίας
ἔχοντες, συνεργήσειν δὲ[4] τά τε πρὸς ἔω πάντα καὶ
τῆς Εὐρώπης ὅσα τῶν ἀπὸ Οὐιτελλίου φόβων
κεχώρισται, καὶ τοὺς ἐπὶ τῆς Ἰταλίας δὲ συμμάχους, ἀδελφὸν Οὐεσπασιανοῦ καὶ παῖδα ἕτερον,
599 ὧν τῷ μὲν προσθήσεσθαι πολλοὺς τῶν ἐν ἀξιώματι
νέων, τὸν δὲ καὶ τὴν τῆς πόλεως φυλακὴν πεπιστεῦσθαι, μέρος οὐκ ὀλίγον εἰς ἐπιβολὴν[5] ἡγεμονίας.
600 καθόλου τε ἂν βραδύνωσιν αὐτοί, τάχα τὴν σύγκλητον ἀποδείξειν τὸν ὑπὸ τῶν συγγεγηρακότων[6]
στρατιωτῶν ἀτιμούμενον.
601   (4) Τοιαῦτα κατὰ συστροφὰς οἱ στρατιῶται

---

[1] ed. pr. : παῖδα mss.   [2] Bekker: ὑπεροχάς mss.
[3] αὐτοὺς most mss. (+ τότε VRC): αὐτοῖς L.
[4] συνεργήσειν δὲ M : συνετηρήσαμεν PAL : text doubtful.
[5] L : ἐπιβουλὴν the rest.
[6] Destinon : συντετηρηκότων "joint guardians (of the
empire)" mss.

---

[a] Or, with the ms. text, " is afforded by the sterling
excellences of princes."

332

the legions of Germany, nor are we inferior in arms
to the troops who have thence brought back this
tyrant. Besides, there will be no need for a contest;
for neither senate nor Roman people would tolerate
the lewdness of Vitellius in place of the temperance
of Vespasian, nor prefer as president a most brutal
tyrant to a virtuous ruler, a childless prince to a
father, since the very best security for peace lies
in a legitimate succession to the throne.[a] If, then,
sovereignty calls for the experience of years, we
have Vespasian, if for the vigour of youth, there is
Titus; the pair of them will combine the advantages
of their respective ages. Nor will the persons of our
choice be dependent solely on the strength which
we can supply, mustering as we can three legions [b]
and the auxiliaries furnished by the kings; they will
have the further support of the whole eastern world
and of all in Europe too remote to be intimidated
by Vitellius, as also of our allies in Italy, a brother [c]
and another son [d] of Vespasian. Of these, one will
gain many recruits from the young men of rank,
while the other has actually been entrusted with
the charge of the city—a fact of no small importance
for any designs upon the empire. In short, if there
is any delay on our part, the senate will probably
elect the very man whom his own soldiers, who have
grown grey in his service, have disgracefully
neglected."

(4) Such was the conversation current in military

---

[b] V, X, and XV (*B.* iii. 65).

[c] Flavius Sabinus, who had served with Vespasian in
Britain, been for seven years governor of Moesia, and now
held the important post of *praefectus urbis* in Rome.

[d] Domitian.

διελάλουν· ἔπειτα συναθροισθέντες καὶ παρα-
κροτήσαντες ἀλλήλους ἀναγορεύουσι τὸν Οὐεσπασιανὸν αὐτοκράτορα καὶ σώζειν τὴν κινδυνεύουσαν
602 ἡγεμονίαν παρεκάλουν. ·τῷ δὲ φροντὶς μὲν ἦν
πάλαι περὶ τῶν ὅλων, οὔτι γε μὴν αὐτὸς ἄρχειν
προῄρητο, τοῖς μὲν ἔργοις ἑαυτὸν ἄξιον ἡγούμενος, προκρίνων δὲ τῶν ἐν λαμπρότητι κινδύνων
603 τὴν ἐν ἰδιωτείαις ἀσφάλειαν. ἀρνουμένῳ δὲ μᾶλλον οἱ ἡγεμόνες ἐπέκειντο καὶ περιχυθέντες οἱ
στρατιῶται ξιφήρεις ἀναιρεῖν αὐτὸν ἠπείλουν, εἰ
604 μὴ βούλοιτο ζῆν ἀξίως. πολλὰ δὲ πρὸς αὐτοὺς
διατεινάμενος ἐξ ὧν διωθεῖτο τὴν ἀρχὴν τελευ-
ταῖον, ὡς οὐκ ἔπειθεν, εἴκει τοῖς ὀνομάσασι.
605   (5) Προτρεπομένων δ' αὐτὸν ἤδη Μουκιανοῦ τε
καὶ τῶν ἄλλων ἡγεμόνων ὡς αὐτοκράτορα καὶ
τῆς ἄλλης στρατιᾶς ἄγειν [βοώσης αὐτὴν]¹ ἐπὶ
πᾶν τὸ ἀντίπαλον, ὁ δὲ πρῶτον τῶν ἐπ' Ἀλεξανδρείας εἴχετο πραγμάτων, εἰδὼς πλεῖστον τῆς
ἡγεμονίας μέρος τὴν Αἴγυπτον οὖσαν διὰ τὴν τοῦ
606 σίτου χορηγίαν, ἧς κρατήσας εἰ παρέλκοι καὶ
βίᾳ καθαιρήσειν ἤλπιζεν Οὐιτέλλιον, οὐ γὰρ
ἀνέξεσθαι πείνης ἐπὶ Ῥώμης τὸ πλῆθος, τὰ δύο
τε ἐπὶ τῆς Ἀλεξανδρείας τάγματα προσποιή-
607 σασθαι βουλόμενος. ἐνεθυμεῖτο δὲ καὶ πρόβλημα
τὴν χώραν ἔχειν τῶν ἀπὸ τῆς τύχης ἀδήλων·
ἔστι γὰρ κατά τε γῆν δυσέμβολος καὶ τὰ πρὸς
608 θαλάσσης ἀλίμενος, κατὰ μὲν ἑσπέραν προβεβλη-

---

¹ ins. ed. pr. with some ms. support : om. PAM (probably
through homoioteleuton).

ª Licinus Mucianus, legatus of Syria (§§ 32, 621), shortly
to be sent to Italy to secure the empire for Vespasian (632,

circles ; and then banding together and encouraging and proclaim Vespasian emperor. one another, they proclaimed Vespasian emperor and urged him to save the endangered empire. Their general had long been concerned for the public weal, but had never purposed·his own promotion ; for, though conscious that his career would justify such claim, he preferred the security of private life to the perils of illustrious station. But on his declining, the officers pressed him more insistently and the soldiers, flocking round with drawn swords, threatened him with death, if he refused to live with dignity. After forcibly representing to them his many reasons for rejecting imperial honours, finally, failing to convince them, he yielded to their call.

(5) He was now urged by Mucianus [a] and the Vespasian secures Egypt. other generals to act as emperor, and the rest of the army clamoured to be led against all opponents. His first object, however, was to secure a hold upon Alexandria. He realized the supreme importance of Egypt to the empire as its granary : [b] once master of it he hoped, by persistence,[c] to force Vitellius to surrender, as the populace of Rome would never submit to be starved. He also desired to annex the two legions [d] at Alexandria ; while he further contemplated holding the country as a bulwark against the uncertain freaks of fortune. For Egypt [e] is at Description of Egypt. once difficult of access by land and on its sea-board destitute of harbours. It is protected on the west

654). His mixed character is tersely sketched by Tacitus (*Hist.* i. 10).
  [b] Alexandria supplied corn sufficient to feed Rome for four months of the year (*B.* ii. 386).
  [c] Or perhaps " if (the war) dragged on " ; *cf. A.* xv. 148 εἰ παρέλκειν δέοι.
  [d] III and XXII, ii. 387 note.   [e] *Cf.* ii. 385 f.

μένη τὰ ἄνυδρα τῆς Λιβύης, κατὰ δὲ μεσημβρίαν
τὴν διορίζουσαν ἀπὸ Αἰθιόπων τὴν Συήνην καὶ
τοὺς ἀπλώτους τοῦ ποταμοῦ καταράκτας, ἀπὸ
δὲ τῆς ἀνατολῆς τὴν[1] ἐρυθρὰν θάλασσαν ἀναχεο-
609 μένην μέχρι Κοπτοῦ. βόρειον δὲ τεῖχος αὐτῆς[2] ἥ
τε μέχρι Συρίας γῆ καὶ τὸ καλούμενον Αἰγύπτιον
610 πέλαγος, πᾶν ἄπορον ὅρμων. τετείχισται μὲν
οὕτως ἡ Αἴγυπτος πάντοθεν· τὸ μεταξὺ δὲ Πηλουσίου καὶ Συήνης μῆκος αὐτῆς σταδίων δισχιλίων,
ὅ τε ἀπὸ τῆς Πλινθίνης ἀνάπλους εἰς τὸ Πηλούσιον
611 σταδίων τρισχιλίων ἑξακοσίων. ὁ δὲ Νεῖλος
ἀναπλεῖται μέχρι τῆς Ἐλεφάντων καλουμένης
πόλεως, ὑπὲρ ἣν εἴργουσι προσωτέρω χωρεῖν οὓς
612 προειρήκαμεν καταράκτας. δυσπρόσιτος δὲ λιμὴν
ναυσὶ καὶ κατ' εἰρήνην Ἀλεξανδρείας· στενός τε
γὰρ εἴσπλους καὶ πέτραις ὑφάλοις τὸν ἐπ' εὐθὺ
613 καμπτόμενος δρόμον. καὶ τὸ μὲν ἀριστερὸν αὐτοῦ
μέρος πέφρακται χειροκμήτοις σκέλεσιν, ἐν δεξιᾷ
δὲ ἡ προσαγορευομένη Φάρος νῆσος πρόκειται,
πύργον ἀνέχουσα μέγιστον ἐκπυρσεύοντα τοῖς
καταπλέουσιν ἐπὶ τριακοσίους σταδίους, ὡς ἐν
νυκτὶ πόρρωθεν ὁρμίζοιντο πρὸς τὴν δυσχέρειαν
614 τοῦ κατάπλου. περὶ ταύτην τὴν νῆσον κατα-

---

[1] τὴν Lat.: ἐπὶ τὴν mss.   [2] Niese: αὐτῇ mss.

---

[a] Assuan.
[b] Koft, on the right bank of the Nile, N. of Karnak;
named perhaps as the place where the river most nearly
approaches the sea. The Red Sea, not including the Gulf of
Suez, actually penetrates considerably farther north.
[c] Tell Farama, alias Tineh, situate at or near what was
once the easternmost mouth of the Nile.

by the arid deserts of Libya, on the south by the frontier separating it from Ethiopia—Syene [a] and the unnavigable cataracts of the Nile—, on the east by the Red Sea, which penetrates as far north as Coptus [b]; while its northern barriers are the land towards Syria and the so-called Egyptian sea, totally devoid of havens. Thus is Egypt walled off on every side. Its length from Pelusium [c.] to Syene is two thousand furlongs [d]; the passage from Plinthine [e] to Pelusium is three thousand six hundred.[f] The Nile is navigable up to the city called Elephantine,[g] beyond which the cataracts already mentioned bar further progress. The port [h] of Alexandria is difficult for ships to approach even in peace-time, the entrance being narrow and diverted by submerged rocks [i] which preclude direct passage. On the left the channel is protected by artificial moles; on the right juts out the island called Pharos, supporting an enormous tower, emitting a light visible three hundred furlongs away to mariners making for port, to warn them to anchor at night some distance off because of the difficulty of the navigation. Round this island

The port of Alexandria

Pharos.

---

[d] *i.e.* about 230 miles, a wholly inadequate figure; the actual distance was *c.* 650 miles.

[e] The Libyan frontier of Egypt, on the coast W. of Alexandria; exact site unidentified.

[f] *i.e.* about 414 miles; this figure is nearly double the actual distance of the sea voyage round the Delta basin (*c.* 220 miles). Strabo 791 is nearer the mark in reckoning the distance by sea from Pelusium to Pharos as 1450 stadia (166 miles).

[g] The island below the First Cataract, opposite Assuan.

[h] *i.e.* the Great Harbour. Strabo, xvii. 791 ff., gives a fuller account of the three harbours.

[i] *Cf.* Strabo 791 πρὸς δὲ τῇ στενότητι τοῦ μέταξυ πόρου καὶ πέτραι εἰσὶν αἱ μὲν ὕφαλοι αἱ δὲ καὶ ἐξέχουσαι.

βέβληται χειροποίητα τείχη μέγιστα, προσαρασ-
σόμενον δὲ τούτοις τὸ πέλαγος καὶ τοῖς ἄντικρυς
ἔρκεσιν ἀμφηγνυμένον[1] ἐκτραχύνει τὸν πόρον καὶ
σφαλερὰν διὰ στενοῦ τὴν εἴσοδον ἀπεργάζεται.
615 ὁ μέντοι γε λιμὴν ἀσφαλέστατος ἔνδον καὶ τριάκοντα σταδίων τὸ μέγεθος, εἰς ὃν τά τε λείποντα
τῇ χώρᾳ πρὸς εὐδαιμονίαν κατάγεται καὶ τὰ
περισσεύοντα τῶν ἐπιχωρίων ἀγαθῶν εἰς πᾶσαν
χωρίζεται[2] τὴν οἰκουμένην.
616 (6) Ἐφίετο μὲν οὖν εἰκότως τῶν ταύτῃ πραγμάτων Οὐεσπασιανὸς εἰς βεβαίωσιν τῆς ὅλης
ἡγεμονίας, ἐπιστέλλει δ' εὐθὺς τῷ διέποντι τὴν
Αἴγυπτον καὶ τὴν Ἀλεξάνδρειαν Τιβερίῳ Ἀλε-
ξάνδρῳ, δηλῶν τὸ τῆς στρατιᾶς πρόθυμον, καὶ
ὡς αὐτὸς ὑποδὺς ἀναγκαίως τὸ βάρος τῆς ἡγεμονίας συνεργὸν αὐτὸν καὶ βοηθὸν προσλαμβάνοι.
617 παραναγνοὺς δὲ τὴν ἐπιστολὴν Ἀλέξανδρος προθύμως τά τε τάγματα καὶ τὸ πλῆθος εἰς αὐτὸν
ὥρκωσεν. ἑκάτεροι δ' ἀσμένως ὑπήκουσαν τὴν
ἀρετὴν τἀνδρὸς ἐκ τῆς ἐγγὺς στρατηγίας εἰδότες.
618 καὶ ὁ μὲν πεπιστευμένος ἤδη τὰ περὶ τὴν ἀρχὴν
προπαρεσκεύαζεν αὐτῷ καὶ τὰ πρὸς τὴν ἄφιξιν,
τάχιον δ' ἐπινοίας διήγγελλον αἱ φῆμαι τὸν ἐπὶ
τῆς ἀνατολῆς αὐτοκράτορα, καὶ πᾶσα μὲν πόλις
ἑώρταζεν εὐαγγέλια [δὲ] καὶ θυσίας ὑπὲρ αὐτοῦ
619 ἐπετέλει. τὰ δὲ κατὰ Μυσίαν καὶ Παννονίαν

---

[1] Niese: ἀφικνύμενον, ἀφικν(ο)ύμενον MSS.
[2] PA: μεριζόμενα L: μερίζεται the rest.

---

[a] The Great Harbour seems to have been only half this
length. The figure named (=c. 3½ miles) can barely be
reached by including the Eunostus Harbour ; the two were
originally separated by the causeway called the Hepta-
stadion, but this had perhaps now disappeared (Strabo 792).

immense walls have been reared by human hands;
and the sea dashing against these and breaking
around the piers opposite renders the passage rough
and ingress through the strait perilous. The harbour inside is, however, perfectly safe and is thirty
furlongs [a] in length. To this port are carried all the
commodities which the country lacks for its welfare,
and from it the surplus local products are distributed
to every quarter of the world.[b]

(6) With good reason therefore was Vespasian
eager to obtain control here, with a view to the
stability of the empire at large. He accordingly at
once wrote to Tiberius Alexander,[c] the governor of
Egypt and Alexandria, informing him of the army's
zeal and how, being forced to shoulder the burden
of empire himself, he desired to enlist his co-opera-
tion and assistance. Having read this letter in public,
Alexander promptly required the legions and the
populace to take the oath of allegiance to Vespasian;
a call to which they both gladly responded, knowing
the sterling quality of the man from his generalship
in their neighbourhood. Tiberius, now having the
interests of the empire entrusted to his charge, made
all preparations for Vespasian's arrival; and quicker
than thought rumour spread the news of the new
emperor in the east. Every city kept festival for
the good news and offered sacrifices on his behalf;
but the legions in Moesia and Pannonia,[d] recently

Tiberius Alexander secures Alexandria for Vespasian.

General acclamation at Vespasian's accession.

[b] Strabo 798 calls Alexandria μέγιστον ἐμπόριον τῆς οἰκουμένης and speaks of the precious wares of which she καὶ
ὑποδοχεῖόν ἐστι καὶ χορηγεῖ τοῖς ἐκτός.

[c] B. ii. 220 note (summarizing his varied career).

[d] The provinces on the south bank of the Danube: Moesia
covering the eastern portion (Serbia and Bulgaria), Pannonia
the western (Austrian and neighbouring territory).

τάγματα, μικρῷ πρόσθεν κεκινημένα πρὸς τὴν
Οὐιτελλίου τόλμαν, μείζονι χαρᾷ Οὐεσπασιανῷ
620 τὴν ἡγεμονίαν ὤμνυον. ὁ δ' ἀναζεύξας ἀπὸ
Καισαρείας εἰς Βηρυτὸν παρῆν, ἔνθα πολλαὶ μὲν
ἀπὸ τῆς Συρίας αὐτῷ, πολλαὶ δὲ κἀπὸ τῶν ἄλλων
ἐπαρχιῶν πρεσβεῖαι συνήντων, στεφάνους παρ'
ἑκάστης πόλεως καὶ συγχαρτικὰ προσφέρουσαι
621 ψηφίσματα. παρῆν δὲ καὶ Μουκιανὸς ὁ τῆς
ἐπαρχίας ἡγεμών, τὸ πρόθυμον τῶν δήμων καὶ
τοὺς κατὰ πόλιν ὅρκους ἀπαγγέλλων.

622 (7) Προχωρούσης δὲ πανταχοῦ κατὰ νοῦν τῆς
τύχης καὶ τῶν πραγμάτων συννενευκότων ἐκ τοῦ
πλείστου μέρους, ἤδη παρίστατο τῷ Οὐεσπασιανῷ
νοεῖν, ὡς οὐ δίχα δαιμονίου προνοίας ἅψαιτο τῆς
ἀρχῆς, ἀλλὰ δικαία τις εἱμαρμένη περιαγάγοι τὸ
623 κρατεῖν τῶν ὅλων ἐπ' αὐτόν· ἀναμιμνήσκεται
γὰρ τά τε ἄλλα σημεῖα, πολλὰ δ' αὐτῷ γε-
γόνει πανταχοῦ προφαίνοντα τὴν ἡγεμονίαν, καὶ
τὰς τοῦ Ἰωσήπου φωνάς, ὃς αὐτὸν ἔτι ζῶντος
624 Νέρωνος αὐτοκράτορα προσειπεῖν ἐθάρσησεν. ἐξ-
επέπληκτο δὲ τὸν ἄνδρα δεσμώτην ἔτι ὄντα παρ'
αὐτῷ, καὶ προσκαλεσάμενος Μουκιανὸν ἅμα τοῖς
ἄλλοις ἡγεμόσι καὶ φίλοις πρῶτον μὲν αὐτοῦ τὸ
δραστήριον ἐκδιηγεῖτο καὶ ὅσα περὶ[1] τοῖς Ἰωτα-
625 πάτοις δι' αὐτὸν ἔκαμον, ἔπειτα τὰς μαντείας, ἃς
αὐτὸς μὲν ὑπώπτευσε τότε πλάσματα τοῦ δέους,
ἀποδειχθῆναι δὲ ὑπὸ τοῦ χρόνου καὶ τῶν πραγ-
626 μάτων θείας. "αἰσχρὸν οὖν," ἔφη, "τὸν προ-

[1] L: in Lat.: om. the rest.

[a] Tacitus, Hist. ii. 85 f. The legions in Moesia were

exasperated by the audacity of Vitellius, more gladly than any swore allegiance to Vespasian.[a] The latter, leaving Caesarea, proceeded to Berytus,[b] where numerous embassies, both from Syria and from the other provinces, waited upon him, bringing crowns and congratulatory decrees from the various cities. Thither too came Mucianus, the governor of the province, to report the popular enthusiasm and that every city had taken the oath.

(7) Now that fortune was everywhere furthering his wishes and that circumstances had for the most part conspired in his favour, Vespasian was led to think that divine providence had assisted him to grasp the empire and that some just destiny had placed the sovereignty of the world within his hands. Among many other omens,[c] which had everywhere foreshadowed his imperial honours, he recalled the words of Josephus, who had ventured, even in Nero's lifetime, to address him as emperor.[d] He was shocked to think that the man was still a prisoner in his hands, and summoning Mucianus with his other officers and friends, he first dwelt upon his doughty deeds and all the trouble that he had given them at Jotapata ; and then referred to his predictions, which at the time he himself had suspected of being fabrications prompted by fear, but which time and the event had proved to be divine. " It is disgraceful," he

Liberation of Josephus from bonds.

III Gallica (see § 633), VII Claudia, and VIII Augusta ; those in Pannonia, VII Galbiana and XIII Gemina.

[b] *Beirut.*

[c] Various *omina imperii* are mentioned by Tacitus (*Hist.* ii. 78), Suetonius (*Vesp.* 5), and Dio Cassius (lxvi. 1). The two last authorities include the prophecy of Josephus ; Weber, *Josephus and Vespasian* 45, believes that they drew upon some common source. *Cf. B.* iii. 404 n.   [d] iii. 401.

θεσπίσαντά μοι τὴν ἀρχὴν καὶ διάκονον τῆς τοῦ
θεοῦ φωνῆς ἔτι αἰχμαλώτου τάξιν ἢ δεσμώτου
τύχην ὑπομένειν," καὶ καλέσας τὸν Ἰώσηπον
627 λυθῆναι κελεύει. τοῖς μὲν οὖν ἡγεμόσιν ἐκ τῆς
εἰς τὸν ἀλλόφυλον ἀμοιβῆς λαμπρὰ καὶ περὶ
αὐτῶν ἐλπίζειν παρέστη, συνὼν δὲ τῷ πατρὶ
628 Τίτος " δίκαιον, ὦ πάτερ," ἔφη, " τοῦ Ἰωσήπου
καὶ τὸ ὄνειδος ἀφαιρεθῆναι σὺν τῷ σιδήρῳ·
γενήσεται γὰρ ὅμοιος τῷ μὴ δεθέντι τὴν ἀρχήν,
ἂν αὐτοῦ μὴ λύσωμεν ἀλλὰ κόψωμεν τὰ δεσμά."
τοῦτο γὰρ ἐπὶ τῶν μὴ δεόντως δεθέντων πράτ-
629 τεται. συνεδόκει ταῦτα, καὶ παρελθών τις πε-
λέκει διέκοψε τὴν ἄλυσιν. ὁ δὲ Ἰώσηπος εἰληφὼς
ὑπὲρ[1] τῶν προειρημένων γέρας τὴν ἐπιτιμίαν ἤδη
καὶ περὶ τῶν μελλόντων ἀξιόπιστος ἦν.

630 (xi. 1) Οὐεσπασιανὸς δὲ ταῖς πρεσβείαις χρη-
ματίσας καὶ καταστησάμενος ἑκάστοις τὰς ἀρχὰς
δικαίως καὶ διὰ τῶν ἀξίων, εἰς Ἀντιόχειαν
631 ἀφικνεῖται. καὶ βουλευόμενος ποῖ τρέπεσθαι,
προυργιαίτερα τῆς εἰς Ἀλεξάνδρειαν ὁρμῆς τὰ
κατὰ τὴν Ῥώμην ἔκρινε, τὴν μὲν βέβαιον οὖσαν
632 ὁρῶν, τὰ δ' ὑπὸ Οὐιτελλίου ταρασσόμενα. πέμπει δὴ Μουκιανὸν εἰς τὴν Ἰταλίαν παραδοὺς
ἱππέων τε καὶ πεζῶν συχνὴν δύναμιν. ὁ δὲ διὰ
τὴν τοῦ χειμῶνος ἀκμὴν δείσας τὸ πλεῖν[2] πεζῇ
τὴν στρατιὰν ἦγε διὰ Καππαδοκίας καὶ Φρυγίας.
633 (2) Ἐν δὲ τούτῳ καὶ Ἀντώνιος Πρῖμος ἀναλαβὼν τὸ τρίτον τάγμα τῶν κατὰ Μυσίαν, ἔτυχεν

---

[1] Niese: περί mss.   [2] Hudson from Lat.: πᾶν mss.

---

[a] Mucianus went ahead with some light-armed troops,
being followed by the 6th legion (Ferrata) and 13,000 veterans
(vexillarii), Tac. Hist. ii. 83.

said, " that one who foretold my elevation to power
and was a minister of the voice of God should still
rank as a captive and endure a prisoner's fate " ;
and calling for Josephus, he ordered him to be
liberated. While the officers were only thinking that
such requital of a foreigner augured brilliant honours
for themselves, Titus, who was beside his father,
said, " Justice demands, father, that Josephus should
lose his disgrace along with his fetters. If instead
of loosing, we sever his chains, he will be as though
he had never been in bonds at all." For such is the
practice in cases where a man has been unjustly put
in irons. Vespasian approving, an attendant came
forward and severed the chain with an axe. Thus
Josephus won his enfranchisement as the reward of
his divination, and his power of insight into the future
was no longer discredited.

(xi. 1) Vespasian, having responded to the embassies and disposed of the various governorships
with due regard to the claims of justice and the
merits of the candidates, repaired to Antioch. Here
deliberating in which direction to turn, he decided that
affairs in Rome were more important than a march
to Alexandria, seeing that the latter was secured,
whereas at Rome Vitellius was creating general
disorder. He accordingly dispatched Mucianus
to Italy with a substantial force of cavalry and infantry ; [a] that officer, fearing the risk of a sea voyage
in the depth of winter, led his army by land through
Cappadocia and Phrygia.[b]

(2) Meanwhile Antonius Primus, along with the
third legion from Moesia, where he was then in

Vespasian sends Mucianus with an army to Italy.

---

[b] Ordering the fleet from Pontus to concentrate at Byzan-
tium, Tac. *ibid.*

δ' ἡγεμονεύων αὐτόθι, Οὐιτελλίῳ παραταξόμενος
634 ἠπείγετο. Οὐιτέλλιος δ' αὐτῷ συναντήσοντα μετὰ
πολλῆς δυνάμεως Καικίναν¹ 'Αλιηνὸν ἐκπέμπει,
μέγα θαρρῶν τἀνδρὶ διὰ τὴν ἐπ' 'Όθωνι νίκην.
ὁ δὲ ἀπὸ τῆς 'Ρώμης ἐλαύνων διὰ τάχους περὶ
Κρέμωνα τῆς Γαλατίας τὸν 'Αντώνιον καταλαμ-
βάνει· μεθόριος δ' ἐστὶν ἡ πόλις αὕτη τῆς
635 'Ιταλίας. κατιδὼν δ' ἐνταῦθα τὸ πλῆθος τῶν
πολεμίων καὶ τὴν εὐταξίαν, συμβαλεῖν μὲν οὐκ
ἐθάρρει, σφαλερὰν δὲ τὴν ἀναχώρησιν λογιζό-
636 μενος προδοσίαν ἐβουλεύετο. συναγαγὼν δὲ τοὺς
ὑφ' αὑτὸν ἑκατοντάρχας καὶ χιλιάρχους ἐνῆγεν
μεταβῆναι πρὸς τὸν 'Αντώνιον, ταπεινῶν μὲν τὰ
Οὐιτελλίου πράγματα, τὴν Οὐεσπασιανοῦ δ' ἰσχὺν
637 ἐπαίρων, καὶ παρ' ᾧ μὲν εἶναι λέγων μόνον τῆς
ἀρχῆς ὄνομα, παρ' ᾧ δὲ τὴν δύναμιν, καὶ αὐτοὺς
δὲ ἄμεινον [εἶναι]² προλαβόντας τὴν ἀνάγκην
ποιῆσαι χάριν καὶ μέλλοντας ἡττᾶσθαι τοῖς ὅπλοις
638 ταῖς γνώμαις τὸν κίνδυνον φθάσαι· Οὐεσπασιανὸν
μὲν γὰρ ἱκανὸν εἶναι καὶ χωρὶς αὐτῶν προσκτή-
σασθαι³ καὶ τὰ λείποντα, Οὐιτέλλιον δ' οὐδὲ σὺν
αὐτοῖς τηρῆσαι τὰ ὄντα.
639 (3) Πολλὰ τοιαῦτα λέγων ἔπεισε καὶ πρὸς τὸν
640 'Αντώνιον αὐτομολεῖ μετὰ τῆς δυνάμεως. τῆς δ'
αὐτῆς νυκτὸς ἐμπίπτει μετάνοια τοῖς στρατιώταις
καὶ δέος τοῦ προπέμψαντος, εἰ κρείσσων γένοιτο·

---

¹ C Lat. Heg. : Κικίλ(λ)ιον the rest.
² ins. L (Lat. ?): om. the rest.
³ Dindorf: προκτήσασθαι L : προσθήσεσθαι the rest.

ᵃ M. Antonius Primus, in the sequel a rival of Mucianus,

command,[a] was also hastening to give battle to Vitellius ; and Vitellius had sent off Caecina Alienus with a strong force to oppose him, having great confidence in that general on account of his victory over Otho.[b] Caecina marching rapidly from Rome met Antonius near Cremona, a town in Gaul [c] on the frontiers of Italy ; but there, perceiving the numbers and discipline of the enemy, he would not venture on an engagement and, considering retreat hazardous, meditated treason.[d] Accordingly assembling the centurions and tribunes under his command, he urged them to go over to Antonius, disparaging the resources of Vitellius and extolling the strength of Vespasian.[e] " The one," he said, " has but the name, the other the power of sovereignty ; and it were better for you to forestall and make a virtue of necessity, and, as you are bound to be beaten in the field, to avert danger by policy. For Vespasian is capable, without your aid, of acquiring what he has yet to win ; while Vitellius, even with your support, cannot retain what he has already."

(3) Caecina's words, prolonged in the same strain, prevailed, and he and his army deserted to Antonius. But the same night the soldiers were overcome with remorse and fear of him who had sent them into the field, should he prove victorious ; and drawing their

Marginal notes: Antonius Primus leads another army from Moesia against Vitellius. Caecina, general of Vitellius, goes over to Antonius.

was now in command of the 7th legion (Galbiana ; Tac. *Hist.* ii. 86), in Pannonia, not in Moesia, as Josephus states ; but he was joined by the Moesian legions, the third (Gallica) taking the lead in revolt : " tertia legio exemplum ceteris Moesiae legionibus praebuit " (Tac. *H.* ii. 85).

[b] § 547.

[c] *i.e.* Gallia Cisalpina, Italy N. of the Po.

[d] Tacitus gives a fuller account, *Hist.* ii. 99, iii. 13 ff.

[e] " Vespasiani virtutem viresque partium extollit . . . atque omnia de Vitellio in deterius " (Tac. *Hist.* iii. 13).

σπασάμενοι δὲ τὰ ξίφη τὸν Καικίναν[1] ὥρμησαν
ἀνελεῖν, κἂν ἐπράχθη τὸ ἔργον αὐτοῖς, εἰ μὴ
προσπίπτοντες οἱ χιλίαρχοι καθικέτευσαν ἑκά-
641 στους.[2] οἱ δὲ τοῦ μὲν κτείνειν ἀπέσχοντο, δήσαντες
δὲ τὸν προδότην οἷοί τε ἦσαν ἀναπέμπειν[3] Οὐιτελλίῳ. ταῦτ' ἀκούσας ὁ Πρῖμος αὐτίκα τοὺς
σφετέρους ἀνίστησι καὶ μετὰ τῶν ὅπλων ἦγεν
642 ἐπὶ τοὺς ἀποστάντας. οἱ δὲ παραταξάμενοι πρὸς
ὀλίγον μὲν ἀντέσχον, αὖθις δὲ τραπέντες ἔφευγον
εἰς τὴν Κρέμωνα. τοὺς δὲ ἱππεῖς ἀναλαβὼν
Πρῖμος ὑποτέμνεται τὰς εἰσόδους αὐτῶν, καὶ τὸ
μὲν πολὺ πλῆθος κυκλωσάμενος πρὸ τῆς πόλεως
διαφθείρει, τῷ δὲ λοιπῷ συνεισπεσὼν διαρπάσαι
643 τὸ ἄστυ τοῖς στρατιώταις ἐφῆκεν. ἔνθα δὴ
πολλοὶ μὲν τῶν ξένων ἔμποροι, πολλοὶ δὲ τῶν
ἐπιχωρίων ἀπώλοντο, πᾶσα δὲ [καὶ] ἡ Οὐιτελλίου
στρατιά, μυριάδες ἀνδρῶν τρεῖς καὶ διακόσιοι·
τῶν δ' ἀπὸ τῆς Μυσίας Ἀντώνιος τετρακισχι-
644 λίους ἀποβάλλει καὶ πεντακοσίους. λύσας δὲ τὸν
Καικίναν πέμπει πρὸς Οὐεσπασιανὸν ἀγγελοῦντα
τὰ πεπραγμένα. καὶ ὃς ἐλθὼν ἀπεδέχθη τε ὑπ'
αὐτοῦ καὶ τὰ τῆς προδοσίας ὀνείδη ταῖς παρ'
ἐλπίδα τιμαῖς ἐπεκάλυψεν.

645 (4) Ἀνεθάρσει δὲ ἤδη καὶ κατὰ τὴν Ῥώμην
Σαβῖνος, ὡς πλησίον Ἀντώνιος ὢν ἀπηγγέλλετο,

---

[1] Lat. Heg.: Κικίλ(λ)ιον mss.
[2] L: αὐτοῖς or αὐτούς the rest.
[3] L: πέμπειν (πέμψειν) the rest.

swords they rushed off to kill Caecina and would have accomplished their purpose, had not the tribunes thrown themselves at the feet of their companies and implored them to desist.[a] The troops spared his life but bound the traitor and prepared to send him up to Vitellius. Primus, hearing of this, instantly called up his men and led them in arms against the rebels ; these forming in line of battle offered a brief resistance, but were then routed and fled for Cremona. Primus with his cavalry intercepted their entrance, surrounded and destroyed the greater part of them before the walls, and, forcing his way in with the remainder, permitted his soldiers to pillage the town. In the ensuing slaughter many foreign merchants [b] and many of the inhabitants perished, along with the whole army of Vitellius, numbering thirty thousand two hundred men ; of his troops from Moesia Antonius lost four thousand five hundred. Caecina, being liberated by him and sent to report these events to Vespasian, was on his arrival graciously received by the emperor, and covered the disgrace of his perfidy with unlooked for honours.

Antonius cuts the Vitellian army to pieces.

(4) In Rome, too, Sabinus [c] now regained courage on hearing of the approach of Antonius, and, muster-

Fights for the Capitol.

---

[a] Details not in Tacitus, who merely states that the soldiers bound Caecina and elected other leaders (*Hist.* iii. 14).

[b] " The occurrence of a fair (*tempus mercatus*) filled the colony, rich as it always was, with the appearance of still greater wealth " ; the sack of the town occupied four days (Tac. *Hist.* iii. 32 f.).

[c] § 598 note. The full story is told in Tacitus, *Hist.* iii. 64 ff. Sabinus attempted to negotiate conditions with Vitellius, who was prepared to abdicate ; but the Vitellianists prevented this, and a collision between them and the followers of Sabinus drove the latter to seek refuge in the temple of Jupiter on the Capitol.

347

καὶ συναθροίσας τὰ τῶν νυκτοφυλάκων στρατιωτῶν τάγματα νύκτωρ καταλαμβάνει τὸ Καπε-
646 τώλιον. μεθ' ἡμέραν δ' αὐτῷ πολλοὶ τῶν ἐπισήμων προσεγένοντο καὶ Δομετιανὸς ὁ τἀδελφοῦ
παῖς, μεγίστη μοῖρα τῶν εἰς τὸ κρατεῖν ἐλπίδων.
647 Οὐιτελλίῳ δὲ Πρίμου μὲν ἐλάττων φροντὶς ἦν,
τεθύμωτο[1] δ' ἐπὶ τοὺς συναποστάντας τῷ Σαβίνῳ,
καὶ διὰ τὴν ἔμφυτον ὠμότητα διψῶν αἵματος
εὐγενοῦς τοῦ στρατιωτικοῦ τὴν συγκατελθοῦσαν
648 αὐτῷ δύναμιν ἐπαφίησι τῷ Καπετωλίῳ. πολλὰ
μὲν οὖν ἔκ τε ταύτης καὶ τῶν ἀπὸ τοῦ ἱεροῦ
μαχομένων ἐτολμήθη, τέλος δὲ τῷ πλήθει περι-
όντες οἱ ἀπὸ τῆς Γερμανίας ἐκράτησαν τοῦ λόφου.
649 καὶ Δομετιανὸς μὲν[2] σὺν πολλοῖς τῶν ἐν τέλει
Ῥωμαίων δαιμονιώτερον διασώζεται, τὸ δὲ λοιπὸν
πλῆθος ἅπαν κατεκόπη, καὶ Σαβῖνος ἀναχθεὶς
ἐπὶ Οὐιτέλλιον ἀναιρεῖται, διαρπάσαντές τε οἱ
στρατιῶται τὰ ἀναθήματα τὸν ναὸν ἐνέπρησαν.
650 καὶ μετὰ μίαν ἡμέραν εἰσελαύνει μὲν Ἀντώνιος
μετὰ τῆς δυνάμεως, ὑπήντων δ' οἱ Οὐιτελλίου καὶ
τριχῇ κατὰ τὴν πόλιν συμβαλόντες ἀπώλοντο
651 πάντες. προέρχεται[3] δὲ μεθύων ἐκ τοῦ βασιλείου
Οὐιτέλλιος καὶ δαψιλέστερον ὥσπερ ἐν ἐσχάτοις
652 τῆς ἀσώτου τραπέζης κεκορεσμένος. συρεὶς δὲ

[1] τεθυμωμένος L Lat.   [2] Bekker with Lat.: δὲ mss.
[3] rapitur Heg.: hence προέλκεται Destinon (cf. Tacitus,
Hist. iii. 84).

---

[a] "vigilum cohortes" (Tac. Hist. iii. 64). Seven corps of
night police had been instituted by Augustus "adversus
incendia," a sort of fire-brigade (Suet. Aug. 30, Dio Cass.
lv. 26).

ing the cohorts of the night-watch,[a] seized the Capitol 18 December
during the night. Early next day [b] he was joined A.D. 69
by many of the notables, including his nephew 19 December
Domitian, on whom mainly rested their hopes of
success. Vitellius, less concerned about Primus, was
infuriated at the rebels who had supported Sabinus,
and, from innate cruelty thirsting for noble blood,
let loose upon the Capitol that division of his army
which had accompanied him (from Germany).[c] Many
a gallant deed was done alike by them and by those
who fought them from the temple ; but at length
by superior numbers the German troops mastered
the hill. Domitian, with many eminent Romans,
miraculously escaped ; [d] but the rank and file were
all cut to pieces, Sabinus was brought a prisoner to
Vitellius and executed, and the soldiers after plunder-
ing the temple of its votive offerings set it on fire.
A day later Antonius marched in with his army ; he Antonius
was met by the troops of Vitellius, who gave battle enters
at three different quarters of the city [e] and perished 20 Dec.
to a man.[f] Then issued from the palace Vitellius The end of
drunk and, knowing the end was come, gorged with Vitellius.
a banquet more lavish and luxurious than ever ;

<hr>

[b] " At dead of night " (*concubia nocte*), Sabinus, owing to the careless watch of the Vitellianists and a rain storm, was enabled to bring in his own children and Domitian and to communicate with his followers (Tac. *H.* iii. 69).

[c] According to the fuller account of Tacitus (*H.* iii. 70 f.) the soldiers acted without orders from Vitellius, now " neque jubendi neque vetandi potens."

[d] Domitian disguised as an acolyte, *ib.* 74.

[e] The forces of Antonius advanced in three divisions : along the Via Flaminia, along the Via Salaria to the Colline Gate, and along the bank of the Tiber (Tac. *H.* iii. 82).

[f] " cecidere omnes contrariis vulneribus, versi in hostem " Tac. *H.* iii. 84.

διὰ τοῦ πλήθους καὶ παντοδαπαῖς αἰκίαις ἐξ-
υβρισθεὶς ἐπὶ μέσης τῆς Ῥώμης ἀποσφάττεται,
μῆνας ὀκτὼ κρατήσας καὶ ἡμέρας πέντε, ὃν εἰ
συνέβη πλείω βιῶσαι χρόνον, ἐπιλιπεῖν ἂν αὐτοῦ
653 τῇ λαγνείᾳ τὴν ἡγεμονίαν οἶμαι. τῶν δ' ἄλλων
654 νεκρῶν ὑπὲρ πέντε μυριάδας[1] ἠριθμήθησαν. ταῦτα
μὲν τρίτῃ μηνὸς Ἀπελλαίου πέπρακτο, τῇ δ'
ὑστεραίᾳ Μουκιανὸς εἴσεισι μετὰ τῆς στρατιᾶς,
καὶ τοὺς σὺν Ἀντωνίῳ παύσας τοῦ κτείνειν, ἔτι
γὰρ ἐξερευνώμενοι τὰς οἰκίας πολλοὺς μὲν τῶν
Οὐιτελλίου στρατιωτῶν πολλοὺς δὲ τῶν δημοτικῶν
ὡς ἐκείνου ἀνήρουν, φθάνοντες τῷ θυμῷ τὴν
ἀκριβῆ διάκρισιν, προαγαγὼν δὲ τὸν Δομετιανὸν
συνίστησι τῷ πλήθει μέχρι τῆς τοῦ πατρὸς
655 ἀφίξεως ἡγεμόνα. ὁ δὲ δῆμος ἀπηλλαγμένος ἤδη
τῶν φόβων αὐτοκράτορα Οὐεσπασιανὸν εὐφήμει,
καὶ ἅμα τήν τε τούτου βεβαίωσιν ἑώρταζε καὶ
τὴν Οὐιτελλίου κατάλυσιν.

656   (5) Εἰς δὲ τὴν Ἀλεξάνδρειαν ἀφιγμένῳ τῷ
Οὐεσπασιανῷ τὰ ἀπὸ τῆς Ῥώμης εὐαγγέλια ἧκε
καὶ πρέσβεις ἐκ πάσης τῆς ἰδίας οἰκουμένης
συνηδόμενοι· μεγίστη τε οὖσα μετὰ τὴν Ῥώμην
657 ἡ πόλις στενοτέρα[2] τοῦ πλήθους ἠλέγχετο. κε-
κυρωμένης δὲ ἤδη τῆς ἀρχῆς ἁπάσης καὶ σεσω-
σμένων παρ' ἐλπίδα Ῥωμαίοις τῶν πραγμάτων
Οὐεσπασιανὸς ἐπὶ τὰ λείψανα τῆς Ἰουδαίας τὸν
658 λογισμὸν ἐπέστρεφεν. αὐτὸς μέντοι [γε][3] εἰς τὴν

[1] μυριάδες PML.   [2] + τότε L.
[3] ins. L: om. the rest.

_a_ He was haled from hiding in the palace, after attempting
escape, to the Gemonian stairs, where he was slain, the corpse
being then dragged to the Tiber (Tac. iii. 84 f., Suet.
Vitell. 17).

dragged through the mob and subjected to indig-
nities of every kind, he was finally butchered in the
heart of Rome.[a] He had reigned eight months and
five days ;[b] and had fate prolonged his life, the very
empire, I imagine, would not have sufficed for his
lust. Of others slain, upwards of fifty thousand
were counted. These events took place on the third
of the month Apellaeus. On the following day
Mucianus entered with his army and restrained the
troops of Antonius from further slaughter ; for they
were still searching the houses and massacring large
numbers, not only of the soldiers of Vitellius, but
of the populace, as his partisans, too precipitate in
their rage for careful discrimination.[c] Mucianus
then brought forward Domitian and recommended
him to the multitude as their ruler pending his
father's arrival. The people, freed at length from
terrors, acclaimed Vespasian emperor, and celebrated
with one common festival both his establishment in
power and the overthrow of Vitellius.

(5) On reaching Alexandria Vespasian was greeted
by the good news from Rome and by embassies of
congratulation from every quarter of the world,[d] now
his own ; and that city, though second only to Rome
in magnitude, proved too confined for the throng.
The whole empire being now secured and the Roman
state saved beyond expectation, Vespasian turned
his thoughts to what remained in Judaea. He was,
however, anxious himself to take ship for Rome [e] as

(marginal notes:) (20 or 21) Dec. Mucianus enters Rome.

Domitian acting ruler.

Vespasian at Alexandria

---

[b] From 17 April to 21 (or 20) December.

[c] Cf. Tac. Hist. iv. 1, 11.

[d] Including one from King Vologesus, offering him 40,000
Parthian cavalry (Tac. Hist. iv. 51).

[e] He had received unfavourable reports of Domitian's
conduct, ibid.

Ῥώμην ὥρμητο λήξαντος τοῦ χειμῶνος ἀνάγεσθαι
καὶ τάχος τὰ κατὰ τὴν Ἀλεξάνδρειαν διώκει,
τὸν δὲ υἱὸν Τίτον μετὰ τῆς ἐκκρίτου δυνάμεως
659 ἀπέστειλεν ἐξαιρήσοντα τὰ Ἱεροσόλυμα. ὁ δὲ
προελθὼν πεζῇ μέχρι Νικοπόλεως, εἴκοσι δ' αὕτη
διέχει τῆς Ἀλεξανδρείας σταδίους, κἀκεῖθεν ἐπιβήσας τὴν στρατιὰν μακρῶν πλοίων ἀναπλεῖ διὰ
τοῦ Νείλου κατὰ[1] τὸν Μενδήσιον νομὸν μέχρι
660 πόλεως Θμούεως. ἐκεῖθεν δ' ἀποβὰς ὁδεύει καὶ
κατὰ πολίχνην [τινὰ][2] Τάνιν αὐλίζεται. δεύτερος
αὐτῷ σταθμὸς Ἡρακλέους πόλις καὶ τρίτος
661 Πηλούσιον γίνεται. δυσὶ δ' ἡμέραις [ἐνταῦθα][3]
τὴν στρατιὰν ἀναλαβὼν τῇ τρίτῃ διέξεισι τὰς
ἐμβολὰς τοῦ Πηλουσίου, καὶ προελθὼν σταθμὸν
ἕνα διὰ τῆς ἐρήμου πρὸς τῷ τοῦ Κασίου[4] Διὸς
ἱερῷ στρατοπεδεύεται, τῇ δ' ὑστεραίᾳ κατὰ τὴν
Ὀστρακίνην· οὗτος ὁ σταθμὸς ἦν ἄνυδρος, ἐπ-
662 εισάκτοις δὲ ὕδασιν οἱ ἐπιχώριοι χρῶνται. μετὰ
ταῦτα πρὸς Ῥινοκορούροις ἀναπαύεται, κἀκεῖθεν

---

[1] L: μετὰ the rest.   [2] om. PA Lat.
[3] om. L.   [4] LC¹: Κασσίου the rest.

[a] Founded by Augustus in 24 B.C. on the scene of his final
defeat of M. Antonius and in commemoration of the surrender of Alexandria ; it lay on the coast some 2½ (Josephus)
or 3½ (Strabo) miles E. of that city (Strabo xvii. 795, Dio
Cass. li. 18).

[b] " Thirty " according to Strabo.

[c] Or " up and across " (διὰ τοῦ Νείλου, not ἀνὰ τὸν Νεῖλον);
he was crossing the Delta and part of the route would be by
canal.

[d] Or " over against."

soon as the winter was over and was now rapidly
settling affairs in Alexandria ; but he dispatched his _{sends Titus}
son Titus with picked forces to crush Jerusalem. _{against
Jerusalem.}
Titus, accordingly, proceeding by land to Nicopolis ^a
(distant twenty ^b furlongs from Alexandria), there _{Itinerary of
march of}
embarked his army on ships of war and sailed up ^c _{Titus from}
the Nile into ^d the Mendesian canton ^e to the city _{Alexandria
to Caesarea.}
of Thmuis.^f Here he disembarked and, resuming
his march, passed a night at a small town called
Tanis.^g His second day's march brought him to
Heracleopolis,^h the third to Pelusium.ⁱ Having
halted here two days to refresh his army, on the
third he crossed the Pelusiac river-mouths, and,
advancing a day's march through the desert, encamped near the temple of the Casian Zeus,^j and
on the next day at Ostracine ^k; this station was
destitute of water, which is brought from elsewhere
for the use of the inhabitants. He next rested at
Rhinocorura,^l whence he advanced to his fourth

^e The " nome " of which Mendes (*Tell er-Rub'*, S.W. of
Lake *Menzaleh*) was the capital.

^f *Tmai* or (Smith and Bartholomew, *Atlas of Holy Land*,
Map 7) *Tell Ibu es-Salam* ; S.W. of Mendes.

^g *San*, the Zoan of the Old Testament, some 20 miles E. of
Thmuis.

^h Heracleopolis Parva ; site now covered by Lake
Menzaleh.

ⁱ *Tell Farama* alias *Tineh* (Biblical Sin, Ezek. xxx. 15),
§ 610.

^j A temple of Zeus-Ammon near the summit of Mons
Casius (*Ras el-Kasrun*), a sandstone range adjoining Lake
Sirbonis and the Mediterranean : Pompey's tomb was on
the hill-side (Strabo xvii. 760).

^k Unidentified.

^l Or Rhinocolura, *el-'Arish*, on the confines of Egypt and
Palestine ; " the river of Egypt," *Wady el-'Arish*, marking
the boundary in Old Testament times.

εἰς Ῥάφειαν προελθὼν σταθμὸν τέταρτον, ἔστι δ'
ἡ πόλις αὕτη Συρίας ἀρχή, τὸ πέμπτον ἐν Γάζῃ
663 τίθεται στρατόπεδον, μεθ' ἣν εἰς Ἀσκάλωνα
κἀκεῖθεν εἰς Ἰάμνειαν, ἔπειτα εἰς Ἰόππην κἀξ
Ἰόππης εἰς Καισάρειαν ἀφικνεῖται διεγνωκὼς αὐτόθι τὰς ἄλλας δυνάμεις ἀθροίζειν.

---

^a *Refaḥ*; Polybius likewise reckons it as the first city of

station, Raphia,[a] at which city Syria begins. His
fifth camp he pitched at Gaza ; next he marched to
Ascalon, and from there to Jamnia, then to Joppa,
and from Joppa he finally reached Caesarea, the
rendezvous fixed on for the concentration of his
forces.

Syria, Ῥαφίας ἣ κεῖται μετὰ Ῥινοκόλουρα πρώτη τῶν κατὰ Κοίλην
Συρίαν πόλεων ὡς πρὸς τὴν Αἴγυπτον (v. 80).

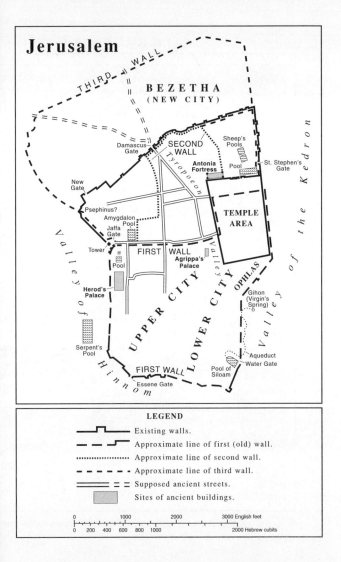

Jerusalem

THIRD WALL

BEZETHA
(NEW CITY)

Damascus Gate

SECOND WALL

Sheep's Pools

Antonia Fortress

Pool

St. Stephen's Gate

New Gate

Tyropoeon

Psephinus?

Amygdalon Pool

Jaffa Gate

TEMPLE AREA

Tower

FIRST WALL

Pool

Agrippa's Palace

Herod's Palace

UPPER CITY

LOWER CITY

OPHLAS

Gihon (Virgin's Spring)

Serpent's Pool

FIRST WALL

Essene Gate

Pool of Siloam

Water Gate

Aqueduct

Valley of the Kedron

Valley of Hinnom

Valley of the Kedron

LEGEND

Existing walls.

Approximate line of first (old) wall.

Approximate line of second wall.

Approximate line of third wall.

Supposed ancient streets.

Sites of ancient buildings.

0	1000	2000	3000 English feet

| 0 | 200 | 400 | 600 | 800 | 1000 | 2000 Hebrew cubits |

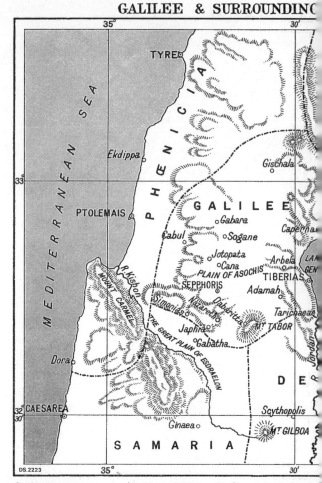

TYRE

PHOENICIA

MEDITERRANEAN SEA

Ekdippa

Gischala

GALILEE

PTOLEMAIS

Gabara

Caperna

Cabul

Sogane

Jotopata

Arbela

LA

GEN

Cana

PLAIN OF ASOCHIS

TIBERIAS

R.Kishon

SEPPHORIS

Adamah

MT. CARMEL

Simonias

Dabaritta

Nazareth

Tarichaeae

Japhia

MT TABOR

THE GREAT PLAIN OF ESDRAELON

Gabatha

Dora

D E

CAESAREA

Scythopolis

Ginaea

MT GILBOA

SAMARIA

DS.2223

Gaulanitis, Batanæa etc.=Kingdom of Agrippa II. Decapolis independ

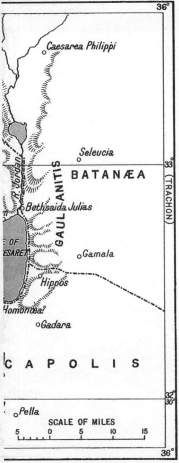

36°

Caesarea Philippi

Seleucia

33°

BATANÆA

GAULANITIS

(TRACHON)

R. Jordan

Bethsaida Julias

E OF
ESARET

Gamala

Hippos

Homonæa?

Gadara

C A P O L I S

32°
30'

Pella

SCALE OF MILES

5   0   5   10   15

36°

ent . The rest under Roman Procurators.

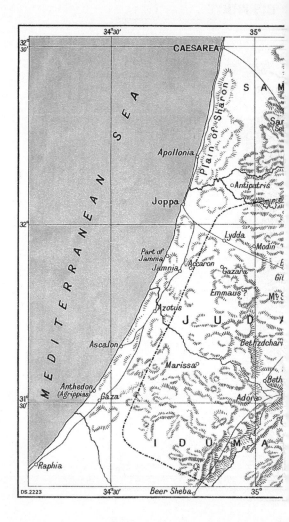

CAESAREA

S A M

Sar
Seb

Plain of Sharon

Apollonia

Antipatris

Joppa

Lydda
Modin

Part of
Jammia
Jamnia
Accaron
Gazara
Gth
Emmaus?
Mt S

Azotus
J U D
Ascalon
Beth zdchari

Marissa
Beth

Anthedon
(Agrippias)
Gaza
Adora

I D U M A

Raphia

Beer Sheba

MEDITERRANEAN SEA

DS.2223

CENTRAL AND SOUTHERN
PALESTINE (50-70 A.D.)

Scythopolis (Beth Shan)
Ginaea
Mt Gilboa
Pella
DECAPOLIS
ARIA
aria
(ste)
Gerasa
Sychem
(Neapolis)
t Gerizim
Archelais
Coreae
Ragaba
Amathus
Jabbok
Borceaus
Acrabeta
Alexandrium?
Phasaelis
Thamna
Isanad
Gophna
Philadelphia
th-horon
eon
Jericho
opus
JERUSALEM
Livias
(Beth Haram)
Heshbon
Bethany
Mt Nebo
Bethlehem
Herodium
Tekoa
Callirrhoe
Machaerus
sur
Hebron
Engedi
ttha
Arnon
larda?
Masada

DEAD SEA
(Asphaltitis)

R. JORDAN

GALAADITIS

SCALE OF MILES
5   0   5   10   15   20